By the same author

Timeless Flight: The Definitive Biography Of The Byrds
Neil Young: Here We Are In The Years
Roxy Music: Style With Substance – Roxy's First Ten Years
Van Morrison: A Portrait Of The Artist
The Kinks: The Sound And The Fury
Wham! (Confidential) Death Of A Supergroup
Starmakers And Svengalis: The History Of British Pop Management

THE FOOTBALL MANAGERS

JOHNNY ROGAN

Macdonald
Queen Anne Press

A *Queen Anne Press* BOOK

© Johnny Rogan

First published in Great Britain in 1989 by
Queen Anne Press, a division of
Macdonald & Co (Publishers) Ltd
66–73 Shoe Lane
London
EC4P 4AB

A member of Maxwell Pergamon Publishing Corporation plc

Jacket photographs – Front: Above – Brian Clough *Colorsport*
                            Below – Sir Matt Busby and Bob Paisley
                            Allsport/Dave Cannon
                     Back: Bobby Robson *Colorsport*

British Library Cataloguing in Publication Data

Rogan, Johnny
    The football managers.
    1. Great Britain. Association football. Clubs.
    Management – Biographies – Collections
    I. Title
    338.7'6179633463'0922

ISBN 0–356–15902–7

Typeset by Selectmove Ltd
Printed and bound in Great Britain by Biddles Ltd, Guildford

In addition to the titular characters in the book, I would like to thank those former players, now managers themselves, whose insights were greatly welcomed. Several other players, who chose not to become managers, nevertheless proved informative and entertaining in their commentaries.

Finally, my task was made that much easier by the support and assistance of Keith Rodger, Ian Foster, Jessie Paisley, Cathy Shea and Donnie Burke, plus Caroline North and Ian Marshall at Queen Anne Press.

Thank you all.

Johnny Rogan

CONTENTS

INTRODUCTION

Who can fathom the crazy world of football management? It is a sphere in which reputations can reach dazzling heights over years of success, then suddenly crumble amid petty accusations and recriminations. There is probably no better example of the changing fortunes of a soccer manager than the salutary case of Sir Alf Ramsey. Elevated to national fame in 1966, he seemed set for life as 'the manager who won England the World Cup'. The sheen had dulled somewhat four years later when England contested the 1970 finals in Mexico, but they were still regarded as a major footballing force. Three years later, following a few erratic results, the proud Ramsey was asked to leave. His achievements had been consigned to the history books and neither his knighthood nor his acquisition of the premier soccer trophy could save his head.

Ramsey's fall reinforced one of the game's oldest clichés: 'The only certainty in football management is the sack'. During the 1960s, newspapers kept abreast of the number of post-war football firings and would eruditely inform their readers about the latest victim and his standing in the statistical scheme of things. Number 686 in this macabre roll call was a young manager named Bobby Robson who had been sacked by his first club Fulham after only seven months. Few expected to hear of him again following such an abysmal start.

When the sacking rate accelerated and passed the 1,000 mark, even the statisticians lost count. Managerial mobility and derailment were rapidly becoming an everyday occurrence and some characters seemed to thrive amid the chaos. Tommy Docherty joked that he had had more clubs than Jack Nicklaus, and was well into double figures before he finally retired. Along the way, he took Rotherham, Aston Villa and Manchester United to relegation and managed Queen's Park Rangers on three occasions, two of which ended with his dismissal. Docherty's resilience and self-promotion combined to distract from his patchy record as a manager, and encouraged clubs to place habitual faith in his reputed charisma. He not only came to personify the journeyman-manager but reminded soccer students that results are not everything. Ironically, Docherty's most celebrated sacking took place at a time when he had probably reached his managerial peak. Having survived the ignominy of taking Manchester United down into the Second Division, he returned with a strong side which upset Liverpool's treble ambitions by winning the 1977 FA Cup. Docherty moved into his fifth year at United and, having at last won a trophy, seemed secure. When it was learned that he was in the midst of an adulterous affair with the club physiotherapist's wife, however, the scandal destroyed his standing at United. Although he later married the lady in question, the embarrassment caused by the liaison was sufficient to cost him his job. Three months after lifting the FA Cup, the discredited Docherty was left to cast a cold eye over the supposed injustice of his fate:

> What I have done has got nothing at all to do with my track record as a manager. I have been punished for falling in love.

He would never win another trophy and finally quit soccer with a cabinet full of newspaper clippings but only one major honour – that rather timely FA Cup.

Docherty's doom is a sharp reminder of how swiftly and unexpectedly the axe can fall. During the period I was researching this book, there were the usual series of sackings including one name whose record, until then, was exemplary. Lawrie McMenemy was widely considered to be one of the best managers of the decade. He had charisma, leadership, communicative skills and a solid temperament. He had taken unfashionable Southampton to a shock FA Cup victory over Manchester United in 1976 and then stormed the First Division. The Saints not only held their own in the top flight but even challenged Liverpool for the Championship in 1984. 'Big' Lawrie was the man, and, always ready for a challenge, he returned to his native Northeast to try to lead Sunderland to greater glory. A disastrous season followed and, amid a barrage of criticism, the once-heroic McMenemy resigned. Suddenly, the big man was yesterday's man. Memories are notoriously short in football.

When I first put pen to paper, the latest hero was an engaging character named Dave Bassett, who had taken Wimbledon from the depths of the Fourth Division to the First Division's top six. He then went to Watford and proceeded to do a 'McMenemy'. He presently resides in the Third Division with Sheffield United and hopes to return stronger than ever. It's a tough life!

One afternoon, half-way through writing this book, I visited the Manor Ground to interview the youngest manager in the Football League, Mark Lawrenson. As a new manager enjoying his first appointment, I thought that Lawrenson might just provide a different angle on this unstable and frustrating occupation and perhaps challenge the viewpoints of my older, more established interviewees. His team, recently relegated Oxford United, had begun the new season in the top half of the Second Division and looked a good bet for promotion. Lawrenson seemed to be well liked by the supporters and players and there was a discernible buzz in the town, as though the public believed that a touch of the Anfield organisation and glamour was about to be bestowed on their ailing team. During our interview, Lawrenson came across as a very confident young manager full of ambition and commitment. He also seemed refreshingly realistic: not only was he aware of the casualty rate among managers, but he continually returned to the theme like a condemned man obsessively checking his own scaffold. There was an endearing fatalism in one of his asides:

> I sink or swim. The majority of managers get the sack. Realistically, it's a question of how long I manage without getting the sack.

The prospect of Lawrenson's sacking seemed far away in October 1988, yet, after leaving the ground, I could not help but dwell on his powerlessness. Beneath the confident veneer, there seemed a man who was ultimately just another employee. This was effectively, although innocently, summed up in his description of the job:

> I deal with the team and most of the work on transfers and players' contracts. Then I have to go to the chairman for a final decision. We have somebody solely responsible for reporting to the chairman on the economic side. The chairman gives a yes or no, or whatever.

With the decision-making and, more importantly, 'the economic side' outside Lawrenson's sphere, it was clear that his ultimate influence on club policy was pretty negligible.

Within a fortnight of our interview, Lawrenson was reported to be angry at the decision of his chairman Kevin Maxwell to sell ace striker Dean Saunders to Derby County for £1,000,000. Lawrenson claimed he was a little upset that he had not learned about the negotiations at an earlier stage. He was on his way to the boardroom, guns-a-blazing, and if he did not receive a satisfactory explanation his resignation would follow. Maxwell proved far quicker on the draw, however, and sacked him on the spot. Plucky Lawrenson, the saviour from Liverpool, was on the scrapheap of soccer after only seven months in management. Club supporters were outraged, the players voiced their upset, the press pledged their support and the initial results suggested that a serious error had been made. From being promotion candidates, Oxford slipped inexorably towards the relegation zone in a matter of weeks. The great furore made no difference, however. The power of the chairman was irreversible.

The fate of Lawrenson is commonplace rather than unique, as the managerial history of the majority of soccer clubs will reveal. The crucial paradox of football management is that the manager is at once seemingly all-powerful and yet powerless. He controls the team selection, pontificates in the media, buys and sells players and may even become a national celebrity. Yet, he may also be little more than a puppet in the hands of a dictatorial director or a charismatic chairman. As events have shown, he can be sacked at any time for a variety of reasons, irrespective of his team's performances. His dismissal may be plainly unjust but there will be no shortage of candidates to take his job. There is no loyalty among managers in football and no sharp-toothed union to boycott, prevent or regulate the merry-go-round of hirings and firings. Faced with the prospect of unemployment or a life outside football, the manager betrays a startling disregard for principle and accepts his next job with an amnesiacal smile of hope and resignation.

One of the more entertaining aspects of visiting a football club is to witness seemingly powerful, awe-inspiring managers reduced to the level of deferential school prefects while addressing their headmaster-like chairmen. The hierarchical structure of football clubs most closely resembles that of a military-style organisation. The chairman is the omnipotent officer, occasionally appearing to monitor events but always ready to interfere if the regiment is threatened. The manager and coach are sergeant majors whose primary role is to motivate and organise the privates for their allotted tasks. It is the common soldier, the football player, who ultimately fights the battle on the pitch and wins or loses the weekly war. Managers readily accept and often revel in their sergeant major persona. They can shout at players as though they were the scum of the earth, safe in the knowledge that even the most temperamental forward is likely to sit there and take it 'like a man'. Indeed, it seems to be expected of a manager that he occasionally provides a 'bollocking' and, should he fail to do so, his squad may call him soft. If a factory foreman were to treat his workers the way managers conduct their relations with players, the wheels of industry would grind to an immediate halt. Players, of course, are neither noted for their militancy nor their intelligence.

The military discipline is reinforced by a fear bred out of familiarity among the various units in the club. Chairmen are treated with the utmost respect by players and managers alike. Even long-serving managers continue to refer to their superiors as 'Mr' or, more amusingly, 'Mr Chairman'. Players are slaves to the same protocol and must never allude to their managers by their Christian names, even though they may have known each other for ten years or even appeared in the same team. Once an individual becomes a manager he is metamorphosed into what is known in the North as a 'gaffer'. More snobbish managers may insist on the 'Mr' prefix (in a vain imitation of their chairman), but most are referred to as 'boss', as if they were South African mine owners.

Behind the closed doors of the dressing room, normally urbane managers often use appallingly coarse language while discoursing with their players. The all-male environment promotes an insidious chauvinism which is evident on team coaches, where certain players are known to gorge themselves on soft porn and boast of their own virility while keenly judging voluptuous women by the redness of their orifices or the shape or size of their breasts. Managers usually turn a blind eye to this type of behaviour as it apparently relieves the players' tensions on a long coach trip. More importantly, it distracts them from that greatest of all soccer taboos: homosexuality. Remarkably, homosexuality has yet to corrupt the footballing fraternity and is completely unknown in the shared baths and dressing rooms of the 92 League clubs. Drugs are the second big taboo and, unlike their American counterparts, English players generally resist the wicked temptation of cocaine and amphetamines. Inevitably, pub gossip will state otherwise, but even the tabloids have had little success in unearthing a major drugs scandal.

Whatever indiscretion a manager commits in the dressing room, whether it be a swear word or a slapped wrist, must never be repeated outside the club walls. Managers are expected to be paragons of virtue with a moral stance befitting the Gladstonian era. Kerb crawling, let alone anything worse, will unseat a manager, even if he is subsequently proven innocent. Divorce is also beyond the pale and even prominent managers such as Vic Buckingham and Tommy Docherty have suffered for interfering with the sanctity of marriage. How strange that a game as rugged and plebeian as football should demand standards of behaviour far above those expected of Cabinet Ministers or even Anglican clergymen.

It is perhaps unsurprising that so many managers appear thoroughly reactionary in their attitudes. Discussions on hooliganism often start reasonably enough but end with earnest suggestions for the re-introduction of national service, the birch, heavy custodial sentences or even capital punishment. Racism is also deplored by the soccer elite, but much needs to be done inside clubs as well as on the terraces. In spite of the influx of black players to the game, we still await the appointment of the first black manager in the Football League. The public image of the sport would surely benefit from such recruitment and the idea of a black in authority might stifle much of the institutionalised terrace racism. Such changes will take time, especially in a sport known for its conservatism. Boards of directors enjoy their autonomy and might feel inhibited about appointing a black manager for fear of causing themselves public embarrassment when the time came to sack him. No doubt they would also realise that their more reactionary-minded players might not be willing to take a 'bollocking' from a black man. For similar reasons, it is unlikely that women will make any inroads into the directorial or managerial arena, although it is intriguing to contemplate a female Jimmy Hill being acclaimed as the new saviour of football. Then again, most successful business women would have more sense than to pour good money into something as unprofitable as a football club, let alone countenance the egotism and posturing that characterises the new breed of soccer chairmen and their pet clubs.

Commercial considerations have brought many clubs into the 20th century, yet the majority still resemble Victorian relics. While cinemas crumble into bingo halls, football clubs stubbornly slouch onwards into the arms of the receiver. They call themselves institutions, part of the fabric of British life, but the falling gates tell their own story. Institutions do not necessarily last: even fish and chip shops seem to be on the way out.

Can football survive in the age of the hamburger? Not without changing: innovations are simultaneously welcomed and reviled. Ideas range from super leagues to artificial pitches, ground-merging and part-time clubs. Meanwhile, the public complains of poor facilities while clinging to a romantic 'Bovril' image of football that demands the retention of old-fashioned terraces, swaying bodies and raucous chanting. Football is inextricably linked to the taste of gobstoppers and Jubblys, and for many it is about as relevant. Nostalgic supporters still stay away in droves.

The proliferation of sackings in football management gives the impression that the job is largely a matter of blind chance. The following case studies provide an alternative perspective by centring on the achievements of ten men whose worth transcended the caprices of club chairmen, financial crises, occasional sackings and personal tragedies to make a lasting contribution to the history of the game. A great manager is defined not merely by the number of trophies he has won, but by his ability to keep a club in the top flight and challenging for new honours, year in, year out. With the exception of Graham Taylor, the man of the future in this study, all the managers from Busby to Robson have savoured and suffered management at the highest divisional or national level for periods in excess of seven years.

I have deliberately restricted this cavalcade of managerial greats to the post-war period when professional management, free from the interference of team-selecting directors, became the norm. It would be criminal, however, not to pay passing tribute to that daddy of all football managers, Herbert Chapman. Chapman was the first great media manager and an adept gambler in the fledgling transfer market. He bought Charlie Buchan for an astonishing £2,000 with the unusual proviso of paying him £100 per goal. The arrangement was typical of Chapman, who enjoyed the reputation of being a big spender as well as an astute purchaser of talent. His tactical prowess was even more impressive and he virtually revolutionised the game with the introduction of a third back. During the 1920s he set Huddersfield Town on the way to three consecutive Championships, although he had moved on to Arsenal by the time they clinched their title treble. Remarkably, Chapman later won three successive Championships with the Gunners in the 1930s to establish himself as one of the most successful football managers of all time.

Chapman's first great club, Huddersfield Town, are currently languishing in the Third Division. That in itself is a reminder of how easily great management can be eroded by time and changing fortunes. Surveying this book it is interesting to note that, in spite of the managerial skills of Busby, Nicholson, Ramsey, Revie, Clough, Robson and Taylor, their former clubs have subsequently each suffered one or more spells in the Second Division. Manchester United, Spurs, Ipswich, Leeds, Derby and Watford could not sustain their form after the gods had gone. That, perhaps, is the way it should be. The emergence of a new elite of soccer clubs may have changed football irrevocably, for it is extremely difficult to imagine Manchester United or Liverpool ever slipping back into the Second Division. However, football history has consistently shown that the unexpected is always possible and it is amazing what bad management can do to a wealthy club even in a short space of time. Conversely, the continued success of clubs such as Wimbledon, Coventry, Norwich, Millwall and, most remarkably, homeless Charlton Athletic, testify to what can be achieved on a low budget. There are still enough sleeping giants in the lower divisions of the League to upset the economic applecarts of Manchester and Merseyside. All they need for starters is a brilliant manager.

SIR MATT BUSBY

THE AMBASSADOR OF EUROPE

Matthew Busby was born on 26 May 1909 in the mining village of Orbiston in Lanarkshire, Scotland. Although far removed from the centre of European conflict, he would directly experience the effects of two world wars. At the age of seven, he lost his father to a sniper's bullet, an everyday tragedy of war which unsettled the family. His mother continued to work hard, fuelled by dreams of emigrating to America, where several of the Busby clan had already settled. Matthew, meanwhile, was progressing steadily at Motherwell Higher Grade School and his form master was confident that he would become a teacher. However, family circumstances undermined that ambition and, at the age of 16, young Busby inevitably followed his colleagues down the mines. The American dream had evaporated along the way as the Busbys encountered visa queues and lengthy waiting lists.

Life in Lanarkshire consisted of a hard day's work at the pit, but football was a popular leisure activity in the area. Busby turned out for the local teams and, much to the disapprobation of his mother, signed professional forms with Manchester City in February 1928. His joy soon turned to disillusionment when he failed to made the grade as either a winger or an inside forward. His failings were effectively summed up in a letter he wrote to his fiancée Jean, which included the revealing line: 'I feel out of my sphere in football'. At one stage, his disenchantment prompted him to pack his bags and leave Manchester, but, on reflection, he decided to stay and fight on. His struggle to find a place in City's team receded with each passing month and by the autumn of 1930 he had lost his place in the reserves. At that point he was almost shuttled off to lowly neighbours Manchester United, but a quibble over transfer fees blighted even that opportunity. Busby's near redundancy as a player was dramatically reversed when an injury in City's third team saw him switched to right half. The positional change revitalised his career and, as his confidence grew, he climbed back into the reserves and finally pushed his way into the first team.

1

Busby's ascendancy was well timed, for City began to emerge as perennial FA Cup battlers. In 1932, they reached the semi-final before losing to Arsenal, but returned stronger the following season to reach Wembley, where they faced the previous year's League Champions, Everton. If we are to believe Busby, the match was lost even before City had kicked a ball. They fell victim to their punctuality, arriving at Wembley so early that the torturous wait undid their nerves. Everton romped home 3–0, the biggest winning margin since 1915. City rose again the following season and looked sharper in reaching the semi-final where they thrashed Aston Villa 6–1. The Wembley hoodoo appeared to be working against them again, however, when opponents Portsmouth scored early in the first half. On this occasion, Busby's team-mates overcame their nerves and, after snatching a deserved equaliser, scored a dramatic winning goal three minutes from time. The archetypal 'Busby Babe', 18-year-old goalkeeper Frank Swift, was so overcome by the tension that he collapsed in a faint following the final whistle. Busby was eulogised in the press as 'the finest right half ever seen at Wembley', a strange epithet for a player who had previously been on the scrap-heap of soccer.

Busby looked likely to reap the rewards of his good press, but his career was hampered by a serious leg injury which kept him out of the game for the best part of a season. In March 1936, he agreed to accept a transfer to Liverpool where he immediately became involved in their fight to stave off relegation. They survived the crisis and during the next couple of seasons pulled themselves safely into the mid-table. City, meanwhile, were crowned Champions only to slide into the Second Division at the end of the next season. However, the vagaries of football fortune were now scarcely relevant as the Second World War terminated the traditional League season for seven long years.

Busby was posted in the Army PE Corps stationed at Aldershot and following the Allied invasion of Italy was despatched to Bari. His former team-mate from Liverpool, Bob Paisley, looked on enviously but failed to get a similar posting. As he wryly put it: 'They never saw an angry man!' What Busby did see was the cream of English football under his personal command, including names such as Joe Mercer, Tommy Lawton, Arthur Rowe, Cliff Britton, Maurice Edelson and Willie Watson. It was a veritable footballers' academy that included not only great ball players like Lawton, but the tactical genius of Rowe. Busby was also fortunate in striking up a friendship with another inspirational trainer named Jimmy Murphy, who would play a crucial part later in his career. Military experience honed the already inchoate managerial skills that Busby had revealed in his couple of seasons at Liverpool. He had already learned the importance of organisation on the field and was now gaining a diploma in man management. Leadership, communication, co-ordination and delegation were army watchwords which also happened to be the requisite skills for managerial success. By the time Busby was demobbed in 1945, his future was already mapped out.

Busby's pre-war playing record and army experience made him an obvious target for clubs in search of new blood. Ayr United offered him a managerial post, but Busby had long since decided not to return to Scotland. Third Division (South) Reading suggested an assistant managership, but this was a time when big city clubs in the North ruled football. Liverpool offered him a five-year contract as coach but, after verbally agreeing to accept the post, he abruptly reneged on the deal when Manchester United intervened with a late offer. Chairman James Gibson was desperate to rebuild the ailing club and provided Busby with what he most desired: the managership of a First Division club. Contracts were exchanged on 22 October 1945 in the unlikely setting of the Cornbrook Cold Storage, a business enterprise which also deputised as Manchester United's headquarters. Old Trafford had been reduced to a derelict shell by the Blitz and required years of renovation before the crowds could again pass through its turnstiles. In the meantime, 'home' games were played at the Maine Road ground of rivals Manchester City.

In spite of these upheavals, Busby was determined to provide United with a high profile and a distinctive identity. From the outset, he envisaged the creation of a highly attractive footballing side whose stylish approach would be rewarded by ever-improving gates. In order to effect such changes, Busby knew it was crucial to eradicate the image of the ivory tower manager then prevalent in football. Fortunately, he was still young and fit enough to train with his charges and soon emerged as one of the game's first 'track-suit' managers. Without compromising his authority, he intended to recapture the spirit of cameraderie that had characterised his Army Corps days. By mucking in with the players he was able to communicate his ideas more effectively, thereby influencing tactical systems and match play.

United needed such vigilance for the club was living under the shadow of a huge £15,000 overdraft which precluded further spending on new players. Busby received an early grounding in football economics and had to balance the books by experimenting with various positional changes. Team captain Johnny Carey was an outstanding Irish international centre forward whom Busby successively switched to wing half and full back. Johnny Aston was also plucked from the forward line and combined brilliantly with Carey to form a match-winning partnership. Busby's budgeting had enabled him to learn that most important of managerial qualities: innovation. The success of his various team changes was reflected in Manchester United's League position at the end of their first post-war season: they finished second to Liverpool, missing the title by a single point.

Manchester United's winning ways boosted the takings at the Maine Road turnstiles at a time when record-breaking crowds were surging into football grounds. As attendances rose dramatically, United's financial worries receded and chairman Gibson looked with confidence to the complete restoration of the club. Unfortunately Busby was still struggling with a makeshift team and a run of poor form saw the side slump temporarily to 16th place in the table. Sensing a crisis, Gibson demanded that Busby buy some star players *post haste*. However, the Scotsman was now too well schooled in the economics of football to take such a rash decision and insisted that the players then on offer at other clubs were ill-suited to United's purposes. He would pounce immediately the right player appeared on the market, but not before. Gibson was so infuriated by Busby's obduracy that he raised his walking stick in exasperated defiance before storming out of the boardroom in a huff. Busby had already demanded total control over team selection and now he was refusing to spend money while United spiralled towards the relegation zone. Gibson could have petulantly sacked his forthright manager, but was level-headed enough to appreciate Busby's worth and soon afterwards expressed his regret about the outburst. From that point onwards, Gibson resolutely supported his employee on all matters concerning the team. This was undoubtedly Busby's most important victory to date and a revealing example of his confidence and single-mindedness in dealing with authority.

Busby's conviction that United's poor form was illusory was proven at the end of the season when they again finished runners-up, seven points adrift of Arsenal. Their revitalisation had coincided with an astonishing FA Cup run, in which they were drawn in turn against six First Division teams. The buccaneering saga commenced at Villa Park, where United overwhelmed their opponents in a breathtaking first half to lead 5–1. However, Aston Villa emerged from the dressing room like men possessed and, in a remarkable display of resilience, pulled back goal after goal until the score was reduced to 5–4. United seemed certain to crack until their gifted, stylish striker Stan Pearson blighted Villa's comeback hopes with a breakaway goal. Following the 6–4 drama, United more comfortably put paid to Liverpool, Charlton and Preston. Hat trick hero Pearson despatched Derby single-handedly in the semi-final thereby taking United to Wembley for the first time in their history.

Busby was no stranger to FA Cup finals, but he did not underestimate the threat posed by Blackpool. The coastal side contained several star players including Stanley Matthews, Stan Mortensen, Eddie Shimwell and Harry Johnston. Clearly, the greatest single threat came from the legendary England international Matthews, whom Busby planned to mark out of the game. Ever the tactician, he took a bold gamble by introducing reserve John Anderson whose brief was to wreak havoc on the right flank. Such planning did not account for a disputed penalty which gave Blackpool an early lead. United equalised, but Blackpool's resident genius Stan Mortensen restored the lead before half-time. The second half ebbed away in frustration for United but their intense pressure was finally rewarded when that powerhouse striker Jack Rowley rocketed in an equaliser. The ubiquitous Pearson netted a third and, rather appropriately, reserve hero Anderson scored a fourth to clinch it. The final went down in history as one of Wembley's finest. Already, Busby was fulfilling his dream of establishing a football team whose name would become synonymous with class and style.

The 1948–49 season saw United again challenging on all fronts but they were frustrated in the League, finishing runners-up for the third successive year, this time to Portsmouth. Hopes of retaining the FA Cup remained high until the semi-final when they lost a tightly-fought replay to the eventual winners, Wolves. Such disappointments were quickly forgotten for, in the autumn of 1949, Old Trafford opened its gates for home fixtures for the first time since the War. United's League form remained fair, rather than impressive, and they finished the season in fourth place, while their FA Cup dreams ended prematurely in the sixth round at Stamford Bridge. Off the field, Busby was encountering problems with some players and a disagreement over team selection led to the sale of talented inside forward Johnny Morris to Derby for £25,000. Irrepressible team joker Charlie Mitten, who took a gamble on making some real money in Bogota, Colombia, was another unfortunate loss. Busby warned him that he would never play for United if he returned, and that is precisely what happened. For all his apparent patience and humanity, Busby could be extremely dogmatic and strait-laced when confronted by insurgents. Only in later years, and when faced with an undisputed football genius, would Busby's scrupulousness be tempered by tolerance.

Manchester United's reputation as perennial runners-up was re-inforced in the 1950–51 season when they were thwarted by Tottenham Hotspur. The new Spurs side had been fashioned by Busby's former Army colleague, Arthur Rowe, whose 'push and run' tactics had swept them from Second Division mediocrity to the League Championship. They remained a formidable threat the following season, but United's consistency finally proved decisive as they won their first title under Matt Busby's management. At Manchester United's Annual General Meeting the mood was buoyant but Busby cut through the complacency with a stern warning: the team required major surgery. It was difficult to believe that much could be wrong with England's League Champions, but within six months Busby's worst fears were realised. Unbelievably, United sank to the foot of the First Division table. Busby shuddered as he recalled how neighbours Manchester City had won the Championship only to suffer the humiliation of relegation the very next season. If United were to avoid the same fate then the ageing team would have to be replenished. Changes were, in fact, already taking place. Charlie Mitten had been replaced by Roger Byrne, who was to establish himself as one of the best full backs in the game. The £25,000 received for the rebellious Johnny Morris was spent on Birmingham's Johnny Berry, who combined with Byrne to replace the great Carey/Aston partnership. Although impressive, such team changes were largely cosmetic, as Busby realised. At the next board meeting he announced boldly: 'I'm going to make the move which will make or break Manchester United'. His plan was not merely ambitious but scarcely believable. Overnight, virtually half the Manchester United side was replaced by untested reserves. Two draws against high-flying Huddersfield and Champions-elect Arsenal convinced Busby that the boys could survive such sudden promotion. Suddenly, unknown names such as Blanchflower, Colman, Edwards and Pegg appeared regularly on team sheets. League performances steadied, then improved as United clawed their way back to finish in eighth position. A football revolution was in the making.

Busby's audacious concept of a soccer crèche had begun as early as the late 1940s when he realised that United's future lay in an adventurous youth policy. This meant not only signing promising local lads, but scouring the country for raw, undiscovered talent. Busby wanted nothing less than a battalion of youngsters whose untutored genius would supply United with sufficient playing power to keep them in the top flight for the next decade or more. His reasoning was partly based on sound football economics: unknown boys did not cost exorbitant transfer fees. Beyond the financial considerations, however, lay the knowledge that such untapped skill could be moulded into a playing pattern of Busby's own choosing. Inchoate, innocent youth could be inculcated with Busby's footballing philosophy, a Corinthian ideal in which open, stylish soccer was fused with an intense club loyalty that transcended individual fame.

Busby's programme required a backroom staff of formidable quality and in this respect he was extremely fortunate. Joe Armstrong was the chief scout responsible for travelling Britain in search of soccer-mad schoolboys and promising amateurs. A retired civil servant, his urbanity and gentlemanly air won over many a cynical and untrusting parent. Armstrong's fledgling players were next placed in the hands of Bert Whalley, a former United centre half who was appointed trainer after an eye injury forced him to retire from the game. Whalley was patient and studious in his approach and helped many an erring lad adapt to the rigours of a professional football club. For those who made the grade, there was the intimidating presence of reserve team manager Jimmy Murphy, the hard man of United whose job was to transform boy wonders into tough professionals. At the top of the pyramid stood Busby himself, the all-knowing, all-seeing first team manager whose favour alone bestowed the chance of soccer immortality.

The system was brilliant in its simplicity with each of the parties complementing the other. New players, whatever their temperament, could always find someone on the staff who understood their problems. The signings themselves were the stuff of legends: David Pegg, the miner's son whose father saw a mirror image of himself in Busby; Eddie 'Snake hips' Colman, whose erotic swivelling movements were said to hypnotise baffled opponents; Duncan Edwards, whose passion for Manchester United overruled the parochial loyalty that had claimed him as a future Wolves centre forward; and Bobby Charlton, who spurned family tradition by not following his uncle 'Wor' Jackie Milburn as the Northeast's favourite son. And there were many more. Busby even made a rare dive into the transfer market for Barnsley's centre forward Tommy

Taylor, who cost £29,999. Within two years the Manchester United team had been regenerated.

During their period in the nursery, the cutely-named Busby Babes viewed their first team manager as an omniscient presence. His appearance at reserve matches engendered an air of tension and expectancy, as though any of them might suddenly be plucked from obscurity and slotted into the first XI. All too often, that was precisely what happened. Mr Busby would ask for a quiet word, inform the young player of his intentions and politely wish him well. Such paternal solicitude had a marked effect on young stars like Bobby Charlton, who clearly revered the great man's meticulousness:

> The one thing I will always remember about him is his ability to memorise people's names . . . The youngest apprentice, the washerwoman, the chap who sweeps out the stand – he knew them all by their Christian names. It may not sound a lot, but it is amazing how good it makes you feel. It emphasises that you are just as much a part of the club as any of the first team players, that you are part of the Manchester United family. This family spirit has been created and nurtured by the boss.

The reconstruction of the team saw a temporary lull in Manchester United's form during 1953–55, although they finished in the top five in both seasons. Their Cup exploits also ended prematurely, and this bad run continued into 1956 when they were unexpectedly defeated 4–0 by Second Division Bristol Rovers. The League race posed no such problems that year and United romped home as Champions, an incredible 11 points clear of their nearest rivals, Blackpool and Wolves. Only two names remained from the Championship-winning side of 1952: Johnny Berry and Roger Byrne.

By 1957, Manchester United had installed floodlights and spent a staggering £200,000 on improving the ground. From a ramshackle tip, they had blossomed into one of the most modern and best-equipped clubs in the country. As ever, this modernity was reflected in Busby's progressive attitude. In the mid-1950s, the European and Fairs Cup competitions were inaugurated and League Champions Manchester United were requested to compete. The previous year the Football League had insisted that Chelsea decline such an invitation and they offered the same stern advice to United. Busby refused to be bullied, however, and insisted that it would be a retrograde step for English football if United declined FIFA's invitation. This was yet another example of Busby's willingness to challenge dusty officialdom in the pursuit of innovation. Manchester United's debut in European competition began impressively enough with a 2–0 away victory over Anderlecht. However, it was the return leg in Manchester that really excited the public imagination for, incredibly, United won 10–0. Even the normally passive Busby was overwhelmed by the team's insolent power and attacking commitment.

Their performance that night completely vindicated the brave decision to compete with Europe's finest.

A second round victory over Borussia Dortmund took United to Spain where they confronted Bilbao. Busby soon discovered why the Spaniards boasted such a brilliant home record when they raced into a 3–0 half-time lead. United reduced the deficit in the final 45 minutes, but still emerged 5–3 down. It was only a sparkling display in the return leg that saved the Reds who narrowly pulled through 6–5 on aggregate. The semi-finals now beckoned and for the first time in English soccer history there was talk of the magical treble: European Cup, FA Cup and League title.

After several disappointing FA Cup seasons, Manchester rediscovered their form, although they almost fell victim to recent bad habits in their third round match against Hartlepools. An emphatic 3–0 lead was suicidally squandered and it required a late goal from Liam Whelan to prevent an embarrassing replay. From that point onwards, United successively overcame Wrexham, Everton, Bournemouth and Birmingham to earn their second Wembley appearance. Now the treble was only a handful of games away.

Busby might reasonably have expected a tough League season with the number of fixtures Manchester United had forced upon themselves. Instead, the team played better than ever, losing only six matches and scoring 103 goals in the process. High-scoring Spurs had dogged them throughout the season but could not match United's record-equalling 28 victories which helped log an impressive 64 Championship-winning points.

The odds on Manchester United capturing the treble lengthened considerably when they were drawn against the holders Real Madrid in the semi-final. Real were an awesome team whose ranks included Di Stefano, Ganto and Kopa, three of the greatest players of their generation. Busby knew the task ahead would be formidable and elected to play a containing game in Madrid. Eddie Colman, of the swinging hips, was given the unenviable job of marking the brilliant Di Stefano and such was his success that United survived the first half. The siege continued, however, and the Reds were beaten 3–1. Their sole reply by Tommy Taylor provided hope for the return, particularly as they had retrieved a similar two-goal deficit from Bilbao. Most observers expected Real to marshal their defence against a Mancunian onslaught, but instead they spurned customary Continental caution and attacked. United were outfoxed by an audacious approach and rapidly found themselves a further two goals down. Having taken an unassailable 5–1 lead, Real could allow Manchester a couple of consolation goals and still emerge the comfortable winners. Busby had received a soccer lesson and the dream of the treble was over.

At least the FA Cup offered attractive consolation in the form of the double, which had last been achieved in season 1896–97 by the very opponents they faced: Aston Villa. It was an intriguing confrontation but with two consecutive Championships behind them, United were firm favourites. FA Cup finals are seldom predictable affairs, however, as Busby was to discover to his horror after only six minutes. Prior to the match, he had sought out Northern Ireland international Peter McParland as the main threat in the Villa attack. Having already scored the semi-final goal that killed off West Bromwich Albion, McParland was anxious to make his mark on the game. After seeing his innocuous header expertly caught by United's Ray Wood, he charged the goalkeeper and both players were bundled to the ground. Wood came off worst with a fractured cheekbone and was removed from the pitch. With no substitutes allowed, Busby was forced to play Jackie Blanchflower in goal, while Wood received treatment. The goalkeeper was clearly incapable of continuing and suffered blurred vision and blackouts for the remainder of the game. Rather pathetically, he was reduced to running along the right flank in the role of a distracting mascot. McParland, meanwhile, continued to pile on the agony with two second-half goals. Although United pulled one back and the incapacitated Wood returned to goal for the closing stages, the only double he received was double vision. McParland emerged as both the hero and villain of the piece and a waggish reporter suggested: 'He bagged two goals and one goalkeeper'. Busby was left crying for another much-needed innovation: the introduction of substitutes.

Manchester United's success focussed considerable attention on Busby. The Great Provider of soccer youth had proven himself a polished ambassador and the Continentals were quick to recognise his pedigree. Both Real Madrid and Bilbao approached him with lucrative offers to manage abroad, but their solicitations were politely declined – Busby had set his heart on establishing Manchester United as Europe's premier club.

Prior to the start of the 1957–58 season he seemed less concerned with lifting the European Cup than emulating Herbert Chapman's feat of winning the League Championship for three consecutive years. The team seemed less inclined to fulfil his wishes, however, and slumped disastrously in the early part of the season, losing seven matches before Christmas. Their defence was not only shaky but porous. Pinpointing the problem, Busby made another rare but decisive foray into the transfer market and, in December 1957, purchased Harry Gregg from Doncaster Rovers for £25,000, a world record for a goalkeeper. Positional changes and the introduction of fresh reserves, including Bobby Charlton, stabilised United and by the New Year they were ascending the table with extraordinary rapidity.

The European odyssey was also progressing steadily with victories over Shamrock Rovers and Dukla Prague. After defeating the Czechoslovakian army team, United were delayed in Prague when fog grounded their flight. In order to fulfil their League commitments in England, thus avoiding a fine and possible deduction of points, the squad was forced to take a circuitous route via Amsterdam. It was a tiring schedule for the players and highlighted the problems of relying upon restricted commercial flights. The club secretary addressed this aeronautical annoyance by chartering a private plane for their next European fixture against Red Star, Belgrade.

The teams met first at Old Trafford where United secured an unconvincing 2–1 victory. Doom merchants argued that such a slim first leg lead would prove insufficient on foreign soil. What they had not reckoned on, however, was Busby's increasing knowledge of the European game. Recalling Real's remarkable away performance against United the previous season, Busby decided to adopt a more aggressive attacking policy in Belgrade. On the night, Red Star pushed forward expecting to confront a defensive wall of players. Instead, United uncoiled like a lethal spring and pulverised their opponents with three first-half goals. Faced with an aggregate score of 5–1, Red Star would have been forgiven for displaying signs of despondency but they showed their true worth in the second half with three goals of their own. United grimly hung on for victory. Their success had owed much to Busby's attacking opening gambit, backed by some uncompromising tackling. The Yugoslav press was not so generous in its assessment and pilloried the Manchester men for their cynicism and unsportsmanlike behaviour. Such barbs were forgotten on the flight home for the side had an urgent Saturday appointment with League leaders Wolves at Old Trafford. Four points separated the teams but a United victory would reopen the title race and revive hopes of that impossible treble. Sadly, it was not to be.

On 6 February, Manchester United's charter plane left Belgrade, stopping off for refuelling at Munich. The passengers disembarked for refreshments and suffered the inconvenience of two false starts before the plane sped on to the end of the runway. At that point, disaster struck. Instead of lifting clear of the ground, the aeroplane plunged through a perimeter fence, collided with a house, lost a wing and sliced itself in two. There were a horrifying 24 fatalities, including eight Manchester United players: Geoff Bent, Roger Byrne, Eddie Colman, Duncan Edwards, Mark Jones, David Pegg, Tommy Taylor and Liam Whelan.

Busby was thrown clear of the crash but suffered a punctured lung which hospitalised him for several months. On two occasions a priest was summoned to administer the last rites. During his ordeal, he seriously considered quitting football and it was only the patient solicitude of his wife Jean that encouraged him to carry on. As he slowly recovered, the enormity of the task before him became almost overwhelming. The team he had nurtured was ravaged and would take years to replenish. The restoration of Manchester United over the decade had now become nothing less than a managerial mission.

Football fixtures are impervious to personal tragedy and it was left to assistant manager Jimmy Murphy to continue the quest for the doomed treble. Predictably, United's League form declined markedly and they plummeted to finish a disappointing ninth. Murphy began to rebuild the team immediately, drafting in Ernie Taylor and Stan Crowther from

Blackpool and Aston Villa, respectively. They were joined by a new generation of Busby Babes, prematurely seized from the reserve cradle and forced to compete in the toughest league in the world. It was fully expected that United would withdraw from their remaining European commitments, but Murphy bravely soldiered on. Astonishingly, the decimated United side retained sufficient strength to overcome AC Milan 2–1 at Old Trafford. However, the effects of the tragedy took their toll abroad where the Italians triumphed 4–0. Busby's courageous acceptance of European football in the face of official disapprobation deserved success but had brought instead disappointment and death.

The FA Cup offered one final hope as, incredibly, Manchester United bulldozed their way to Wembley, driven on by fanatical supporters whose frenzied cries inspired the team to superhuman displays against emotionally intimidated opponents. Sheffield Wednesday, West Bromwich Albion and Fulham were executed in turn and there was a genuine belief that United could triumph over formidable Bolton Wanderers in the final.

The recuperating Matt Busby dragged his weary body from the Rechts der Isa Hospital in Munich to attend the Cup final. He intended to inspire the players with a galvanising team talk, but the occasion proved so emotional that he was forced to leave the dressing room. The youngsters attempted to live up to the reputation of their illustrious predecessors in what was a doomed struggle. Bolton were far from daunted by Manchester United's young warriors, having already punished the pre-Munich side 6–0 in an early season game. The renowned England international Nat Lofthouse silenced the United faithful with a fierce goal in the third minute, and Bolton soon threatened to increase their lead. Somehow Manchester United survived and, urged on by the partisan crowd, seemed capable of producing more miracles. Instead, they suffered a sickening sense of *déjà vu*: memories of the previous year's final came flooding back as Nat Lofthouse repeated Peter McParland's trick of barging the goalkeeper. Both Harry Gregg and the ball ended up in the back of the net and the referee awarded a goal. Bolton Wanderers had won the FA Cup.

While football honours had eluded Manchester United, Busby received official recognition for his courage and services to sport by being awarded the CBE. He was convalescing in Switzerland at the time of the award but promised to return to Old Trafford prior to the new League season. Always a master of public relations, Busby decided to drum up support for Manchester United by coaxing Real Madrid to Old Trafford. The Spanish side had just won their third successive European Cup and were probably the most famous football team in the world. For guest appearances they usually charged around £12,000, but in deference to Busby they waived a large percentage of their fee. Real's generosity did not extend as far as actually allowing United to win the game. Instead, the Manchester public was treated to a soccer feast Spanish style with Real overwhelming their opponents 6–1. The chasm of quality between the two sides provided some clue as to how far United needed to progress in order to challenge Europe's finest.

Upon resuming his managerial seat, Busby immediately entered the transfer market, purchasing Albert Quixall from Sheffield Wednesday for a record-breaking fee of £35,000. United hit a bad patch before Christmas but their form improved dramatically in the New Year when they took 23 out of a possible 24 points. Such Championship form saw them rise to challenge League leaders Wolves. In spite of scoring 103 goals, however, United could not undo their poor form earlier in the season and ended as runners-up. For Busby, it seemed an astonishing achievement but he knew that the grand run was only temporary – United still needed new top class players.

It was not only Manchester United that required Busby's assistance in the months following his return to football. Scotland had fared badly in the summer World Cup finishing bottom of their group. Determined to restore national pride and in search of a miracle man to improve results, they turned to Busby. Although he was still struggling to recover from his Munich injuries, the Manchester United supremo unexpectedly accepted the post. Young Scottish players who attended his team talks were amazed by his tactical awareness and familiarity with the playing strengths and weaknesses of their opponents. In an era when Scottish international managers were still known for their aloofness, Busby displayed a polite and ingratiating attitude towards his squad. Dave Mackay remembers Busby's team talk with great affection:

> He stood at the top of the table and looked so impressive. He had that wonderful, deep voice. We all knew Matt Busby but assumed that he wouldn't know us. When he said 'Dave', I didn't know who he was talking to. There was no 'Mackay' or anything like that. He'd say 'Dave' as if he'd known you for years. He made me captain of Scotland and I was only 23. Why he made *me* captain, I don't know! He even gave me a room of my own because he thought a captain should be treated a little differently from the others. He impressed me more than any manager I ever met.

Scotland's first fixture under Busby's charge was against Wales at Ninian Park on 18 October 1958. Busby characteristically recruited a number of new players including 18-year-old Denis Law, the youngest Scottish cap of the century. The squad prepared for the match at Reading's football ground and Busby surveyed the proceedings with a critical eye. Dave Mackay was delicately side-footing penalty kicks when his manager suggested: 'I like to see a penalty *struck*'. The Scotland captain obediently altered his approach and began rocketing balls into the back of the net much to Busby's smiling appreciation. On the evening of the match there was drama in the very first minute when Scotland's Bobby Collins was felled in the six-yard area. The referee showed no hesitation in awarding a penalty. Mackay stepped up to the spot and blasted the ball towards the top corner of the net, only to sink in dismay as the Welsh keeper parried his effort aside. Fortunately, his miss did not prove costly, for Scotland won convincingly 3–0. Immediately after the match Busby took Mackay aside and apologised for deflecting him from his normal penalty-taking procedure. It was a remarkable act of humility from a manager who was not too proud to admit his fallibility, even in the celebratory atmosphere of an emphatic victory.

Busby's tenure as Scotland manager was short-lived, mainly because the pressures of reviving Manchester United's fortunes proved to be all-consuming. For the next two years, the team finished in seventh position, a respectable enough placing in the circumstances, but far from Championship form. United's aristocratic reputation had been usurped by a brilliant Spurs side masterminded by another great manager, Bill Nicholson. In 1961, Tottenham achieved the feat that had eluded Busby by winning the double and already some football critics were suggesting that they were England's greatest ever club side. The myth of the Busby Babes had long since ceased to be the chief topic of football conversation.

Busby attempted to improve Manchester United's performances with the aid of a cheque book. Never renowned as a buyer of talent he now plunged into the transfer market to replenish a formless side. Characteristically, he placed quality before economy and the players he assembled were formidable propositions: Maurice Setters, Tony Dunne, David Herd and Pat Crerand. It was still not enough. The changes affected United's form and they slumped to 15th in the table. A chance to retrieve old glories was also lost in the FA Cup when they succumbed to Spurs' dazzling attack in the semi-finals. Busby concluded that he needed more firing power in the front line.

The goalscoring flair that had eluded United since the beginning of the 1960s was rekindled with the arrival of Denis Law. The Scottish striker had exported his skills to Italy but, after 12 controversial months at Torino, was anxious to return home. The negotiations to win his hand proved tortuous in the extreme and, after three failed attempts, the implacable Busby was forced to shatter the British transfer record. He now had a £300,000 team but paradoxically they plummeted towards the Second Division. Busby's reaction to the relegation blues was to tell the players that they would win the FA Cup. His incautious boast was rapidly transformed into a self-fulfilling prophecy as United expertly dismantled Huddersfield, Aston Villa, Chelsea, Coventry and Southampton before overwhelming Leicester 3–1 in the memorable final of 1963.

A match of no less importance was United's 'relegation derby' against neighbours Manchester City. Denis Law's former club urgently needed both points whereas United required only a draw. When Alex Harley scored early in the first half Busby suddenly found himself with potentially the most expensive Second Division side in League history. The prospect of such an anomaly was eradicated in the second half when Law was felled in the area and Quixall converted the most important penalty of his life. The final score was 1–1. Manchester United had survived.

It had been a particularly eventful first season for Denis Law: he had won an FA Cup winners' medal, scored in the final, and effectively consigned his previous English club to the Second Division. Throughout the drama, Busby had hovered in the foreground like a protective, encouraging parent. In common with so many other players from the period, Law appreciated the unique qualities of an exceptionally gifted manager:

> I had never met anyone else like him in the game . . . Busby seemed to care about your life off the field as well as how you performed on it. Were your digs all right? Your family? Your wife? Your children? It got through to me that here was a man who took a great deal of interest in his players' private lives. It made players run through brick walls for him because they knew that he had their interests at heart. The longer you knew him, the more you felt for him, which was why he had everybody doing the things they did.

Contrary to Law's eulogy, Busby did not win the unqualified support of everybody in the team. After losing the Charity Shield to Everton, he was confronted by a sturdy rebel in the form of little Johnny Giles. The Irishman found it difficult to accept Busby's decision to demote him from the first team for a spell in the reserves and their disagreement culminated in his transfer to Leeds United for a bargain £34,000. The sale was probably the biggest mistake of Busby's managerial career for Giles soon emerged as the centrepiece of Don Revie's awesome side. For a relatively paltry transfer fee, United had surrendered one of the greatest footballers of all time. What they might have won with his midfield genius tantalises the imagination. The Giles episode provided another revealing glimpse into Busby's psychology. Here was a player who had been guilty of nothing more serious than challenging the absolute authority of his manager, but for that crime alone he was banished. It was the same ruthless dogmatism that had prevented Charlie Mitten from regaining his place and seen the talented Johnny Morris despatched to Derby. Busby always insisted that no player could seem bigger than the club, but even as Giles journeyed to Yorkshire, there lurked in the reserves a lad who would challenge that assertion to its logical extreme.

George Best had arrived at the club in the summer of 1961 as a 15-year-old apprentice. Homesickness immediately drove him back to Belfast but he soon returned to a life of boot polishing, floor sweeping, and junior football. For the next two years Busby watched his progress with ever-increasing amazement. The boy's potential seemed unlimited. His speed, determination, dribbling skill, heading ability and goalscoring instinct were already way beyond his years and his natural nonchalance added an engagingly arrogant dimension to his play. On 14 September 1963 he was thrust into the first team and impressed Busby again by his absolute lack of fear and willingness to chase every ball. By 1964 he was a regular in the first team and well on the way to becoming a national celebrity. Initially, Busby succeeded in curbing his wilder instincts but before long Best would don the mantle of a rebel and challenge the very ethos of the club to its foundations.

United's victory in the 1963 FA Cup brought European competition back to Manchester for the first time since the Munich disaster. The Cup Winners' Cup campaign began solidly enough with a 7–2 aggregate victory over Holland's Tilburg Willem II before United faced the holders Spurs. A 2–0 defeat at White Hart Lane left the critics guessing, but Busby's improved squad made no mistake in the return, winning 4–1. Suddenly, there was premature talk of United competing for another treble as they moved steadily towards the FA Cup semi-finals and challenged strongly in the League. The first leg of the Cup Winners' Cup quarter-final against Sporting Lisbon was nothing less than a rout. The Portuguese attempted to outfox their opponents by playing the offside trap, but the manoeuvre backfired and United rammed home four goals to register one of their easiest European victories.

Most of the players felt that Sporting were a mediocre side that would offer little resistance in the return. And so it seemed when Law shaved the post early in the first half of the second leg at Lisbon. At that point, the Portuguese shook free their defensive shackles and poured into United's half raining down on goal in a desperate attempt to retrieve their lost pride. Busby's team was soon reduced to the level of a hungover village pub side as Sporting scored goal after goal before finally winning 5–0. It was the most abysmal European performance in Manchester United's history and a salutary lesson on the dangers of complacency abroad. At least Busby was guaranteed further European competition in 1964, although not in the way he would have preferred. United were defeated by West Ham in the semi-final of the FA Cup and had to settle for a Fairs Cup place after losing the League race to Liverpool.

The 1963–64 season had proved a turning point for Manchester United. Having won the FA Cup in the previous season they showed themselves capable of competing strenuously on three fronts. The failure to secure a trophy was less important than the fact that they were capable of competing for so many. At last, Busby convinced himself, his squad had the necessary blend of youth and experience to mount a convincing Championship assault. In addition to the new generation of reserves, Busby already boasted a brilliant attacking formation with Law, Best and Charlton, and a solid defence featuring Crerand, Brennan and Stiles. United needed strength as well as flair, for the First Division was becoming more rugged and defence-minded with each new season. They looked likely title winners until Christmas 1964 when they faced the might of newly-promoted Leeds. The Yorkshire side won 1–0 at Old Trafford and soon usurped United's place at the top of Division One. Both teams ended up chasing the double and met again in the semi-finals of the FA Cup. A goalless draw almost degenerated into a brawl as the physical Reds conceded close to a score of free kicks. It did them no good, for Leeds won the replay 1–0. Busby was now facing a repetition of last season's series of near misses, as Leeds powered towards the League title. A third crucial meeting between the clubs, this time at Elland Road, saw Manchester take both points and revive their Championship pretensions. Leeds faltered just enough in their final fixtures to allow Busby's men to snatch the title on goal average. By a whisker, Manchester United were back in the European Cup.

After parading the League Championship trophy, Busby had some post-season Fairs Cup commitments to complete. While sparring with Leeds, the Reds had trudged their way to the semi-finals of the Inter-Cities competition where they faced the formidable Hungarian side Ferencvaros. Weary from a long season, United struggled to win the first match at Old Trafford 3–2. Their defence seemed solid enough to withstand the return in Hungary, however, but their temperament brought a heavy rebuke when Pat Crerand was sent off. Ferencvaros won 1–0 and tied the aggregate score. The rule allowing away goals to count double had yet to be introduced into the competition, so United were granted a replay. A toss of the coin decided the venue in Ferencvaros' favour and this advantage was to prove crucial. Another tight match in Budapest saw a tired United outplayed and the Hungarians shaded the match 2–1. It was Busby's fourth unsuccessful attempt to win a European trophy. The only consolation was the knowledge that further Continental competition beckoned in the forthcoming season.

In June 1965, Busby was dismayed to learn of the death of his chairman Harold Hardman. He was the second incumbent to pass away during Busby's reign and a sad loss to the club. The post was filled by the ageing director Louis Edwards, who offered Busby the same unqualified support as his predecessors had done. Although Manchester United had restored a lost stability, the club was not without its problems on and off the field. The inflammatory Denis Law appeared to be confusing disciplinary points with League points and was no stranger to heavy fines and suspensions.

Even more alarming to Busby was the increasing waywardness of his clubhouse genius George Best, who had emerged overnight as a nightclub celebrity. No longer the preserve of football columns, Best's nocturnal activities had spilled over into the general news section. His good looks, Beatle-styled hair, flashy clothes and rumoured romances made him a paparazzi favourite and a godsend to gossip writers throughout Fleet Street. The one person alarmed by these developments was the patriarchal Busby. He warned Best that his excessive partying would ruin his footballing career and frequently reprimanded him behind closed doors. Perhaps realising that the Belfast boy was a misunderstood genius, Busby adopted a kid gloves approach which many felt was ill-advised. He genuinely liked Best, who invariably seemed non-confrontational and contrite whenever he was hauled up to his manager's office to explain away his latest misdemeanours. It was clear that he was damaging the club's conservative image, but his football skills were such that he could fill Old Trafford on his own. For most of his soccer life Best remained a law unto himself and challenged his manager's authority like none before or since. Perhaps his most remarkable snub was failing to turn up for his own disciplinary hearing at the FA. Busby, who was there to give mitigating evidence on his behalf, was left with the embarrassment of explaining away an inexcusable transgression. Such discourtesy would have taxed any manager's patience beyond endurance, but somehow Busby held faith with the Irish rebel. Obviously, punishments were meted out. Best was lectured, fined and suspended, but always forgiven. In an astonishing display of managerial protectiveness, Busby even invited him to share his home, but Best chose to go his own way. The fate of George Best suggests that Busby's reformative tactics were ultimately unsuccessful. Other managers were quick to suggest that Busby's patience may have been misplaced but, interestingly, Bob Paisley was not among them:

> We all have a little failing somewhere. If you look at Matt and ask where he might have failed you immediately think of George Best. But could anybody have handled him? It's a shame that his talent wasn't fully used because after the age of 26 he just played around. But if Matt Busby couldn't handle him *nobody* could.

The importance of Best to Manchester United was never better exemplified than in their immemorial quest for the European Cup. The 1965 campaign had begun confidently enough with convincing victories over Helsinki and East Berlin's ASK Vorwaerts. However, these were mere tasters to a spectacular quarter-final showdown in which United faced the former holders Benfica. The Portuguese side included the wizard Eusebio who made his presence felt during the first leg at Old Trafford by scoring the opening goal. United rallied, but in a hard-fought contest could only emerge with a threadbare 3–2 lead.

Benfica returned home confident that they could overpower their opponents in the return leg. Football sages reluctantly agreed with the prognosis and most did not give United a cat's chance in hell of surviving. Benfica were regarded as invincible at home where they had not lost for over seven years! Such statistics were lost on Busby who, as so often before, used the tension of the away return to Manchester United's advantage. Rather than soaking up punishment for the duration of the contest and playing on the break, Busby decided to repeat the old Real trick of impudent attack. He advised United to settle for a quarter of an hour before bombarding Benfica's goal with sustained attacking football. Such tactics were perfectly suited to a player of Best's carefree temperament, but he lacked the patience to restrain himself for Busby's required 15 minutes. In fact, he scored two goals in the first 12 minutes, which so inspired United that they added a third shortly afterwards, leaving Benfica shell-shocked and demoralised. More thrills followed in the second half as United cantered towards an unbelievable 5–1 victory. Even more remarkable was the attitude of the crowd. Instead of lifting the beleaguered Benfica a treacherous group of fans incessantly chanted 'El Beatle' every time the heroic Best pounced upon the ball. At the end of the match, Busby was shocked to see a man with a knife heading menacingly towards the Belfast Adonis. Suddenly, it seemed that United were to pay for their famous victory with the ritual slaughter of their favourite son. The alarm passed, however, when it became clear that the 'attacker' was simply an overeager fan determined to secure a lock of Best's dark Beatle hair as a souvenir. Even in Portugal, Best was now a god.

In April 1966 Busby set out for his third European Cup semi-final. The opponents were the relatively unknown Partizan Belgrade who, despite containing a glut of internationals, were rated well below Benfica. Surely United would win this one. The Belgradians proved tough opposition, however, and won their home leg 2–0, leaving the Reds with much to do in the return. The cause had not been helped by a nagging injury which incapacitated George Best, who was afterwards forced to retire for the remainder of the season. The return at Old Trafford was a sell-out as crowds gathered to see if Busby could rekindle the Munich dream. It was not to be. Partizan provided a text book example of defensive Continental play and although Nobby Stiles penetrated their back line late in the game, that elusive equaliser would not come. It had undoubtedly been Manchester United's best chance yet of reaching a European final and Busby could not help feeling that the opportunity had been squandered. Salt was rubbed into the sores three days later when United narrowly lost to Everton in the FA Cup semi-final. In a season which had promised so much, United and Busby had ended up with nothing.

The summer of 1966 saw Busby at his lowest ebb since Munich. The disappointment of failing to win the European Cup bit deeper than anybody could have imagined. In a totally uncharacteristic and bitter admission of defeat, Busby confided in Pat Crerand: 'We'll never win the European Cup now'. The eight-year burden of attempting to realise the Munich dream had clearly taken its toll, so much so that Busby privately threatened to quit football. What changed his mind was the positive attitude of his wife, Jean, backed by the undeniable knowledge that Manchester United were now a Championship-winning team. The striking power of Law, Best and Charlton seemed guaranteed to prise open any defence in the First Division and was worth supporting for at least one more season. The melancholic cloud had passed. Almost.

Even while Busby considered the future of his great new side, the mutinous Denis Law was threatening to leave Manchester United. His contract was due to end in August 1966 and, in order to retain his services, Law demanded that the club pay him a re-signing fee and substantial wage increase. It was a high-handed move, but Busby was not afraid to call his bluff. The press reported, in barely concealed amazement, that the Manchester maestro had put Law on the transfer list. The Scottish striker was dismayed to learn that his plan had backfired. Shocked by the realisation that he might have to leave United, he hurriedly made his peace with Busby, who was pleased to accept an apology for the cheeky manoeuvre. The episode typified Busby's toughness with players when he felt they had overstepped the mark.

The attempt to win the League title and re-qualify for Europe began in earnest during the autumn of 1966 when Busby signed goalkeeper Alex Stepney to replace the incapacitated Harry Gregg. By replenishing the squad, Busby was cleverly insuring against winter injuries and preparing his troops for an arduous campaign. After an average start, United dug in their heels and hit peak form around Christmas. A major setback in the fourth round of the FA Cup, where they lost at Old Trafford to Second Division Norwich, merely strengthened their resolve to clinch the Championship. In the event, they remained unbeaten in the League after 16 December to secure their seventh title with 60 points. After two years, Busby was back on the trail of the European Cup.

Even with a Championship-winning squad, Busby was anxious to improve United's prospects with another star signing. Celtic, who had recently achieved a place in the history books by becoming the first British club to win the European Cup, boasted a fearsome striker called Jimmy Johnstone, but Busby could not persuade him to leave Parkhead. Busby next turned his attention to the English clubs, but nobody was available that he fancied. The pressure of obtaining new stars was alleviated by United's excellent form in the League where they swiftly opened a formidable points lead. Meanwhile, the European adventure was progressing quietly. Hibernian of Malta were despatched 4–0 at Old Trafford and the return leg was less a competition than an excited gathering of the Maltese Manchester United fan club. Far from encountering angry supporters, the United players were mobbed by well-wishers and autograph hunters. The friendly reception was a tribute to the Corinthian image that Busby had created for United back in the 1950s. Unfortunately, the return match did not live up to the club legend, although the Maltese no doubt took some consolation from holding their Mancunian idols to a goalless draw.

The next round presented a far greater challenge in the form of Sarajevo of Yugoslavia. For the first time since Munich, United boarded a charter plane to travel to the match and were the worst for wear upon arrival. A hard-fought tie ended in deadlock, although not without some furious protests from the Yugoslavians, who felt that they had been robbed of a goal. The scenes were intimidating enough to prompt Busby to write off the fixture as his 'worst footballing experience'. The return was not a sparkling affair either: United won 2–1 against a Sarajevo side reduced to ten men and still capable of scoring. This was hardly the form expected of a side hoping to become European Champions.

On paper, United's next European fixture against Gornick Zabrze of Poland should have proved even tougher. Fortunately, they encountered the Poles in a sluggish state, still recovering from their mid-season break. At Old Trafford, United secured a solid 2–0 first leg lead with Brian Kidd scoring the crucial second goal in the final minute. Before setting off for the return Busby again decided to wade into the transfer market with a presumptuous bid for West Ham's World Cup hero Geoff Hurst. A message was left for manager Ron Greenwood indicating that United were willing to pay £200,000 for the striker. Busby requested his Upton Park counterpart to telegraph a message with a 'yes or no answer'. The brusque Greenwood took Busby's words literally and immediately despatched a telegram to Poland containing the curt message: 'Busby, Manchester United, Gornik. No. Greenwood'. Without the additional flair of Hurst, Busby was wary of throwing everyone into attack in the return against Gornik and so played a tantalising cat and mouse game. Stiles was called upon to adopt the feline role terrifying attackers with his lethal tackling. Although Gornik's Lubanski broke through to score, United had done enough to hang on and win their way through to the semi-final.

There was an unnervingly eerie element to the semi-final draw which saw United paired alongside Real Madrid, just as they had been in 1957. Fortunately for Busby, Real were past their prime although their experience and lingering power could not be underestimated. United discovered this to their cost in the first leg when they laboured to snatch a fragile 1–0 lead. With Law troubled by a leg injury and shortly to be hospitalised, Manchester seemed ominously short of firing power for the return engagement. Faced with the likelihood of losing his fourth consecutive European semi-final, Busby elected to play a defensive formation, leaving only Kidd and Best upfront for an unlikely breakaway goal. The ploy failed to unsettle the free-flowing Real who swiftly scored twice. An own goal by Zoca brought hope to the Mancunians, but this was swiftly negated when Amancio struck to take the Spaniards to a 3–1 half-time lead. United seemed dead and buried although, in reality, they were only one goal behind on aggregate. This was the morale-boosting message that Busby attempted to impart to his demoralised squad, but, as Bobby Charlton confesses, it was difficult to believe:

> We were 3–1 down at half-time and getting murdered. They were playing great, we were playing badly. We were feeling shattered with no one saying a word because it was all too bad to be true. Then the boss walked in. 'Come on lads', he said. 'We can still do this'.

In a bold attempt to improve United's play Busby reversed his previous instructions and ordered his players to revert to their customary attacking game. After the break, Sadler, in a striker's role, reduced the deficit to 3–2. With 15 minutes left, United and Real were equal on aggregate when Best passed to the Munich veteran Bill Foulkes who, fittingly, netted the winner. Busby's attacking gamble had worked. According to Charlton, the semi-final victory over Real Madrid was Busby's greatest moment in football, even more stupendous than the forthcoming final against the great Benfica.

As the 1968 season reached its close there remained a distinct possibility that Busby might once again see United squander their chances of winning a trophy. Strongly fancied to retain the League title, they allowed Manchester City to draw level and eventually surrendered the Championship to their rivals by two points. The need to win the European Cup was now paramount.

On 29 May 1968, Manchester United walked out onto the Wembley Stadium pitch to the sound of 100,000 roaring, chanting fans. In theory, home advantage weighed heavily in Manchester's favour, but their opponents Benfica were no strangers to Wembley having lost the European Cup final there in 1963 against AC Milan. The Portuguese had played in three other finals, winning two of them, and were undoubtedly one of the most accomplished sides in Europe. The absence of the injured Denis Law severely weakened United's striking thrust and underlined the need for patient building from the back. Busby wisely employed the ferocious Stiles to mark Eusebio out of the game and hoped that Benfica's defenders would prove less effective against the rampaging Best. In the event, both stars were contained in the first half, although the speedy Eusebio eluded Manchester's back four on one occasion and hit the crossbar. The deadlock was broken after 65 minutes when the hot-footed Bobby Charlton made novel use of his head by glancing the ball into the net. United hung on until the 80th minute when Graça scored a highly-deserved equaliser. Busby now considered that Benfica might snatch a late winner and his worst fears were almost realised when the impeccable Eusebio was left with only Alex Stepney to beat. In that moment, the European dream faded from Busby's eyes and he turned away in despair. Eusebio needed only to place the ball but elected to destroy United with a spectacular, fiercely-hit shot. Stepney had a half chance to narrow the angle and somehow managed to get his fingertips to the ball. For the second time in the match Eusebio had failed to bury United by a matter of millimetres. Busby breathed a sigh of relief when the referee blew for the end of 90 minutes.

Manchester United seemed spent during the full-time interval, but Busby urged his boys to establish control in midfield and keep attacking. The tactics proved extremely profitable and before long Best was finding acres of space. A weaving run past several opponents, including the keeper, saw Best arrogantly deposit the ball into the Benfica net. Shortly afterwards the lead was increased by Brian Kidd who had the good fortune to score on his 19th birthday. Appropriately enough, Busby's favourite son, Bobby Charlton, completed the scoring to put the tie beyond doubt. A match that Manchester United had come so close to losing had ended 4–1 in their favour. Charlton collapsed in tears at the final whistle and both he and Pat Crerand later missed the celebratory banquet due to stomach cramps. It turned out to be a joyous day for Busby, the fulfilment of a dream that had seemed irrevocably destroyed on a Munich airfield in 1958. Now at last his mission was complete.

The coda to the European Cup victory was inevitably anti-climactic. Like his Cup-winning predecessor, Jock Stein, Busby insisted on allowing his team to play in the unofficial World Club Championship against the present kings of South American soccer. This two-match battle of the giants had degenerated into a soccer war in recent years, with violence, intimidation and lackadaisical refereeing playing as important a part in determining the result as the actual football. Manchester United's opponents were Estudiantes, a team made up of young students. They sounded deceptively innocuous but Busby soon discovered the true depths of their physical aggression. There was some hint of what was to come when Nobby Stiles was pilloried as 'El Assassin' in the local press. Even in the programme notes he was disturbingly referred to as 'brutish, bad intentioned and a bad sportsman'. Clearly, the Argentine press had not forgotten his World Cup escapades. While the vitriolic press suggested that Stiles and United were heading for a public mauling, the local people were far from unpleasant or aggressive, either before or during the match. Sadly, the same could not be said of Estudiantes. They played at their cynical worst, gratuitously fouling their opponents in a vain attempt to secure a psychological advantage. For all their efforts, they produced only a 1–0 lead whereas a display of pure football might have provided a more substantial victory. Busby was content enough to emerge with such a slim defeat, although he was less pleased about the sending off of Nobby Stiles whose sole transgression was an impolite gesture to the referee. Such niggles were expected to be righted in the return at Old Trafford, but Busby had not banked on Estudiantes producing their secret weapon: football. Within five minutes of the second leg opening, the students of Argentina had astounded their Mancunian professors with an opportunistic goal. United diligently sought to reduce the alarming deficit, but could only manage a late goal by Willie Morgan. By then, Best and Medina were exchanging punches and left the field in disgrace. The entire fiasco was a pitiful way for Busby to prepare for his imminent retirement.

It was not until January 1969 that Busby finally announced that he was stepping down as Manchester United team manager. In his 60th year, he clearly felt that the squad would be better served by a younger, track-suited manager. The truth was that there was little left for Busby to achieve as Manchester United supremo. He had fulfilled that single driving ambition of lifting the European Cup and his odyssey had been publicly acknowledged with the award of a knighthood. The rest could only prove anti-climactic as Busby discovered half-way through the following mediocre season. So it was that former Manchester United chief coach Wilf McGuinness took over the reins while Busby promoted himself to general manager. McGuinness's troubled reign lasted just 20 months before poor results prompted his dismissal. Busby returned to steady the team but soon retired once more to accept a directorship. Since then his beloved club has experienced a series of managers all promising much but providing relatively little. Far from reclaiming the European Cup that Busby so prized, the Red Devils have not even won one League Championship since 1967. Their failure to secure the premier domestic trophy, and thereby qualify for inclusion in the European Cup, puts Busby's managership in an even more favourable light. His successors cannot complain of a lack of resources or public support, for Busby provided both in abundance. What he could not bestow, however, was the experience gained in establishing and nurturing Championship-winning teams. Manchester United's shortcomings in that respect have proven at times surprising, irritating and downright embarrassing.

The statistics of major honours and near misses testify to Manchester United's pre-eminence under the expert guidance of Matt Busby: they were five times League Champions and seven times runners-up; they reached the FA Cup final four times, winning the trophy twice; they were the first English club to win the European Cup and that came after they had lost four semi-finals. During the period of Busby's management, Manchester United won more League points and Cup games than any of their competitors and provided more international players with close to 300 appearances between them. By any standards these remarkable results and records are exemplary, yet they tell only part of the story. For Busby did not merely create one great team but helped fashion four, during a 23-year reign of triumph and tragedy. There is little doubt that, were it not for the Munich air disaster, the above roll of honours would have stretched still further. Busby's success in rebuilding a decimated Championship-winning team and tirelessly pursuing the European Cup dream are a tribute to his persistence and dedication over two decades in football management.

From a historical vantage point, the managerial quality that impresses most was his consistent and courageous innovation: Busby destroyed for ever the concept of the ivory tower manager by empathising with his players and joining them on the field in training; he loosened the grip of interfering directors in the crucial matter of team selection; he overruled the myopic objections of soccer's hierarchy by accepting European competition; he pursued an adventurous youth policy as a means of achieving consistent excellence without undue expenditure; he campaigned for the introduction of substitutes at a time when ten men were expected to carry on regardless; he was among the first to realise that England would be bled of its top players unless the footballing authorities sanctioned freedom of contract; and throughout his career he championed attractive, attacking football as the best means of maintaining long-term support from an increasingly discriminating public. His philosophy of the game was positive, consistent and invariably ahead of its time. Matt Busby was a trailblazer whose managerial achievements dominate the second half of 20th-century British football.

BILL NICHOLSON

THE POWER AND THE GLORY

William Nicholson, the seventh of nine children, was born on 26 July 1919 in the seaside town of Scarborough, North Yorkshire. Although he could not complain about his pleasant surroundings, Nicholson was effectively marooned in a resort bereft of soccer tradition. With no big local side to support, youths had to look beyond football terraces for leisure satisfaction. In an age before the advent of television when even cinema visits were regarded as a luxury, most kids made up their own games. Scarborough offered one obviously large attraction with its sumptuous beach, but young Nicholson was unable to swim. Boredom, rather than burning commitment, encouraged him to spend most of his waking hours on the streets: 'The only attraction was to kick a ball about – a tennis ball, a little rubber sponge or even a paper ball. Anything . . . morning, afternoon or night, if possible'.

Nicholson's hard-working parents did not discourage this obsessive interest in football but made sure that he attended school regularly and were no doubt pleasantly surprised when he won a scholarship to the prestigious Scarborough Boys' High. Bill was doubly pleased, for his secondary school played organised football and boasted some of the best teams in the area. The new boy slotted into the under-14 side as a centre half, and his ball-playing skills were much in evidence during the eagerly awaited Saturday afternoon matches. The High School teams were allowed to practise on a pitch adjacent to Scarborough Football Club and Nicholson admits that such reflected glory fuelled his ambition to achieve professional status. He dreamed of earning £5 a week, although he was unsure what could be done with such a kingly sum. The dreams continued throughout adolescence when Nicholson won a place in the school senior team. His physical attributes were now under question, however, and the PE master decreed that such a slight frame would have to be switched from centre half to inside forward. From that moment onwards, Nicholson's soccer-playing pretensions retreated in the starkly realistic face of an uncertain future. He remained at school until 16, then quite a late age, but he was no academic. Ironically, the High School education that had promised so much was placed in cold perspective when Nicholson was reduced to working in a laundry. He still kicked a ball occasionally and featured in his local junior side, but his progress was unspectacular. The Scarborough and District Minor League now appeared to be the summit of his footballing ambition. The immemorial dream of playing in a Football League side suddenly seemed both presumptuous and delusory, and as Nicholson confessed: 'When I left school thoughts of becoming a professional faded completely'.

Nicholson would probably have remained languishing in Scarborough were it not for the timely intervention of Tottenham Hotspur's chief scout Bill Ives. He had received some favourable reports about the lad and backed his judgement sufficiently to offer Nicholson a £2-a-week apprenticeship. In the circumstances, the offer was a godsend, although Nicholson had good reason not to be over-optimistic. Like many big clubs, Spurs signed starstruck youngsters as though they were going out of fashion, and few ever made it to the first team. Interestingly, Nicholson attended the same trial as young Bob Paisley, who had the foresight to question Spurs' terms before making the brave decision to reject the Londoners in favour of amateurs Bishop Auckland. Nicholson betrayed no such reticence and maintained an endearing, if naive, faith in Tottenham Hotspur for the remainder of his footballing career.

Pre-war apprentices were expected to earn their money the hard way, working from 8am-5pm with a one-hour lunch break. The youngsters were seldom allowed anywhere near the dressing room and fraternisation with the players was strictly taboo. Soccer was sandwiched grudgingly between long hours spent tending the pitch and painting the roofs of the stand. Some of the lads felt so starved of football that they would stuff empty £5 money bags with paper and eagerly kick them through the White Hart Lane corridors. Even this boyish escapade was severely frowned upon by their superiors who appeared to prefer decorating skill to football artistry. Hard-working Nicholson made a reasonable start, but the training staff soon realised that he was nothing more than an average inside forward. After one-and-a-half years, it seemed unlikely that he would ever experience first team football but, as so often happens, a happy accident caused a positional shuffle. Nicholson emerged from the debris as a full back and then performed so competently that, within six months, he found himself promoted to the first team. This was a period of stability and progress for the 19-year-old who swiftly adopted Tottenham as his home. He married a local girl who insisted upon being known by her affectionate, and oddly ambiguous nickname, 'Darkie'. The couple settled in a house near the ground and, despite changing financial circumstances, stayed in the area permanently.

The War interrupted Nicholson's promising playing career, but he put these missing years to good use. He was rapidly promoted to sergeant in the Durham Light Infantry and spent much of his time instructing troops in physical education. This not only ensured that he was always fit, but enabled him to develop coaching and communicative skills which would later pave the way for a successful managerial career. Nicholson was astute enough to continue his coaching activities long after the War and won an FA badge under the expert instruction of England manager Walter Winterbottom. Without realising his prospects, Nicholson was already on the way to becoming a first-class manager and top flight coach.

Following his demobilisation from the Army, Nicholson returned to a new Spurs team and was somewhat taken aback when manager Joe Hulme announced that he would henceforth be a centre half. Nicholson protested that, at 5 feet 9 inches, he was too small for the job but Hulme was insistent. Cruelly, the first fixture in this new position saw Nicholson facing up to the great Chelsea centre forward Tommy Lawton, against whom he had last played in the wartime inter-command matches. When Lawton saw Nicholson lining up in his new unfamiliar position, he laughingly exclaimed: 'What are *you* doing here?' Naively, Nicholson made no attempt to disguise his fears and confessed that he was wary of playing at centre half. A more opportunistic opponent would have used this knowledge to intimidate the re-positioned player but Lawton was unusually sympathetic and boosted Nicholson's confidence with some well-chosen words. The reassuring tone settled Nicholson's nerves and he later admitted: 'I don't think I ever played a better game than that at centre half'.

Spurs were nothing more than a middling Second Division side in the late 1940s, but in 1948 they found themselves on the brink of FA Cup glory. A fortuitous draw saw them paired alongside teams from their own Division until the semi-final, when they faced formidable Blackpool. The First Division side boasted two of the era's most famous internationals, Stanley Matthews and Stan Mortensen, but, in spite of such superiority, it was Spurs that held a precarious 1–0 lead with three minutes of the match remaining. The Tottenham fans were rehearsing their Wembley chants when Matthews neatly intercepted a bad pass and crossed to Mortensen who netted a late equaliser. Spurs were psychologically shattered. Unable to lift themselves in extra time, they allowed Blackpool to assert their First Division pedigree and Mortensen ended the day with a hat trick. It was one of Nicholson's saddest moments as a Spurs player and the whole scenario was destined to be re-enacted five years later.

Prior to the 1948 Cup saga, Nicholson had been moved across to right half, a position in which he felt most uncomfortable. He was frequently given the run around by superior players such as Jimmy Hagan whose pace and passing skill left opponents stranded. Undeterred by Nicholson's initial problems, Spurs manager Joe Hulme insisted that he would settle and was eventually proven right. In his new role Nicholson was about to enter the most successful phase in Tottenham's history.

The appointment of Arthur Rowe as manager in 1949 saw Spurs arise from the doldrums of the Second Division to become one of the most feared teams in the country. Their secret lay in a simple but ingenious tactic which required players to push the ball forward as quickly as possible and race into space to collect the return pass. The dazzling push and run attacks made mincemeat of the opposition and in the spring of 1950, Spurs clinched promotion with a scorching 61 points.

As a coaching enthusiast Nicholson was greatly impressed by Rowe's innovative tactics and repeated his instructions as though they were a litany: 'Make it simple, accurate and quick', 'simplicity of purpose', 'utility of ability'. Rhyming watchwords and 27 Second Division victories were not enough to convince the soccer powers that Spurs were anything other than average opponents. The three previous post-war Second Division Champions had proven an ineffectual bunch and two of them were relegated in the very season that Spurs re-emerged in the top flight. Rowe was undeterred by such statistics, however, and soon bamboozled the leading teams in the country with his tactic of playing football at a breakneck pace. Defences found this impossible to handle and it was not uncommon for Spurs to have four players alongside whoever held the ball and possession was maintained by short, speedy, accurate passes. The tactic retained its efficacy throughout the season and Spurs celebrated their grand return by lifting the Championship in 1951.

Nicholson's most memorable season since entering football was completed when he was chosen to represent England at international level against Portugal in May 1951. It was a debut straight out of *Roy of the Rovers*. As the referee blew his whistle, Nicholson moved upfield and received a timely pass from Stan Pearson. From 25 yards out, the Spurs right half struck the ball towards the Portuguese goal and watched in frozen amazement as the ball glided into the net five feet from the post. Nicholson had scored his first goal for England after only 19 seconds on the pitch! The final result was 5–2 in England's favour but the heroic Nicholson was not rewarded with a second cap. The legendary Billy Wright claimed the place as his own and proved impossible to dislodge, so Nicholson's 19-second goal was his first and last for his country.

In the days before the European Cup, the English League Champions were starved of Continental competition. However, Nicholson was fortunate enough to accompany Spurs on a trip to Brussels where they drew with the talented FK Austria 2–2. The match had been billed as the Championship of Europe and certainly lived up to its name. Nicholson later recalled that it was the finest game of his soccer-playing career.

Rowe's great push and run side lasted two more years before a decline in player fitness and a management upheaval took its inevitable toll. Spurs threatened to retain their Championship in 1952 with some scintillating football, but Rowe could not prevent Matt Busby's perennial bridesmaids Manchester United from finally clinching the title. The following season Spurs slipped to mid-table but their progress in the FA Cup was impressive. They survived tough replays against Preston and Birmingham before again facing Blackpool in a dramatic semi-final. It was a game uncannily similar to its 1948 counterpart with a late Blackpool goal once more destroying the Wembley dream. The culprit was Spurs' Alf Ramsey, whose lack of pace presented Jackie Mudie with an easy winner literally seconds from full-time. The Tottenham players fell into a muted depression back in the dressing room as if realising that this was their last chance of glory.

The influential Arthur Rowe did not return for the new season, having retired due to ill health. His replacement, Jimmy Anderson, was a Spurs veteran in his mid-60s. Anderson was respected throughout the club and the players enjoyed the stories of how he spent his boyhood days scrambling under the turnstiles to watch his beloved team. His infatuation and persistence had made him the youngest assistant trainer in Tottenham Hotspur's history and the eventual climb to the managerial throne was seen as a deserved reward for decades of service. Like many managers in the early 1950s, Anderson was primarily an administrator, but his decisions were generally sound. He appointed Bill Nicholson as chief coach and oversaw a superlative training staff headed by Cecil Poynton and Jack Coxford. What Anderson could not do, however, was arrest the natural decline of an ageing team. Such luminaries as Roy Burgess, Eddie Baily and Alf Ramsey had all seen better days and soon moved on. Meanwhile, Spurs' fortunes foundered to such an extent that they slipped to 16th in the table.

The critics initially blamed Anderson for Tottenham's sudden decline and cried for the return of Arthur Rowe's push and run tactics. Rowe was briefly reinstated but ill health blighted his comeback, leaving Spurs in more trouble than ever. The unfortunate Anderson was left to pick up the pieces and nurse ailing Spurs through three transitional years. Push and run was already anachronistic, killed off by defences retreating down the centre and closing up space. The Tottenham forwards had lost their speed and became easy prey for full backs who man-marked rather than chased the ball. Anderson rode the crisis with bullish aplomb, convinced that Spurs would rise again. Nicholson, meanwhile, watched from the sidelines, eagerly awaiting a new generation of talented players.

The promotion of Danny Blanchflower to team captain at least ensured that Tottenham had inspired leadership on the field, but by 1956 even that was causing problems. The loquacious Northern Ireland international had his own ideas and was not above challenging Anderson's absolute authority. Events reached a head during the climax of a surprisingly impressive FA Cup run. In the sixth round at West Ham, Blanchflower had indisputably saved Spurs from defeat by reshaping the side and pushing a defender into attack. He tried the same arrogant trick in the semi-final against Manchester City but his bold gamble could not prevent Spurs from losing 1–0. Blanchflower's meddling caused whispers at Spurs, who now faced an exhausting battle against relegation. During an Easter bottom-of-the-table dogfight against Huddersfield, Blanchflower again altered the playing pattern and Spurs suffered a calamitous home defeat. Believing that his influence had been usurped, Anderson reacted strongly by stripping Blanchflower of his captaincy. Amid the crisis, Spurs somehow scrambled to safety finishing 18th in the table, just two points from relegation.

Anderson's faith and perseverance were finally rewarded in 1957 and 1958 when Spurs rose phoenix-like to finish second and third, respectively. Blanchflower had re-emerged as the hero of the team winning the Footballer of the Year title in the process. Following two successive seasons in the top three, the portents looked favourable for another Championship trophy, but Anderson was not caught up in the expectant euphoria. He realised that the side was again in urgent need of major surgery and spoke eloquently on the importance of establishing a successful youth policy. Obviously, he was considerably influenced by the impact of Matt Busby's youthful Manchester United and saw no reason why Spurs should not create a similarly effective footballing nursery. Following discussions with Nicholson, Poynton and Baxter, Anderson promised the imminent formation of a formidable youth team. In August 1958, a mass trial took place at the Cheshunt training ground attended by 50 eager youngsters. Spurs were on the brink of another golden era.

Anderson's grand plan was never likely to reach fruition during his own reign for his health was poor. He had been suffering from phlebitis for some time and then bronchitis rendered him ineffectual during the closing weeks of the 1957–58 season. Although he realised that Spurs' high League position was flattering, the extent of their decline in the opening weeks of the new season was alarming. By mid-October they had taken only eight points from their first 11 games and slipped to a disappointing 16th in the table. Their lacklustre performances were compounded by a series of bizarre injuries which read like a witch's curse. Star signing Cliff Jones had broken his leg soon after arriving and was consigned to the terraces for the remainder of the season. Within days of that setback, reserve goalkeeper Ron Reynolds sliced off part of his finger in a car crash. Unbelievably, the returning veteran Ted Ditchburn, dislocated a finger shortly afterwards, leaving Spurs looking more forlorn than ever. Anderson had seen enough and realised that the struggle ahead required the stamina of a young man. After 50 years' employment at Tottenham, the old warhorse at last retired.

10 October 1958 was an eventful day in the footballing career of Bill Nicholson. During the morning he was greeted as usual by Anderson, then told: 'Put on your coat and go to see the vice-chairman'. When Nicholson asked why, Anderson playfully refused to elaborate suggesting only that Mr Wale would reveal all. Minutes later, Nicholson was flabbergasted to be offered the job as Spurs' new manager:

> I didn't know what to say because I was unprepared for anything like this . . . I had no inclination to take up management with all its worries and hazards. In my capacity as assistant manager and coach with Spurs I already had one of the best jobs in football.

Before Nicholson could even come up with a suitable reply, Wale ushered him from his office with instructions to consider the offer and relay his decision to the board before the next home fixture. After recovering from the shock, Nicholson began to appreciate precisely why he had been selected as the primary candidate. Firstly, he knew the set-up at Spurs as well, if not better, than anybody else at the club. Secondly, having worked alongside Anderson, he was in the perfect position to implement the youth policy and team changes that were necessary to ensure First Division longevity. What most impressed the board, however, was Nicholson's extra-curricular activities. During the previous two years, he had served beneath England manager Walter Winterbottom, taking control of the under-23 side and helping with the preparations for the 1958 World Cup. In an era when track-suited managers were coming into vogue, Nicholson was perfectly placed to take over from his desk-bound predecessor.

Nicholson's appointment was confirmed on 11 October. The only assurance he required from the board was that he should have complete control of team selection. Remarkably, there was no mention of any contract and nor would there be. Stubbornly independent, Nicholson was content to stand or fall on his ability to win matches.

The players had already changed into their kit when chairman Fred Bearman entered the dressing room to introduce the new manager. The suddenness of the appointment visibly shocked several members of the team, but that was nothing compared to what happened on the pitch. Everton had come to White Hart Lane expecting to meet a side in poor form, instead they found themselves 6–1 down by half-time. There was no respite in the second half and, incredibly, the match ended 10–4, with Bobby Smith scoring four of Spurs' goals. The remarkable result was so unexpected and eminently newsworthy that it dwarfed the far more important announcement of Anderson's retirement.

Nicholson had made the perfect managerial debut and witnessed the highest League aggregate score in football history. One week later the goal rush continued in a thrilling 3–4 victory over Leicester at Filbert Street. The new manager found himself overwhelmed with critical plaudits, yet he knew that Tottenham's transformation was illusory. Pink champagne went flat at White Hart Lane on 15 November when Leeds United grabbed a 3–2 victory. From that moment onwards Spurs went into irreversible decline. Between 22 November and the New Year they took only one point from seven matches and looked likely candidates for the Second Division. Nicholson took drastic action by bravely omitting star striker Danny Blanchflower, who was reprimanded for not spending sufficient time assisting Spurs' bombarded defence. On the first Saturday of 1959, Bill Dodge stepped into Blanchflower's boots and Tottenham beat Blackburn 3–1. Confidence was momentarily restored but by the time Blanchflower returned from exile in the reserves, Spurs were back in trouble. Glaring newspaper headlines unambiguously predicted the worst: 'Spurs Will Take The Drop'. Nicholson held faith, however, and on 2 March Spurs showed their fighting spirit in holding Champions Wolves to a draw at Molineux. A final surge saw them drag their weary limbs up the League ladder to finish a relieved 18th. It was a tough season but at least Nicholson was still a First Division manager.

While the relegation battle raged, Nicholson had been seeking reinforcements north of the border. His experience with under-23 teams and various FA XIs ensured that he was a prolific discoverer of talent and one lad whom he had earmarked for Spurs was Hearts' wing half Dave Mackay. Nicholson knew Hearts' trainer Johnny Harvey from his days in the forces and his proud boasts were not to be underestimated. The stumbling block to the proposed signing was manager Tommy Walker who rejected Nicholson's advances outright. The Spurs manager was then distracted by the unsuccessful pursuit of Swansea's Mel Charles, who ended up in the clutches of rivals Arsenal. With the mid-March transfer deadline approaching, Nicholson again contacted Walker who suddenly seemed more amenable. No doubt he was influenced by Mackay's alarming proneness to injury. The wing half had already broken his foot three times that season so there was a strong temptation to sell before his market value plummeted. The entire deal was completed during a 24-hour period in which Nicholson took the night train to Edinburgh, arrived at the ground at 10am and left with Mackay's signature at midday. The Hearts captain remembers his £32,000 transfer with a mixture of humour and astonishment:

I was shocked! There had been nothing in the papers and nobody had said Spurs were interested in me. I had no inkling until Tommy Walker phoned to tell me that Bill Nicholson was coming to the ground to speak to me. I was captain of Scotland, and Hearts were a very successful team. I had no intention of going anywhere else and hadn't considered English football. In fact, a friend of mine was planning to buy a pub and I was going to take a share in it. But Bill seemed a nice, straight guy. He told me exactly what he expected of me. It's true that I was only taken on the rebound. If Mel Charles hadn't gone to Arsenal I don't know where I'd have gone. Mel Charles hardly played at all – a bad cartilage and he was finished. I was very lucky – this is fate in life.

Mackay arrived in time to help Spurs through the last few games of a troubled season and soon established himself as a strident force in the dressing room. A fiercely competitive player and dedicated trainer, he impressed the workaholic Nicholson and formed a complementary partnership with the more studious Blanchflower. Mackay's arrival heralded a new era in Spurs' history and in later years Nicholson claimed that the Scot was his best ever signing.

During the close season, Nicholson finally sorted out Tottenham's goalkeeper jinx. Young Johnny Hollowbread had replaced the injured Ron Reynolds and Ted Ditchburn, but Nicholson felt it was crucial to sign a more experienced keeper. His target was Scotland's talented Bill Brown, who came highly recommended from northern scout Jock Richardson. As with Mackay, Nicholson met initial resistance from Dundee manager Willie Thornton, but an improved offer opened the way. Another night train to Scotland was sufficient to secure Brown for a bargain £14,500. Nicholson was also responsible for bringing back exported star Tony Marchi from Juventus for less than half the sum received by Spurs two years before. The spate of transfer activity inevitably led to several departures and Tottenham said goodbye to the remaining old guard: Ted Ditchburn, Joe Spicer and Tommy Bing. The link with the great Championship-winning side of the early 1950s had ended.

The start of the Bill Nicholson era coincided with a surge of public interest in Tottenham Hotspur. Although the complete antithesis of the eloquent, media-minded manager, Nicholson continued to attract press scrutiny with his flurry of signings and new ideas. At the end of his first season, Spurs again hit the headlines when it was announced that they were to visit the USSR. The trip was a glorious public relations exercise in which culture shock played as important a part as the actual football. Huge crowds greeted the yet-to-be-mighty Spurs during the ten-day visit and there were some wonderfully lurid descriptions of Russian food. Slavonic steak and chips and endless sightseeing tours apparently took more out of the players than their exertions on the pitch. Considering the inexperience of the squad in foreign climes, the results were impressive: they defeated Moscow Torpedo and Dynamo Kiev and only lost to Russia Olympic. The Russian sojourn brought a new spirit to the team, and a special cameraderie wrought from the experience of mucking together in an unfamiliar environment. Dave Mackay recalls sharing injury tales with the recovering Cliff Jones and spending hours translating his own broad Scottish accent into equally incoherent colloquial Welsh. By the end of the tour, the squad had learned the truth of a Nicholson axiom: 'A good team is a healthy team'.

In August 1959, Nicholson fielded the most expensive side in Spurs' history for their opening game at St James' Park. Fortunately, it was their soccer skills rather than their £182,000 price tag which impressed the Geordie public. At one of the best-supported grounds in the League, previously faltering Tottenham won 5–1. On 18 September they visited mighty Manchester United and once again emerged 5–1 winners. The glut of goals made even sceptics take notice of the table-topping pretenders, but what would Spurs do against gritty Portsmouth? Nicholson answered that question the following week with a third 5–1 drubbing. Modern day tabloid journalists would probably claim that the Russians had fed Spurs a secret dose of steroids, but their 1959 counterparts believed that the real miracle worker was Olympic weightlifter Bill Watson, who had been recruited to knock the boys into shape. Work-mad Nicholson explained how Spurs had taken the First Division apart so quickly and comprehensively:

We started our pre-season training even before we went to Russia. While in Russia we decided there would not be much in the way of entertainment so we decided to work. We trained every day and even an hour before every match.

While super-fit Spurs continued to entertain crowds with their new high-powered football, Nicholson was still seeking out fresh talent. Backed by the board, he doubled the scouting staff and provided incentive bonuses to step up the production line of class signings. The emphasis was now on youth as Nicholson reiterated the rhetoric of his Busby-influenced predecessor, Jimmy Anderson.

The ever-efficient Scottish representative Jock Richardson provided the next key player in the form of Falkirk's young international, John White. Nicknamed the 'Ghost', White was an extraordinarily difficult player to mark and although far from robust, his stamina was exceptional. Whatever fleeting doubts Nicholson may have had about his physical stature were brushed aside when he learned that the lad was a cross-country champion. The fitness fanatic in Nicholson could seldom resist the charm of a workhorse. He also realised that the induction of White, another Scot alongside Mackay and Brown, would strengthen the team spirit. Chelsea and Leicester had already expressed interest in the boy, so Nicholson had to move quickly and decisively. His cordial relationship with manager Tommy Younger ensured that Spurs were allowed a bid, and Nicholson took no chances by offering over £8,000 more than either of his rivals. It was an astute move which prevented the three clubs from embroiling themselves in a closely fought, long-winded auction. Younger was so impressed with the solid £20,000 bid that he did not require Nicholson to make his customary night train trek to Scotland. Instead, the Falkirk manager delivered his major asset in person and enjoyed a trip around White Hart Lane in the process.

The White signing confirmed Nicholson's initial reputation as a cheque book manager, much to his annoyance. He feared that impressionable youngsters might convince themselves that Tottenham bought rather than nurtured players. In order to dispel that myth he kept referring to his ever-progressing youth policy and claimed that Spurs already had a budding genius in their lower ranks. His name was Frank Saul.

In spite of Nicholson's protestations, home grown youth was still outweighed by imported talent. December saw the arrival of Les Allen, a Chelsea reserve, whom the Spurs supremo believed could be a great goalscorer. Goals were already becoming synonymous with this embryonic Spurs side and, although they could not sustain their grand opening to the season, they continued to fight hard for the title. The FA Cup offered an alternative route to glory, but Spurs looked far from impressive in their fourth round match against Fourth Division Crewe who drew 2–2 at White Hart Lane on a cold Saturday in January. Sitting on the bench, Nicholson knew that his team were very fortunate to have avoided defeat and demanded a more committed performance in the return. The population of Crewe was understandably optimistic about the team's chances of pulling off a memorable giant-killing act, but Nicholson's criticisms had obviously bitten hard into the pride of his side. On 3 February, Crewe witnessed a goal feast which rapidly developed into a greedy massacre as Spurs sated themselves with a 13–2 victory. For the second time since Nicholson took over, Spurs had written themselves into the soccer history books. The celebrations were forestalled one round later when Tottenham went down 3–1 to Blackburn on a muddy Ewood Park pitch that Nicholson claimed was unfit to host such an important match.

Back in the League, Spurs surprisingly foundered at home and suffered a terrible Easter in which their Championship chances evaporated. Burnley narrowly won the title, pipping Wolves, with Tottenham a frustrating two points adrift in third position. Although they had yet to win a trophy, this new Spurs side had established its claim to greatness in some of the most memorable matches of the season. Nicholson was already convinced that the best was yet to come.

Although Spurs were applauded as the most improved team of 1959–60, their goalscoring exploits paled alongside runners-up Wolverhampton Wanderers, who missed the League and Cup double by a single point. Guided by the 'Iron Chancellor', Stan Cullis, Wolves ably challenged Manchester United as the most successful team of the 1950s. Like Nicholson, Cullis was a fitness fanatic with a profound tactical knowledge of the game. With the assistance of a statistician, Wing Commander George Reep, Cullis concluded that the long ball game, characterised by quick and frequent passes into the penalty area, brought the best chance of victory. The method was simple, unambiguous and crude, especially compared to the aristocratic flamboyance of Manchester United and the midfield majesty of Spurs, but nobody could deny Wolves' effectiveness. Their raiding wingers unsettled some of the best First Division defences which tended to crumble beneath an avalanche of goals. The tragic Munich air disaster had decimated their great rivals Manchester United, leaving Wolves to reign supreme during the closing years of the decade. In the three seasons between 1957 and 1960, they scored an incredible 312 League goals, never failing to reach their century over 42 matches. The point that cost them the double, also prevented a hat trick of Championships, which underlines the extent of their domination. Few could have guessed that they were about to be eclipsed by a North London side which less than two years previously had lurked on the brink of relegation.

The building of a new Super Spurs was accomplished at their seven-acre training ground in Cheshunt where the players practised during the close season for four-and-a-half hours per day. Nicholson neatly mingled road walks and cross-country runs with plenty of five-a-sides and match ball practice. Set pieces were rehearsed *ad infinitum* until Nicholson was convinced that the squad was razor sharp. Inevitably, the discipline of endless repetition did not appeal to every player, as Mackay recalls:

Danny Blanchflower was quite happy chipping and running around, but it can be boring for players. If you're taking free kicks and corners you can't involve everybody. We worked a lot, kept fit and always knew exactly what to do at corners and stoppages.

Nicholson's extensive training sessions were rewarded with a splendid sequence of results as Tottenham produced their best start to a season in over 40 years. While their challengers stared in amazement, Spurs won their first 11 League games with searing displays of open, attacking football. By far the most significant result was a 4–0 drubbing of Wolves at Molineux which effectively symbolised the transference of soccer power from the Midlands to North London.

Nicholson was taking nothing for granted and blasted Spurs when their winning streak ended with a tame 1–1 draw against Manchester City. He was much more annoyed on 3 December when his free-scoring team squandered a four-goal lead against Champions Burnley and surrendered a point. By the New Year, however, Spurs had lost only one match (away to Sheffield Wednesday) and enjoyed a comfortable ten-point lead at the top. Seldom in football history has a side played with such insouciant confidence and even the first whispers of a prospective double did not faze the squad, as Mackay remembers:

It didn't affect me personally and I don't think it bothered the others. I'd never played in such a confident team. If we went to Manchester United we were going to win. We weren't just trying to gee ourselves up by saying, 'We can win this!' We honestly believed that we were better than all the rest.

Ironically, it was at Manchester United that Spurs failed to score for the first time that season, going down 2–0 on 20 January. They remained Championship certainties, however, and with 15 games to go, required only 18 points to equal Arsenal's First Division record of 66 points. From February onwards, the FA Cup loomed large in Tottenham's mind and they were sufficiently distracted to suffer their first home defeat of the season at the hands of Leicester. A month later they lost 3–2 to middling Cardiff but these were aberrations amid a winning streak which none of their rivals could match. The League title was finally clinched on 17 April when Spurs avenged their defeat against Sheffield Wednesday. They had won 31 of their 42 matches, scoring 115 goals in the process. It was an incredible record, marred only by a dilatory performance against previous Champions Burnley, who won 4–2 at Turf Moor and thereby prevented the Londoners from surpassing that magical 66 points total.

Spoilers Burnley threatened to derail Spurs' double hopes in the FA Cup semi-final, but were never given a chance. Nicholson's team enjoyed a precious psychological advantage for the Lancastrians had just suffered a heavy midweek defeat against Hamburg in the European Cup. Travel-weary and unable to lift their spirits, they went down 3–0. Spurs were now only one match away from the double.

The Wembley confrontation promised to be an interesting affair, not least because Tottenham faced their erstwhile League conquerors Leicester, managed by the hugely-underrated Matt Gillies. Unfortunately, the match was spoiled by a Les Allen tackle on Leicester right back Les Chalmers who was rendered ineffectual for the remainder of the game. The Wembley hoodoo had again claimed a victim and without the option of a substitute, Gillies could only hope that Leicester might hang on. They frustrated Spurs throughout the first half but could not prevent Bobby Smith from bludgeoning the ball into the roof of the net in the 69th minute. Terry Dyson put the result beyond doubt seven minutes later and unlucky Leicester trudged off the field in disillusioned defeat.

Tottenham Hotspur were now immortalised in the annals of football history: the first team to achieve the double in the 20th century. For all their tremendous success, Nicholson was strangely subdued. Having won the double he grudgingly admitted to the press that he was 'satisfied up to a point'. As Dave Mackay observed: 'Bill never seemed to be very excited. Even though he was very pleased he could never show it the way other people could'. Hours later, at the Savoy Hotel, the phlegmatic Spurs manager gave an after dinner speech which was wistful and bitter rather than celebratory. Instead of concentrating on the greatness of Spurs, he lapsed into condemnation of mercenary youngsters and grasping parents and appeared thoroughly disillusioned with what he sarcastically termed 'progress'. Amusingly, it was left to Ernest Marples, the Minister of Transport, to put Tottenham's achievements in triumphal perspective with a timely tribute:

> It is not only what you have achieved but the manner in which you have achieved it. You have shown us the arts and graces of the game with a great deal of poise, balance and rhythm. You have tried always to play football and I do congratulate you.

Marples' reflections rightly pinpointed an oft-neglected feature of the Spurs double-winning team: their sportsmanship. There are other forgotten statistics beyond goals and points totals, and it still seems scarcely believable that this team endured an intensely competitive season in the English First Division yet received only one booking and conceded just one penalty. Perhaps even more than Matt Busby's Manchester United, they personified the Corinthian ideal of fair play which would all too soon be replaced by a harsh new cynicism. There was a certain lost innocence in the memory of that Savoy banquet where the players celebrated to the sounds of the Tottenhamites' 'Tip Top Tottenham Hotspur' and enjoyed the cabaret antics of guest stars Harry Secombe and Roy Castle. It would not be long before the players reassembled at Cheshunt to prepare for their next goal – the European Cup.

Tottenham's close season workouts brought them early success in the Charity Shield where they defeated an FA XI which was virtually a surrogate England team. Morale was high for the Continental jaunt and there was even some short-lived speculation that Spurs might compete in both the European Champions and European Cup Winners' Cup competitions. According to FIFA rules, Tottenham were eligible for both, but logistically, such a campaign would have been virtually impossible. The superior status European Champions Cup was the obvious choice and it was to provide some dramatic footballing moments. The first match, behind the Iron Curtain, was against Gornik of Poland. In spite of their recent ascetic regimen in Russia, the Spurs players found it difficult to adjust to living conditions in Katowice and performed poorly in the match, losing 4–2. The return leg took place a week later at White Hart Lane and the capacity crowd was stunned when the Poles scored an early goal to register a seemingly unassailable 5–2 aggregate lead. Nicholson had transformed Spurs into a goalscoring machine and seldom had their skills been more liberally required than on that evening. They responded magnificently and with almost embarrassing ease swept aside Gornik to win 10–5 on aggregate.

Tottenham continued to prosper in their subsequent matches against Feyenoord and Dukla Prague, but the European campaign was seriously affecting their League form. Three days after the Gornik match they lost 2–0 to Notts County; the Feyenoord saga was followed by a lacklustre draw against Sheffield Wednesday; and after beating Dukla Prague, they suffered a disastrous 6–2 defeat by Manchester City. Even as early as 1961, Nicholson was discovering the strains and distractions that face a team regularly playing big games abroad. In order to strengthen the squad, he set off on his own European adventure in search of AC Milan's star striker, Jimmy Greaves. En route, Nicholson encountered the same lengthy prevarication from the Italians that Matt Busby had suffered during his relentless pursuit of Denis Law. After several run arounds, tortuous haggling and amended offers, AC Milan finally surrendered their resident genius for £99,999.

It was several weeks before Greaves finally made his League debut on 16 December 1961. Logic suggested that after two months' lay-off and no match practice the prodigal Londoner would make an anti-climactic start. Instead, he scored a hat trick as Spurs pummelled Blackpool 5–2. Match-rusty Greaves won over the White Hart Lane crowd at once with a devastating display of controlled football, highlighted by some breathtakingly accurate passes and that one-touch clinical finishing which was already his trademark. The media immediately adopted Greaves as a national soccer hero and lavishly described his Tottenham debut as 'the dawn of a new era'.

In spite of giving the country's goalscorers a 13-match start, Greaves ended the season as the League's highest scorer with 25 goals in 29 matches. His lethal touch revived Spurs' flagging League aspirations and for a time they threatened strongly to retain the Championship.

Unfortunately, the glamour games in Europe and the FA Cup took their psychological toll, and Tottenham frequently slipped up against lesser League opposition. Following a 1–1 draw with Cardiff in February, even Nicholson lost his patience: 'They were just treating the game as an exhibition, showing off and tip-tapping the ball about'.

By Easter, the Championship was all but lost and Spurs ended in third position, four points adrift of Champions Ipswich. Alf Ramsey's recently promoted side had outfoxed the First Division and won both their games against Spurs. Nicholson was left to mull over the statistical realisation that had Tottenham won either of those fixtures, the Championship would have been theirs.

The possibility of a League/FA/European Cup treble dwindled further away when Spurs were bundled out of the Champions Cup by Benfica. Both legs were controversial affairs and the press claimed that Tottenham had been robbed by some questionable refereeing decisions. Nicholson was stoical about the defeat, although he had good reason to be bitterly despondent after Spurs had come so close to forcing a play-off. Now only the FA Cup stood between Spurs and a barren season.

Despite some erring League performances against questionable opposition, Spurs proved consistently decisive in their Cup victories. Plymouth (1-5), West Bromwich Albion (2–4), Aston Villa (2–0) and Manchester United (1–3) were disposed of without the debilitating drama of a replay, leaving Spurs relatively fresh to contest the final against Burnley. The Lancastrians were then at the peak of their powers and, like Tottenham, had challenged strongly for the double. Wembley could therefore boast a clash of the titans featuring the teams second and third in the First Division. What promised to be a classic confrontation was given extra grit by the memory of Burnley's semi-final defeat against Spurs the previous year. With both sides desperate to salvage a trophy, the tension was especially high and, according to Mackay, the unemotive Nicholson was feeling the strain:

> Bill's a very tense man. I think the tension got to Bill more than the players. He'd always try to hide it but he was very keyed up. Fortunately, we were very confident and even with semi-finals we could handle it.

The 1962 Cup final proved something of an anti-climax, although the Greaves/Smith partnership played extremely well and the crowd saw some goals as Spurs emerged 3–1 victors. They were the first team since Newcastle to win the Cup in successive seasons, an achievement which deserved applause but, characteristically, Nicholson was far from satisfied. He dearly wanted Tottenham to win the trophy in glorious fashion and not even the sight of three goals could convince him that the game was anything other than a poor spectacle. His post-match comments were particularly revealing: 'Today's performance was probably the worst in the whole of the Cup competition but nobody can deny that

Tottenham Hotspur won the Cup on merit – even today!' It is hard to imagine any other FA Cup-winning manager speaking with such frankness and honesty, but Nicholson would never exaggerate Tottenham's strengths. While his contemporaries deluded themselves in victory and defeat with barbed rhetoric or fantastic excuses, Nicholson remained ruthlessly candid. He was probably the most self-critical manager in soccer history.

1962–63 was very much the last hurrah for several members of the great double side. It was also one of the toughest seasons in League history as blizzards and freezing temperatures brought a record number of postponements and ground closures. On treacherously icy surfaces, Tottenham continued to play their traditional attacking game, knocking in an incredible 111 League goals, a figure none of their rivals could match. Given the harsh, wintry conditions, one might have expected Nicholson to adopt a less adventurous policy, but as Mackay stressed, the manager invariably refused to compromise his positive footballing principles:

> What I admired about Bill was that if you went to Manchester United and won 1–0 but played badly he would be very disappointed. Other managers wouldn't care if the opposition had hit the bar ten times and they'd only scored from one attack. But Bill did care. Often after we'd won a game he would be moaning and groaning.

For their bravery and flair Tottenham deserved to win the Championship, but it was the more cautious defence of Everton that ultimately clinched the title in May 1963.

There was some consolation for the erstwhile double winners in the European Cup Winners' Cup. Up until that point, no British club had won a European trophy and Nicholson was determined to once again make history. Emphatic aggregate victories over Glasgow Rangers and Slovan Bratislava took Spurs to a semi-final clash against OFK Belgrade which was most notable for its unruliness. Tottenham clinched the two-leg tie 5–2, but not before Greaves was sent off in an incident which almost produced a brawl. It was no matter. Spurs had already gone further than any British club in Europe and now faced the intimidatory might of Atlético Madrid in the final.

Nicholson faced a major problem in selecting a team, for Mackay was out with a severe stomach upset and Blanchflower had injured his leg. Realising that Spurs needed an inspirational leader on the field Nicholson gambled on Blanchflower's durability and he managed to survive the 90 minutes with the aid of a painkilling injection. The match saw Spurs in the ascendant during the first half with two early goals courtesy of Greaves and White, but when Atlético replied with a penalty it seemed that the Londoners might wilt. Instead, they knuckled down to their customary attacking game and scored three more goals to register an incredible 5–1 victory, the highest tally ever recorded in a

European final. Even the over-critical Nicholson had to admit that he was satisfied this time.

After four years of consistent success, the ageing Spurs side disintegrated during 1964. Key players such as Blanchflower, Marchi, Dyson, Allen, Baker, Smith and Brown all said their farewells, having each played an important part in Tottenham's illustrious history. Sad though their leavings were they were nothing compared to the tragic loss of John White. It was during the close season on 21 July 1964 that Nicholson received a call informing him that White had been killed by lightning. The ever jovial, supremely fit young man had visited Crews Hill Golf Club for some solitary practice when a freak thunderstorm interrupted his play. While shielding from the rain under a tree he was struck by a lightning bolt and died from heart failure. Nicholson and trainer Cecil Poynton were called in to identify the body, which was later cremated. The tragedy had a profound effect on Nicholson, who seldom expressed emotion. Mackay remembers the players' astonishment at seeing this glimpse of the private man during a team meeting later in the season:

> When he started to talk about seeing John White he broke down and had to go into the toilet. It was very unusual for him to break down like that.

Mackay's surprise at Nicholson's show of emotion emphasises the degree to which the manager distanced himself from the players on a personal level. Professionally, he was totally involved and even in later years retained his standing as an energetic track-suited manager. Unusually, he dressed and showered with the team but never fell into the trap of considering himself 'one of the lads'. Mackay cannot recall once seeing him having a drink at the bar and described him as 'almost teetotal' during his years at Tottenham. While other managers at least wound down towards the close of a tough season, Nicholson maintained his hectic schedule, year in, year out. Mackay and his team-mates came to accept his extraordinary stamina and dedication with an air of amused perplexity:

> Bill was a smashing guy but he took life so seriously. Over the years he never changed. Bill was always the same: a dourish man, very distant. He was straight as a die, 100 per cent honest and 100 per cent Spurs. That was important. Spurs never came second to his own interests. He worked for them like a Trojan. Even going past the club at 8 o'clock at night you'd see his light was still on. What he had to do up there I've no idea, but nobody in football worked harder than Bill Nicholson.

Nicholson's obsessive work rate may have been largely self-generated as a means of convincing himself that he was indispensable as a manager. His over-thorough approach betrayed all the hallmarks of a manager weighed down by statistics and the ever-present worry of surrendering chunks of power. Yet, it would be wrong to suggest that Nicholson found it impossible to delegate on important matters. He worked effectively with assistant manager Eddie Baily for many years and during the Blanchflower era listened attentively to his captain's suggestions. Spurs' scouting representatives were also well-chosen and Nicholson placed great store on their advice. Attention to detail and a willingness to back his faith in a player with a sizeable cheque brought him a reputation as one of the more astute traders in the managerial game. The gradual erosion of the old order threatened to end Tottenham's hard-won standing in the upper echelons of the League, but during the mid-1960s they still flitted on the outskirts of the title race. During those transitional years Nicholson recruited a string of impressive players including Pat Jennings, Alan Mullery, Alan Gilzean, Terry Venables, Cyril Knowles, Joe Kinnear, John Pratt and Mike England. It was this new team that brought Spurs their last trophy of the decade in 1967.

Few football critics expected Spurs to salvage anything from another average season which seemed to have run its course by Christmas. After a promising opening run of League wins Tottenham had fallen apart in November 1966, losing home games to West Ham, Blackpool and Aston Villa. The fact that the latter two teams were later relegated gives some clue to the state of Spurs' football. Nobody expected a major resurgence from Spurs in the New Year but, by the end of April, Tottenham could look back on an 18-match unbeaten run from which they had emerged as one of the most consistent teams in the League. Their poor pre-Christmas spell prevented them from mounting a serious challenge for the double yet they finished a creditable third in the table, only four points behind Champions Manchester United. The winning streak had extended to the FA Cup and excitement grew as Spurs booked their place at Wembley where they had last appeared in 1962. It was the first ever all-London final, with Tommy Docherty's young Chelsea side tipped by many to win their first Cup trophy.

The exuberant Docherty was the complete antithesis of dour Nicholson: garrulous, witty, demonstrative and eminently quotable. He was already renowned as one of the game's great talkers and had that rare quality of being able to motivate ordinary players to take on the world. His confidence was born of a fearless and fiery impulsiveness which also made him prone to incautious effusion and occasionally disastrous error. A Docherty appointment could mean promotion and glory to an ambitious team but it could equally spell relegation. Egocentricity, tinged with a degree of self-destructiveness, marked him out as a flawed, but always exciting, manager. Chelsea was his first and longest stay in management and under his guidance the team had emerged as the best in London. They had finished above Spurs in the top five of the table for the past two years as well as reaching two FA Cup semi-finals during the same period. It was an impressive record and although Spurs had retrieved their League standing as the premier London team during 1967, their heaviest defeat of the season had been inflicted by Chelsea. The portents looked good for a closely fought and thrilling final. Once again, however, Nicholson was to suffer a feeling of anti-climax.

The ever brash Docherty had belatedly decided to change the tactical system that had beaten Spurs so effectively in the League by removing his sweeper. This was music to Nicholson's ears, but the threat remained that Chelsea would outwit Spurs with their youthful pluck and fitness. Nicholson effectively precluded this possibility by encouraging his side to slow the tempo. Tottenham probed the Chelsea defence with cool determination and a defensive discipline that would have been scorned by their double-winning predecessors. It was not a particularly pleasing spectacle but the result was impressive enough. As half-time beckoned, Pat Jennings, having just made a great save from a fierce drive by Charlie Cooke, drove the goal kick into the opposing half where Alan Mullery unleashed a hard shot which spun off the body of burly Chelsea defender Ron Harris. The ball fell to Jimmy Robertson who blasted Spurs in front on the stroke of half-time. It was one of the worst psychological moments to concede a goal and Chelsea never recovered. With 22 minutes remaining, Robertson again found himself in the action and passed to Frank Saul who hit a second to ensure victory. It was a memorable moment for the lad whom Nicholson had always claimed was the jewel in Spurs' youth team. He had never won over the White Hart Lane crowd or established a regular first team place, but in that moment Saul vindicated his manager's original pronouncement of faith. Chelsea rallied in the closing stages and pulled a goal back four minutes from time, but it was too late to tilt the game. Nicholson had won his third FA Cup in six years.

The Spurs manager again regretted that the final lacked grandeur although his tactical approach contributed to such an outcome. Several of the players were surprised by the unhurried pace of the game and Joe Kinnear summed up the public's feeling in an unintentionally contemptuous aside: 'I thought it was an easier game than the semi-final'. Dave Mackay agrees with this assessment and still argues that Chelsea were mentally ill-prepared:

> We weren't as good a team as we were in the early '60s. Tottenham were a bit over the hill, especially me! Yet we were very confident. Chelsea were an excellent team then, but on the day it was too much for them. They just didn't play well. The Chelsea lads froze and didn't fulfil their potential. It was the biggest example of tension I'd seen. We won 2–1, but it was really *much* easier than that.

Spurs remained a sturdy First Division side in the closing years of Nicholson's reign but their form was too erratic for Championship contention. Football had undergone a profound change, and in the wake of England's World Cup victory the emphasis switched to defence. Spurs, the attacking aristocrats of the early 1960s, were often an easy touch for better drilled teams playing with points-winning parsimony. Nicholson had hoped to create another great Tottenham side, but he could never match the power of Leeds who had emerged from the Second Division after the Londoners' double to take football into a new era. Although Nicholson ostensibly remained a great advocate of attacking football, he was no dinosaur and changing times forced him to alter his tactics and concentrate more on defensive matters. Mackay argues that somewhere along the line the old Spurs magic was mislaid:

> The only weakness Bill had was when he became less confident in his team. He brought the opposition more and more into it. We worried about what we had to do against certain players whereas before they were expected to worry about us. He started to think more about tactics and how to stop other people from playing. When I first came to Tottenham nobody ever said: 'Get a sheet on Liverpool or whoever and see how they play'. We didn't bother about them. We didn't respect them. But suddenly he was worrying about other teams.

The truth was, of course, that Tottenham had to change or risk extinction. Without a team as great as the double side, they could hardly hope to take on the might of Leeds United or Liverpool, whose organisation, methodology and cunning rendered impotent all but the most prepared. So it was that Nicholson countered dossiers with dossiers. As Mackay ruefully concluded: 'That's the way football went in general'.

Another change in Nicholson was his growing estrangement from the team. Over the years a generation gap had developed as the manager lost touch with the players' desires, interests and motivations. Everybody at Spurs admired the boss, but his world view was rapidly becoming outdated. He waged a losing war against long hair, flared trousers and casual clothes and saw no place for pop star androgyny on the football field. His assistant, Eddie Baily, still used Second World War metaphors in his training sessions and became increasingly disillusioned upon discovering that his men carried hair-dryers rather than bayonets. The other big gripe was money: high-powered agents were negotiating all sorts of deals for their gauche charges, who seemed desperate to make a killing before their careers ended at 35. Their motives were eminently sensible but Nicholson detected connotations of greed and, more alarmingly, a declining passion for the game. He would probably have played soccer for nothing. How many stars in his squad could truthfully say the same? It was a depressing thought.

The interaction between manager and player was further affected by escalating transfer fees. Increasingly, players knew their worth and the best of them expected to be applauded for their skills. Improved status and pride required a degree of patronage that Nicholson was always incapable of providing. He had never been an extrovert character and bestowed praise grudgingly. The new gods in the Spurs team, such as young Steve Perryman, never came to terms with this aspect of Nicholson's character. Even when Perryman played the proverbial blinder, the most effusive response he received from his manager was a curt: 'Well done son'. Good performances were greeted with unsmiling acceptance and towards the close of Nicholson's managerial career Perryman felt neglected and over-criticised.

Perryman's troubled period with Spurs was not unique. Nicholson was always a tough taskmaster and sought to eradicate what he considered flaws in a player's temperament or tactics. He quarrelled frequently with the great Jimmy Greaves over the man's lackadaisical attitude towards training but, fortunately, the ace goalscorer was a humorist incapable of bearing a grudge. Alan Gilzean, a likeable chap, was another target, blasted for his unorthodox style of play; Terry Venables found problems scoring and was soon transferred with an unimpressive record; even Pat Jennings was castigated for a couple of seasons for having played as though someone had smeared butter on his gloves. All the above received the rough end of Nicholson's tongue and most went on to become far better players. Perhaps Nicholson should have been more approachable and understanding of the needs of the younger players, but a personality cannot be changed overnight. Moreover, for the previous generation, Nicholson's greatest strengths had been his consistency and his constancy. As Mackay noted: 'Bill never changed. He was always 100 per cent Spurs'.

Nicholson was too efficient a manager to allow Tottenham to surrender their standing among the League heavyweights. They remained in the top half of the table from 1968-74 and the old glamour was restored with some star signings. World Cup hero Martin Peters replaced the faithful Jimmy Greaves whose career was swiftly reaching a premature end. Nicholson had hoped to find a new Greaves in Martin Chivers, who arrived in a record-breaking transfer deal which saw the departure of Frank Saul. Chivers did emerge as a prodigious goalscorer in the early 1970s, but not before some spectacular clashes with his manager. Nicholson found his star moody and sullen and could not come to terms with his seemingly lazy attitude towards the game. Chivers was the stereotypical gentle giant who lacked the necessary aggression to intimidate the opposition into submission. In one memorable derby match against Arsenal he ran up to a red-shirted rival and congratulated him on the Gunners' excellent performance. The lack of competitive grit infuriated the military-minded Eddie Baily and brought constant rebukes from Nicholson. Like Perryman, Chivers was depressed by his manager's dour acceptance of victory and complained: 'You never praise us when we do well'. Certainly, Nicholson was no flatterer, but it would be a mistake to describe him as uncaring. He tried to convert Chivers to his way of thinking and even broke his first rule of management by treating the troubled star as a special case. For all his apparent remoteness, Nicholson cared about the players, but they were always seen as subservient to the interests of the club.

Nicholson's dedication to Spurs convinced over-optimistic critics and rival managers that the team could mount another title challenge. Invariably, however, bad form and erratic away performances ensured that Tottenham stayed in the shadows of Leeds, Liverpool, Arsenal and

Derby. The glory days were far from forgotten though, and Nicholson exploited Spurs' ability to rise to the occasion in various Cup competitions. The expedient League Cup, with its guarantee of a European place, kept Tottenham in the headlines throughout the early 1970s and brought some much-needed silver to the White Hart Lane trophy room. The 1971 final of the League Cup saw Spurs facing Third Division Aston Villa. Lower division sides had an unnerving habit of upsetting the odds, as Arsenal had recently discovered to their cost against Swindon. Nicholson kept Spurs vigilant to the dangers of over-complacency and they won 2-0. European glory now beckoned.

During the close season of 1971, Nicholson made his last big buy as Tottenham manager with the £190,000 signing Ralph Coates. Although highly rated by Nicholson, the Burnley striker found it difficult to settle into the Spurs team and was roundly criticised by the press. Like several other imported stars, he was frequently ridiculed by members of his own side, a trend that Nicholson deplored. More than once, the fair-minded Tottenham manager accused his players of failing to support the new boy, whose goalscoring flair was sorely needed.

It was another disconsolate star, Martin Chivers, who emerged as the hero of the 1972 European campaign. For the only time in soccer history, the two-leg UEFA Cup final was contested between two English sides, Tottenham and Wolves. Chivers' two goals at Molineux virtually clinched the trophy for Spurs, who drew the return 1-1 to lift their second Continental cup. Only Leeds United had previously boasted two European trophies and Spurs' victory was an important psychological boost for future sides competing abroad.

Spurs looked likely candidates to retain the UEFA Cup in 1973 until they met Liverpool in the semi-finals. The Merseysiders had knocked Tottenham out of the FA Cup in 1968 and 1971 and history was about to repeat itself. Cruelly, Spurs surrendered their trophy without losing a match, for they were dismissed on the 'away goals count double' rule. There was consolation in the League Cup, however, where they beat Norwich in a best-forgotten final. Some felt Tottenham's performance was an insult to their grand tradition of exciting football, but the fans were content enough with the acquisition of another cup.

By 1973-74, time had caught up with Nicholson's last Spurs side and they struggled in the League before finally climbing to 11th position. Their cup flair remained intact, however, and further glory was promised in the UEFA final against Feyenoord. The Dutch side contained several leading internationals and it was their experience which secured a valuable first leg draw at White Hart Lane. Nicholson was not confident about the return and betrayed little surprise when Spurs lost 2-0. The events on the pitch were overshadowed by the appalling behaviour of the Tottenham fans who rioted on the streets of Rotterdam. There were further problems on the terraces which prompted Nicholson to make a censorious public address: 'You hooligans are a disgrace to Tottenham Hotspur and a disgrace to England. This is a football game not a war'. The riotous display ended with 200 injuries and 70 arrests. For Nicholson, this unwanted glimpse into the uglier side of modern football underlined how far he had travelled. The glory days of the double-winning side and their sportsmanlike supporters had been replaced by an increasingly rebellious squad of money-minded players and animalistic fans. The generation gap between Nicholson and the modern day Tottenham Hotspur was revealed to him on that terrible evening. His heated broadcast had failed to pacify the rioters just as his team talks were no longer inspiring the players. As he was soon to lament: 'There is no longer respect'.

Nicholson had intended to leave Tottenham Hotspur in quiet celebration, but the Rotterdam riot spoiled the script. Instead of retiring with a record-breaking third European trophy, Nicholson reluctantly decided to carry on in a vain attempt to strengthen his squad. During the close season he admitted that Spurs were probably remiss in failing to sign promising younger players but he later revealed that the real problem was greed. Several promising transfer deals were scrapped when star players demanded under-the-counter payments of between £7,000 and £10,000 to offset their tax liability. Nicholson spoke frankly about the iniquities implicit in this unwelcome trend:

> We have certainly lost players because of what has happened. All our players are treated the same from the seniors to the juniors. If I had to give somebody an under-the-counter payment to join Spurs – even if I really wanted the player – I would not because players that are already here would deserve the same. Home-made players are worse off. They get less out of the system than anybody. I have had some of the really great players in my office and they never asked me for a penny more than they were entitled to – nothing that wasn't written into their contracts. Jimmy Greaves was one of the biggest names but he never asked for a penny.

Nicholson's nostalgic reference to Greaves was poignantly apt for it was his modern day counterpart who was causing additional problems. While visiting players demanded back-handers, those within the club grew restless and ace striker Martin Chivers let his disenchantment over pay spill over into a bitter public outburst: 'I never want to play for Spurs again'. The threat was not carried out but, with or without Chivers, Tottenham looked a sorry sight. They began the new season in desultory form against Ipswich. It was the lowest gate for a home match since the War, and Spurs lost. Alarmingly, the defeats continued as once-great Tottenham slumped to bottom of the table with their worst start to the season in 62 years. Hours before their fourth successive League defeat at the hands of Manchester City, Nicholson resigned. The following day he held a news conference to explain why he was leaving Tottenham Hotspur after 39 years, including 16 seasons as manager:

> I feel my retirement is in the best interests of the club. It will give the chance to someone new with new ideas to instil new enthusiasm. It

could also shake up the players themselves. They might think they will have to work that little bit harder or they will be out.

Looking back, I've had possibly too much authority. I've taken on too much work. I've done everything and it's difficult to fight with players one minute and the next minute to take them out on the park and expect them to play for you. When I first started I would get out of the office to be with the players and no phone call would bring me back. But a club needs organisation, there's training routines to work out, disputes with players to draw me into the office now. I've been a manager a long time. I was once asked how long I thought a good manager could go on for and I replied five to seven years – well, I've gone over double that and feel very tired.

In later years Nicholson confirmed that weariness was the major factor contributing to his retirement, but there were other reasons, most notably a profound disillusionment with several members of his team:

Players have become impossible. They talk all the time about security but they are not prepared to work for it. I am abused by players when they come to see me. There is no longer respect.

Nicholson commendably sought to ease Spurs through a torturous transitional period by nominating his own replacement. He privately interviewed both Danny Blanchflower and Johnny Giles, hoping that they might join Tottenham as manager and coach, respectively. His choice of successor was characteristically excellent, but the board of directors were indignant at his presumptuousness in pursuing such matters without their prior approval and rejected both candidates in favour of the former Arsenal player Terry Neill. Nicholson had lost the respect of several players and now he was snubbed by his own chairman, Sydney Wale, who did not consider Blanchflower or Giles worthy of an interview. The ex-Spurs and Northern Ireland captain duly turned up to witness the symbolic passing of the managerial crown and left with ill-disguised disgust:

Bill Nicholson and Eddie Baily were treated like office boys, wandering around not knowing what was going on. I had assumed that Bill Nicholson had their blessing in helping to find the new manager. He had assumed it too, going about it in his usual thorough way, doing his utmost for the club, using his experience to make it easier for the directors. That they had examined the written applications without him I found difficult to believe. Why were the directors not using his experience? What did they know about management? And why did they not keep him informed? If they could not trust him, who could they trust?

Nicholson had hoped to continue with Spurs in an advisory capacity but he soon learned that there was no place for him in the new set-up. Retaining his dignity, he claimed that he had no complaints and made no reference to the derisory sum that Spurs had offered as a golden handshake for 39 years' service. His assistant, Eddie Baily, who also found himself out in the cold, was rather less reticent about his feelings concerning the money:

> I won't say how much it was but I will say my reaction was one of disgust. I am a very disappointed man. I am very sad that a club to which I have given so many years of loyal service should treat me like this.

The circumstances of Nicholson's departure from Spurs is one of the sorry episodes in football management history. Here was a man who had devoted his life to a club being ushered out with all the grace that a temporary menial could expect. The experience of four decades in football seemed irrevocably lost but, fortunately, there was a happy ending. The ever-perceptive Ron Greenwood plucked Nicholson from the twilight of soccer retirement to assist ambitious West Ham. It was a satisfactory arrangement that lasted a year. In the meantime, Terry Neill's two-year stint at Spurs ended in resignation. His replacement, Keith Burkinshaw, was astute enough to realise the value of an elder statesman and, backed by a fresh board of directors, reinstated Nicholson as a scouting consultant. Amid the shuffle, the previously luckless Eddie Baily also found himself returning to football as chief scout at West Ham. A scriptwriter could not have devised a more appropriate conclusion.

Nicholson enjoyed the less taxing role as consultant and was instrumental in the signings of most of the next generation of Spurs stars including Tony Galvin, Graham Roberts, Gary Mabbutt, Osvaldo Ardiles and Ricardo Villa. His continued presence at Tottenham brought prestige and continuity and provided an object lesson for other clubs in how to utilise the services of a retiring manager. On a personal level, Nicholson was able to appreciate football from an entirely new perspective. Throughout his managerial career he had been not merely a workaholic but an incessant worrier whose tension was all too often tangible. A generation of Tottenham players vowed never to enter management after observing a day in the life of Nicholson. It was therefore a pleasant surprise for one former player to spot his old manager sipping a whisky and looking happier and calmer than he had ever remembered. It somehow seemed a fitting conclusion to an extraordinarily successful and hard-working career.

SIR ALF RAMSEY

WHEN TWO WORLDS COLLIDE

Alfred Ramsey was born in 1920, the son of a hay and straw dealer. His youth, spent almost exclusively in the dreary suburb of Dagenham, was characterised by a rigid conventionality and fussy orderliness that imprinted upon him the mark of a parvenu. A humble, hard-working, homespun boy, whose idea of a big day out in 1934 was a visit to the cinema, Ramsey urgently needed dreams of football fame to unfetter his imagination. His brothers played a crucial part in honing his soccer skills and he rapidly climbed the Indian rope of schools' football. A solitary scout from Portsmouth noted his emerging talent and encouraged him to sign amateur forms. Unfortunately, Pompey's commitment did not extend as far as actually allowing him to play for the club. He was spared any further spells in the shadows by the outbreak of the Second World War which saw him assigned to an anti-aircraft unit. While there, he played in an Army XI against a visiting Southampton team unschooled in the importance of military morale. The distinctly uncharitable Saints earnestly set about their task of annihilating the soldiers 10–0. Ramsey emerged from the debris clutching fresh amateur forms and a pat on the back from Southampton manager Bill Dodgin. Between bouts of military service, Ramsey was called upon to employ his untried talents as a reserve centre forward. He began spectacularly enough by giving away a penalty to Luton, but still managed to hold his place. After endless practice sessions strenuously attempting to improve his rather suspect pace, the 26-year-old was elevated to the first team. Dodgin, meanwhile, astutely moved him to right back, where he developed an uncanny forte for precision passing from defence to attack. His role model during this period was the ageing Manchester City international Sam Barkas, whom he later claimed changed his entire footballing life.

Ramsey's tireless work rate reflected an all-embracing passion for the game. A quiet, taciturn personality, he would be transformed into an effervescent zealot when talk turned to football matters. Even at this early stage, Ramsey was quite capable of staying up until the

49

early hours discussing players and re-enacting tactical permutations to amused, puzzled and, not infrequently, bored listeners. Like Brian Clough, Ramsey lived and breathed football at a time when the 'science' of the game was still in its infancy. There is perhaps no better test for a player and future football manager than to suffer the pressure of a Second Division promotion race. The tantalising prospect of a return to the top flight, and all the potential glory that this implies, inevitably produces a dog fight which taxes players' nerves and commitment to extreme levels. Ramsey's first full season with Southampton in 1947–48 brought all the expected hopes and agonies as chances came and went before the Saints finally finished in third place behind promoted Birmingham and Newcastle. A frustrating season ended with Ramsey joining the England 'B' team on a European tour. Four months later he won his first cap in a memorable encounter with Switzerland which saw England emerge 6–0 victors.

Exposure to the international stage sharpened Ramsey's skills considerably and by early 1949 he again found himself leading Southampton towards the promised land of the First Division. His active involvement in that campaign ended abruptly when he was injured in a friendly match against Portsmouth. The loss of Ramsey forced Dodgin to reorganise the side and before long the incapacitated right back was deemed expendable. Dodgin, rather tactlessly, informed his promising find that it would be extremely difficult to recover his place in the first team. The news upset Ramsey sufficiently to seek a transfer and, after rejecting Sheffield Wednesday, he joined Second Division Spurs in an exchange deal estimated at £21,000. There was no end-of-season joy for his ex-club who again found themselves missing out on promotion, this time by a single point.

Ramsey's arrival at Spurs coincided with a new phase in the club's history. The man behind the revolution was Arthur Rowe, a local boy who had played at Tottenham throughout the 1920s before becoming a coach and finally replacing Joe Hulme as manager. Rowe was a master tactician at a time when methodical approaches were frowned upon. He specialised in snappy slogans, which were drummed into players' minds and learned like a catechism. His ideas were simple, effective and well-executed. Rowe was fortunate in inheriting a team that included no less than three great managers of the next era: Vic Buckingham, Alf Ramsey and Bill Nicholson. Buckingham was the quintessential managers' manager: amazingly methodical, infuriatingly garrulous and entertainingly long-winded in his tactical theorising. In their own ways, all three players were managerial prodigies of the great Rowe whose 'push and run' was shortly to become a tabloid watchword.

The push and run style involved short, quick passes played at lightning speed with great accuracy. Its effectiveness largely depended upon players' stamina and Rowe was again fortunate in having fitness fanatics like Nicholson and Ramsey in his side. Although Ramsey was never a brilliant right back and lacked aggression and speed, he was a master of positional awareness and frequently anticipated situations before more experienced players. An unusually pensive footballer, he was uncannily quick to spot space and his deadly accuracy as a passer often created crucial openings, usually at critical points in a match.

The teamwork engendered by Rowe ensured that Spurs took the Second Division by storm. Ramsey's third consecutive fight for promotion ended triumphantly with Tottenham Hotspur collecting 61 points, nine ahead of their nearest rivals. Ironically, Ramsey's old team, Southampton, again faltered at the final hurdle missing promotion on goal average.

Rowe's buoyant side caused as much havoc in the First Division as they had on their way out of the Second. The push and run style was awkward to play against and Tottenham had become such a well-drilled team that they lost only seven League matches during 1950–51 and duly clinched the Championship. An incredible run of games without injury saw Spurs emerge as one of the most consistent sides of the early 1950s with Ramsey missing only five matches in three seasons. Before long, he took over the captaincy and simultaneously established himself as a regular member of the England squad.

Ramsey's international career could not have begun at a more opportune moment, for England were about to enter the World Cup for the first time. The organising body, FIFA, decreed that the Home International Championships should serve as a qualifying eliminator and generously allowed the top two teams to proceed to the final round. While England gladly accepted this arrangement, the perversely nationalist Scottish FA refused to allow their team to attend the finals unless they headed the Championship group.

Such petulance was to cost them dearly. With the teams level on points, England trekked to Hampden Park, carefree in the knowledge that they were Brazil bound. Scotland required a draw to share the Championship and mollify the Scottish FA, but the pressure proved too much. Ramsey, making his debut in a Home International, watched dispassionately as Scottish hopes were vanquished by a single goal. Desperate appeals were lodged at the SFA to reconsider their decision, but they remained defiantly intransigent. British hopes now rested entirely upon England's performances.

The managerial brain behind England in 1950 was Walter Winterbottom, a former schoolmaster who came to prominence as the FA's director of coaching. An articulate, learned football theorist, Winterbottom's coaching ideas were to have a profound effect on the national game. Unfortunately, his managerial power was severely circumscribed by the FA selection committee which was ultimately responsible for choosing the international team. The selection process was haphazard, capricious and partisan, with committee members and club directors nominating their own players or the media hero of the month. Winterbottom was powerless to challenge this strange system and his professorial stoicism was all too often reflected in the *laissez faire* attitudes of certain key players. Nevertheless, he commanded great respect within the game, particularly from tactically-minded internationals like Ramsey, who would later build upon his innovative ideas.

British football was cocooned in self-delusion during the early 1950s, a fact demonstrated by the bookmakers' conviction that England would win the World Cup. Even though they were playing on the other side of the world against unfamiliar teams in an energy-sapping climate, the football world decreed that England were joint favourites (alongside brilliant Brazil) to lift the Jules Rimet trophy. The campaign began comfortably enough with a 2–0 win over Chile. The next match seemed anti-climactic by comparison, as England faced the United States of America, a nation that had failed to take football to its heart and appeared in the competition almost as an afterthought. The confrontation elicited scant interest from the media and the apparent inevitability of the result was reflected in the attitude of the American players who indulged themselves in an all-night party prior to the match. What happened the following day represented nothing less than the greatest upset in British football history. The unfancied Americans scored in the 37th minute and, despite ferocious attempts to equalise, England failed to break down their shambolic but resolute defence. Ramsey and his fellows were forced to drink the cup of humiliation to its rankest dregs. For the man chosen to restore England's glory in the 1960s, it was a psychologically devastating debut.

The jingoistic belief that England were still great now rested solely on their unbeaten record at Wembley. Ramsey himself retained that fragile record by scoring a late penalty in a 2–2 draw against Austria and repeating the trick in a tightly-fought contest against a Rest of the World XI in November 1953. He returned once more to witness the ultimate mortification at the hands of the brilliant Hungarians who swept aside England's lingering pretensions as a footballing force with a staggering 6–3 Wembley triumph. A return match in Hungary ended 7–1, a scoreline that destroyed the myth of English invincibility for evermore.

Ramsey's decline as a player coincided with that of England and Spurs. The once-great push and run side suffered a major setback when Arthur Rowe's health steadily deteriorated during 1953–54. The system that he had inaugurated finally proved fallible when certain team members could no longer maintain absolute fitness. It was clear that the manager had proved overloyal to ageing players, several of whom smoked like chimneys and rapidly lost their form. Although there was an attempt to forestall the fragmentation of this great side, a period of mid-table mediocrity beckoned. Rowe was replaced by Jimmy Anderson, another Tottenham old boy in his mid-60s. His first decision as manager was to drop Ramsey, who found himself replaced by a new discovery – Danny Blanchflower. Realising that there was no way back at 34, Ramsey decided to market his experience by seeking a management post.

The one club that expressed interest in acquiring Ramsey's services was a recently relegated East Anglian outfit whose prospects were indisputably dire. Ipswich Town had hit the big time in 1938 when they won promotion to the Third Division (South). There they remained for 15 gruelling years in which they clung tenaciously to their modest position before unexpectedly breaking into Division Two. Dreams of further progress were snuffed out after only one season when they slipped back into their Third Division nether world. Few expected to hear from them again.

Ramsey's brief was to revitalise the dejected side and this he achieved with surprising rapidity. A lowly 59 points enabled them to creep back into the Second Division at the first attempt and for the next three years they hovered around mid-table while their canny manager plotted his next move. Before long, Ramsey had assembled a solid yet curiously anonymous squad consisting of young players and bargain buys from lower division clubs. The team was characterised by an intense loyalty to a manager whose status as a former international brought a much-needed vicarious glamour. What Ramsey instilled in his players was a naive belief that they could compete in the top flight in spite of their modest footballing talents.

Ramsey's resuscitative act could not have been effected without the application of a systematic, tactical innovation. This consisted of a rudimentary 4–4–2 formation built around two wingers, Jimmy Leadbetter and Ray Stephenson, who were employed as a midfield decoy to create space for strikers Ray Crawford and Ted Phillips. The plan transformed humble Ipswich into a veritable scoring machine and they ended the 1960–61 season with 100 League goals and the Second Division Championship.

The improbable rise of Ipswich was greeted with condescension by the top clubs and derision from the popular press. They were immediately dubbed 'Ramsey's Rustics' and the country yokel image was reinforced by a discernible anonymity. There were no internationals in the team and the club's meagre resources meant that the players were receiving a modest £25-a-week wage. Ramsey kept a tight hold of the purse strings and decided against strengthening the side during the close season. His single purchase was Dixie Moran whose £12,000 fee exceeded the cost of the entire Ipswich team. Ramsey could only look with envy at his former team-mate Bill Nicholson, who had just achieved the 'impossible' double with a Spurs side whose estimated value was in excess of £250,000. By contrast, Ramsey had to be content with a first XI which would fetch no more than £30,000 on the transfer market. It was scarcely surprising that most hard-hearted commentators viewed Ipswich as relegation fodder long before they had kicked a First Division ball.

When Ipswich lost their first game 4–2 to Manchester City they looked a ragbag of second-rate artisans. Ramsey resolutely stuck to his tactical plan, however, and the results steadily improved. Ipswich joined the First Division pacemakers and, against the odds, they stayed the course. The Ray Crawford/Ted Phillips partnership seemed capable of scoring at will and between them they notched up an impressive

61 goals. The vigilant Walter Winterbottom noted Crawford's progress with interest and before the season was over the young centre forward was selected to play against Austria and Eire. The most unfashionable side in the First Division could now boast their first international cap.

More important to Ramsey and Ipswich was the state of the First Division title race. The ultimate test occurred on 21 October when the East Anglians entertained the all-conquering Tottenham Hotspur. On paper, it was no contest, but Ipswich's progress was sufficiently alarming to impress upon Bill Nicholson the need for caution. Prior to the match, he had intended to instruct his midfield to accompany the wandering Stephenson and Leadbetter, thereby allowing the full backs to nullify the Crawford/Phillips striking combination. Uncharacteristically, however, he changed his mind at the last minute and Spurs played their traditional attacking open game. Gaps inevitably opened in their defence and Ipswich emerged 3–2 victors. Nicholson repeated his error in the return match at White Hart Lane where rampaging Ipswich triumphed with an amazing 1–3 scoreline. These results effectively prevented Spurs from retaining the Championship and they had to be content with the FA Cup. Nicholson still argues that his tactical *volte face* robbed Spurs of achieving the improbable glory of two consecutive doubles. It is a provocative argument that neglects the reality of Tottenham's declining League form. They finished with 52 points, 14 less than the previous season when they had also won ten more games. Ramsey's Ipswich had timed their ascent at the perfect moment and ended the season as League Champions with 56 points, the lowest winning total of the decade. In retrospect, they were fortunate to emerge at a transitional period in football history when Manchester United hit the doldrums and those great 1960s sides, Liverpool and Leeds, were still stuck in the Second Division preparing for imminent glory. Whether Ramsey's tactics would have withstood the onslaught of Shankly's Red Army or Revie's Robots is doubtful, but having outwitted the sagacious Nicholson and twice beaten Spurs, nobody could deny Ipswich their opportunistic Championship.

Ramsey's fortuitous habit of being in the right place at the right time worked to his advantage in 1962. While the press marvelled at his miraculous achievement in masterminding Ipswich's League title, the perpetually troubled Walter Winterbottom was nearing the end of his reign as England manager. Since England's disgraceful performance against the USA in 1950, Winterbottom had overseen three World Cup campaigns. In 1954, an untaxing qualifying draw had taken England to the quarter-finals where they were annihilated by Uruguay. Four years later, in the wake of the Munich air disaster, England failed to reach the final stages after losing to the USSR in a group play-off. Winterbottom's fourth World Cup in 1962 was marred by the lackadaisical attitude of several starstruck players overawed by the great Brazilians who comfortably disposed of England 3–1. It was clear that a more professional, disciplined approach was needed if England were to exploit their home advantage in the next finals. Winterbottom had been a great ambassador of the game but a change was urgently needed, particularly in the thinking of the anachronistic selection committee and administrative board.

Before surrendering his post, Walter Winterbottom nominated his successor: Jimmy Adamson. Rather surprisingly, however, the Burnley manager declined the invitation, not wishing to leave his northern home. Logic suggested that the FA should next approach the most successful managers then operating in League football. Bill Nicholson's credentials included the legendary double, two FA Cups and, most crucially, a period in charge of the under-23 team during Winterbottom's tenure. Such qualifications, although undoubtedly impressive, did not prevent the FA from completely ignoring the Spurs supremo. The same fate befell that stern disciplinarian Stan Cullis, another great tactician whose long-ball game had brought Wolves two Championships and two FA Cups. Instead, the FA turned their attention to the wonder manager of the moment who had taken Ipswich to an unexpected Championship. In October 1962, they approached Ipswich chairman John Cobbold requesting permission to interview Ramsey for the vacant England post. The offer was irresistible, not least because Ramsey was suddenly struggling. The East Anglian Champions had slumped to third from bottom in the First Division as rival clubs grew wise to their tactics. Without a strong budget, youth policy or scouting system their prospects were grim and in 1963–64 they conceded 121 goals, finished bottom and suffered relegation. By then, Ramsey was safely ensconced at Lancaster Gate, no doubt relieved that he had escaped a sinking ship. As ever, his timing was perfect.

Ramsey's first contact with his England squad occurred prior to their European Nations Cup match against France. The meeting was cordial and informal, but the players did not respond to Alf's half-time admonitions. France won 5–2, the first team to score five against England since Yugoslavia in 1958. Ramsey clearly had a great deal of work ahead but, unlike Winterbottom, his hands were not tied by a capricious selection committee. From the outset, he established total control over team selection and won a reputation for not suffering fools gladly. The first two Wembley matches, against Scotland and Brazil, were eminently forgettable, but before long Ramsey hit a winning run which hinted at genuine greatness.

During the summer tour of 1963 Ramsey experimented with wingers to spectacular effect. Terry Paine and Bobby Charlton wrought havoc abroad and the sequence of victories over Czechoslovakia (2–4), East Germany (1–2) and Switzerland (1–8) still sound astonishing. Charlton's hat trick against the Swiss emphasised his early emergence as one of the undisputed greats in the squad and Ramsey expended considerable effort ensuring that he trained harder and mastered set pieces such as corner kicks. It was a period of long-overdue optimism for English football and even the normally cautious Ramsey found himself caught up in the euphoria. In an oddly uncharacteristic effusion, he effectively placed his head on a block by proclaiming to a London press conference:

> England will win the World Cup in 1966. We have the ability, strength, character and, perhaps above all, players with the right temperament. Such thoughts must be put to the public, and particularly to the players, so that confidence can be built up.

It was, indeed, a tremendous act of faith in the players and the first public indication of his indisputable belief in old-fashioned English glory.

Ramsey's star remained in the ascendant for the remainder of 1963 with successive victories against Wales, a FIFA XI and Northern Ireland. The latter was another triumph for England's wonderful wingers and the 8–3 scoreline suggested that a perfect formation had already been found. Certainly, a consistent side was beginning to emerge with Bobby Moore, Ray Wilson and Gordon Banks settling in comfortably at the back and the heroic Jimmy Greaves claiming his place as a leading goalscorer. Yet, Ramsey was strangely unsatisfied and continued to experiment, with initially unflattering results. A New Year defeat at the hands of Scotland saw Greaves relegated to the bench in favour of the workmanlike Roger Hunt. It was the first sign of Ramsey's willingness to sacrifice individual flair in the quest for a more balanced, cohesive team unit, and the plan backfired. Unsurprisingly, Greaves was recalled for the next match against Uruguay and played a vital part in setting up the two winning goals by Johnny Byrne. With wingers still in vogue, England travelled to Lisbon for a friendly in celebration of the Portuguese FA's 50th birthday. It would have been a prestigious match for Portugal to have won, yet they went down 4–3, overwhelmed by the attacking flair of an English side at their apparent zenith. A 4–2–4 line-up now seemed the most likely formation on which Ramsey would pin his World Cup hopes.

The victory in Portugal was not achieved without some ructions in the England camp. On the eve of their departure from London, several players had broken curfew in order to visit a local restaurant. When they returned in the early hours they each discovered a mysterious symbolic message from Ramsey. Their passports had been placed carefully on their beds, a sure sign of Ramsey's displeasure as well as a provocative reminder of all that was at stake. Oddly, no more was said about the matter until they arrived in Estoril whereupon Ramsey rounded on the truants. The star-studded gathering of Gordon Banks, Bobby Moore, Bobby Charlton, Johnny Byrne, George Eastham and Ray Wilson sat like obedient kids while Ramsey rammed home his message:

> I don't admire what you've done. If I had enough members here to make up a team, none of you would play, you'd all be on the plane on the way home. I realise I can't do this in the circumstances. Make sure it doesn't happen again.

The players were sufficiently intimidated by Ramsey's stone-faced disapprobation to take heed of his warning. Only two of the miscreants, Byrne and Eastham, would fail to line up for the Wembley World Cup final.

Although it is generally assumed that Ramsey ruled his players with a rod of iron, the squad was not without its rebels. Even the staunch Moore felt that the road work demanded of the team was excessive and voiced his complaint to deaf ears. Ramsey had the dictatorial art of listening to advice but failing to act upon it. Even the most recalcitrant players soon realised that there was no point in crossing their manager on football matters. In the end it was Ramsey's obduracy and consistency which won the loyalty of the squad. His unflinching self-belief and willingness to pursue a new tactical plan, unpopular and misunderstood at home, would shortly test his managerial and diplomatic skills as never before.

The realisation that the much-praised 4–2–4 formation was not a blueprint for World Cup success occurred during a salutary South American tour. The visit was preceded by a deceivably good omen when England thrashed the USA 10–0. The result was an exorcism of the 1950 World Cup defeat when a disbelieving news agency had mistranslated the USA's momentous 1–0 victory into a 10–1 thrashing. This time the telegraph wires did not lie. Excitement mounted at the prospect of England audaciously snatching the cutely-named 'Little World Cup' and finally putting paid to South American invincibility at home. It was to prove a fatuous dream. In their opening match against Brazil, England were outrun, outclassed and finally humiliated 5–1, with Pelé emerging as man of the match. Although Ramsey was aware of the Brazilians' lightning skills, even he was unprepared for such a devastating demolition job. Responding to the crisis, he dropped five players for the next match against Portugal, from whom England managed to scrape a 1–1 draw. The strength and scope of South American football was placed in a more alarming perspective by Brazil's next fixture. Against England, they had looked invincible, yet they proved no match for the cynical tactically-minded Argentinians who rendered Pelé redundant and won emphatically 3–0. Their substitute was the brilliant Antonio Rattin, the best man-to-man marker of his era. His performance alone was enough to alert Ramsey to the dangers that awaited England in their next match. Not unexpectedly they lost 1–0, outmanoeuvred by Argentinian guile. The diversity of the Argentine formation, which successively moved from 4–2–4 to 4–4–2 and 4–3–3 made Ramsey's methodology seem simplistic by comparison. What the South American visit confirmed was that Ramsey's England required further surgery and a major tactical revision.

The setback in South America insidiously permeated England's hitherto excellent home form and from October 1964 their results worsened dramatically. Ineffectual draws against Belgium, the Netherlands, Scotland and Yugoslavia and narrow wins over Northern Ireland, Wales and Hungary saw a promising side degenerate into a second-rate team. With one year's preparation left, the side looked worse than ever and hit a new nadir in October 1965 by managing to lose 2–3 against lowly Austria at Wembley. It was a confusing game in which Bobby Charlton switched from the wings to midfield and Jimmy Greaves failed to produce his customary striking flair; only afterwards did it emerge that the Spurs star was stricken with jaundice. His condition worsened to such an extent that he was forced out of the game for ten weeks with no guarantee of recovering full fitness in time for the finals. Meanwhile, criticism of Ramsey intensified. Erratic results had erased the happy memory of his early reign and prompted several critics to insist that it was now impossible for England to win the World Cup.

Unbeknown to his critics, Ramsey was in the middle of a tactical rethink which was to alter the England line-up drastically. Despite the disappointing result against Austria, he continued to experiment with Charlton in midfield and seemed reasonably satisfied with England's defence. The problem lay in attack. The continued absence of Greaves encouraged Ramsey to utilise a 4–3–3 formation for the visit to Spain and, surprisingly, England won 2–0. In retrospect, it was a turning point in Ramsey's managerial career. The team that day included no less than nine players who would later appear in the World Cup final. The unlucky couple were George Eastham and Joe Baker, soon to be replaced by Martin Peters and Geoff Hurst.

The 4–3–3 system was employed to enable Ramsey to use a select number of players both in defence and attack. It was a flexible system capable of stopping the gaps that had been so noticeable in the recent South American debacle. Like the Argentines, Ramsey had hit upon a tactic that could not only accommodate but ultimately overcome the differing styles of play that England would face in their improbable quest for World Cup glory. It soon became clear, however, that a 4–3–3 formation without wingers was far from infallible. On a muddy Everton pitch, Poland strenuously secured a 1–1 draw, forcing Ramsey back to the drawing board. For the next few months, the England manager would chop and change as each new match produced further baffling questions.

On 23 February 1966, England unwittingly played a mock World Cup final against West Germany with George Cohen scoring the only goal. Only five of the eventual finalists appeared for England that day but significant among their number was debut boy Geoff Hurst. The West Ham striker retained his place for the 4–3 defeat of Scotland at Hampden Park. This was England's most promising result since Spain and the end of a disastrous run against the Scots whom they had last beaten five years before in a 9–3 drubbing at Wembley. Surprisingly, this winning side was not retained for England's next match against Yugoslavia, the last home fixture prior to the finals. Instead, Ramsey experimented with a more traditional combination, spearheaded by the triumphant return of Jimmy Greaves. Almost inevitably, Greaves opened the scoring and England won comfortably 2–0, the best team performance for months. Ramsey could not fail to have been impressed by those raiding wingers Terry Paine and Bobby Tambling, not to mention the successful debut of Martin Peters. And what price Bobby Moore? He was conspicuously absent and apparently in danger of losing his place.

Press speculation about the fate of Bobby Moore coincided with his loss of the West Ham captaincy. He remained in the shadows for some time while Ramsey continued to experiment with the squad in order that the majority of players received top-flight experience. Ramsey's critics were confused by all the changes, particularly in light of the excellent performance against the Yugoslavians. Here was a team with robust, old-fashioned wingers and Jimmy Greaves at his brilliant best. It was a fascinating line-up that looked powerful enough to win the World Cup in its own right. With one month to go, however, Ramsey remained as tight-lipped as ever.

Having completed their fixtures at home, the England squad was transported to Lilleshall, a remote town in rural Shropshire. There, they underwent the psychological transformation that was to mould them into a unified team. Several of the players joked about Lilleshall, some even compared it to a prisoner-of-war camp. The analogy was not as outlandish as it seemed. Ramsey had regimented his troops like a no-nonsense commanding officer and their daily schedule was synchronised with all the precision of a military timetable: breakfast, training, recreational games, afternoon tea, dinner, a cowboy film, ovaltine and bed. What might have been a stifling environment inexplicably worked wonders on team morale. Although they were allowed a drink only one night in 18, the players knuckled down to the Ramsey regime and virtually acted out the romanticised role of stiff-upper-lipped imprisoned officers. There were no cliques, no prima donnas and no discernible jealousy. Ramsey had effectively achieved what several subsequent England managers have vainly sought – a family atmosphere characterised by camaraderie and old-fashioned selfless sportsmanship. As a manager, Ramsey was loyal and solicitous yet simultaneously remote enough to be a stern disciplinarian and sufficiently poker-faced to keep everyone guessing about their status in the squad.

The England squad emerged from Lilleshall revitalised and in peak form. A lightning foreign tour brought some fortuitous results and showed Ramsey's determination to continue experimenting with formations and players. Without Moore or Greaves, England took apart Finland 3–0, yet Ramsey announced an incredible nine changes for the next match against Norway three days later. An emphatic 6–1 victory, with Greaves bagging four goals, appeared to confirm the Tottenham marksman's place, but the spectre of his illness had not been forgotten. The tour ended with convincing victories over Denmark and Poland and a firm conviction among the players that they really could win the World Cup. Ramsey's adventurous strategy of using a host of different players meant that there was tremendous scope for strategic changes at short notice. Neither unforeseen injuries nor unorthodox formations could now upset a team which was capable of effortless reorganisation and adaptation. The word 'team' was a misnomer for Ramsey boasted a fully-fledged protean squad whose tactical canniness might even surprise the awesome Argentines.

Throughout the memorable 1966 World Cup finals, Ramsey looked imperious and efficient, yet he also seemed strangely out of tune with the times. 1966 was the year of swinging London, when the King's Road and Carnaby Street were awash with brightly-coloured geometric T-shirts, Union Jack shopping bags and heavy-spending American tourists. The political rallying cry 'Let's Go With Labour' continued to extol the promise of a much-desired emancipation from the strait-laced conservatism of earlier years, while cleverly paying gratuitous homage at the apparently inviolable altar of youth. With England universally acclaimed as the world capital of fashion and pop music, it was appropriate that the country should also become pre-eminent in football. Everything had been perfectly scripted right down to the hit film of the year, which was suitably titled *Alfie*. The tirelessly waggish Jimmy Greaves had taken great delight in adapting the movie's theme song in order to provide an ironic commentary on his manager's unpredictability. On the team bus, players would double up as the cheeky centre forward chirped: 'What's it all about, Alfie?' Perhaps part of the humour came from the realisation that Ramsey was so far removed from the character portrayed by Michael Caine in the film. Caine's Alfie revelled in his cockney accent, hip permissiveness and outrageous frankness – the quintessential mid-'60s modern man. By contrast, Ramsey was old-fashioned, extremely retiring and deeply sensitive about his working-class origins. Through elocution lessons he had attempted to cultivate a BBC newsreader's posh voice in a vain attempt to improve his social status. His over-ambitious phraseology merely made him more unapproachable than ever and journalists in particular regarded his cold formality as insufferably snobbish. None of the players could justifiably claim that they knew or understood the man, but most had seen glimpses of the private person beneath the pompous public persona. In lighter moments, Ramsey could be an engaging social companion, drinking brown ale, eating jellied eels and even joining in the occasional sing-song. He was also adept at speaking to the players in a language they understood and was not averse to sprinkling his studiously refined vocabulary with swear words. Unfortunately, he never played the common man with the media and therefore could only rely on public support when he was winning. Such was his record in 1966, however, that nobody could deny that he was the man. The anachronistic Ramsey was again in the right place at the perfect time.

As befitting the host nation, England kicked off the World Cup finals on 11 July. A tame, goalless draw saw them incapable of breaking down a resilient Uruguayan defence, whose priority was clearly survival rather than victory. Fortunately, England could afford such setbacks for their group opponents were considerably less daunting than those of rivals Brazil, Argentina and West Germany. Nevertheless, stubborn Mexico provided a stern test until Bobby Charlton scored a thunderous goal with Roger Hunt adding a second. England confirmed themselves as group champions with an emphatic 2–0 victory over France, although the game was marred by an appalling tackle from Nobby Stiles which prompted FIFA to demand his head. Ramsey refused to be swayed by such protestation and insisted that the bullish defender would not be sacrificed to appease football officialdom. While the furore over Stiles raged, Ramsey was left to ponder a far more worrying legacy from the controversial encounter with France: Jimmy Greaves had sustained a serious leg injury.

Greaves' long battle, first against jaundice, then injury, finally cost him his place in the finals when Ramsey elected to stick with Roger Hunt and Geoff Hurst. Even more significant than Greaves' exit was Ramsey's ultimate decision to select a team without wingers. Contrary to popular misconception, it was not a deliberate ploy from the outset of the tournament, but a decision which evolved logically from playing a variety of formations. In the group matches against France, Mexico and Uruguay, Ramsey had employed Ian Callaghan, John Connolly and Terry Paine on the flanks, but a noticeable lack of goals testified to the need for a wingerless 4–3–3 formation with twin strikers in the middle. It was an unorthodox system for the period but its very unfamiliarity was to prove crucial in propelling England towards the brink of glory.

The quarter-final stage of the World Cup brought together a motley collection of the great and the humble: Argentina, England, Hungary, North Korea, Portugal, Uruguay, the USSR and West Germany. Those perennial World Cup campaigners Italy slumped to embarrassing defeats against North Korea and the USSR and departed for home in disgrace. Even more surprising was the fate of favourites Brazil, beaten by Hungary and Portugal and finally exposed as an ageing team whose great young star, Pelé, was literally kicked out of the competition. Even Stiles' unforgivable transgression against the French seemed less reprehensible than the callous savaging of Brazil's finest. The unseemly side of footballing physicality, already brutally displayed by England and Portugal, was shortly to reach its cynical zenith courtesy of marauding Argentina.

England v Argentina was probably the most memorable game of the entire competition, for it brought together two stylistically contrasting football nations, each renowned for their inimitable aggression on the field. As ever, pinpointing the villain of the piece was largely a matter of interpretation. The Argentinians clearly regarded off-the-ball intimidation as clever gamesmanship and conducted themselves like theatrical television wrestlers, eager to give their opponents a dig in the ribs on the referee's blind side. Similarly, blatant time-wasting and incessant arguing with officials were seen as part of the jolly game and had long since been an everyday occurrence in South American football. What the English saw as cynical, dirty and savage, the Argentinians merely regarded as efficient, expedient and ultra-professional. Conversely, while England prided themselves on their terrier-like tackles and 'hard but fair' marking, the Argentinians perceived such tactics as blatant fouls, audaciously committed in full view of the referee. That the official decreed some of these tackles as perfectly legitimate seemed even more perplexing and encouraged the Argentinians to amplify their own intimidatory tactics. So it was that two soccer nations battled it out, each playing the game by their own rules. England's destiny lay less in their soccer skills than in the nationality of the referee who was European rather than South American.

Rudolf Kreitlein was much praised for the way he handled this fiery quarter-final, but he won few friends in Argentina. The game was remorselessly physical from the outset, with England committing almost twice as many fouls as their aggressive opponents. For their part, Argentina landed many more kicks on their opponents off the ball and heaped verbal abuse upon Kreitlein at every opportunity. The chief offender in the psychological humiliation of Kreitlein was Argentina's statuesque captain, Antonio Rattin, who towered over the diminutive German referee and appeared to be using his height and undoubted argumentative skill to undermine every decision. That Kreitlein could not understand a single word was both irrelevant and advantageous. The language barrier enabled Rattin to amuse his colleagues by demeaning the referee's authority with insulting banter and he was not above using explicit hand language to emphasise his opinion of the German. Rattin's football was even more astonishing than his verbal skill. Majestic in his ball control and precision passing, he trotted contemptuously across the pitch like a world class international playing against a pub side. Without breaking sweat, he had displayed footballing prowess beyond the imagination of England's artisans. When brilliance was not enough, the remarkable Rattin reverted to the professional foul, hacking down any player who presumed to challenge his authority in defence. Inevitably, he was booked. Still he berated the referee, challenging decisions and intervening on behalf of his players when they were cautioned. This, he felt, was a captain's prerogative but Kreitlein was growing weary of the deliberate provocation. When Rattin protested loudly about the booking of Luis Artime, Kreitlein snapped and ordered his antagonist off the field. It was a remarkable decision which Rattin initially refused to accept. The game was delayed for seven minutes during which the Argentine team threatened a mass walk-out in support of their captain. Police intervened and eventually the reluctant Argentinian giant accepted his fate, slowly walking away with the arrogant air of a ruthless gunslinger. In spite of his love of westerns, Ramsey had no sympathy for Rattin and regarded the controversial decision as perfectly just. The referee was surprisingly willing to discuss the matter and subsequently informed the world's press:

I had taken Rattin's name once, then cautioned him. He said nothing I could understand, but I could read in his face what he was saying. He was following me around the field shouting at me, but although he towered over me I was not afraid of him. I had no alternative but to send him off.

Kreitlein's words testify to the sheer power of Rattin, whose intimidatory countenance was apparently sufficient in itself to provoke a sending off. The incident was a godsend to England who feared Rattin more than any other player in the competition. Following the restart, however, they threatened to upstage the Argentinians and an appalling tackle by Hunt was worthy of instant dismissal. Riding their luck, England attempted to force home the advantage during the second half but the ten-man Argentine team rose to the occasion and played more brilliantly than ever. They looked capable of winning, let alone forcing a replay, but their bad day ended when Hurst broke free to score a late winner. As the match ended, George Cohen and Alberto Gonzalez attempted to bring some dignity to the occasion by swapping shirts, but in a disgraceful act of bad sportsmanship, the petulant Ramsey intervened and physically prevented his player from completing the exchange. He was unrepentant later that day when he appeared on television and coolly asserted: 'We still have to produce our best football. It will come against a team who come out to play football and not act like animals'. Ramsey's intemperate and provocative outburst was rightly denounced by the FIFA Disciplinary Committee, which wrote an official letter of complaint to the FA. The Argentinian team and officials also received a censorious broadside from FIFA, not only for their indiscipline and insurrection on the field, but also for an alleged attack on the hapless referee after the game had ended. It was a tawdry conclusion to one of the most fascinating confrontations in World Cup history.

The South Americans trudged home outraged by the double standards of European football. While Uruguay (defeated by West Germany) and Argentina had each suffered bookings and sendings-off that ultimately decimated their hopes, their aristocratic counterparts Brazil had played fair against a brutal Portuguese side which, unchecked by officialdom, had mercilessly destroyed Pelé. It was hardly surprising that the South American confederation saw fit to complain about these anomalies and chief among their grievances was FIFA's reluctance to take direct action against the inflammatory Ramsey.

England's long-term hopes of winning the World Cup were substantially increased when FIFA agreed to switch their semi-final from Goodison Park to Wembley. Apart from home advantage, they now had ground advantage, having already played Uruguay, France, Mexico and Argentina on the same surface. Significantly, the three remaining semi-finalists – Portugal, West Germany and Russia – had played everywhere else but Wembley, having been successively farmed out to Villa

Park, Goodison Park, Ayresome Park, Roker Park, Old Trafford and Hillsborough. In spite of such handicaps, England's next opponents, Portugal, had good cause for optimism. They had defeated favourites Brazil and boasted the tournament's leading goalscorer in the highly acclaimed Eusebio. England, of course, had yet to concede a goal and, having survived Argentina, felt capable of conquering the world.

Against the odds, the Portugal v England semi-final proved a thoroughly sporting affair with both teams committed to open, attacking, foul-free football. England secured a 2–0 lead, but were pegged back by a Eusebio penalty and nervously survived a Portuguese barrage before the referee's whistle ended their agony. Ramsey was predictably pleased by the footballing display he had witnessed but, still stinging from the controversy caused by his comments on Argentina, kept his post-match summation brief. Without fear of contradiction, he concluded: 'This was England's greatest performance since I became manager'.

On 30 July 1966, England made their sixth consecutive appearance at Wembley Stadium for the final. By contrast West Germany were appearing in London for the first time in the competition. The scales were weighed heavily in England's favour, but as every FA Cup watcher could testify, Wembley finals show scant respect for bookmakers' odds. In the event, both teams were evenly matched and surprisingly willing to play reasonably adventurous football. Ramsey's West German counterpart, Helmut Schoen, had done his homework well and despatched Franz Beckenbauer to mark England's danger man, Bobby Charlton. Amusingly enough, Ramsey had done precisely the same and such was each player's dedication to the task that the one neutralised the other, like opposing kings on a chessboard. Consequently, it was England's new boys, Geoff Hurst and Martin Peters, who were provided the opportunity for unexpected glory. England began confidently, but the Germans struck first with an opportunistic goal from Helmut Haller. For the first and only time in the competition, Ramsey's men were trailing. Their concern was alleviated within six minutes when Hurst latched on to a hastily taken free kick from Bobby Moore and headed an emphatic equaliser. With the play switching from end to end and half-time looming, German striker Sigi Held shot from 30 yards forcing Gordon Banks to make one of his characteristically excellent saves. It was an enthralling first 45 minutes.

England attempted to seize control of the match during the early stages of the second half, but Germany looked threatening on the break. Finally, the weight of pressure told and in the 78th minute Martin Peters took advantage of a lucky rebound to give England a 2–1 lead. As the minutes ticked away, German attacks grew more frequent and frantic, but the result seemed beyond doubt. English supporters were already blowing whistles and arrogantly claiming that they had won the Cup when Wolfgang Overath hoisted a ball into the penalty area which ricocheted to Jack Charlton who was immediately penalised for blocking Sigi Held just outside the area. The resulting free kick saw

England lapse into a state of near panic and while they earnestly erected a defensive wall, the ball thundered this way and that before landing at the feet of Wolfgang Weber who made no mistake. With only seconds remaining, West Germany had clawed their way back from oblivion. England were still in a daze as the referee blew for the restart and then, almost immediately, indicated that full-time had elapsed. For the first occasion in a World Cup final the teams were forced to endure the agony of extra time.

Ramsey was admirably calm when he walked onto the pitch to confront the players who had let victory slip by a matter of seconds. While the England trainers, Les Cocker and Harold Shepherdson, busily sponged down players and passed around refreshing containers of water, Ramsey eyed the opposition. He noted that their socks were already down around their ankles, a sure sign of fatigue. Coolly, he instructed his own men and, in as businesslike a manner as possible, suggested: 'Look, you've beaten them once, now go out and do it again'. His words were enough to convince the players that hard work and concentrated running would inevitably produce further rewards. Grasping the psychological initiative, they rose to their feet and showed off their stamina to the tiring Germans. Now all they needed was another goal.

The crucial goal came early in the first period of extra time. Spotting an opening, Geoff Hurst unleashed an ambitious driving shot which whisked past goalkeeper Hans Tilkowski, hit the crossbar, bounced on the goalline and was swiftly headed away by Wolfgang Weber. None of the English players had seen precisely what happened in those split seconds yet several raised their hands, optimistically signalling a goal. The rules clearly state that the entire ball must be beyond the white goalline to register a score and the referee Gottfried Dierist was left with the unenviable task of ruling upon an incident that he had not seen. Reluctantly, he consulted his Russian linesman Tofik Bakhramov, whose view also had been obstructed. Ludicrously, neither official could understand the language of the other so, without explanation, the linesman pointed to the centre spot. It was a heartbreaking moment for the West Germans who accepted the ruling with remarkable stoicism. Instead of intimidating the referee or threatening to leave the pitch in disgust, they simply continued as though nothing had happened. Slow motion television replays subsequently revealed chalk marks rising with the ball after impact with the goalline, a strong enough suggestion that West Germany had been robbed. Refusing to accept the seemingly inevitable, the Germans found new inspiration with the striking force of Sigi Held and Willi Schultz, but tired legs weakened their finishing. As the match limped to a close, Moore pushed a ball to Hurst who ran upfield while the referee stared at his watch and the stadium erupted in a crescendo of whistles. The BBC commentator, Kenneth Wolstenholme, could not believe England's good fortune as the German players ground to a halt. 'They think it's all over', he cooed, before humorously adding, 'It is now!', as the buck-toothed Hurst shot the ball into the top corner of the net to claim his hat trick. The goal was immediately followed by the final whistle, and while the players slumped to the ground in exhaustion and relief, the England bench exploded into life. Track-suited trainers and delighted reserves jumped for joy and fisted the air in jubilant triumph. Only one of their number remained seated throughout the joyous proceedings: Alf Ramsey.

Although the crowd chanted his name and several players affectionately pulled him onto the pitch, the phlegmatic England manager refused to join the team on a lap of honour. Dignity, combined with the modest assertion that it was *their* Cup, prevented him sharing the glory. Back in the dressing room he shook hands with every member of the squad, offering warm congratulations, but there were no hugs and kisses. It was, quite simply, a job well done.

The day after winning the World Cup, Ramsey was approached by two journalists requesting a brief interview. Although the pair had steadily supported him throughout the recent tournament his response was icily curt: 'Sorry, it's my day off'. So began the steady deterioration in his relationship with the media that would eventually cost Ramsey his job. In late 1966, however, such a notion would have been unthinkable. Ramsey was a national hero and soon received a knighthood for his services to soccer. His improved status probably made him more independent than ever, although he treated his squad with the same solicitude of earlier times. Even after his investiture, he insisted that the players still call him 'Alf'. Such modesty was in striking contrast to his aloof and uncooperative public persona.

Ramsey's track record from 1966–70 was quite impressive. In 34 internationals, England won 20 and lost only four. Interestingly, one of their defeats was against the old enemy West Germany in a friendly match in Hanover. The result was psychologically significant, for the Germans had never beaten England before, their best effort being a 3–3 draw in Berlin back in 1930. Although the gap between the great powers in international soccer was rapidly diminishing, Ramsey still had one of the best squads in the world. He boasted that England could retain the Jules Rimet trophy in Mexico and even suggested that his present team was better than the 1966 model. At least the latter comment was largely correct. Ramsey had retained the core of his great side (Banks, Moore, Ball, Bobby Charlton, Hurst and Peters) and familiarity wrought strength and consistency. Above all, England were an extremely difficult side to score against, as their match statistics revealed. Like most English managers, Ramsey had become increasingly concerned with defence and placed his faith in a gritty 4–4–2 formation which brought favourable results but few goals.

Many soccer pundits tipped England as likely winners of the 1970 World Cup in Mexico ignoring the fact that no European team had ever won the trophy in South America. The squad received a rousing send-off when their recording of 'Back Home' zoomed to the top of the charts. Its success was symptomatic of the period. Since 1966 footballers had risen in media consciousness from the level of inarticulate sports personalities to quasi-pop stars.

Although the time seemed right for further English glory, Ramsey's squad found itself besieged by problems throughout the Mexico sojourn. First, there was the 'Bobby Moore affair', a comedy of errors in which the England captain was taken away for questioning having allegedly stolen some jewellery from a hotel shop in Bogota. The allegation was completely unjustified but proved sufficient to ruffle a squad already concerned with such matters as acclimatisation and altitude. However, Ramsey's imperious cool was perfect for calming his own players, particularly the troubled Moore who responded admirably to the crisis.

Unfortunately, Ramsey's diplomacy did not extend to effective public relations. His stinginess with his time upset the Latin American press and their mood was reflected by the general public. The fact that England insisted on carting around their own food supplies was regarded as unnecessarily insular, but when it was discovered that they had imported cans of orange juice, the fruit-loving Mexican people felt justifiably insulted. Ramsey could have deflated the criticism with some unctuous praise but instead fell into the trap of commenting adversely on the Guadalajara pitch. His indiscretion was again interpreted as a personal rebuke. Meanwhile, other nations were busy currying favour with the locals, posing patiently for photographs and providing carnival paper hats and souvenir rosettes. Brazil even threw in some free seats for the Mexican kids, a brilliant PR stroke which won them a new generation of supporters. Ramsey ignored all this ballyhoo, naively underestimating the collective power of a hostile crowd.

The attitude of the English press was more difficult to fathom. There is a theory that Ramsey's antipathy towards the press was cemented in Mexico. In order to assist journalists with their deadlines, he had agreed to name his final squad in advance. Obviously, the information was in strict confidence, but one man allegedly broke the embargo by informing a player before Ramsey could have his 'quiet word'. As a former England international revealed: 'Alf Ramsey never trusted another journalist after that. That was the day they started to put the knife in'.

England's performances in their Group C matches were solid but unspectacular. A goal from Geoff Hurst in a pedestrian display against Romania brought two points. . . and then there was Brazil. On the eve of this crucial match, Latin American fans declared a war of noise on England's hotel in an attempt to rob the players of vital sleep. However, such nefarious tactics were hardly necessary given the opposition. Brazil, the unquestionable stars and eventual Champions of the World, were playing football of a standard far above their nearest rivals. It was to England's eternal credit that they lost the match by a single goal, particularly as they were playing in the noon-day heat with temperatures high in the 90s. Several players lost over half a stone in that match alone. While England deserved credit for their resilience, the lack of goals was worrying. In their final match, against Czechoslovakia, they required an Allan Clarke penalty to provide a workmanlike victory. The 4–4–2 system was proving difficult to operate effectively in the stamina-sapping heat which led some observers to criticise Ramsey's tactics. The cries of condemnation grew shriller following the epic quarter-final against West Germany in Leon.

West Germany had yet to drop a point in the competition and boasted the leading goalscorer in the majesterial Gerd Muller. An arguably superior side to the 1966 finalists, they were eager to bury the memory of Wembley and looked strong outside contenders for the Cup. The game promised to be a classic, and so it was. England dominated West Germany for much of the game and, with 20 minutes remaining, held a seemingly unassailable 2–0 lead, courtesy of Alan Mullery and Martin Peters. The score appeared to vindicate Ramsey's tactical system and it was expected that England would simply close up shop. Against most teams this would have been possible, but West Germany were renowned for their resuscitative powers and willingness to fight lost causes. The masterful Franz Beckenbauer increasingly dominated the midfield and finally broke through to outwit the deputising Peter Bonetti and reduce the deficit to 2–1. At this point, Ramsey replaced Bobby Charlton with Colin Bell, an eminently sensible decision given the need to preserve the ageing player's energy for the semi-final. As the minutes ticked by, West Germany pushed forward with an indefatigable spirit reminiscent of their 1966 counterparts. In a clever attempt to seal the defence, Ramsey brought on Norman Hunter in place of Peters. With only minutes remaining, however, Uwe Seeler scored to take the match into extra time. What appeared sound substituting had backfired, although no critic could rightly say that West Germany would not have scored if Ramsey had left the side unchanged. The memories of 1966 came flooding back with England forced to retrieve a game that they had seemingly already won. This time round, however, West Germany would not be denied. Franz Beckenbauer and Wolfgang Overath had already proven the most lethal midfield partnership in the entire tournament and it was their industry that allowed striker Gerd Muller to win the match with a characteristically opportunistic goal.

The England team was distraught after the game having convinced themselves that lapses in concentration had robbed them of certain victory. The unfortunate goalkeeper Peter Bonetti was inconsolable. To his credit, Ramsey maintained his imperturbable demeanour and took time to console and thank his players for all their efforts. Even in defeat his loyalty to the squad was unquestionable.

There was one final irony to the unhappy Mexico saga. While the players wept, England's first choice goalkeeper was in celebratory mood back at the hotel. Confined to his bed with a stomach complaint, Gordon Banks was watching the match on delayed transmission television. England were still leading 2–0 when the team trooped in like a funeral procession. It took Banks several minutes to realise that he was not the victim of a cruel practical joke. England had indeed surrendered the World Cup in the most unlikely circumstances.

In retrospect, the 1970 World Cup campaign was far from disastrous. In reaching the quarter-finals on South American soil, England had done no worse than their critics could reasonably have expected. West Germany's agonising 4–3 defeat against Italy was equally heartbreaking and confirmed their world class, while Brazil's 4–1 Championship victory suggested that they were from another planet. Ramsey's oft-quoted and much-misunderstood comment after the final ('We have nothing to learn from Brazil') was both perceptive and accurate. Mere English mortals cannot follow in the tracks of sun gods.

The initial post-Leon years saw a slight upswing in Ramsey's fortunes for between 1970 and 1972 England played ten matches, winning eight and drawing two. The results suggested that the team was equipped to succeed in both the European Nations Cup and the 1974 World Cup. It was a happy delusion finally broken at Wembley in April 1972 when the West Germans returned to rewrite history with a 3–1 victory. From that point onwards, Ramsey's critics slowly moved in for the kill. Looking at the England side Brian Clough muttered: 'If Ramsey knows what his squad for Europe is going to be, the man's either crackers or a genius'. Manchester City manager, Malcolm Allison, was equally perplexed by his choice of players and suggested dismissively: 'Ramsey lives in his own football world'.

For the remainder of his reign, the aloof Ramsey fended off critics and suffered the frustration of seeing his team playing reasonably well only to founder on the big occasion. A World Cup qualifying group featuring Wales and Poland hardly seemed the sternest of tests, but when England drew with the former and suffered a 2–0 defeat in Katowice, the unthinkable became all too possible. England were only one match away from failing to reach the World Cup finals. Despite the erratic results, many maintained that Ramsey's charisma would lift the players sufficiently to defeat Poland. A marvellous 5–0 victory over Scotland at Hampden Park and a devastating 7–0 thrashing of Austria indicated that there was no lack of firing power. Sadly, the dream ended on a cold November night when Poland held England to a 1–1 draw at Wembley. A shock goal from Domarski in the 57th minute provided the death blow and although Allan Clarke converted an equalising penalty, a winning goal remained frustratingly elusive. Even Ramsey's few supporters were forced to admit that England had lost their standing in Europe. That lesson was rammed home one month later when Italy registered their first ever victory on English soil. The newspaper headlines said it all: 'Alf's Final Humiliation'.

Without media support, Ramsey was in a precarious position for he had few allies at Lancaster Gate. The amount of revenue that England had lost by failing to appear in the World Cup finals was sufficiently sickening to prompt the FA to consider the 'Future of Football'. A committee was formed for this purpose on 14 February 1974 and for the next two months Ramsey's fate hung in the balance. Perhaps realising that the axe was nigh, Ramsey embarked on an uncharacteristically vigorous public defence, complaining about the non-availability of club players and indicating that his job had become impossible. In March, he presented the FA with a three-point plan to improve England's performances, requesting three days' preparation for friendly games and a week's grace for European and World Cup qualifying matches. He even suggested that the England team must achieve internal cohesion by playing an international match every month throughout the season. His demands were punctuated by a provocative slogan: 'There has to be a decision – club or country?'

Ramsey's forthright response to the footballing authorities and ungrateful media came too late to save his head. On 19 April he was informed by chairman Sir Andrew Stephen and FA secretary Ted Croker that his services as England manager were no longer required. Even today, Ramsey feels bitter about the shabby treatment he received from the old men of Lancaster Gate:

> It was the most devastating half-hour of my life. . . I stood in a room almost full of staring committee men. It was just like I was on trial. I thought I was going to be hanged. . . Typically, I was never given a reason for the sack.

Ramsey was equally displeased by his £15,000 'golden handshake' feeling that after 11 years' service he deserved better.

The disillusionment that Ramsey felt following his fall can be measured by his activities thereafter. Rumours abounded of his intention to accept a post at Athletic Bilbao with a starting salary of £40,000 per annum. Soon afterwards there was an approach from struggling Portsmouth but Ramsey refused to be drawn. Instead, he involved himself in building and sports equipment firms, having apparently turned his back on football. A change of heart occurred in January 1976 when he accepted a directorship at Birmingham. His love of the game sustained his interest and by September of the following year he assumed a new role as caretaker manager. Ramsey had no delusions about the post which he stressed was strictly temporary: 'I am convinced that the standard of football has declined. I will only do this job until a permanent manager is signed because there is no future in me at 57'. The Birmingham fans and players clearly felt otherwise. Within two days of his appointment, the team won 2–1 at Middlesbrough collecting their first points of the season. A 3–0 victory over Newcastle the following week had journalists rushing to their typewriters to proclaim the good news – Ramsey was back. Two months later he resigned his directorship and became Birmingham's full-time manager although he still insisted on being referred to as a 'consultant'. The honeymoon lasted five months before Ramsey realised that it was time to quit. A 4–0 defeat at Coventry in March 1978 saw the erstwhile England manager publicly criticising his players for a 'thoroughly bad performance'. It was probably the most uncharacteristic action of his managerial career.

History has not been unkind to Sir Alf Ramsey. Once reviled for his blunt-edged aloofness, he is now better remembered for his integrity, honesty and patriotism, qualities that are becoming increasingly rare in the ruthless arena of modern football. Ramsey's greatest epitaph, however, lies in the continued loyalty of his World Cup stars. Like a stern but beloved schoolmaster, none of his ex-pupils have a bad word to say about him. We may never see his like again.

BILL SHANKLY

YOU'LL NEVER WALK ALONE AGAIN

William Shankly was born on 2 September 1913 in the mining village of Glenbuck, near Ayrshire, the youngest son in a family of ten children. That he became a footballer is scarcely any wonder, for the entire clan was steeped in soccer tradition. Two of his uncles played for Rangers and Portsmouth and Preston and Carlisle, respectively, and their exploits inspired the soccer-hungry nephews. All four of Shankly's brothers achieved some success as footballers and their gallery of clubs included Ayr, Alloa, Barrow, Southend, Carlisle, Sheffield United, Luton and Portsmouth. Brother Bob Shankly was the first to strike out into the uncharted area of football management and over a period achieved considerable success in Scotland, overseeing several clubs including Falkirk, Dundee, Hibernian and Stirling Albion. The realisation that footballing life need not end on the pitch had a profound effect on Bill whose zealousness for the game was already all-consuming.

Shankly began his working life down the pit until an all-too-common mine closure made him unemployed. Fortunately, a few months later Carlisle United offered him a trial. He played against Middlesbrough reserves in a nightmare match which ended 6-0. Even such a heavy defeat could not disguise Shankly's obvious footballing skill and he was immediately offered professional forms. One distinct advantage he had over any of his rivals was the presence of an uncle, Billy Blyth, on the Carlisle board, but Shankly always denied any suggestion of nepotism. His performances as an amateur would inevitably have attracted other clubs and Carlisle were fortunate to draw first blood. In spite of his awareness of football's short-term career prospects, Shankly convinced himself that he could reach the top of his profession. He claimed to have believed that football was his 'destiny', but such faith in predestination did not prevent him from training remorselessly. A fitness fanatic with a religious fervour for football, his charismatic presence on the field soon attracted the attention of vigilant scouts and it was not long before a new offer took him further south.

Carlisle finished 19th in the Third Division (North) at the end of the 1932-33 season and it was clear that their ageing side of former stars was in for a long slog. Within two seasons they would finish bottom of their Division with a paltry 32 points, but by then Shankly had moved on. His break came in July 1934 when newly promoted Preston began searching for young talent to enhance their prospects in the First Division. Shankly was initially taken aback by the meagre financial remuneration that accompanied his move to the top flight, but the chance to play First Division football finally proved irresistible and he accepted his £8-a-week wage.

Preston ended their first season back in Division One in the classic mid-table spot, winning and losing 15 games and notching up 42 points from 42 matches. Their Cup run was more promising, but ended in the sixth round when they narrowly lost to finalists West Bromwich Albion. Shankly was impressed with his team's battling skill and two years later they were given the opportunity to avenge themselves against West Brom in the semi-finals. Preston made no mistake and routed the Midlands club 4-1 to book their first FA Cup final at Wembley in 1937. Their opponents, Sunderland, were a formidable side, having won the Championship the previous year. After seeing off Third Division Millwall in the semi-finals, their confidence was sky high and Preston, missing their regular goalkeeper through injury, were overrun 3-1.

Like many losing Cup finalists, Preston vowed to return the following year and win the trophy. The team worked harder than ever in training, pushed on by skipper Tommy Smith whose namesake would later play a similar role in captaining the great Liverpool side of the 1960s. Preston's industry paid off and they duly returned to Wembley, beating the First and Second Division Champions, Arsenal and Aston Villa, along the way. The final was a drab affair but Preston emerged victorious courtesy of a George Mutch penalty. The characteristically exuberant Shankly was predictably the first player to lift Mutch off his feet in celebration after the ball reached the net. It was a memorable year for Preston who finished third in the First Division, only a handful of points away from the double. Before the season ended, Shankly also made his debut as a Scottish international in a team which included three other Preston players: Andy Beattie, Tommy Smith and George Mutch.

Preston seemed likely candidates for further glory but their progress was interrupted by the Second World War. Shankly was now 26 and at the peak of his playing career. The War effectively ended the footballing lives of most players over 25, but Shankly was determined to prove himself the exception. During his RAF years he kept himself remarkably fit, training constantly and falling back on the Scottish Presbyterian work ethic which cried 'More industry – and no boozing'. Just before the War ended, he married a Glaswegian girl, Agnes Fisher, nicknamed 'Nessie', who, despite her lack of interest in football, became his greatest supporter.

Shankly returned to Preston after the War but was already preparing for his future by qualifying as a masseur. Such a diploma would facilitate his entry into coaching and management which he knew was not far away. For the present, he soaked up as much enjoyment from the game as time would allow. He was fortunate to play for a couple of seasons alongside the legendary Tom Finney, a wonderfully adaptable and prolific goalscorer whom Shankly revered. In later years, he would regale his own players with tales of Finney's brilliant ball play and always maintained that the Preston hero was the greatest soccer god of all time.

Preston returned to post-war football with a respectable placing in the First Division but were surprised by the emergence of unexpected Champions Liverpool. The Merseyside team included a wing half named Bob Paisley, who would later play a crucial part in Shankly's managerial career. As ever, Preston were uncannily consistent: seventh in the League with 47 points for two consecutive seasons and twice quarter-finalists in the FA Cup. Shankly was captain by this time but, in common with Tom Finney, began to play less as age and injuries took their toll. Knowing that his playing days were ending, Shankly was anxious to break into management at the earliest opportunity and successfully applied for a post at his old club, Carlisle. Leaving Preston was a sad and bitter affair, for, by taking the Carlisle job, Shankly forfeited his benefit match and began his new career out of pocket. The Preston board's decision rankled with Shankly for many years and he later described the episode as 'the biggest letdown of my life in football'. He no doubt saw some poetic justice when Preston were dramatically relegated from the First Division at the end of the season.

Shankly began his circuitous route to managerial glory on the rough road of the notoriously competitive Third Division (North). With only one team from 24 guaranteed promotion, there was inevitable heartache and frustration for the also-rans. Shankly's main aim was to instil pride into a club whose financial resources were limited. He was not a manager to stand on ceremony but gladly mucked in with the juniors, polishing boots, sweeping dressing rooms, painting walls and cleaning the pitch. Inspired by the motto 'Cleanliness is next to godliness', he buttonholed the directors and demanded that the players receive a new playing kit. The request was granted.

Shankly's unselfish approach immediately translated itself to the younger players and before long he became something of a father figure to them. His aim was to inspire rather than denigrate and he studiously avoided the trap of picking favourites. Whatever personality clashes occurred could always be resolved if a player was genuinely committed to the club. The paternal respect that Shankly elicited from the team was reflected in his favourable rapport with the supporters. For a time he became a local celebrity, like a professional radio comedian. The homely atmosphere that Shankly brought to the club boosted gate receipts and the team responded with gradually improving displays on the field. From mid-table in his first season, they became promotion contenders during 1950-51, but ended up in third place, nine points adrift of all-conquering Rotherham.

The disappointment of missing promotion, coupled with a lack of financial resources, persuaded Shankly to switch clubs, but this was no soft option. When he arrived at Grimsby in 1951, the team had just been relegated from the Second Division and their prospects were grim. Their main advantage over Carlisle was a willingness to buy players and Shankly soon made some clever forays into the transfer market nabbing Jimmy Hernon and Wilf Mannion. His main contribution to Grimsby was restoring the confidence of players still haunted by the stigma of relegation. By altering their training and practice sessions, he encouraged the team to enjoy their football again and abandoned taxing physical workouts in favour of ball control exercises and practice matches. He drilled players on the importance of using the ball and encouraged the team to experiment with set pieces. It was the familiar story of a new man revitalising the side, and Grimsby responded with a concerted push for promotion which brought them the runners-up position behind Lincoln. At that moment Shankly must have felt that he would never escape from the Third Division (North).

After two years at luckless Grimsby, Shankly and his wife grew homesick for Scotland and decided to narrow the geographical gap by moving further north. It was a surprisingly regressive career move for Shankly who found himself trying to save a lowly Third Division club far worse off than Carlisle or Grimsby. Workington had finished bottom of their League in 1952 and could only raise enough effort to lift themselves one place higher the following year. Shankly realised his brief was a tough one but accepted the task. He brought his customary positive approach to the club, spent wisely and dragged them up the table until they finished a commendable eighth. His work was far from complete, but before the end of the next season an unexpected offer presented itself which could not be ignored.

Andy Beattie of Preston and Scotland, had gone on to manage Huddersfield, fresh and confident after promotion from the Second Division. Following an excellent start back in the big time, however, they rapidly lost ground and Beattie suddenly found himself managing a team with one foot in the relegation zone. Seeking strength in numbers he had already enlisted coach Eddie Boot and now sought an inspirational assistant to save the club and his job. Shankly needed little persuading for he regarded Beattie highly and saw the move as a brilliant opportunity to taste First Division management. Although he was initially a mere assistant in charge of the reserve team, Shankly's ambition was boundless. The beneficent Beattie had offered what amounted to a co-management deal, explaining that he would give his partner greater responsibilities in time, even if they moved on to better clubs. In principle, it was a set-up not dissimilar to that which existed between Brian Clough and Peter Taylor where the distinctions between manager and assistant became increasingly blurred.

What made Shankly's job as assistant more palatable was the quality of the players that passed through his hands. The senior side was growing old so Huddersfield spent considerable time searching for and grooming youngsters. Their inspiration was undoubtedly the great Matt Busby whose legendary 'Babes' had proven to the football world that youth could be harnessed to greatness. In April 1955, Andy's younger brother Archie went on a scouting mission which culminated in the discovery of a teenage prodigy whom Shankly would later develop into one of the greatest players of his generation. The kid was 15 years old, weighed only eight stone, wore National Health spectacles and suffered from a disconcerting squint. Although he looked the complete antithesis of a robust footballer, his ability on the field was sensational and Huddersfield wasted no time in signing him as an amateur. Shortly afterwards, an eye operation corrected his squint, improved his footballing vision and literally changed his life. A precocious display in a Youth Cup final against Manchester United brought him to the attention of Matt Busby, who soon after offered Beattie £10,000 for the player. It was a staggering offer for the period, but the Huddersfield manager knew the worth of his priceless prodigy and refused to sell the boy named Denis Law.

While Shankly was enjoying developing the youth side and reserves, the first team continued their dangerous flirtation with relegation and came unstuck in May 1956. Ironically, it was Beattie's and Shankly's old team Preston that forced the nail into their First Division coffin by losing to relegation rivals Aston Villa. Shankly's hero, Tom Finney, had even missed a penalty to complete the unhappy drama. Demoted on goal average, Huddersfield prepared for life in the Second Division, confident that their youth policy would bring swift reward.

Sadly, an upswing in Huddersfield's fortunes did not come quickly enough for Andy Beattie. Four months into the new season he attended a meeting with the board of directors and resigned his post. Shankly, meanwhile, had been stringing together some excellent results with the reserves and, unaware of Beattie's fate, found himself thrust into the managerial chair. It was an unfortunate end to a promising partnership, but Beattie would reappear later in the Shankly story to play an important role in the success of Liverpool.

One month after Beattie's resignation, Huddersfield averted another crisis when they finally signed Denis Law as a fully-fledged professional. There were whispers that he might be wooed away by some bigger predators but Shankly's rhetoric won the day. Law remembers Shankly, as most people do, for his dry wit, cute turn of phrase and football fanaticism. With Law he occasionally tended to play the Scottish patriarch admonishing the lad to 'Be tidy, clean and healthy'. Such instant aphorisms came easily to his lips as did the free advice, 'Never mind your strengths, work on your weaknesses'. Law needed little persuading for he loved the game with a newcomer's passion. The youngster thrived on managerial enthusiasm and almost drove himself into injury by his incessant work rate. When his limbs were finally wrenched out of joint, he discovered a different Bill Shankly, uncaring to the point of callousness. As Law hobbled out of the treatment room one afternoon, Shankly briskly walked past in the other direction without uttering a word. For Shankly, Law was a god on the field but, once injured, he became a leper.

Shankly's answer to Law's fragility was characteristically eccentric. He placed the lad on a strict diet of milk and rump steak, arguing that it would transform him into a bulging Adonis. A boxing enthusiast, Shankly had once read that American heavyweights devoured steak during their fight preparations so decided that all good footballers should do the same. Whether the diet made any substantial difference to his player's footballing skills or fitness is questionable, but it was excellent psychology. If a player was not a giant, then Shankly at least insisted that he think big. Fortunately, Law had a touch of arrogance in his play that appealed to Shankly's grandiose style. As the teenage prodigy later observed: 'He gave you confidence and made you feel cocky'.

Denis Law was not the only talented youngster in Shankly's squad. Ray Wilson, Gordon Low, Les Massey and Mike O'Grady all came through the ranks during the same period. Wilson, like Law, was a veritable honeypot for aspiring rival managers and Shankly found himself constantly fending off offers from such big timers as Stan Cullis, Ted Drake and Harry Catterick. It says much for Shankly's enthusiasm that the boys remained at the club throughout his tenure.

In late 1959, Huddersfield were playing promotion-chasing Cardiff when Shankly was approached by Liverpool chairman, T V Williams. With an air of jollity, he asked: 'How would you like to manage the best club in England?' Shankly reeled in mock astonishment before eagerly enquiring the details of Matt Busby's shock resignation. Williams played along with his wry humour and patiently pointed out that he was referring to Liverpool not Manchester United. Shankly released a sigh of indifference, but it was clear to Williams that he was interested in the post. The two men agreed to keep in touch and Shankly was given several weeks to reach a decision. It was his second opportunity to become Liverpool's manager, for he had attended an interview back in 1951 when Don Welsh was given the post. Now, suddenly, he found himself in a much stronger position. In some ways it was surprising that Williams considered Shankly a candidate, for his record was far from impressive. Huddersfield had potential and boasted some outstanding young players but they were still stuck in the middle of the Second Division. Shankly had a reputation for boasting about his sides, but he had never actually won anything or mounted a serious First Division challenge. Liverpool, by contrast, had finished in the top four for four consecutive seasons since being demoted in 1954 and looked certain to return to the First Division before long. Their prospects had not been helped by an unfortunate turnover of managers during the 1950s. Theoretically, all they needed was a degree of stability to climb that one extra place for another taste of First Division football. The journeyman Shankly could not resist the lure of a big city club and decided to take another chance.

Shankly's first managerial decision at Liverpool concerned the fate of the backroom boys who included Bob Paisley, Reuben Bennett and Joe Fagan. Although the new manager had already decided that sweeping changes were required at the club, the staff were spared the axe. Bob Paisley recalls that first staff meeting with some affection:

> Bill was a man after my own heart. If he'd go out on the field he'd always try to win. He did the sensible thing at Liverpool by getting to know the training group and seeing who was looking after the reserves. He said he liked what he saw, and asked us all if we would stay. We jumped at it!

Shankly's willingness to retain the staff was to have far-reaching consequences for the club for it put in motion a sense of continuity and stability which was to make Liverpool a football institution.

Shankly's reign began with a 4-0 defeat, but for once he managed to bite his tongue and avoid any snap condemnation. Instead, he set about rebuilding the club in his own inimitable way. The apprentices were provided with paintbrushes and pitchforks and ordered to redecorate every building and transform the Melwood training field. Even Bob Paisley, a former bricklayer, found himself cementing new girders onto the stand. Nobody at Anfield was too proud for manual work and Joe Fagan and Reuben Bennett often toiled alongside the juniors without complaint. Everyone felt that they were part of the club, and some even felt that they had built it. Shankly's 'cleanliness is next to godliness' philosophy was working wonders on morale, although he remained unsatisfied. During those early months he gave the impression that he would dearly love to knock down the entire ground with a bulldozer and start from scratch.

Shankly's clean-up campaign extended to the players' room. Before long, the clean-up became a clear-out as half the team was off-loaded. After impatiently serving his time with lesser clubs, the ambitious Scot was in no mood for easy compromises. Liverpool had some money in the coffers, but extracting advances from the parsimonious directors strained Shankly's rhetoric to the limit. He cajoled, pleaded, argued, rationalised, threatened and begged, but the directors were cocooned in complacency and caution. For two consecutive seasons Liverpool finished third in the Second Division, although each time they were several points adrift of the leaders. They had now spent six successive seasons in the top four and Shankly was convinced that such near misses were the result of directorial indifference. The board, however, was content with Liverpool's standing as a solid Second Division club and tended to see promotion as a lucky bonus. That attitude finally changed thanks to Shankly's obdurate persistence and the arrival of an ambitious new director, Eric Sawyer.

Sawyer was impressed by his manager's earnestness and almost religious belief in Liverpool FC. Convinced that such a man could take the club back to the top he promised strong financial support. Shankly responded immediately and snapped up Ian St John from Motherwell for £37,500. The Saint soon showed his worth as a centre forward by scoring a hat trick against Everton in his first match. Such an achievement was enough to make him an instant hero of the Liverpool faithful. The fact that Everton had scored four in the same match and won the Liverpool Senior Cup was conveniently forgotten. Shortly after St John's arrival, Shankly returned to Scotland to barter for Ron Yeats, an intimidating giant guaranteed to bolster Liverpool's centre field. After some prevarication, Dundee United reluctantly surrendered their asset for £30,000. Shankly was overjoyed. He was overwhelmed by Yeats's size and skill and loved to tell tall tales about his great find. Surprised journalists were summoned to Anfield and actually invited to walk around the bemused player while Shankly beamed: 'He is a colossus'. Before they left, several reporters were told that Yeats had previously worked in an Aberdeen abattoir where he had once killed a raging bull with his bare hands. What would he do when he hit the First Division?

Yeats and St John spearheaded Liverpool's next promotion assault which saw them clinch the Second Division Championship in 1962 with 62 points. Shankly was impressed with the contribution of his new stars but never liked favouring individual players at the expense of the team. From the outset, he considered Liverpool as a single 11-man unit and could not abide prima donnas. In later years, however, he looked back at those early days with some nostalgia and concluded that St John and Yeats were the driving forces which first won him glory. He was not alone in this belief, which was echoed in a derogatory chant sung by Liverpool's keenest critics, the Everton supporters: 'We hate Bill Shankly and we hate St John but most of all we hate Big Ron'.

Liverpool did not storm the First Division in their 1962-63 season but finished a modest eighth. Towards the end of the title race they had been concentrating on the FA Cup having progressed to the semi-finals at the expense of London teams Arsenal and West Ham. A 1-0 defeat by Leicester robbed Shankly of a Wembley clash against Manchester United, but he was far from despondent. Young players such as Tommy Smith, Peter Thompson and Ian Callaghan were waiting in the wings to strengthen a team that already had Championship potential.

Winning a place in the Liverpool first team was no easy task since, in spite of their reputed physicality, few players suffered long term injuries. Shankly always claimed that this was a tribute to their intense concentration on the field. He hated players worrying about trivialities which might in some superficial way distract them from their game. As a result, everything at Liverpool was run with clockwork efficiency and a routine established that has lasted to this day. Like Don Revie, Shankly believed in providing his boys with first-class hotel accommodation, the best kit and transport available and excellent training facilities. Occasionally, his fastidiousness bordered on the eccentric. A glutton for consistency, he insisted that all hotels provided the same dinner for the entire team: tomato soup, steak, and fruit and cream. He thought nothing of imposing his tastes on others and remained unchallenged for years. Lord help any Liverpool lad who turned out to be a vegetarian.

The 1963-64 season ended with Shankly achieving a lifelong footballing ambition: the League Championship. Liverpool had come through a tough season with a modest 57 points which was enough to kill off the challenges of Manchester United, Everton and Spurs. Shankly was proud of his achievement, for this was the age of the charismatic manager and the teams below him boasted the guiding brilliance of Matt Busby, Harry Catterick and Bill Nicholson. One name missing from the scenario was not far away. Don Revie's Leeds United had taken the Second Division Championship and were about to emerge as Liverpool's greatest rivals over the next decade.

Liverpool celebrated their Championship win with an end-of-season trip to America. Shankly sanctioned the tour, but after completing the arrangements turned to Bob Paisley and said: 'You take charge. I'm not going over'. Never a great traveller, he intensely disliked flying but eventually agreed to endure the long plane trip. His entire attitude to America was curiously ambivalent. A boxing devotee and fan of 1930s American gangsters, he spoke enthusiastically about visiting Jack Dempsey's bar and viewing Al Capone's old car. Once on US soil, however, he grew restless and irritable. Paisley offered to take him out for a drink on the first evening only to be told: 'No, it's a bit late'. Bob laughed upon realising that his boss had neglected to put back his watch. 'It's all right, Bill', he teased. 'It's only half past seven'. Shankly looked puzzled, then expressed horror at the idea of interfering with Greenwich Mean Time. Refusing to accept idiotic foreign hours, he remained out of time with his colleagues for the duration of the trip. 'He'd give out the team sheets at three in the morning', Paisley recalls with a wry, painful smile. As the tour progressed, Paisley witnessed other xenophobic eccentricities from his partner. On one occasion, he damned the Americans for their ignorance when somebody failed to recognise the insignia on his club blazer. When he realised that virtually nobody had heard of Liverpool FC, the Champions of England, he was appalled and seemed quite hurt. With one game left to play, Paisley was abruptly called home having received the sad news of his mother's death. Shankly agreed to stay with the team but eventually left ahead of time. The disillusionment he experienced in America would shortly be increased tenfold when Liverpool sampled Continental competition.

The European Cup was the Holy Grail for British football managers in the early 1960s and, like many, Shankly was convinced that his team could lift the trophy. His campaign began in earnest with an 11-1 aggregate victory over K R Reykjavik, followed by a brilliant tactical triumph over Anderlecht. Shankly had seen most of the Belgian side, which included a number of internationals, and decided to outfox them by using Tommy Smith as both an inside left and right half. Anderlecht were uncomfortable with Liverpool's 4–4–2 system and finally succumbed 4–0. What seemed an easier task against Cologne went the full distance and, after two stultifying goalless draws, a play-off was arranged. The match forced each side to take greater risks but after extra time a 2–2 draw was the final outcome. Under European rules this meant that the tie had to be decided by the crudest of means: the toss of a coin. Liverpool's luck won the day and convinced Shankly that their name was already written on the European Cup. He awaited the semi-final draw with interest, unaware what nightmares lay ahead.

The distraction of playing European football had seriously affected Liverpool's chances of retaining the League Championship and they ended the season in seventh place. There were no such problems in the FA Cup, however, apart from an early scare in the fourth round when they were held 1–1 at Anfield by lowly Stockport County. Amazingly, this was the only home match that Shankly ever missed during his years at Liverpool. He had travelled abroad to spy on Cologne and returned to London during the evening, unaware of the result. Accosting a porter he enquired whether there had been any shock results in the FA Cup and was told that Peterborough had beaten Arsenal 2–1. Perusing the porter's newspaper he noticed that Liverpool had been held and stormed off in a huff crying: 'Liverpool drawing with Stockport, what do you call that if it isn't a shock?' The players had hell to pay when Shankly returned to Anfield, but they responded well, overcame Stockport 2–0 in the replay, and went on to defeat Bolton and Leicester. The semi-finals offered a far stiffer test, for they included the top three teams in the League. Liverpool drew the weakest of those three, Chelsea, and won 2–0, leaving Manchester United and Leeds to battle for a place in the final. Leeds pulled through, thereby ensuring that a new name would be added to the list of FA Cup winners.

The 1965 FA Cup final was not a particularly memorable match as both Leeds and Liverpool erred on the side of caution. After only nine minutes, however, an incident occurred which almost spelled disaster for Shankly's men. Left back Gerry Byrne collided with Leeds' Welsh giant Bobby Collins and landed clumsily on the pitch. Trainer Bob Paisley provided treatment, then discovered to his dismay that the lad had broken his collar bone. With no substitutes allowed in football at the time, Byrne could either be taken off or allowed to continue in near agony. Fearing the consequences of being reduced to a ten-man team, Shankly consulted with Paisley on the bench and Byrne played on. A dour 90 minutes produced no result, but in extra time the injured Gerry Byrne laid on a cross for Roger Hunt which ended in a goal. Leeds gamely resisted but eventually went down 2–1, with Ian St John scoring the winner. For Shankly, that victory represented his greatest moment in football. The Liverpool Kop choir were in full chorus throughout the afternoon and established a bond with Shankly that was to remain cordially intact for the remainder of his life.

Three days after their Wembley triumph, Liverpool resumed the trek for European glory in a semi-final clash against Inter-Milan. The Italians were understandably intimidated by the intense atmosphere at Anfield which was made crazier when Liverpool walked on to the pitch carrying the FA Cup. The Kop danced in jubilation with Shankly urging them on. It was a brilliant exercise in crowd psychology and it left the Italians completely undermined. Liverpool romped to a 3–1 victory while Inter-Milan coach Helenio Herrera hung his head in dejection.

The return leg at the San Siro Stadium was to prove Shankly's saddest and most bitter experience in football. The local Italian press had stirred up bad feeling by complaining about Liverpool's gamesmanship at Anfield and suggesting that their supporters had acted like baying animals. The Inter-Milan fans needed little prompting in exacting revenge. As Liverpool emerged from the tunnel they were greeted with hostile jeers, several bottles and a series of smoke bombs. Shankly feared the worst but instructed the team to concentrate on their football. Events on the pitch consistently went against the away team and the Liverpool bench was appalled by the standard of refereeing. After Tommy Lawrence had gathered an innocuous cross, a Milan player charged the keeper knocking the ball from his hands and thumping it into the net. Liverpool's angry appeals were brushed aside and the score was upheld. When a second goal was netted from an indirect free kick, Shankly found himself facing the prospect of a play-off. Suddenly, Liverpool came alive and scored a breakaway goal themselves which the referee disallowed. It was the last straw for the pyrogenous Tommy Smith who grabbed hold of the Spanish official and threatened a punch. Amazingly, he was neither dismissed nor booked. The match continued its ugly course until the inspired Milan scored a third goal to thwart Liverpool's bid for glory. Shankly refused to be visibly downcast after the match and informed his players that they were still the greatest team in the world. Although he promised to return in triumph, European competitions were to remain an unhappy hunting ground during the Shankly years. The bad experience in Italy reinforced his xenophobia which may have proven a factor in inhibiting later European performances. Bob Paisley confirms Shankly's ambivalent attitude towards foreign competition:

> He'd have loved to have won the European Cup, but we didn't get near it when he had the team. He detested foreigners and hated going to these places. You couldn't find a foreign player that could play. He used to always call them phoneys. If he'd got one himself things might have worked out, but he was never keen on them.

Shankly's successes in the League and Cup transformed him into football's most famous personality during the mid-1960s. Unlike many of his dour and over-cautious colleagues he was never short of a word for the media and his sayings became legendary. His wit would emerge in instant quips and amusing aphorisms, the most famous of which was the outrageous contention: 'Football is not a matter of life and death – it's much more important than that'. The witticisms were generally spontaneous, although there is evidence of twice-told jokes. Both Geoff Twentyman at Carlisle and Huddersfield captain John Toddington recall Shankly using an identical half-time talk. On each occasion his side was trailing by a glut of goals and, eager to discover an explanation or scapegoat, he rounded on the captain. The poor lad was blamed for defensive lapses, ineffectual marking and anything else that came into Shankly's mind. After exhausting his arsenal of criticisms, he abruptly condemned the captain for losing the toss at the kick off! 'What did you call?' he enquired knowingly. 'Heads', replied the puzzled lad. 'Ah! You don't call heads!' grimaced Shankly, as though the skipper had made a fundamental footballing error. The players laughed uproariously at this riposte but their manager retained his stern countenance. He was a brilliant straight-man and so eccentric in his outbursts that few players could be absolutely certain when he was joking or being serious.

1965–66 was another vintage season for Shankly. Liverpool's League progress was steady, allowing them the luxury of pursuing the European Cup Winners' Cup with increased confidence. Their list of Continental scalps was impressive and included Juventus, Standard Liège and Honved. After overcoming Celtic in a tense semi-final, Liverpool looked set for their first European title. Shankly was anxious to win the trophy not merely for its prestige, but to compensate for a disappointing run in the FA Cup. The holders had come unstuck as early as the third round when Chelsea avenged their semi-final defeat of the previous year. Undeterred, Shankly pinned his hopes on an historic League and European double. Nearest rivals Leeds ebbed away in the closing stages of the title race leaving Liverpool as Champions with a solid 61 points. Perhaps the most remarkable aspect of this latest title campaign was that Shankly used only 14 players throughout the season, and one of those, Bobby Graham, made a cursory single appearance in their final League match. Other managers, hampered by injured players, looked on enviously at Shankly's super-fit squad. Liverpool's extraordinary performance that season was a testament not only to their skill, stamina and strength but their canny vigilance in avoiding clumsy errors. As Shankly observed, the best players have a knack of protecting themselves.

The Cup Winners' Cup final was an anti-climax for Shankly, as Liverpool played below their usual high standard and were outmanoeuvred by Borussia Dortmund. Even bigoted Bill could not find much to complain about in the Germans' 2–1 victory. Turning defeat to advantage, he realised that Liverpool were now one of the more experienced English clubs in Europe and the League title meant another shot at glory. What promised to be Shankly's most sustained attack on the European Cup to date foundered early the next season. There was a tough first round fixture which took Liverpool behind the Iron Curtain to play the Romanian side Petrolul Ploesti. A highly competitive two-leg match ended 3–3 on aggregate forcing a play-off in Brussels which Liverpool won 2–0.

It proved nothing more than a false reprieve before execution, for in the next round Liverpool faced Ajax Amsterdam and the deadly skills of teenage prodigy Johan Cruyff. Ajax would not emerge as three-time European Cup winners until the early 1970s but even in this embryonic stage they were capable of giving Liverpool a soccer lesson. At the Olympic Stadium, the Merseysiders were trounced 5–1 and clearly had no answer to the sweeping Dutch attack. Shankly spent most of the match sitting on the bench sarcastically complaining about the fog which had rendered his players invisible. There was one amusing moment in the proceedings when the wily Liverpool manager sneaked onto the darkened pitch and lectured his players about the need to tighten up the defence. The scoreline suggested that his illegal words had made little impact. After the match, Shankly was as confident as ever and insisted that Liverpool were the better team. As they left the ground he turned to Bob Paisley and said: 'If this is European football they can keep it. It's too defensive for me!' Paisley resisted the temptation to remind his xenophobic friend that Ajax had just scored five goals. Against all logic, Shankly protested that Liverpool would wipe out the four-goal deficit in the second leg at Anfield, but he was only fooling himself. Liverpool drew 2–2, thereby losing 7–3 on aggregate. It was left to Celtic to win the European Cup that year, a competition that Liverpool would not compete in for another six years.

Although Liverpool stayed in the top five of the First Division for the remainder of the 1960s, they failed to win another trophy. Overshadowed by the emergence of Don Revie's Leeds United, who played equally tight defensive football but offered more guile in midfield and greater flair in attack, Shankly was forced to reappraise his team's prospects. There was no crisis at Anfield, but even at their best Liverpool had lost the edge to Leeds. Events reached a head during the 1968–69 season when the Merseysiders lost only six League games, logged 61 points, but still found themselves half a dozen points behind their Yorkshire rivals. Shankly maintained Liverpool's consistency throughout this period, but Leeds were even more consistent and seemed to be improving with each passing season. Clearly, if Liverpool were to re-establish their supremacy in the 1970s, a new side would have to be created. Shankly realised the need for progress but was unwilling to dive recklessly into the transfer market and so chose to bide his time. Always on the lookout for untutored talent he kept a vigilant eye on the lower divisions and made two crucial signings in 1967.

Emlyn Hughes was a fiery young kid, eager to impress and arrogant enough to grab an opportunity at the first time of asking. Shankly happened to witness his debut in the League, playing for Blackpool against Blackburn, and was astonished by the lad's undisguised aggression. Always appreciative of fiercely competitive players, the Liverpool supremo instantly offered £25,000 for the untried teenager.

Blackpool were unmoved by the offer having already secured a sizeable fee for Everton-bound Alan Ball. Shankly kept in touch, however, and eventually bagged Hughes in February 1967 for £65,000. It was to prove one of his best investments. An even more astonishing bargain followed during the summer when Shankly spent £18,000 on an unknown goalkeeper from Scunthorpe. Ray Clemence would not only ably replace Tommy Lawrence at Liverpool but was destined to become the long-time number one goalkeeper for England.

Brilliant though the above signings turned out, Shankly was far from infallible in the transfer market. That same year he purchased the promising Tony Hateley from Chelsea for a stiff fee of £96,000. The outlay was never recouped on the playing field as Hateley fell prone to injury and survived for barely a year at Liverpool. In September 1968 he was despatched to Coventry and during that same week Shankly caused a sensation by splashing out a phenomenal £100,000 on a Wolves reserve player, Alun Evans. Shankly's critics claimed the fee was grossly exorbitant and questioned the sagacity of signing an inchoate 18-year-old who could not even command a first team place at Wolves. The maestro responded to the doubters with characteristically bullish spite: 'If Wolves had asked £200,000 I would have been prepared to pay it'. Like Hateley, Alun Evans also failed to become part of Liverpool's long-term plans and a series of injuries saw him return to the Midlands, where he joined Aston Villa. Shankly's Midas touch appeared to be corroding alarmingly and other new players such as Peter Wall and Stuart Mason (bought in a package deal from Wrexham) came and went without making much impact.

While the new signings faltered, Shankly clung confidently to his old school of Hunt, St John and Yeats, all of whom were pushing 30. Soccer pundits continued to press the beleaguered Liverpool manager on the need for class replacements but he rose to the defence of his ageing team and refused to administer further cuts: 'They are playing with the enthusiasm of schoolboys, even after all these years, and have not lost their appetite for success. They still want to win something'.

Although the spirit was willing, Liverpool's speed and strength were diminishing with each passing year. In retrospect, Bob Paisley argues that Shankly was guilty of allowing sentiment to rule his managerial decisions:

> Bill was a softie at heart. If he ever had a failing it was that. He didn't like to upset players that had done so tremendously well for him. But like everybody else they get old. Some of them were ready to go and, really, it would have been better to have given them a chance to move to another club and get some money.

Of course, most of the Liverpool old guard had become as attached to Anfield as their manager, so the learning process proved particularly painful.

By the end of the 1960s even the Liverpool faithful were growing impatient about the lack of recent trophies, so Shankly took drastic action. The turning point was the sixth round of the 1970 FA Cup when Liverpool were knocked out by lowly Watford. This humiliation hastened the departure of several former stars and paved the way for the emergence of new boys such as John Toshack and Steve Heighway. Amid the purge, such Liverpool greats as Yeats, St John and Lawrence found that they had been dropped for the first time in their careers.

Shankly's method of laying off players could be endearingly coy. Prior to a team selection, he would accost his victim and express concern about the player's health. 'You look a bit tired, son!', was a favourite opening line, followed by the benevolently euphemistic advice: 'I think you could do with a rest'. Occasionally, Shankly would be caught out by his own rhetoric if his chosen substitute fell ill. In such circumstances, the 'rested' player would have to be driven out of his state of Shankly-induced hypochondria by contradictory reassurances. Far from requiring a rest he would be abruptly transmogrified into a god among players, the fittest man in the team and the only footballer that Shankly could rely upon. Such inconsistencies brought amusement rather than anger from the team, for Shankly was blessed with the ability of being able to get away with murder. The redoubtable Ian Callaghan was no stranger to 'Shankly doublethink' having experienced the phenomenon during his first season at Liverpool. Although a fitness fanatic, his capricious manager became worried by the way the tireless Callaghan ran himself ragged every Saturday afternoon and then pushed his body to the limit during training. Convinced that the boy was overworking himself, he took him aside one afternoon and suggested a more relaxed approach. The following week the workaholic Callaghan reluctantly decided to accept the advice but when Shankly saw him apparently easing off during training he shouted: 'Let's have you!'

Notwithstanding his inconsistencies, Shankly was never less than decisive in his actions and demanded the same of others. His partnership with Bob Paisley remained unspoiled by a single bad word, in spite of their occasional differences of opinion. Shankly respected absolute conviction, even when it ran counter to his own beliefs. The quite forcefulness of Paisley played its part in influencing the choice of teams and Shankly was always open to suggestions concerning new purchases. Trainer Reuben Bennett was a shrewd judge of a player but sometimes his very thoroughness ran counter to Shankly's whims. On one occasion, the trainer was asked his opinion of a potential buy and gave a lengthy appraisal pointing out various merits and faults, until Shankly wearily cut him off. 'Aw, there you go again!' he accused, misinterpreting Reuben's analysis as procrastination. As Paisley smilingly observed: 'With Bill you *had* to say yes or no. If anybody sounded unsure he just didn't want to know'.

The recruitment of John Toshack and Steve Heighway in 1970 reduced the average age of the side and encouraged Shankly to experiment more freely. Unafraid to whet new blood in the First Division he made the bold decision to establish a new Liverpool within two years. The transition was less painful than might have been expected, for Liverpool retained their place in the top five and began to enjoy a good run in the FA Cup. Musing on the future of the Reds, Shankly let slip a revealing comment:

> We have the youngest staff we've ever had, in fact, overall. But we're still looking for one more player. He could be among the youngsters at present on our books or he could be making his way with another club. We'll keep looking, weighing things up – and when we decide which is our man, that will complete the jigsaw.

Shankly found the boy of his dreams in May 1971 when Kevin Keegan signed for Liverpool. The man responsible for discovering Keegan was Shankly's old friend from the Preston and Huddersfield days, Andy Beattie. Since joining Liverpool as a part-time scout, Beattie had made several excursions on Shankly's behalf but none as momentous as that trip to Scunthorpe where the 18-year-old Keegan transfixed his eye with scintillating soccer skills and a strength of purpose that belied his diminutive stature. At first, Shankly found it difficult to believe that Beattie was not exaggerating, especially as two other clubs had passed over the boy wonder. Eventually, Liverpool's chief scout, Geoff Twentyman, visited Scunthorpe followed by Bob Paisley and Joe Fagan. Each agreed that Keegan had enormous potential and, with Bobby Robson threatening to pounce on behalf of Ipswich, Shankly dramatically intervened to claim his prize. Robson later admitted that he did not rate Keegan at that time and feared that his lack of inches and small frame would inhibit his progress. Shankly was not so myopic. A new era in Liverpool's eventful football history was about to commence.

Within days of Keegan's signing, Liverpool returned to Wembley in a vain attempt to prevent Arsenal from winning the double. The game stuttered into extra time before Steve Heighway opened the scoring. Shankly was convinced that the Cup was won, but late goals from Eddie Kelly and Charlie George enabled Arsenal to break the Leeds/Liverpool duopoly and register only the second double of the century. The London side also wrecked Liverpool's title hopes the next season when Derby sneaked the Championship. This was Shankly's sixth consecutive year without a single trophy on the Anfield shelf, but the tide was turning. A tremendous late run in the Championship race had suggested that Liverpool would be a force in the following season, and so it proved.

The revitalised Liverpool re-enacted their mid-1960s glory at the end of the 1972–73 season by claiming the Championship. Although it was not his greatest title win, Shankly admitted that it was the most satisfying. With a team of young players Liverpool produced their own version of the double by becoming the first team to top the League and bag a European trophy in the same season. The UEFA Cup final was a two-leg affair against the star-studded German side Borussia Moenchengladbach. Rain played a decisive part in determining the destination of the trophy when the first match at Anfield was abandoned after 30 minutes. Liverpool looked lacklustre that evening but the wily Shankly had spotted a crucial flaw in Borussia's defence which his scouting team had inexplicably missed. The German back four were unusually immobile and suspect to high, long-range crosses. In the rearranged fixture, Shankly instructed his men to bombard Borussia with a non-stop aerial assault and this ploy worked to devastating effect. Three first-half goals overwhelmed the Germans and, although they tightened up their defence after the interval, the damage had already been done. The debilitating effects of a torturous English League season caught up with Liverpool in the return match and, despite the aggregate advantage, Shankly genuinely feared that his team might lose. While he watched disconsolately from the bench, Borussia tore into the heart of Liverpool's defence and scored two goals. Then the unbelievable occurred. A flash of lightning, a roar of thunder and the pitch was soon awash. On this occasion, the referee allowed the game to continue and the rain robbed the Germans of their shooting power. Liverpool ended the match as 3–2 aggregate winners having played in conditions ideally suited to a team familiar with wet English winter afternoons. Even if there was an element of rainy luck in the proceedings, nobody could deny that after years of European competition Liverpool thoroughly deserved their first Continental trophy.

The new boys at Anfield quickly grew accustomed to their manager's distinctive match preparations which usually took the form of breast-beating eulogies on the power and glory of Liverpool Football Club. During tactical talks at their Melwood training ground, Shankly would carefully set up a board of miniature red and white players. Confusingly, the opposition were always cast in Liverpool's colours, a superstition that Shankly never bothered to explain. The talks were seldom long-winded for Shankly showed scant respect for any opposition. Towering over his board of miniatures like an angry god, he would verbally assassinate the team in red, sparing no reputations and deriding their presumptuousness in visiting Anfield. The routine was the same whether the team under fire was Stockport County or Manchester United. Even before the attentive Liverpool players had settled in their seats, the opposing forward line would be plucked from the board and deposited into his track-suit pocket. 'You don't even have to worry about them', he would sneer before lunging into the inadequacies of the midfield and defence. As his rhetoric reached uncontrollable heights, he would abruptly lose patience and, with a dismissive sweep of the hand, bulldoze the entire miniature team from the board. Regaining his poise, he would casually announce: 'Now that we've dealt with them, this is what you should do'.

Such contempt for the opposition would reach its apogee on the following Saturday afternoon when the famous 'Shankly psychology' enveloped the Liverpool team. The manager seemed positively manic on such occasions, rushing into the dressing room, with eyes sparkling and hands rubbing together in unconcealable glee. As ever, the big news was that the opposition looked frightened to death. A stream of dismissals would follow: 'I've just seen their goalkeeper and he doesn't look as if he's slept for a week. He looks older than me!' Even the number 12 did not escape Shankly's evil eye: 'The substitute is as white as a sheet. He's petrified. I hope they put him on in the second half because I'm telling you now, he definitely doesn't want to go on'. Summing up the opposition's hopes, Shankly would wryly conclude: 'They've come here happy to go away with a respectable 1–0 defeat, let's hit them for five and teach them a lesson'. Although all the players were used to Shankly's hyperbole and quaint mythologising, the effect on team morale was inestimable. After laughing at Shankly's jokes and lapping up his praise they would walk onto the pitch temporarily convinced that they truly were the greatest side in the world.

Shankly fully expected Liverpool to retain the Championship in 1973–74, but he had not reckoned on a last hurrah from Leeds United who took the footballing world by storm in establishing a 29-game unbeaten run from the beginning of the season. Although Liverpool kept chasing and closed the enormous gap considerably in the latter stages, Leeds would not be denied their second-ever Championship. These two giants of football were due to clash in the sixth round of the FA Cup until Leeds were sensationally dismissed by Second Division Bristol City. Liverpool duly overcame the West Country side and, after a replayed semi-final against their old bogey team Leicester, finally returned to Wembley. Their opponents were mid-table Newcastle, a team with a wonderful Cup tradition, having won the trophy three times during the 1950s. Sentimental critics tended to favour the Northeasterners while more objective scribes concluded that the match would be a tight affair possibly requiring a replay. In the event, Liverpool dominated the game from start to finish, scoring three goals without reply. It was the culmination of Shankly's achievements over the years and the Kop faithful demonstrated their feelings by despatching two boys who were photographed literally kissing Shankly's feet.

Shankly was strangely subdued following the Cup final for, unknown to his colleagues, he had made the momentous decision to retire. According to Paisley, Bill was always making such pronouncements, but this time the consequences were more serious. Having won the League and Cup in successive seasons with an entirely new squad, Shankly felt that his work was virtually complete. He had already written himself into the annals of football history and, although further success was beckoning, he wanted to leave Liverpool on a winning note. The temptation to continue the quest for the European Cup somehow proved resistible even though Shankly longed to emulate the feats of his two old friends, Jock Stein and Matt Busby. Such immemorial ambition might have kept him in the game for another decade, but after a lifetime devoted entirely to football he suddenly felt very tired. Unlike most of his contemporaries, Shankly had no consuming passion or interest outside the game and ultimately nothing to distract him from the long-term pressures of top-flight management. As Bob Paisley observed:

> I don't think anybody was as obsessive about football as Bill. I put everything into the game but I sometimes liked to do other things. But Bill couldn't get away from it for one hour! There comes a time when football has to be put aside but he could never do that.

Bill Shankly's departure from Liverpool climaxed in a testimonial which proved another milestone in his career. What seemed a happy ending, however, grew sour soon after, when Shankly fully realised the implications of his decision and discovered that he was no longer needed at Anfield. He criticised the club in print for their alleged tardiness in inviting him to away matches and detected disapproving signs when he visited the team during training at Melwood. Whether this was oversensitivity on Shankly's part or calculated coldness from a club trying to bury a legend is a matter of conjecture. Perhaps part of the problem lay in understanding precisely what Shankly wanted or expected after his retirement. There is certainly evidence to suggest a change of heart in the months following his testimonial. The reluctant new manager Bob Paisley had accepted the job under duress and initially attempted to persuade Shankly to reconsider before offering him an untaxing consultative post:

> When I got the job I said, 'Would you be available to have a look at some people?' He could have taken Nessie up to Scotland, looked around for players and got his expenses. I wanted to keep him involved but he got sickened off. It had got on top of him.

Paisley refutes any suggestion that Liverpool may have treated his colleague shabbily. He recalls that 'tickets were always in the box' awaiting Shankly's collection and a directorship was virtually his for the asking. Sadly, it was not to be. An intensely proud and sensitive man, Shankly would never have dreamed of putting himself forward for a place on the board, but fully expected to be invited. Clearly, he felt that the club was guilty of indifference. Beneath his disenchantment was the knowledge that he may have acted too hastily in announcing his retirement. Paisley maintains that he came to regret the decision in the light of Liverpool's unparalleled success after his departure:

> He was no sooner out than he wished he'd never done it. I gave him the opportunity to reconsider but he said, 'No! I want out altogether'. Then, when I got away too well for him he became a bit jealous and we didn't see much of him.

Indeed, Shankly caused a stir among long-time Liverpool supporters by turning up at rival grounds. He was enjoying spectator football, visiting old friends, chatting to employees and meeting fellow managers. Paisley believes that certain clubs poached free advice from the great man who could never resist discussing football with anybody. However, it is doubtful whether Shankly was ever indiscreet enough to spill the secrets of Anfield for he never lost his affection for the club. At least any visits to rivals Manchester United were to prove harmless thanks to the integrity of Matt Busby. As Paisley noted: 'Matt was always good, he'd tell us!'

Bill Shankly's lifelong love affair with football ended on 29 September 1981 when he suffered a fatal heart attack at Broadgreen Hospital, Liverpool. He was 67. A memorial service in Liverpool was attended by a massive congregation longing to pay tribute to the man who had transformed the city into the football capital of Europe. Among the mourners was pop singer Gerry Marsden, an ardent Liverpool fan whose third number one hit had provided the Kop with their personal anthem. During the service he led the congregation in a moving and distinctly elegiac rendition of 'You'll Never Walk Alone'. It was a fitting valediction.

DON REVIE

TANTALUS BECOMES MAMMON

Don Revie was born on 10 July 1927 in a two-bedroomed terraced house in Bell Street, Middlesbrough, close to the famous Ayresome Park ground. The Depression bit deep in the Northeast and Revie's father, a joiner, was frequently unemployed. Football provided a much-needed distraction from the bleakness, but even here a lack of money proved stifling. With a scarcity of such rudimentary luxuries as a real ball, Revie and his friends were often reduced to kicking around a bundle of rags in order to pass the time. The hard times taught Revie the value of thrift and in later years he became well known as one of soccer's soundest economists.

At the age of nine, Revie was promoted to captain of his school soccer team, an honour which prompted his father to present the boy with his first pair of football boots. The purse strings continued to loosen as the decade progressed. By the late 1930s, Revie's father and elder sisters had all found steady work, but the family was still not without its problems. At 12 years of age, with his secondary school life barely underway, Revie suffered the bereavement of his mother. Faced with a deserted household at 8 am, the brooding youngster would leave early for school and relieve the tedium by aimlessly kicking a ball against a wall. These solitary hours of ball practice were soon to transform him into a highly promising player.

Until 1939, Revie had been content to play for Newpark Boys Club, but with his teens approaching he suddenly found himself head-hunted. The amusingly titled 'Middlesbrough Swifts' were so impressed with the lad's skills that they poached him from Newpark for the not unconsiderable sum of five shillings. It was Revie's first experience of the transfer system and it greatly appealed to his financial imagination.

Great soccer maestros are sometimes influenced by the first manager they encounter, but few would have guessed that one of Revie's greatest innovations was borrowed from his gaffer at inconsequential Middlesbrough Swifts. Manager Bill Sanderson regularly held extra-curricular team meetings in the cramped surroundings of his council home. An engine driver by trade, Sanderson was something of a train spotter when it came to dissecting rival teams and his peculiar speciality was the preparing of highly detailed dossiers outlining the strengths and weaknesses of the opposition. Revie marvelled at these carefully produced documents which conjured up visions of secret service files containing vital information on enemy activities. Sanderson's scheme of soccer spying was a revelation which reduced genuinely frightening teams to the level of fallible, all too human, opponents, who could be overcome by a superior game plan. The dossier could not guarantee victory over a vastly superior side but it was the psychological equivalent of a two-goal start. At Middlesbrough Swifts, Revie learned the crucial lesson that methodology rather than blue-in-the-face ranting, was the true secret of great management. The role of the manager was not merely to inspire his team, but to unlock the secret weakness of the opposition and exploit their flaws with merciless efficiency. The biblical aphorism 'know thine enemy' became a soccer watchword to Revie and would later enable him to transform a relegation-threatened Second Division side into one of the most feared and highly organised teams in the 100-year history of League football.

After leaving school at 14, Revie served his time as an apprentice bricklayer and two years later made his League debut with Leicester City. He figured prominently in their great Cup run of 1949, scoring twice in the shock 3–1 defeat of Portsmouth. During the match, Revie suffered a nosebleed which resulted in a haemorrhage that could have cost him his life. It proved serious enough to rob him of a place in the Wembley final, which Leicester narrowly lost to Wolves 2–1. That same year the unlucky Cup hero married Elsie May Leonard Duncan, the niece of his team manager, John Duncan. By his own admission, Revie became one of soccer's journeymen, moving for a spell to Second Division Hull before reaching his peak as a player with Manchester City in the mid-1950s. It was there that he became a household name as the proponent of the famous 'Revie Plan', a tactic built around the innovative use of a deep-lying centre forward. In truth, it was not Revie who introduced the plan, but Manchester City manager Les McDowell who had borrowed the idea from the all-conquering Hungarians. The grand scheme at first foundered with an ignominious 5–0 defeat at Preston but McDowell persevered and the method eventually provided Revie with sufficient space to utilise his formidable passing skills. City ended the 1955 season as FA Cup runners-up and Revie received the Footballer of the Year award. A year later, he returned to Wembley to lift the Cup in a 3–1 win over Birmingham. A tally of six England caps completed an eventful playing career.

In his twilight years on the field, Revie briefly moved back to the Northeast for a two-year sojourn at Sunderland before Leeds intervened with a timely £14,000 offer in 1958. The money that Revie had accumulated in transfer deals was a record for the time and underlined his astuteness as a soccer businessman. The move to Elland Road proved to be the most crucial transfer of his footballing career. Since their promotion to the top flight, two years previously, Leeds had established themselves as solid mid-table candidates, but their status seemed far from secure. One year after Revie's arrival, they slipped back into the Second Division and were soon heading towards the Third. It was at that point that the Leeds directors made the eminently logical decision to appoint their autumnal midfielder as club manager. Revie's greatest champion at this time was chairman Harry Reynolds, a wealthy businessman who took a gamble on his retiring club captain rather than seeking an already established manager:

> I immediately took to Don. I assessed him as I would anyone in the business and I found he had the right qualities and the right ideas. . . I could tell he was the man for the job. But he had no experience of management and some people felt that this was not a good thing.

The scepticism was not unreasonable. Leeds were only three points away from the relegation zone when Revie took over and the average gate had slumped to a depressing 7,000. They desperately required a miracle worker. Against the odds, Revie maintained their Second Division status and they finished in 17th place.

During the close season of 1961 the ever efficient Revie sought the counsel of the most successful manager of the era: Matt Busby. The revered Manchester United maestro gave him invaluable advice for securing team loyalty: 'All you have to do is treat your players well, be honest with them and never lie to them. In return, they'll do anything for you'. Revie took this advice to its logical extreme, exercising a managerial solicitude which his jealous rivals would later deride as 'mollycoddling'. However, Revie's psychology was to prove remarkably effective in winning the respect and intense loyalty of a squad of players, virtually all of whom came through the youth ranks. Self pride and an indestructible belief in the power of Leeds were the hallmarks of the team which began the 1963–64 season intent on winning promotion to the First Division. Revie instilled this new confidence by boldly changing the club strip to all white in honour of Real Madrid. He also boasted to amused reporters that Leeds would one day emulate the achievements of that legendary Spanish side. The overreaching gestures coincided with the unfortunate adoption of Continental cynicism, characterised by an obsessive determination to avoid defeat at any cost. Such tactics brought Leeds a reputation as a ruthless, dirty side, but there was no doubting the success of their expedient policy. They ended the 1963–64 season as Second Division Champions with only three defeats (a new League record) and the highest divisional points total since the great Spurs side of 1919–20. The statistical facts were sufficient warning to First Division opponents that Leeds would be a tough side to beat the following season.

With a minimum of spending on new players, Revie had already assembled a formidable defensive team which included Billy Bremner, Jackie Charlton, Norman Hunter, Paul Reaney and arguably his most important signing as a football manager: Johnny Giles. Giles had come to Elland Road from Manchester United in 1963 for a bargain £32,000 and soon combined with Bremner to form one of the finest midfield combinations of the decade. The Irishman rapidly replaced the ageing hero John Charles and was called upon to live up to Revie's billing as 'the greatest inside forward of his generation'. With Norman ('I've never deliberately set out to injure an opponent') Hunter and 'Big' Jack Charlton marshalling the defence, Leeds conceded only 34 goals in their promotion-winning season. In spite of their notoriety as an unrelentingly physical side, Revie saw no reason to change the formula for First Division opponents. Occasionally, he promised that attacking flair would be forthcoming once Leeds had established themselves in the top flight, but precisely when Revie envisaged that time to be was never clear. Tactically, Leeds clung to their hard man image as a means of intimidating opponents and staking their claim for major trophies. It was difficult to imagine how it could have been otherwise for their reputation went before them and the players soon realised that a role once assumed is not easily discarded. Former Leeds centre forward Alan Peacock argues that the blatantly aggressive style was perpetuated partly as a means of combating retaliatory attacks from equally aggressive rivals:

The method business was overplayed but did suit Leeds well. The flair was there. Giles and Bremner had as much flair as you'll see anywhere, but for a variety of reasons they weren't allowed to bring it out. One of the troubles was that Leeds were branded as a kicking side. We found that when we got into the First Division teams were out to kick us before we kicked them. If we played a bit hard in return we got the blame.

Leeds' opponents were not quite as generous in their assessments, although few could dispute the impact that the Yorkshire team had made in its first year back in the top flight. Rather improbably, the newcomers had threatened to usurp the soccer aristocracy by winning the double, and they came agonisingly close to succeeding. In the FA Cup, they dismissed both Everton and Manchester United in tense replays before finally succumbing to Liverpool in a final decided 2–1 in extra time. The League Championship was even more heartbreaking with Leeds losing the title to Manchester United by 0.686 of a goal! It was only the fourth time that the Championship had been decided by the convoluted mathematics of goal averages. The rivals had won, drawn and lost an identical number of games, but, surprisingly, it was Leeds' defensive record which was significantly inferior to that of their Manchester opponents. The Championship race had strongly favoured Leeds until as late as 16 April when Manchester United had avenged their Cup defeat with a killing 0–1 victory at Elland Road. Don Revie hardly needed reminding of the significance of that result or that Leeds' points total was the largest accumulated by any runners-up in the history of the League.

The image of Leeds as perennial runners-up grew steadily during the next three seasons. Having being ousted by Manchester United in 1965, they excelled them the following year, but still ended up second, this time to their alternate rivals Liverpool. The next season was even more frustrating. Manchester United retrieved the Championship, while Leeds were involved in chasing treble honours. Their League campaign foundered, five points behind United; they lost to Chelsea 1–0 in a tightly fought FA Cup semi-final and surrendered 2–0 to Dynamo Zagreb in a two-leg European Fairs Cup final. For Revie, an intensely superstitious man, the portents must have seemed positively alarming. If he needed confirmation that the football gods were playing some sadistic game with Leeds then the mounting list of lost trophies was evidence enough.

During 1967–68, the bizarre coincidences continued to multiply. Leeds again found themselves involved in an overambitious treble-chasing campaign and the results made ominous reading. Once more their Championship challenge faltered and they finished five points behind League winners Manchester City; they again reached the semi-final stage of the FA Cup and the result was the same as the previous year, a 1–0 defeat. With the Fairs Cup final again beckoning, the historical inevitability of defeat suddenly seemed irresistible. What saved Leeds from themselves was their unexpected pursuit of a fourth trophy, the little-loved League Cup. Unkindly derided as 'Hardaker's folly', the competition had been given a new lease of life when the Fairs Cup committee agreed to accept the winners (provided they were First Division pedigree) into Europe the following season. This carrot proved sufficient to attract the interest of the big clubs and it was Leeds who emerged as winners with a 1–0 victory over Arsenal. After four years of near misses, Revie had won his first major trophy as a manager. Within a few months he added a second when Leeds became the first British club to win the Fairs Cup, narrowly defeating Ferencvaros 1–0 over two legs. At last, it seemed, the Leeds hoodoo had been broken.

The European Fairs Cup final had taken place in Budapest during mid-September and Leeds were sufficiently distracted by the journey to suffer a hangover the following Saturday when they lost their first League match of the season to rivals Manchester City. Although they led the table in late October, critics searching for signs of fallibility found rock-solid evidence when unfancied Burnley dismantled Revie's robots with a scarcely credible 5–1 victory. Far from upsetting Leeds, however, this setback merely increased their competitiveness. Unbelievably they were undefeated in their remaining 28 League fixtures and completed the season as Champions with a record-breaking

67 points. The extent of their professionalism was probably best exemplified in the return match with presumptuous Burnley where they made a point of winning 6–1. Even their severest critics conceded that no team had ever won the Championship with such efficiency. In losing only two matches in a 42-match season, Leeds created an all-time League record which testified to the iron strength of their defence. With Norman Hunter adopting a more adventurous role in midfield and the quality of passing between Giles, Bremner and their forwards reaching a perfection of precision, there was no longer any doubt that Leeds were poised to emerge as one of the greatest footballing sides of the modern era. During the post-Championship euphoria, Billy Bremner reiterated the dreams of his inexhaustibly ambitious manager:

> I won't rest content until Leeds are acknowledged to be a great side, fit to rank alongside Real Madrid, Benfica and Manchester United. I believe it will take us three or four more years to achieve this, but it can be done. I want us to have won everything in sight. . . to be better than anyone else.

Revie's sights were even more firmly set and he casually announced that Leeds' next aim was the European Cup, World Club Championship and, almost as an afterthought, the FA Cup.

Like all great managers, Revie was not content to consolidate, but actively sought to improve his squad, even at their apparent peak. At the beginning of the 1968–69 season, he had promised a more adventurous, attacking approach away from home and although Leeds had markedly improved in this respect, it was not sufficient to quell the criticism of 'football purists'. Rather uncharacteristically, Revie was willing to concede that his Champions were still over-cautious in away games, '. . . it takes time to adapt to a new system. Our approach work has deserved more goals than we've actually scored'. What Leeds needed, Revie concluded, was one missing ingredient: flair.

The birth of a new super Leeds occurred during the close season of 1969 when Revie made another of his rare but spectacular forays into the transfer market with the purchase of Leicester striker Allan Clarke for a record-breaking £165,000. Clarke maintains that the prospect of European glory heavily influenced Revie's decision:

> What he was buying was a goalscorer. He'd won the First Division Championship and was looking to Europe. He felt he needed a lad who could knock in 20 goals a season and I was his man.

Leeds now possessed a strike force worthy of comparison with their brilliant midfield and defence.

The 1969–70 season started promisingly but not particularly authoritatively, for Leeds had to wait until 29 November before reaching second place, five points behind Everton. Even at this early stage, the Championship was looking decidedly like a two-horse race as the chasing pack fell further and further behind. Always threatening a major Championship bid, the Everton team, which included Alan Ball, Colin Harvey and Howard Kendall, was playing its most fluid football of the decade. It was clear to Revie that another formidable points total would be necessary to prevent the title from transferring to Goodison Park. If he required a good omen then the award of an OBE on 1 January was probably not insignificant. As if on cue, Leeds began the New Year with the most dazzling display of power football since their emergence from the Second Division. On 3 January they beat leaders Everton 2–1, and soon afterwards the Merseysiders found themselves knocked out of the FA Cup by Sheffield United. No such problems for Leeds, who disposed of Swansea and then ended the dreams of non-League Sutton with a clinically efficient 6–0 soccer lesson. A visit to third-placed Chelsea further tested Leeds' Championship aspirations in what was unquestionably the match of the day. What the television cameras recorded that afternoon was a performance of such magnificence that it seemed otherworldly. Although playing some of their best football of the season, Chelsea could only watch helplessly as their rivals turned on an exhibition of passing skill and lethal finishing to win 2–5. It was enough to convince the television pundits of something they had long suspected – that Leeds were the best club side in the world. Having taken the League leadership from Everton on goal average, the impossible dream of the European Cup, FA Cup and Championship treble suddenly seemed a distinct possibility.

Throughout February and March, Leeds continued to battle their way through to the semi-finals of both the FA and European Cups, while Everton enjoyed the less demanding task of concentrating on their League challenge.

In virtually any other season Leeds' sheer force of will might have fulfilled the treble dream, but in 1970 it was a nigh impossible task. The already overcrowded English League season had been cruelly truncated in order to allow Sir Alf Ramsey the luxury of preparing England for their defence of the impending World Cup. As a result, treble-chasing Leeds were left facing a mountainous fixture pile-up so ludicrous in its proportions that postponements seemed inevitable. Unfortunately, League secretary Alan Hardaker refused to be swayed by Revie's pleas and decreed that the matches must be played as scheduled. On 21 March, Leeds were ten games away from the treble, but six of their fixtures, including vital FA Cup and European Cup ties, had to be completed within the next fortnight. The nightmare grew to surreal proportions when Leeds chose this very moment to re-enact their epic 1964 FA Cup confrontation with Manchester United. Once more a goalless draw was followed by a hard-fought replay but on this occasion Leeds could not achieve the crucial breakthrough. Desperate to avoid the unthinkable – another replay – they surged forward kamikaze-style in extra time, but their opponents refused to yield. From that point on, the treble had ceased to become a matter of football excellence, but purely a sadistic theatre of team exhaustion masquerading as competitive spirit.

Inevitably, injuries increased amid the chaotic series of matches that followed. Among the victims was Paul Reaney who suffered a broken leg at a critical stage of Leeds' campaign. Meanwhile, Bremner and his cohorts limped on, finally putting paid to Manchester United and securing a place at Wembley. The marathon FA Cup tie had enabled Everton to turn the screw another thread by forcing Leeds to maintain top form in their League outings. The Yorkshire team managed to defeat Wolves, but by the Easter weekend they were suffering physical and mental fatigue. With a crucial European Cup semi-final only days away, Revie gambled on a side which now included six reserves. The match against Southampton proved a watershed. Leeds lost 3–1, and as if to comment on their sheer exhaustion, Terry Yorath and Jack Charlton both scored own goals in the final 20 minutes. Two days later Revie fielded an entire reserve side at Derby which predictably lost 4–1. Everton were now the Champions. The quest for the treble had ended in bitterness, frustration and exhaustion.

Leeds were still sluggish from the previous days' endeavours when they entertained a buoyant Celtic at Elland Road on 1 April. They were awoken abruptly when the visitors scored a shock goal within 40 seconds of the start. Once more, Leeds dragged their tired bodies through 90 minutes of high-powered drama, but their desperate assault on the Celtic goal failed to produce an equaliser. The second leg at Hampden Park was scheduled several days after the FA Cup final and seemed designed to test Leeds' endurance qualities to the obscene limit.

Don Revie continued to wear his threadbare 'lucky' suit and raincoat, unaware that their talismanic qualities had long since proved hopelessly redundant. Old rituals continued as before with the manager massaging the legs of Bremner and Hunter prior to every match and studiously compiling detailed dossiers on even the most anodyne opponents. With their few remaining League games reduced to the level of practice matches, Leeds had the long-awaited luxury of several days' rest prior to their Wembley visit. It was an important recuperative period during which Billy Bremner accepted his Footballer of the Year award and Revie looked forward to receiving the equivalent managers' trophy. Always aware of the importance of public relations, Revie reminded his critics how far Leeds had come: from being defensively-minded First Division artisans they had reached their present apotheosis as immaculately skilled football artists. He earnestly promised the public that Leeds would improve upon their previous Wembley finals against Liverpool and Arsenal by playing entertaining and attacking soccer of the highest quality. His detractors were sceptical of such uncharacteristically romantic rhetoric, but Revie proved as good as his word. On the day of the final his players were admonished with stirring rapture: 'Go out and show people what a great team you are'.

The 1970 FA Cup final was rightly hailed as the finest since the mid-1950s, with Leeds firmly in control and Chelsea reduced to never-say-die breakaways. After Jack Charlton opened the scoring the smooth-running Leeds machine seemed to be heading for a comfortable victory until goalkeeper Gary Sprake fumbled a 25-yard shot from Peter Houseman which slid bizarrely beneath his left arm into the net. Leeds recovered their poise during a furious second half in which winger Eddie Gray emerged as Man of the Match with a series of telling runs. When Mick Jones's low left-foot drive flashed past goalkeeper Peter Bonetti, Chelsea seemed dead and buried, but an Alan Hutchinson header four minutes from time won them another reprieve. Extra time failed to produce a result, so Leeds were forced into yet another unwanted replay. Their stoical manager could only rue the countless lost chances which included three stupendous efforts that scarred the woodwork only to be scuttled away by the harried Chelsea defence. For once the pat post-match quip 'I have never seen the lads play better' sounded dispassionately genuine. Football experts echoed Revie's epithet and beneath such headlines as 'The Cruel Cup' eloquently pronounced that no team in the history of the competition had dominated a final to such a degree and failed to win.

Prior to the FA Cup replay, Leeds faced the awesome prospect of defeating Celtic at Hampden Park. Encouraged by the Wembley performance, Revie was convinced that the tie could be saved and his quest for European glory realised. Rather fittingly, it was captain Billy Bremner who stunned the Scottish crowd with a fiercely hit aggregate equaliser in the first half. Celtic's pressure remained unrelenting while Leeds for once welcomed the opportunity of forcing a replay which would take them back to Yorkshire. It was not to be. The footballing gods again tantalised Leeds with false hopes before clubbing them into submission with another fatal blow. This time the victim was their erratic goalkeeper Gary Sprake, who collided with a Celtic player and ended the season on the injury list. Demoralised and outplayed, Leeds saw their lingering hopes vanquished by a Bobby Murdoch goal. With the European dream shattered, Revie had every cause to rail against malevolent Fortune and the footballing authorities for their part in Leeds' downfall, but instead he confounded his critics by unexpectedly bestowing unctuous praise on Jock Stein's victorious team:

> Celtic were great at Elland Road, and were out of this world before their own fans. Now you can go to Milan and carry off the European Cup for the second time. I hope to be there with some of my men to cheer you on. This is a match we don't want to miss.

The mellifluous lilt could not fully mask what sounded suspiciously like another example of expertly-timed Revie PR. Always the master of contradiction Revie was at once the consummate soccer cynic and the gushing, magnanimous loser.

With the FA Cup replay against Chelsea, Leeds' main concern was salvaging some silver from a heart-breaking season. Their perennial bridesmaid routine had become an enthralling soap opera for the anti-Leeds general public but within the game they still commanded respect. That passionate football proselytiser Bill Shankly was sufficiently moved to admit: 'I feel the deepest sympathy for Leeds. There's something crazy about a situation in which the greatest team in England are struggling to win one trophy'. That Shankly should imply, however obliquely, that Leeds were greater than his beloved Liverpool was praise *in extremis*. But his fear that Leeds might be beaten by their own ambition proved well founded. The second joust with Chelsea had all the familiar ingredients of a Leeds mini-drama: an early goal to the Yorkshire side, a great deal of pressure and possession, another Chelsea breakaway goal and, inevitably, extra time. The sickening prospect of yet another replay was barely more merciful than what finally occurred – a late Chelsea goal. The treble candidates were left with nothing save the glory of perverse endeavour.

Football critics and rival managers found themselves divided on the sagacity of attempting the impossible treble. Many believed that Leeds would have won a major trophy had they not diffused their efforts by greedily attempting to scoop the pool. Such reasoning left Revie cold. He firmly believed that Leeds were more than capable of winning everything, a view also held by Billy Bremner and his team-mates. All that Leeds required were some quality reserve players to boost the squad during spells of injury and clear cut results that did not necessitate endless replays and a fixture pile-up. What Revie no doubt craved was an easier run-in in the League, a throwback to seasons not so distant when Ipswich, Burnley and Chelsea had secured a Championship with 56, 55 or even 52 points. A runaway lead in the League would allow Leeds the odd slip during those vital periods when they might be involved in taxing semi-finals or stamina-sapping Continental jaunts.

Revie's remarks at the start of the 1970–71 season seemed rather puzzling. When asked to predict next year's Champions he ignored the obvious contenders such as Everton and Liverpool and tipped 14–1 outsiders Arsenal. The Gunners had emerged with a young team under expert tactician Bertie Mee and Revie was quick to spot their Championship potential. By Christmas, his pre-season prediction seemed ominously threatening and soon the Championship was once more reduced to a two-horse race. Champions Everton, another young side tipped by many to emerge as Leeds' successors, had slipped inexplicably and disastrously to mid-table while Liverpool found the pace of the race too frantic for their liking. Only Arsenal seemed capable of catching Leeds and, as the weeks passed, this task became increasingly more difficult. After 31 League matches Leeds romped seven points clear at the top and looked certain Champions, although Arsenal still had a couple of games in hand. It was during this period that the Leeds machine momentarily developed engine trouble. Unfancied Fourth Division Colchester entertained the leaders at Layer Road and in fairy-tale fashion found themselves 3–0 up at half-time. The Yorkshiremen stormed back to 3–2 but could not prevent what was then described as the biggest upset in FA Cup history. The humiliation permeated their League form and a couple of surprise defeats gave Arsenal renewed hope. Revie was quick to restore order, however, and a 3–0 thrashing of Wolves revealed Leeds at their arrogant best. Continued success in the Fairs Cup convinced everybody that the fluke Colchester result could not prevent a consolation European and Championship double. Revie remained confident, yet cautious:

> The competition at the top is ferocious and neither Arsenal nor us can afford to slacken. I think it will take 66 or 67 points to clinch the title. Needless to say we must fancy our own chances now with points in hand.

Revie's reading of the Championship race was not far wrong for, against the odds, Arsenal, like Everton before them, kept on winning. With Easter approaching, Leeds' worst nightmares returned to haunt them. Injuries and illness combined to decimate the team and for the second successive season Leeds faced the prospect of confronting plucky Derby County with a reserve side. No less than 11 players were unavailable, a crisis that sent Revie scurrying to Alan Hardaker begging for a postponement. Hardaker remained unconvinced. He always suspected Revie of bending the rules and was tired of Leeds' quibbles over fixture congestion, rescheduled matches, conflicting international demands and 'unsuitable' referees. Revie was outraged by Hardaker's obdurate attitude and, no doubt fearing another League fine if he fielded a reserve side, reluctantly enlisted the incapacitated Hunter, Madeley, Jones, Davey and Bates. Remarkably, Leeds beat Derby 1–0, a result which hardened Hardaker in his conviction about Revie's gamesmanship. In private, he marvelled sarcastically at the wonders of medical science in Yorkshire where players seemingly at death's door could emerge from their sick beds and play like gods. What Hardaker conveniently forgot, however, was the crucial absence of such international stars as Bremner, Gray, Clarke, Sprake and Cooper. No Championship-chasing team would willingly play without its midfield captain, star striker and goalkeeper! Sprake and Gray were still on the bench when Leeds went to Portman Road and destroyed Ipswich 2–4.

These astonishing results suggested that Leeds had survived their injury crisis and fought off Arsenal's distant challenge. With seven games left Leeds were six points clear of Arsenal, who needed to win three games in hand just to draw level. The Gunners' continued involvement in the FA Cup made their task even more daunting and many predicted that they would abandon their League aspirations before Easter. Leeds, however, were not free from Cup commitments themselves. A narrow victory over Vitoria Setubal brought them into their final phase, which included a two-leg Fairs Cup semi-final clash with old rivals Liverpool.

While everybody expected Arsenal to submit, they continued their winning run eating up games in hand with narrow victories and edging closer to the Champions-elect. Leeds, meanwhile, beat Liverpool at Anfield and still looked favourites for the Fairs Cup and League double. The return of Billy Bremner strengthened the team but a couple of minor slips, including a dour draw with Huddersfield encouraged Arsenal's fighting spirit. The Easter programme showed the contenders at level pegging until an all-too-familiar doom laden headline proclaimed: 'Sheer Tragedy for Don Revie and Leeds'.

On Saturday 17 April 1971 the most controversial goal of the season all but destroyed Leeds' hard-fought campaign for the title. Referee Ray Tinkler overruled a linesman's flag to allow what seemed a blatant offside which resulted in a Jeff Astle goal. Overwhelmed by the frustrating injustice of another lost Championship, the Leeds supporters invaded the pitch and 23 fans were arrested. Recoiling from the furore, Revie seemed dumbstruck at the evident ruination of nine months' hard work and tersely exclaimed: 'I have never been so sick in all my life'. Rival manager Bertie Mee, whose team benefited from the Leeds disaster, reiterated Revie's sentiments in a weary aside: 'I feel damn sick about the whole issue'. The Football Association was not so sympathetic and decreed that Leeds must play their first four home games of next season on neutral ground. The events of 17 April were therefore to have a profound bearing on the direction of the Championship in both 1971 and 1972.

With Arsenal jubilantly threatening a League and Cup double, Revie marshalled his men for a final assault. The Londoners' winning streak was dramatically halted when Leeds defeated them at Elland Road and regained top position. Leeds then completed their League programme a point clear of Arsenal who had one match left to play. The Gunners travelled to north London rivals Spurs and took both points to clinch the title; five days later they rubbed salt into Leeds' wounds by audaciously overcoming Liverpool at Wembley to secure the double. Leeds had amassed a staggering 64 points and yet failed to win the Championship. Their points total made them the most successful runners-up in League history, beating the record previously held by themselves in their promotion year. Revie was left with the chilling realisation that his team's points total would have won the Championship in all but four of the seasons since 1945.

A consolation victory in the Fairs Cup final ensured that Leeds ended the season with at least one trophy but the feeling of anti-climax was tangible. During the close season, soccer sceptics convinced themselves that Leeds were about to enter a period of decline. The theories were nine parts sophistry but there was validity in some of the conclusions. Leeds were, undoubtedly, an ageing team and had consistently suffered the psychological blow of losing trophies at the final hurdle. Their motivation and morale suddenly seemed suspect and the players were grilled by journalists anxious to discover signs of world-weariness. The old Leeds professionalism remained impregnable, however, and Allan Clarke's reaction to his interrogators typified their mood of boastful defiance:

Over the top? You must be joking. We finished second in the League last year. We won the Fairs Cup against some of the best opposition in Europe. Does that sound as if we're past our best? Personally, I think we haven't reached our peak!

Clarke's perkiness could not disguise the obstacles that faced Revie in his eighth Championship campaign. In establishing Leeds as perennial League challengers, Revie relied heavily on home advantage as a means of amassing points. Like Liverpool, Leeds seemed virtually unbeatable on their own ground and few teams travelled to Elland Road with delusions of victory. For the first four home games of this season, however, the FA had forced Leeds to travel to Hull, Sheffield and Huddersfield, far away from the cauldron of fear that had traditionally intimidated the opposition into early submission. With Leeds effectively playing 25 of their 42 League matches away from home, their rivals were given a veritable head start. Not surprisingly, Leeds faltered during the early stages of the Championship race and the loss of Clarke and Jones robbed them of a much needed striking force. Unbelievable defeats at lowly Southampton and Coventry dented their pride sufficiently to prompt a serious post mortem. Billy Bremner was disarmingly frank about their fluctuating form:

> We had a lot of injuries. But I've got to be honest: there was more to it than that. A lot of the boys, myself included, had lost our enthusiasm for the game. We weren't hungry enough. Ability-wise, we were still very good but we were content to play with the ball. We weren't winning it enough when the other side had it.

Revie's response to mediocre form was a series of team talks and small group discussions specifically engineered to thrash out tactical problems and instil motivation. The presence of Les Cocker, probably the greatest trainer of the era, reinforced the psyching-up process in which the players convinced themselves that they were the greatest team in the world. The result was a 14-match unbeaten run which, by Christmas, took Leeds into second position, five points behind runaway leaders Manchester United.

Early in the New Year, several teams were in the hunt for the Championship but it was Leeds whose play was reaching new peaks of adventure and skill. The same critics who had dismissed Revie's squad earlier in the season were now extolling their virtues as entertainers and football maestros on a par with the best Continental sides. Throughout February and March Leeds played their most astonishing football to date, overwhelming their main rivals with breathtaking displays of artistry and arrogance. Word spread rapidly that this was a new Leeds, more deadly in its attacking flair than any previous incarnation. The Championship challengers were temporarily overwhelmed: Derby thrashed 3–0; Liverpool quashed 2–0 at Anfield; recent leaders Manchester United demoralised 5–1. The greatest humiliation, however, was reserved for struggling Southampton who were teased, taunted and frustrated by a dazzling display of precision football during which Leeds strung together over three dozen passes without interruption, having already established an unassailable 7–0 lead. For Revie, the team had at last reached the impossible pinnacle that he had promised eight years before. He now claimed that Leeds were as great as Real Madrid in their prime.

The euphoria that surrounded the new 'Super Leeds' extended to their stupendous FA Cup run. Soon they were in the quarter-finals facing a potentially tricky match against improving Spurs. It was another superb attacking display executed with machine-like precision. Revie, usually calm in victory, could not contain his excitement: 'The way they knock the ball about so well amazes even me. This is what you work for, for many, many years to see them play like this'.

Among the cluster of teams challenging for the Championship, Leeds alone faced the prospect of continued FA Cup commitments. That, combined with their unfortunate start to the season, explained why they were not already Champions. After defeating the old enemy Arsenal 3–0, Johnny Giles had seen enough to make an announcement far more extravagant than even his manager's recent effusion:

> I played against Real Madrid at their best for Manchester United and I would frankly say that we are a better side. Real Madrid had some outstanding individuals – players like Di Stefano, Puskas, Gento and Santamaria – but their defence was a bit suspect and their full backs were weak. We are a better all-round side because we are strong in all positions. It's true we haven't won the European Cup but it was easier for Real Madrid because they dominated Spanish football and their entry was almost automatic. We've been called a machine and we take that as a compliment to our teamwork. It's the players who make the machine work.

The denouement to the 1971–72 season exposed a plot worthy of a thriller writer. Four teams were involved in an epic struggle for the Championship with Manchester City having completed their programme in first place as follows:

Manchester City	played 42	57 points
Liverpool	played 40	56 points
Derby County	played 41	56 points
Leeds United	played 40	55 points

Paradoxically, City were already out of the race because Derby were set to play Liverpool making it mathematically impossible for Manchester City to steal the Championship. Meanwhile, Chelsea manager Dave Sexton added to the drama by refusing to rearrange a match with favourites Leeds which had been scheduled in the same week as the Cup final. It was no matter. Leeds defeated Chelsea, Derby overcame

Liverpool and suddenly Revie's quest for the double was two matches away.

The centenary FA Cup final was far from a classic, but Leeds were sufficiently well drilled to negate Arsenal and repeat their 1–0 League Cup victory of four years before. Winning the FA Cup for the first time is usually an excuse for tumultuous celebration, but Leeds were forced to quell their euphoria. Revie had recently returned from his latest joust with Alan Hardaker with some alarming news: due to UEFA Cup fixtures and internationals, the League president was unable to re-schedule Leeds' last match of the season. Regrettably, they would have to face Wolverhampton Wanderers 48 hours after their Wembley exertions. Revie was aghast. He feared that his players would be mentally exhausted following the final, but a glance at the League table proved reassuring:

Derby County	played 42	58 points
Leeds United	played 41	57 points
Manchester City	played 42	57 points
Liverpool	played 41	56 points

With their superior goal average, Leeds merely required a draw at Molineux to emulate Arsenal's double of the previous season. The bookmakers consulted their calculators and offered some unattractive odds: Leeds 10–11 favourites; Liverpool 11–8; Derby 6–1.

Revie was taking no chances. Meticulous to a fault, he created an unlikely record by making Leeds the only FA Cup winners in history not to turn up for their own celebratory banquet. Amazingly, they boarded their coach at Wembley Stadium and headed straight for Wolverhampton. Not a word of protest was heard from the team, as Allan Clarke reveals:

> We could have stayed on in London, relaxed a bit, had a few beers, attended the banquet and travelled on Sunday morning. But the Wolves match was just as important as the Cup. He already had our minds on the job on Monday. That's the way the man worked and we weren't going to argue with the gaffer.

The Wembley workout had not left Leeds untouched by injury, and the following day Giles, Gray and Clarke went to nearby West Bromwich Albion for treatment. Desperate to compete for Leeds' greatest glory they were dubiously declared fit.

In spite of Revie's concern, nobody seriously believed that Leeds could lose at Wolves. The Midlanders, placed safely in mid-table, had little incentive to win the game beyond professional pride and would probably be distracted by their forthcoming UEFA Cup final against Spurs. A hard, containing game would surely kill off Wolves without undue effort. On paper, it looked less like a double than a doddle.

By the Monday evening, the atmosphere at Molineux was charged with tension. Leeds overcame their nerves and attempted to secure midfield possession while Wolves inexplicably raised their game way beyond the call of duty. Observers noted that they were playing like men possessed, as though their lives depended on winning this fixture. Their tackles were uncompromising and their running indefatigable. Logic dictated that they should be wary of sustaining injuries and eager to conserve energy, but their play was relentless in its ferocity and pace. Even the referee seemed amazed by Wolves' commitment, and afterwards he admitted: 'It was one of my hardest games for years'. Contrary to need or charity, punishing Wolves won 2–1 in a match that was as mysterious as it was controversial. Only marginally less surprising was the news that losing Cup finalists Arsenal had held Liverpool to a goalless draw that same night. Rank outsiders Derby were therefore crowned Champions.

Revie had set his heart on challenging for the European Cup in 1973 and the Wolves defeat was the worst setback of his managerial career. The players were equally depressed. Two days before, they had won the FA Cup for the first time in Leeds' history but the celebrations had been forestalled because of the double. Now there was nothing to celebrate. Forlorn and dejected, the players trooped back to the Queens Hotel in Leeds and drowned their sorrow until four in the morning. Their mood was effectively summed up by Allan Clarke: 'It was as if we had won nothing. We wanted that League Championship so badly'.

In the next few days, Leeds found that they had unexpectedly won the sympathy of a once antagonistic public. Revie argued persuasively that the latest Leeds tragedy was due to the intransigence of Alan Hardaker. The bureaucratic indifference of the imperious League secretary prompted others to take up Revie's grievances. Bobby Charlton was downright appalled at the decision which had forced his brother's team to play a Championship decider under such duress: 'Sometimes I wonder whether the people who make these decisions know what it's like to play in a Cup final.' Even Jimmy Hill, an inveterate critic of Leeds, joined the chorus of condemnation: 'It is shameful that Leeds were asked to play their final League match only two days after appearing in the FA Cup final'. While the controversy raged on, Revie accepted his third Bell's Manager of the Year trophy. It was small consolation. How could he forget the sadistically scheduled Wolves fixture or the ground closure that had cost Leeds four crucial home games? It was enough to make him a bitter man. The football authorities had robbed him of his greatest glory.

Revie's anguish did not prevent Leeds from starting the 1972–73 season as firm favourites for the Championship. However, on the opening day of the season at Chelsea, they received a sharp reminder of past ill omens. Goalkeeper David Harvey and striker Mick Jones were both carried off with injuries during the first half and a depleted Leeds, with Lorimer in goal, suffered a 4–0 defeat. Off the field, Leeds were forced to relive the Wolves nightmare when the *Sunday People* printed a story alleging that there had been an attempt to fix that crucial match. Three Wolves players admitted that they had been approached and offered bribes of up to £1,000 in return for 'throwing' the match. Beneath the seriousness of the allegations, however, there was a strong element of farce. Two of the players suggested that inducements had been offered while they were actually on the pitch. They claimed there were odd instructions to 'take it easy' and a hint that financial rewards would follow. 'I know it wasn't meant as a joke', cried the Wolves players involved. The allegations were tantalisingly unsubstantiated by any concrete proof of corruption and merely strained the reader's credulity by their outrageous eccentricity. The unlikely spectacle of international players cavalierly risking a life ban and approaching opponents in such a stupid and offhand manner prompted no comment from the paper's investigative team. Nor, indeed, was there any explanation as to how or when the money might be paid. Presumably, the gullible Wolves players were expected to risk all, cheat and keep their fingers crossed that a backhander might be forthcoming after the match. The entire episode as described seemed faintly ludicrous but if there was any corruption from outside, it certainly cost Leeds dearly. Wolves played above themselves and the Yorkshire side were even denied what seemed an obvious first-half penalty. The assessor's report of the match revealed a handling offence, but the referee had denied the appeal. Interestingly, the officials sternly refuted any suggestion that they had been alerted to the danger of a fix. As for the supposed fixers, their identities remained unrevealed.

The FA responded to the scandal by conducting an immediate investigation in conjunction with the CID. The matter was later placed in the hands of the Director of Public Prosecutions, but no evidence to support the newspaper allegations was disclosed and after eight months the inquiry was dropped. Revie's reputation remained unsullied by the affair and the scandal that never was soon faded from public memory. Few would have guessed that five years later this yellowing story would again make front page news.

A troubled opening season gradually brightened for Leeds and Revie when they found themselves in the enviable position of challenging for yet another treble. Memories of the 1970 fixture pile-up did not deter Revie from stressing that he would field his strongest team in every competition. By March, Leeds were heading towards FA Cup and Cup Winners' Cup semi-finals, but seemed less likely to pull away from Liverpool and Arsenal in the Championship race. A growing list of suspensions caused Revie unwanted selection problems and some erratic results followed. Meanwhile, Liverpool consolidated their League lead leaving Leeds to look towards a more likely Cup double. Having overcome Derby in the quarter-finals of the FA Cup, Leeds avoided Arsenal in the semi-final draw and the stage was set for the first 'repeat final' of the century. The psychological blow of facing their erstwhile double destroyers Wolves did not prevent Leeds from securing a hard-earned 1–0 victory. Relieved to be back in the final for the third time in four seasons, Leeds fully expected to meet the Arsenal side that they had already twice beaten at Wembley. Unbelievably, however, the Gunners were outmanoeuvred by lowly Sunderland. Revie could hardly believe his luck. In what promised to be the most one-sided Cup final for years, England's premier club side had merely to beat Second Division opponents.

Prior to the final, soccer pundits gathered for the traditional televised predictions. For once, the team of experts reached a unanimous decision: Leeds were certainties for the Cup. Romantic talk of Cup upsets was brushed aside by the garrulous Brian Clough who opined that once the ball reached the back of the net, as it inevitably must, Sunderland's dream would be extinguished. Nobody cavilled at that. The experience and professionalism of Leeds was so irresistible that Sunderland's guts and endeavour seemed irrelevant by comparison.

Revie's faith in Lady Luck was again proven ridiculous by the Wembley result. Sunderland, all blood and thunder, took a 32nd minute lead and grimly hung on. For all their class Leeds could not demolish a well-organised and gutsy side who resisted a sterling second-half assault to emerge triumphant as the first Second Division Cup winners for 42 years. Revie had a mere 11 days to swallow the bitter pill of defeat before the compensatory European Cup Winners' Cup final against AC Milan. Leeds' morale was further dented by injuries and suspensions which had left them with a shadow of a team. Without the inspirational midfield presence of Bremner and Giles, the opportunism of deadly striker Clarke, or the wizard runs of winger Gray, there was little hope of a 'Super Leeds' revival. In the event, a fourth minute goal killed off Leeds in a disappointing and gruesomely-fought match. Revie was left to relive the trauma of 1970 with a treble campaign that had finally brought nothing.

The mystery of Leeds' consistency had been matched only by their recurrent fallibility. True, they had won a League Championship, a couple of Fairs Cups, a League Cup and an FA Cup, but five trophies in nine seasons seemed scant reward for all their efforts. Beneath the trophy shelf lay a staggering catalogue of losses: three FA Cup finals and two semi-finals; three European finals and two semi-finals, and a heartbreaking League record of eight near misses. Observing their League statistics, football critic Brian James provided a salutary footnote to the lost Championships: '378 First Division matches have brought Leeds 213 victories and 522 points; a mere 18 points at the right moments and they would have been victorious on six occasions'. In attempting to rationalise Leeds' bad luck, James duly noted the fixture pile-ups, injuries, suspensions and occasional lapses before hitting upon an intriguing theory:

But how much is the animosity and controversy that has surrounded Revie's side at the outset a factor to be considered? The legacy is now of several years' standing but Leeds continue to be the most criticised as well as the most consistent English team. . . In detail, the Yorkshire side are suspected of putting pressure on referees, by questioning decisions and over-acting, that they feign injuries to disrupt the play. Guilty or not, they have made enemies in the game. One is tempted to suggest that this has gone against them over the seasons; that opponents have set their hearts on beating Leeds United; that those 18 lost League points might have been gathered against a background of less ill-feeling. It can be no coincidence that Liverpool – who play no more attractively, who have arguably fewer stars and who are no innocents – were acclaimed in their League triumph. Clough's comment that 'if my side couldn't win, I'd want Shanks and Liverpool to have that title' merely echoed the thoughts of others.

James's observations were uncannily apposite for Clough's immemorial antipathy towards Leeds was about to bring censure from the Football Association. During the close season, the ever controversial Derby manager had suggested, apparently in all seriousness, that Leeds should be forcibly relegated to the Second Division. His extraordinary outburst typified the resentment felt by a few managers towards what Revie could rightly claim was the most consistent and powerful side in the history of English football. Nevertheless, the vitriolic comments had been fuelled by genuine disciplinary problems which caused Revie considerable concern. What the 1972–73 season proved was that Leeds had not lost the title through fixture pile-ups alone but needless suspensions that had robbed them of key players at vital moments. Clearly, a change of attitude was not only desirable but necessary.

In an attempt to stop dissension on the field, Revie had previously ordered his players not to argue with the referee. Billy Bremner was to become their sole representative in 'seeking a courteous explanation' and was even decorated with an armband to signify his seniority. Unfortunately, the experiment had backfired as several referees felt that the fiery Leeds captain was already vocal enough without being given what seemed to them a charter to argue the toss on every occasion. Revie's next move was to request the FA to despatch an assessor to Leeds' away matches and provide detailed reports of incidents involving his players. Like everything else in his life, the Revie clean-up campaign was systematically planned and executed.

During the close season, the ageing Leeds side underwent extra training in preparation for yet another assault on the Championship. Amazingly, Revie seemed more purposeful and determined than ever. Minutes after losing the Cup final he had begun talking about next year's trophies and warned the players: 'I'll make you sweat blood'. Now he was sharpening their competitive instincts with workouts, wooden spoon awards and emphatic instructions to take the land by storm with clean attacking football. As a wide-eyed Allan Clarke admitted: 'We did sweat blood! There was no limit to his ambition. That sums the man up'.

The press remained unaware and unconcerned about the latest Revie reformation. It was generally agreed that the 1972–73 season represented Leeds' last hurrah and rumours intensified that Revie was preparing to leave Yorkshire. Lucrative approaches from Everton and the Greek national team fuelled the speculation, and Revie wavered for a few days before finally accepting a handsome counter offer from the Leeds board. It was to prove a wise decision.

Contrary to their critics' predictions, Leeds exploded into the 1973–74 season with attractive, open football backed by an invincible superiority that was breathtaking to behold. Sweeping their challengers aside they completed the Christmas programme still unbeaten and nine points clear of Liverpool. Along the way a host of cocky managers had hogged the sports pages earnestly predicting that they would end the Leeds run. Almost invariably, their teams were thrashed. By early 1974 even the doubters had ceased cavilling. Several top managers maintained that Leeds had discovered football's Holy Grail of invincibility and would make history by completing the 42-match season undefeated. The Championship seemed a formality even at the half-way stage, but the indomitable Bill Shankly was armed with a ready quip: 'It's a marathon not a sprint'. Later the Liverpool supremo added portentously: 'Leeds will be beaten and when they are, we'll be ready'. It was to be a long wait.

Early in the season Revie had decided to concentrate on the Championship, reiterating his unfulfilled ambition to win the European Cup. A third round defeat in the UEFA Cup competition was seen as a blessing in disguise and Revie even seemed dismissive of the FA Cup. Amazingly, he stated that Leeds would only commit themselves to the competition with a ten-point League cushion. Now that such a ludicrous gap had become a reality Leeds seemed likely candidates for the double.

A fifth round FA Cup match at Bristol City gave Leeds a real fright, but they snatched a late equaliser to take their Second Division opponents to Elland Road the following Wednesday. Nobody paid much attention to this afternoon fixture until the unbelievable news filtered through: unbeatable Leeds had lost 1–0. How could a team that was still undefeated in the League after seven months and 29 games lose at home to a Second Division side? Surely, it could only be a fluke, a lapse of concentration that would soon be forgotten. Despite their professionalism, however, this embarrassing setback sorely dented Leeds' morale. Four days later they visited Stoke for their 30th League game and scored two goals early in the match which should have been sufficient to secure an easy victory. Instead, the Potters spurred themselves on, won 3–2 and suddenly Leeds' marvellous run was over. The Championship still seemed safe, with Liverpool eight points adrift, but suddenly Leeds almost fell apart. A narrow victory at Manchester City was followed by a 1–0 defeat at Anfield which gave Liverpool renewed hope. The cumulative weight of years of disappointments became almost tangible on the slightly stooped figure of Don Revie during the succeeding weeks. The following week they lost 1–4 to Burnley – the worst home defeat since Revie had arrived in 1962. One week later, West Ham hammered another nail into the coffin with a 3–1 scoreline. It was unbelievable. From a virtually unassailable position at the top of the First Division, Leeds were threatening to throw away the Championship. In the past they had suffered odd lapses and fixture pile-ups, but for the first time since arriving in the First Division, they seemed to have lost their nerve. Liverpool continued to press their psychological advantage and newspaper columnists claimed that Leeds had cracked. Ten years of top class professionalism are not lost in a month, however, and Revie successfully managed to steady his troops in the face of a complete collapse. The crisis passed. Leeds did not lose another game and when Liverpool themselves fell to Arsenal, the Championship finally returned to Elland Road. It was symptomatic of a golden era of competitive football that even after a 29-match unbeaten opening run, Leeds still had to fight until late April before securing their second Championship.

Revie's dream of leading Leeds into a European Cup final was ultimately undermined by his own ambition. The departure of Sir Alf Ramsey from the post of England team manager provided an opportunity which was irresistible. Revie's obvious interest in the post caused a considerable stir at the FA who clearly had nobody of his calibre or track record among their applicants. The job was effectively his for the taking. Only his old enemy Alan Hardaker opposed the appointment, subtly suggesting that the FA needed their heads examining.

The Leeds board regretfully accepted Revie's resignation then demanded substantial compensation. The FA baulked at the price tag which exceeded that paid for any player in the history of British football. However, shortly afterwards, in a mysterious *volte face*, the Leeds board agreed to forego compensation and asked only for a contribution towards the appointment of a successor. Their problems were not made easier by the departure of trainer Les Cocker, who joined his old manager one month later.

The Leeds team rapidly fragmented after Revie's departure, although they had one final tilt at glory in the European Cup final. Characteristically, they dominated the match before falling foul to a couple of breakaway goals. It was another sad anti-climax for a team that had achieved so much, yet lost so much more.

It is difficult to gauge what might have happened if Revie had remained with Leeds. Like Matt Busby, he might in time have built another Super Leeds from the youth ranks. Unlike his successors, he would surely have been allowed the opportunity to implement changes over a longer period and replace key players at crucial moments.

Matt Busby pictured shortly after his appointment as manager of
Manchester United in October 1945.   *Colorsport*

Bill Nicholson, the hardest working man in football, made White Hart Lane his second home. *S & G Press Agency Ltd*

February 1963, RAF
Stanmore, Middlesex.
Newly-appointed
England manager
Alf Ramsey (left)
prepares his side for
their first match under
his command
S & G Press Agency Ltd

Jock Stein. The strain of
a lifetime in football is
indelibly etched on his
face.   *Bob Thomas*

The sartorially elegant Don Revie flanked by his long-serving captain,
Billy Bremner. *Colorsport*

Bill Shankly receiving the decoration he prized most – a Liverpool scarf proclaiming him the eternal King of the Kop.   *S & G Press Agency Ltd*

Brian Clough mimes his disgust at Nottingham Forest's 2-1 defeat by Liverpool in the semi-final of the 1988 FA Cup. *Bob Thomas*

Bob Paisley: 'I was never quiet on the pitch'. *Colorsport*

The Agony of Ecstasy. Bobby Robson celebrates England's 8-0 thrashing of humble Turkey.   *Bob Thomas*

Graham Taylor, the man who is widely tipped to be the next England boss.
Syndication International

Instead, he left behind a legend and found himself eulogised, not only by his original side, but the few players he had bought along the way, such as Allan Clarke:

> We were upset when he left Leeds, but we couldn't deny him that right. At club level, he was the best manager I ever played for. He did everything for us, fathered us, left nothing to chance. Anything we wanted, he'd do for us. He was that sort of guy. Right the way through the club they admired him. He got the utmost respect from *everybody* – the players, administrative staff and the commercial side. He was the gaffer.

Tough, yet caring, Revie had established a club whose consistency and passion was matched only by Manchester United and Liverpool. The consummate family man, he built up a strong relationship with all his players and their wives and families. Cards, presents and tickets for West End shows were liberally bestowed on players' relatives just to make them part of the Revie family. Revie was a legend when he left Leeds and had he stayed on and won the European Cup in 1975 many would have hailed him the greatest football manager of all time. Sadly it was not to be.

Revie opened his international managerial career by attempting to persuade Alan Hardaker to postpone Saturday League matches involving England players prior to key international games. The Football League secretary was unmoved but suggested diplomatically: 'You never know what might happen in the future'. At a sportsmen's lunch, Revie translated that vague comment into a firm promise and soon found himself back in conflict with the League secretary, who publicly refuted the suggestion. Their relationship remained tetchy for the duration of Revie's managerial career.

Despite Hardaker's frequently voiced criticism, Revie performed outstandingly in his first year as England manager, eagerly experimenting with an 81-man squad in an attempt to discover the perfect team. Following an impressive opening 3–0 European Championship victory against Czechoslovakia, Revie dropped three players and suffered a goalless draw against Portugal. Further reshuffles followed and, in March 1975, Alan Ball was awarded the captaincy for the 100th international match at Wembley. With 11 players from ten different clubs, England registered their first win over West Germany since the 1966 World Cup. Team morale and public expectation were high, yet Revie remained cautious: 'There is a lot to do yet, but at least the foundation is there'. One month later, England hammered lowly Cyprus with Malcolm Macdonald scoring all five goals. When England won the return in Limassol with a 4–2–4 formation their passage to the European Championship seemed assured. After six months under Revie's aegis, they had yet to concede a goal. The Home Championships that year also saw the squad emerge victorious, killing off Scotland 5–1 at Wembley to clinch the title.

Although Revie's results were exemplary, his frequent team changes invited censure from certain quarters. After being unceremoniously dropped against Wales, Kevin Keegan walked out of the team, forcing Revie to use all his powers of diplomacy to reinstate the indignant star just in time to contribute to the slaughter of Scotland, but others were not so lucky. Erstwhile captain Alan Ball had been left out in the cold and was still sulking about the curt dictated letter he had received from Revie's office. Chelsea star Alan Hudson was similarly aggrieved about losing his place and his League form suffered as a result. Revie remained unrepentant about his mutability policy which he seemed to perceive as a character-strengthening test:

> I want men who are proud to put on an English shirt. I don't want any players with me in the World Cup who go running for the plane home if they are left out of one match.

The image of Revie as a heartless hirer and firer was fallacious. At Leeds, he had a reputation as the most solicitous manager in the business and tales abounded of his dedication to the players' welfare. Birthday cards, congratulatory bouquets for pregnant wives, investment advice and even a personal weekly soap massage were all part of the Revie way. In an astonishing accolade, Allan Clarke once said of his paternalistic manager: 'He would do anything for his team. I think he would even die for them'. Of course, as England manager it was impossible to achieve the same degree of personal involvement with his players, so Revie altered his strategy accordingly. The players he retained were rewarded with a new pay structure based on an elaborate series of bonuses. Instead of the flat fee system by which internationals received £1,000 per match Revie successfully pushed for a £5,000 award for a European Championship final appearance, plus a further £2,000 bonus for reaching the quarter-finals and an additional £1,000 for victories in the semi-final and final. Old-fashioned patriots lamely accused the FA of prostituting football with these incentive payments but Revie forcibly dismissed such naive thinking with the verbal thrust of a politician:

> When I ask players to pull on an England shirt I expect them to do it for the pride of playing for their country. But football is a short career and the players' rewards should be proportionate to the amount of money the national association collects as a result of their efforts.

If Revie's fight for better pay conditions bought loyalty from his players, it was not reflected in the opening results of the 1975 season. Rather brashly, Revie had selected an attacking formation for the return match against Czechoslovakia in Bratislava. The tactic brought England an early lead through Mick Channon but the Czechs replied twice and effectively opened up their tight qualifying group. After one year and nine international matches, Revie had suffered his first defeat. One month later, a tame 1–1 draw against Portugal edged England out of the European Championship. Revie's fallibility was now beyond doubt.

The reversal of fortune brought fresh brickbats from old enemies. Alan Hardaker complained that the players were distracted by talk of 'money, money, money', a view endorsed by Alan Ball and Malcolm Macdonald who claimed that Revie had no sense of national pride. It was a provocative putdown that did not entirely tally with Revie's actions. Outwardly oblivious to patriotic sentimentality, he could also be infuriatingly jingoistic. As early as his first match supervising England he had encouraged the Wembley faithful to adopt 'Land Of Hope And Glory' as their theme song in what many saw as a self-conscious return to the spirit of 1966. It was part of Revie's complex nature that nationalism and player power could sit so easily together. A similar dualism could be observed in his religious asides. For those who remembered the ruthless cynicism of early Leeds it was difficult to accept the strains of saintly humility that flowed so mellifluously from Revie's pen. In the London *Evening Standard* he sounded more like a spiritual guru than a hard-nosed football manager:

> Some players don't realise how lucky they are. They should go down on their hands and knees every night and thank God they are doing something which they love and are being well paid for at the same time.

Alan Ball remained unconvinced by the nightly prayers, lengthy dossiers, tactical training and innocent bingo sessions that Revie so prized. Still smarting from his dethronement as captain, he continued to rail against the England manager and even accused him of nurturing a team of yes-men: 'Some of the players are donkeys. Give them a lump of sugar and they run all day and play bingo all night'. Revie was far too clever a PR person to fall into the trap of exchanging verbal blows with his former captain. Instead, he adopted a dignified tone and elegantly deflected the vitriol by expressing his genuine sadness that a player of such reputation should so thoughtlessly ridicule his fellow internationals.

Revie's positive public profile could not disguise England's shortcomings as a World Cup side. With only one match played since the Lisbon setback, they attempted to retain the Home International Championship in May 1976 but Scotland registered a timely revenge. The failure to win a minor domestic competition did not augur well for the World Cup qualifying rounds in which England were due to face Italy. However, any despondency was immediately forgotten when the campaign began with an emphatic 4–1 victory over Finland in Helsinki. The return leg at Wembley was expected to produce an avalanche of goals in order to pressurise the traditionally defensive Italians. Instead, England could only muster a paltry 2–1 win, and worse was to follow. A world-class Italian side virtually quashed their hopes of qualifying with a 2–0 victory in Rome. Revie now faced the daunting task of not merely beating the Italians but dramatically improving his country's dismal goal difference. Always a clever and opportune propagandist, his New

Year message to the football world revealed a morale-boosting optimism tinged with the knowledge that England's game was too primitive for the world stage:

> We face two World Cup games, home and away, against Luxembourg and a possible Wembley decider against Italy. The task is far from impossible. Our destiny is in our hands. My own concern is to marry the best of our domestic game with a realisation that what we produce at home every Saturday is not ideal for international competition. At home we give the fans what they want – football played at 100 miles an hour. We have been bred on that kind of all-action game and in its own way it typifies the English game. But at international level I doubt if this is where we can achieve progress. We need to slow down and work more at the skilful aspects of our game.

What Revie had always desired was a team steeped in the glorious tradition of Real Madrid and, although this had largely been achieved at Leeds, the England squad was never moulded to his satisfaction. Like Ramsey, he had attempted to find a formation that would suit the players and frustrate Continental opposition but the dream remained unrealised. One week after his festive announcement, England were trounced 2–0 at Wembley in a friendly against the Netherlands. Revie compared the Dutch with the Hungarian wizards of the 1950s and frankly admitted: 'They taught us tonight how far we've got to go'. It was a clear admission, if one was needed, that England were no longer a major force in international football. Those who expected short-term miracles from Revie had conveniently forgotten that England were not even deemed worthy of a World Cup seeding.

In March 1976, Revie was approached by the United Arab Emirates about the possibility of managing the national team. Although he took no immediate action concerning the offer there were several good reasons for not dismissing it out of hand: England's World Cup prospects were indisputably grim and Revie was convinced that he would lose his job should they fail to qualify; the flak that he was receiving in the press had intensified since the Holland match and was adversely affecting his family life; finally, the Arabs would offer enough money to guarantee a financially comfortable retirement. Such temptations must have played on Revie's mind as England stumbled to their seemingly inevitable demise.

A 5–0 victory over Luxembourg flattered to deceive, for England still relied upon Italy incurring heavy losses. Five weeks later, a disastrous display in the Home Championships snuffed any lingering hopes that Revie might yet revitalise the side. While the Wembley crowd voiced their disapproval of Scotland's 2–1 victory, Revie was supposedly heading for Helsinki to observe the Italians in training and attend their qualifying match against Finland. Unknown to the FA, however, he secretly flew to Dubai to discuss terms with the United Arab Emirates. After returning to London he travelled on to Helsinki to watch another depressing Italian victory before joining the England party on their South American tour. This went surprisingly well with England remaining undefeated against stiff opposition. One might have expected Revie to be blasé about these games, knowing that he had already secured his future and had nothing left to prove or lose. Instead, he was as tough as ever and acted as though the matches were League Championship deciders. It was typical of his contradictory character and remarkable professionalism that he should continue to work hard and mull over a team that he was already preparing to abandon.

Buenos Aires was the setting for Revie's most peculiar strategy to date. After requesting an audience with Dick Wragg, the chairman of the FA International Committee, the England manager abruptly announced his intention to resign. In a brilliant display of sophistry and cunning, Revie attempted to convince Wragg that the decision was a magnanimous gesture which would help the FA. They were surely intending to sack him sooner or later anyway, so his resignation would save them the bother. His leaving at the earliest opportunity was, he argued, 'in the best interests of the team'. In return for this bloodless execution, Revie merely required £50,000 compensation to cover the remaining two years of his contract. He also suggested a similar arrangement be offered to his faithful second-in-command Les Cocker. It was, by any standards, an extraordinary proposition. Here was Revie threatening a breach of contract, but engineering his exit in such a way that the FA should feel obliged to recompense his disloyalty. Moreover, he felt his evident cheek was completely justified in the circumstances:

> I hadn't accepted the Emirates job at that time. I felt that I had done enough for the FA in many ways to warrant compensation. When I had been with the FA I had put my head on the block many times, at games at Wembley for example. All the press lads used to say to me that if I had not been banging the drum to get people into Wembley. . . then things would have been bad. I think we got a lot of people in there, but also I brought money into the FA through sponsorship – and could have got a lot more. That is why I felt I was entitled to compensation.

Certainly, England gates improved markedly during Revie's reign and both the FA and the players benefited greatly from his sponsorship deals and bonus schemes. He was probably the most financially astute manager that England ever employed and his bartering with Wragg demonstrated the qualities of a seasoned business tycoon.

Revie's ambitious manoeuvring depended upon the FA agreeing that his departure was a splendid idea. Not surprisingly, they took the opposite viewpoint. In spite of the recent poor results and negative press they expressed continued confidence in his managerial abilities. The request for compensation had predictably fallen on deaf ears. Even if Revie was doomed to be dismissed, as he believed, the FA would never have laid themselves open to ridicule and accusations of suicidal administration by leaving the England manager's post vacant at such a crucial point in a World Cup campaign.

The FA officials convinced themselves that Revie would complete his commitments but he had already made up his mind. Having failed to cajole the FA into paying compensation he next turned to another source of easy money: the press. Although the United Arab Emirates were offering a magnificent tax-free starting salary of £60,000, excluding bonuses, Revie was determined to clean up in England by selling the sensational story of his departure to the *Daily Mail*. Secret negotiations commenced and Revie expertly extracted a small fortune for what was undoubtedly the sports story of the year. On 11 July, the *Daily Mail* scooped Fleet Street and flabbergasted the FA with their front page bulletin in which Revie emerged as a broken man forced to choose between the love of his family and the love of his country:

> I sat down with Elsie [his wife] one night and we agreed that the job was no longer worth the aggravation. It was bringing too much heartache to those nearest to us. Nearly everyone in the country seems to want me out. So I am giving them what they want. I know people will accuse me of running away and it does sicken me that I cannot finish the job by taking England to the World Cup finals in Argentina next year. But the situation has become impossible.

The pathos was not fully appreciated by the FA which did not receive Revie's letter of resignation until later that morning. Clearly, he had not wanted to spoil the *Mail's* brilliant exclusive. The following day, the cloak and dagger tale of Revie's Arabian appointment hit the stands and sent the FA scurrying to their solicitors. In the meantime, Revie's reputation plummeted to a level where the public reviled him as a traitor to the game. The manner of his leaving rankled the pompous patriots of Fleet Street who responded to public antipathy by hastening his fall from grace. In his leaving address, Revie had spoken of the intolerable pressures placed upon him as England manager, but they were as nothing compared to what followed in the wake of his departure. With his reputation already wounded, Revie was a marked man. At first the criticism was mild and took the form of indignant comments from the FA peppered with some predictably scathing words from the wry Alan Hardaker: 'Don Revie's decision doesn't surprise me the slightest. Now I can only hope he can quickly learn to call out bingo numbers in Arabic'.

The jokey tone soon turned more serious when the *Daily Mirror* and the *People* began delving into Revie's managerial past. By September, his reign at Leeds had become synonymous with corruption. The old Wolves scandal was regurgitated with fresh 'evidence'. Further allegations from manager Bob Stokoe and former Leeds goalkeeper Gary Sprake implied a chain of bribery going back as far as 1962. The ever-critical Alan Ball joined the growing list of detractors by penning an autobiography in which he included a revealing chapter telling how he had received financial inducements from Revie on the suitably sinister Manchester Moors. Revie wearily denied all the allegations and threatened legal action, but the long-awaited libel cases never reached the High Court. However, the former Leeds captain, Billy Bremner, who found himself implicated in the alleged Wolves briberies, eventually scotched the rumours and won substantial libel damages in excess of £100,000.

While Revie prepared for his lucrative sojourn in Dubai, the FA charged him with bringing the game into disrepute. Revie refused to attend the hearing in which he was suspended indefinitely from any involvement in FA-controlled football until he appeared to face their complaints. One year later, Revie's solicitors announced that he was at last ready to face the commission and the hearing was set for 18 December 1978.

Ironically, the case immediately preceding Revie's was that of his old enemy Alan Ball, who was fined £3,000 for bringing the game into disrepute by claiming that he had accepted a £300 inducement from the former Leeds manager, who still refuted the allegation.

The Revie hearing commenced with two formidable objections from the accused. Firstly, his counsel argued that the FA had no jurisdiction over their client and, secondly, they objected to the presiding presence of Sir Harold Thompson, whose post as FA chairman arguably favoured the plaintiffs and destroyed his impartiality. Both these objections were brushed aside and the unhappy saga continued. The single light note in the proceedings occurred when Revie's counsel attempted to deflate the seriousness of his leaving with an amusing footballing pun:

> We are not dealing with saints, although we have had the Southampton Football Club represented here. I don't suggest we are dealing with great sinners. We are dealing with ordinary professional footballers, managers and the rest, and to expect a meticulously high standard that might be more appropriate to the House of Convocation in Canterbury or York in this scenario is, in my submission, too extravagant by far.

The standards that the FA expected were underlined by the verdict: Don Revie was banned from English football for ten years.

The severity of the judgement encouraged Revie to fight on and the case was taken to the High Court in November 1979. There, Revie staked his claim for damages and demanded that the court declare his ban illegal. Jimmy Hill gave evidence on Revie's behalf, while Jock Stein and Lawrie McMenemy testified to the precariousness of a football manager's position. The crux of the case increasingly hinged upon the alleged hostility of FA chairman Sir Harold Thompson, whom Revie's barrister described as 'prosecutor, witness, judge and jury'. Revie himself related an amusing anecdote of one of his earliest meetings with Sir Harold who reputedly suggested: 'When I get to know you better Revie, I will call you Don'. Revie instantly punctured the knight's pomposity by retorting: 'When I get to know you better Thompson, I will call you Sir Harold'. The judge listened to a lengthy series of complaints against Thompson, none of which impressed him. He concluded: 'Mr Revie is a very prickly man and I think he has been brooding on imagined wrongs'. Nevertheless, there was no escaping the real likelihood of bias that existed as a result of Thompson's presidency over the tribunal. As the judge observed:

> I think he should not have done so, and particularly after the situation was pointed out to him at the hearing, as it was. . . In either event the decision of the commission with its heavy penalty cannot stand.

With that, Mr Justice Cantley rightly quashed the ten-year ban.

Before savouring his victory, Revie heard himself described as 'selfish' and 'very greedy' and must have cringed at the judge's scathing summing up:

> Mr Revie was the English team manager. He held the highest post of its kind in English professional football and he published and presented to the public a sensational and notorious example of disloyalty, breach of duty, discourtesy and selfishness. His conduct brought English professional football, at a high level, into disrepute.

In submitting a claim for costs, Revie's barrister suggested that little warmth had been shown towards his client, to which the judge tetchily replied: 'I haven't exhibited any more than I can help'. Nevertheless, the FA was ordered to pay one third of Revie's costs plus the entirety of their own. FA general secretary Ted Croker estimated that their total losses were in the region of £141,000.

For Revie, the judgement represented another important financial victory. Years earlier, in 1972, he had signed an ingenious contract with Leeds United which guaranteed him a nine-year consultancy job from 1 January 1980 at a salary of £10,000 a year. The post involved him attending only four board meetings a year and he was now free to take up the position. Meanwhile, the United Arab Emirates job had already offered him the most lucrative contract in the history of football. Further remuneration followed with the managership of Al Nasr (1977–80) and the National FC Cairo. His much-criticised breach of contract, although upheld, cost him a nominal £10 in damages. The avaricious ex-England manager had good cause for celebration.

Looking back at the sorry episode of Revie's resignation, it is difficult to avoid the conclusion that he was simply myopic and self-destructive. Pressure, he claimed, prompted his decision, but the leaving brought more anguish than a dozen England jobs. He clearly underestimated the depth of ill-feeling provoked by his abrupt desertion and as a result suffered terrible damage to his reputation. Ironically, it was all so unnecessary. Had he delayed his decision for a further four months, when England defeated Italy and narrowly failed on goal difference to qualify for the World Cup, any criticism would have been tinged with sympathy. His detractors will maintain that greed played the major part in hastening his departure, but the actual timing was not particularly clever in financial terms. If he had stayed with England for those vital last months he might even have won everything – the Arab money, compensation from the FA and a relatively quiet exit. How extraordinary that a man so skilled in public relations should misread the times so disastrously.

The frustrating illogicality of Revie's fall summed up his footballing career. He was always a contradiction: an attacking player and advocate of open football, he adopted the possessive stifling style of the Continentals to fulfil his managerial ambitions; a family man with a sentimental streak for birthday cards and flowers, he was also a soccer cynic, capable of inculcating players with the unsavoury aspects of gamesmanship; he had a cold, scientific brain and was famed for his labyrinthine dossiers and love of methodology, yet he was always a prisoner of superstitious ritual. Revie was unique and although he was not missed by England, Leeds could never replace his genius. In later, bleaker days, several of his old players returned to Elland Road in increasingly desperate attempts to rekindle the glory days. It is not insignificant that the core of Revie's team – Hunter, Bremner, Clarke and Cooper – are still active as League managers, while Giles, Yorath and Charlton have achieved success on the international platform. The old Revie professionalism has left a rich and distinctive managerial legacy.

Revie returned to the front pages in August 1987 in the most undesirable circumstances. Medical specialists confirmed that he was suffering from motor neurone disease. Faced with the possibility of imminent death, Revie was admirably defiant: 'I aim to do all I can to raise as much as I can for research into the disease. It's not all doom and gloom'. That same indomitable spirit was conveyed in a message from Billy Bremner who urged his gaffer to keep fighting 'just like you told the players to in our great days together'.

On 26 May 1989 Don Revie finally lost his battle against the incurable wasting disease which had robbed him of a long and happy retirement. Always a superstitious man, he would probably have been struck by the uncanny coincidences that attended his demise. The day of his death came on the 80th birthday of Sir Matt Busby, whose advice he had sought upon first venturing into soccer management. When the sad news was announced on the radio I was in the macabre position of proof-reading this chapter on Revie's footballing life. That same evening soccer history was taking place as Liverpool and Arsenal clashed to decide the League Championship. It was the first time this century that the top two sides had met in the final fixture to determine the destination of the title. Like Leeds United in 1972, Liverpool had already won the FA Cup and would clinch the double by avoiding defeat in their final League fixture. It was not until the closing seconds of the game that Arsenal scored the goal which deprived Liverpool and resurrected memories of

Leeds' worst footballing moment. With an identical number of points and a similar goal difference, Liverpool had lost the double by probably the slimmest mathematical margin in soccer history. Revie, who had surrendered the double in similar circumstances, seen one Championship taken away by 0.686 of a goal and another snatched away by Arsenal in a torturous final fixture, would have sympathised.

As memories of Leeds' greatest days came flooding back, tributes from former players poured in. Terry Yorath provided a particularly apt valediction:

> He was a great man. I am very saddened by his death. He built up Leeds into one of the best clubs this country has ever seen, and the training he gave us for football and life in general is something that we will never forget.

Revie's funeral was conspicuous for the absence of soccer officialdom. Even the once acerbic press deplored what they felt was the 'FA's final snub'. Appropriately, the cream of Leeds' great 1970's side turned up to pay their respects and remind us of Revie's pre-eminence among soccer managers. A final poignant comment from former England captain Kevin Keegan begged for a long overdue reassessment of Revie's contribution to football:

> It saddens me that the public at large had, and still have, the wrong impression of him. He was kind, generous and caring. When he left the England job, he did the right thing for his family but did it wrongly. He knew it and was big enough to admit it. He'd have been as successful as Alf Ramsey with England if the players had been good enough. We weren't.

JOCK STEIN

THE PATRIARCH OF SCOTTISH SOCCER

Jock Stein was born on 5 October 1922 in Burnbank, a mining area in Lanarkshire, Scotland. Unlike most of the characters in this book he was not a footballing prodigy but a slow starter whose interest in the game did not blossom until manhood. Like all of his friends, he played his share of junior football and, after a false start with Burnbank Athletic, turned out regularly for Blantyre Victoria. Amateur football was regarded as little more than a pastime by most of the participants and Stein was no exception. He expressed no ambition to turn professional and rightly regarded his soccer talents as fair but unexceptional. After leaving school, he worked briefly in a carpet factory before defying his over-protective mother by following the family tradition and becoming a miner. He continued to play football at weekends, enjoying the camaraderie among the mining folk who so loved the game.

The popularity of soccer in the area produced a legion of future club players including three figures who lived only a few miles apart: Matt Busby, Jock Stein and Bill Shankly. That three of the greatest managers in British soccer history were not only contemporaries but near neighbours is no mere coincidence. They each displayed a no-nonsense, hard-working, disciplined passion for the game as well as an acute understanding of the problems facing the average man in the street. Their ability to communicate and inspire stemmed from a shared conviction that soccer was a simple game that required no elaborate coaching jargon or academic pretension. Players said of Stein, Busby and Shankly that their team talks were so direct and uncomplicated that they could be understood by a ten-year-old. Their other great asset, of course, was a sensitivity to the type of problems that destroy footballers: alcohol, gambling and womanising. Marriage, thrift and abstinence characterised the lives of this Scottish triumvirate and it was an example that players respected and often imitated. Both Stein and Shankly shared the social mores of their Lanarkshire and Ayrshire mining communities, which vehemently denounced alcohol while showing a peculiar tolerance towards gambling. Stein was typical of the breed: a superstitious betting devotee and a lifelong teetotaller.

Although very much a product of his community, Stein did not subscribe to the sectarian prejudice that was an all-too-familiar parasite on the body of Scottish football. Such tolerance manifested itself in his private life to the extent that he married a Roman Catholic girl, Jean McAuley. Her non-denominationalism was even more remarkable. She not only failed to insist that her fiancé take instruction, but she also chose to risk the harrowing prospect of eternal damnation by marrying in a non-Catholic church. Any couple willing to face the burden of a mixed marriage in such a society showed considerable courage, if not foolhardiness. Stein would later show that same attitude of indifferent defiance in marrying himself to a traditionally Catholic football club, Glasgow Celtic.

The outbreak of the Second World War curtailed normal fixtures in the Scottish and English Leagues as well as draining clubs of most of their key players. Stein, at least, was spared military service claiming exemption as a miner. With many small professional soccer clubs searching for competent players to replace active servicemen, the 20-year-old Stein was approached by Albion Rovers and, following a trial, signed with the Second Division club in 1942. In the second post-war season, the club dramatically hit the big time by winning promotion to the Scottish First Division. By this time, Stein had been appointed to team captain and was known as a solid but slow centre half with a forte for straightforward yet effective marking. Given Albion's limited resources and distinct lack of glamour, promotion promised only temporary glory. The following season they plummeted back down, losing 25 of their 30 fixtures, conceding 105 goals and finishing 14 points below their relegated partners Morton. It was a humbling experience.

Throughout this period, Stein continued to work as a collier, although his involvement in football was growing stronger with each passing year. He was an active campaigner for higher wages, a role which sometimes caused friction between himself and the Albion Rovers officials. After eight years he was obviously in need of a change of club to revitalise his atrophying soccer career. Fortunately, an offer was at hand.

A former Albion team-mate impetuously recommended Stein's name to a Welsh club and, in 1950, he adventurously elected to accept an invitation to join non-League Llanelli Town. The substantially higher wages proved an irresistible incentive, but Stein was forced to endure long spells away from his family. As a 28-year-old footballer with an uncertain future it would have been ludicrous to surrender his home base, so Jean remained at their Hamilton council home while her husband lived in local digs. The arrangement was unsatisfactory, however, so after a few months the entire family moved to Wales. Their vacant house in Hamilton, meanwhile, became an easy target for burglars and this so upset the family that Stein decided to return to Scotland. He officially informed the Llanelli Town manager of his intentions but, even as he was speaking, the homesick Scot was made aware of an extraordinary proposition: Glasgow Celtic had expressed a keen interest in acquiring his signature. It was one of several uncanny coincidences in Jock Stein's life. Just as he had resigned himself to returning down the pit he was miraculously deflected by a completely unexpected and unsolicited offer.

The man responsible for bringing Stein to Parkhead was scout Jimmy McGuigan who had noticed the bulky centre half during his Albion Rovers days. Celtic urgently required a replacement in the reserves and McGuigan suggested Stein as a competent pro who could instil confidence and self-belief in the youngsters. So, on the basis of his temperament rather than playing skill, Celtic signed Stein in December 1951. Within two months he had made the centre half position his own in a dramatic promotion to the first team. Stein's surprise elevation was prompted by a series of injuries which left the first XI depleted. Seizing the opportunity, he retained his place through consistently excellent performances which brilliantly masked his playing deficiencies. A clever reader of the game, Stein always played to his strengths and his positional awareness compensated for a worrying lack of pace. Although less talented than his team-mates, the Lanarkshire lad rose rapidly and unexpectedly to the position of vice-captain. The appointment was based entirely on his organisational abilities and willingness to direct play on the field. While other players concentrated on their own game, Stein's eyes seemed to be everywhere, assimilating information, measuring individual performances and clinically punishing tactical weaknesses. Already, he had an encyclopaedic knowledge of the Scottish football scene which was capable of providing the kind of vital information that can tilt the balance in a tightly-contested match. More importantly, he possessed that indefinable quality of leadership which encouraged even noticeably superior players to respond to his advice. A series of team injuries had propelled his lucky rise to the vice-captaincy and another was to take him still further. When captain Sean Fallon broke his arm Stein found himself in charge of the side and Celtic's fortunes improved dramatically thereafter. Under Stein's tutelage, team talks became obligatory and post-match discussions were encouraged as a forum for voicing complaints and improving morale. From a shambolic, carefree unit, Celtic were slowly transformed into a highly efficient, well-organised team. Their mediocre form in the League was rapidly forgotten as Stein prepared them to contest the 1953 Coronation cup, an Anglo-Scottish tournament featuring several prestigious clubs. Outsiders Celtic rapidly disposed of Arsenal and Manchester United and went on to beat Scottish Champions Hibernian in a memorable final. It was Stein's first trophy and brought renewed pride to a side anxious to rediscover past glories. Chairman Bob Kelly satiated himself on public relations outings, appearing with Stein at supporters' clubs and charity functions where the gleaming Cup was displayed as a symbol of Celtic's long-awaited renaissance.

Kelly's critics were apt to cry 'fluke' and rightly pointed out that Celtic's involvement in the Coronation Cup had been determined by ground capacity rather than League form: winning a minor competition could not obscure the fact that they were still a middling side. Stein was convinced that the Coronation momentum could be continued and Celtic responded with a sustained attack on the Championship in the 1953–54 season. After winning 20 of their 30 fixtures, they clinched the title and amazed the Scottish footballing fraternity by battling through several tricky away fixtures to clinch the double, beating Aberdeen 2–1 in the Scottish Cup final. From non-League football in 1951, Stein had risen in under three years to captain a double-winning side. It was a soccer script worthy of Hans Christian Andersen.

The exuberant Bob Kelly rewarded his players with a free trip to the World Cup finals in Germany, where they witnessed the humiliation of Scotland at the hands of Uruguay. It was Stein's first experience of Scottish nationalism producing ludicrous expectations from a team ill-equipped to compete at world level. He returned home having learned a valuable lesson: courage and confidence cannot compensate for poor organisation and tactical naivety.

The double-winning Celtic side found the 1954–55 season a much tougher proposition as they had suddenly become the team everybody wanted to beat. Nevertheless, they mounted another Championship challenge only to falter in the latter stages as Aberdeen pulled clear. A repeat Cup final seemed likely when Celtic and Aberdeen were not drawn together in the semi-finals, but the latter eventually lost a replay to humble Clyde. Stein was confident that his team could overcome such easy opposition, but a fragile single goal lead was dramatically surrendered in the last minute of the final. Clyde went on to capture the Cup in a replay and Celtic were left with nothing. All things considered, it had been an eventful season for Stein which, with better luck, might have ended in another double. The team was confident of achieving further success and in their opening match of the 1955–56 season destroyed rivals Rangers 4–1 at Ibrox. It was a superlative performance which promised further glory, but within a matter of days Celtic suffered a severe setback: Rangers reversed their defeat with a 4–0 victory at Parkhead and in the process Stein suffered a serious ankle injury. An operation failed to right the condition and the Celtic star was left with a limp which precluded any further active involvement in the game. The loss of their captain was a terrible blow to Celtic's morale and precipitated a decline in form which continued until the mid-1960s.

Stein's enforced retirement at 34 was not tragically premature, although it raised doubts about his working future. Fortunately, Celtic chairman Bob Kelly intervened with an offer of a coaching job which Stein accepted. The post was eminently suitable for the former Celtic captain who had been enlisted originally with a view to assisting the younger players. Now he was totally in control of their careers and poised to exert a profound influence on the future of the club. Stein had an exceptional rapport with his boys and was able to impart his experience of the game in simple language and easily-understood tactics. Without forcing his charges to play beyond their abilities, he developed their confidence and inculcated an appreciation of the team ethos. In time he might have produced a squad of dedicated teenagers capable of challenging Matt Busby's Babes, but the role of trainer was frustratingly restrictive in its power and encouraged Stein to move on.

Inflamed with a confidence in his ability to oversee a first team, Stein reluctantly left Celtic, convinced that the board would never appoint a Protestant as manager. Thanks to a recommendation from journalist Jim Rodger he secured a post at Dunfermline Athletic, then on the brink of relegation. Nobody expected or demanded Stein to play the saviour, for Dunfermline were surely doomed. With only six matches left to play, they needed maximum points from their remaining fixtures merely to survive. Following his appointment in March 1960, Stein promised to do his best, but fully expected a prolonged spell in the Second Division. His first match as a full-time manager was a baptism of fire against his old club Celtic. Remarkably, Dunfermline immediately reversed their recent disastrous run and won the match 3–2. The amazement of Dunfermline fans was rapidly transformed into stark disbelief as their team duly won all their remaining fixtures and cheated what had seemed to be certain relegation. Stein had begun his managerial career with an indisputable miracle. In saving the team from the drop, he had unwittingly produced a club record for consecutive wins. It was probably the most successful managerial debut in football history.

Stein's initial contribution to Dunfermline was to revitalise the youth policy and strengthen the reserve side to create a small but effective squad. With the board's permission, he ventured into the transfer market and bought Tommy McDonald and Willie Cunningham from Leicester. These astute buys were to play a vital part in Dunfermline's progress, with Cunningham rapidly establishing himself as first team captain. A tough League season ended with Dunfermline in 12th place, having avoided the usual drama of relegation roulette. If their League performance was acceptable then their progress in the Cup was little short of extraordinary. Effortless away victories at Berwick and Stranraer took them to a third tie where they faced almost certain oblivion against classy Aberdeen. Amazingly, however, they not only survived the tie at Pittodrie but defied form and logic to win 3–6. A comfortable 4–0 rout of Second Division Alloa followed, taking Dunfermline into their first ever Scottish Cup semi-final. Testy St Mirren held on for a goalless draw but succumbed 1–0 in the replay. Suddenly, Stein found himself in the enviable position of overseeing a Cup final side in his first year as a manager. Equally improbably, his opponents turned out to be Celtic. A *Roy of the Rovers* scriptwriter was obviously at work.

Dunfermline received no easy breaks in the final and found themselves pinned into their own half by a lively Celtic attack intent on putting Stein in his place. A late injury saw Dunfermline reduced to ten men and during the closing stages of the match they clung on desperately for the final whistle. Celtic's power and pedigree seemed certain to clinch the replay, but it was not to be. After dominating much of the game they fell victim to two breakaway goals which presented the Cup to Dunfermline. It was a remarkable result and an astonishing achievement by Stein, reminiscent of his starring role in Celtic's double year.

Dunfermline's fairy-tale Cup win transformed the team from relegation fighters into Championship contenders. Stein boosted their confidence during team talks and brought pride to a club not previously associated with greatness. Before long, players were sporting club blazers and ties, much to the satisfaction of their garrulous chairman, David Thomson, another avid Stein supporter. Even at this early stage, the Big Man was employing managerial techniques more usually associated with his illustrious successors. Like Brian Clough, he insisted on knowing everything possible about his charges, including any secret weaknesses that might adversely affect their play; like Bill Shankly he deflated individual egotism by praising the collective strength of the team; like Don Revie he established a family atmosphere at the club and was permanently available to discuss any organisational or personal problem. In an age of ivory tower managers, Stein was clearly years ahead of his time.

The 1961–62 season was a year of consolidation for Dunfermline and a chance to experience European competition. Their first Cup Winners' Cup outing took them to Dublin and back, where they dismissed the amateurs of St Patrick's Athletic 8–1 on aggregate. A taste of the unknown followed when they faced Vardar Skoplje, a Yugoslavian side who came to Dunfermline full of hope but departed 5–0 losers. Stein could afford to surrender the replay 2–0 and still have time to experiment with new players. The quarter-final draw served up Ujpest Dosza of Hungary, a formidable side whose nation had recently demolished England 6–3 at Wembley and virtually altered the course of European football overnight. Stein, like many of his contemporaries, was a devotee of Puskas, Hidegkuti, Kocsis and the rest, and must have feared the worst against skilful Ujpest. Nevertheless, Dunfermline put up a tremendous fight in Hungary and, in a see-sawing game, eventually emerged with a creditable 4–3 defeat. Such a performance on foreign soil augured well for the second leg, but the Hungarians were not intimidated by their trip to Scotland and won convincingly 1–0. The defeat had proven educational, if nothing else, and left Stein eager to return to Europe at the earliest opportunity. Dunfermline looked to the Scottish Cup for a second successive trophy but were ousted in the fourth round by improving St Mirren. The setback did not deter their League progress and eventually they squeezed into fourth position and secured a place in next season's Fairs Cup.

Apart from the opportunity to experience Continental football, the Fairs Cup provided the possibility of renewing hostilities with the 'auld enemy' by drawing one of the leading English clubs. Dunfermline's attendance figures shot up when the news filtered through that they were paired with Everton in the first round. The Merseysiders had finished fourth in the League, and Dunfermline were confronting them in their Championship season. With the exception of recent double-winning Spurs, they could not have hoped for a more lucrative draw. Stein was taking no chances and instructed his side to avoid any reckless attacking displays at Goodison Park. Already, he had adopted Continental patience in playing a match over two legs. Everton were thwarted by Dunfermline's physical resilience and had to be satisfied with a slender 1–0 first leg lead. Dunfermline played even more tigerishly in the return, and frustrated the Merseysiders who finally lost concentration and conceded two goals. It was an amazing victory, not merely for humble Dunfermline and their wonder manager, but for every club in Scotland. In defeating the Champions-elect of England, Stein had struck a blow for national glory which momentarily transformed him into a modern day Robert the Bruce.

The Everton result softened the blow of a 4–0 trouncing by Valencia of Spain in the next round. The Scots had seemed totally out of their depth abroad, but Stein promised a stirring battle in the return leg. He was not wrong. Incredibly, Dunfermline reduced the deficit and in a stupendous display of attacking football caused Valencia to panic. The aggregate score was 6–6 and Stein's side were again shipped abroad for a replay in Portugal. Away from the hostile Scottish climate, Valencia recovered some of their lost poise and narrowly scuttled through 1–0. Stein's disappointment was mollified by the memory of their earlier dramas in which Dunfermline had established their name as an unpredictable and highly dangerous side. Sadly, they could not book a return trip to Europe the following season. A Cup defeat at the hands of Aberdeen and a middling eighth place in the League killed the hope of further Continental exploits.

Europe was not entirely lost to Stein during 1963, for he received a surprise invitation from the *Daily Express* to accompany Kilmarnock manager Willie Waddell on a trip to Italy. The purpose of the visit was to witness at first hand the training methods of the highly influential Inter-Milan coach Helenio Herrera. The Dunfermline board was happy to sanction the trip, realising that Stein might learn something valuable. What he saw were tactical strategies beyond his imagination. Herrera treated his players with almost military discipline and moved the Inter team across a football pitch like figures on a chess board. Upon his return, Stein began to experiment with attacking full backs and converted captain Willie Cunningham into a fledgling sweeper. The tactical shifts not only improved Dunfermline's League form but produced some highly entertaining exhibitions in the Cup. Little Fraserburgh were thrashed 7–0, East Stirling humbled 6–1 and Ayr humiliated 7–0. Nobody wanted to meet Dunfermline in the semi-final, which speaks volumes for the progress made in the three years since Stein took over the team.

The highly-publicised Cup victories convinced Stein that the time was right to move to another club. Football results are always unpredictable and a manager's worth is seldom noted unless his team are in the ascendant. With three years' experience, Stein knew that he was ready for greater things and gambled upon a fresh start. The blow was too much for poor Dunfermline who lost their semi-final to Rangers and narrowly missed qualifying for the Fairs Cup. Stein, meanwhile, accepted an offer from Hibernian, whose recent record paled alongside that of Dunfermline. What the Edinburgh side could not offer on the field was ably compensated for by their far greater financial resources. It was a set-up in which Stein's managerial magic was to prove particularly potent.

Hibernian, once a formidable side which won successive Championship titles in the early 1950s, had slumped to mid-table, betrayed by bad form and diminishing crowds. Stein's brief was to inject confidence into the team, win back the apathetic supporters and add some much-needed trophies to the club sideboard. His first meeting with the board of directors proved promising, for it was evident that their ambition matched his own. Stein established an instant rapport with chairman Harry Swan, an advocate of European football who was determined that Hibs should succeed in Continental competition. Never a manager to miss the chance of making an instant impression, Stein concluded that it was time for Hibs to retrieve some of their lost glory. It was too late to make progress in the League or Scottish Cup but another opportunity unexpectedly arose during the close season. The Scottish footballing authorities had decided to inaugurate a short-lived trophy called the Summer Cup which served as a moneyspinner for the lesser clubs in the League. The big guns, Celtic and Rangers, had declined an invitation to compete for the trophy, but Stein was sharp enough to realise that his new side would benefit from their omission. Almost inevitably, Hibernian were drawn against his former club Dunfermline and the match went the full distance before a replay favoured the Edinburgh side. Stein's boys soldiered on to the final drawing 4–4 with Aberdeen over two legs. A replay finally broke the deadlock and Hibernian emerged 3–1 winners to claim their first trophy in over a decade. The honour was small but it reflected favourably on Stein's management. Once more, he was acclaimed as a wonder worker guaranteed to provide success the moment he swanned through the club doors.

The Summer Cup victory served as a morale-booster which continued into the next League season. The usually indifferent Hibs suddenly found that they were winning matches and seemed booked for a healthy position in the table. Not content with such progress, Stein sought to reap further PR glory by persuading the board to finance a friendly game against Real Madrid. The legendary Spanish side were one of the biggest draws in football and their services did not come cheap, but Euro-crazy Harry Swan could not resist the lure of Continental competition. Plucky Hibernian duly paid £12,000 to entice the Spaniards over and the newspapers did the rest. A packed audience saw their presumptuous side win 2–0, a result which flattered the standard of football in Edinburgh. False confidence can prove a godsend to any struggling team, however, and thereafter Hibs played above themselves almost as though they were carrying the mantle of European Champions. Within days of the Real upset they travelled to Ibrox and overcame title-chasing Rangers 4–2. On the strength of a Mickey Mouse cup and a glamorous friendly, humble Hibs had discovered the swagger of potential Champions. The crowds flocked to Easter Road, united in the belief that their team was on the brink of greatness. Other clubs responded with renewed interest in Hibernian players, inflating their value on the transfer market and enabling Stein to sell paltry stock for a sizeable profit. The resurrection of Hibs was a classic example of Stein's understated managerial stealth. He knew that the directors and fans were hungry for success, so his initial strategy had been to throw them a few decorative fancies. The main meal was intended to follow next season.

Stein's track record was now so impressive that bigger clubs were beginning to believe he had a managerial Midas touch. Celtic's chairman Bob Kelly had been watching the Big Man's development with interest and concluded that the time was right to strike. At the end of February 1965, he approached Stein with an offer he could hardly refuse – the managership of Glasgow Celtic. The decision was inevitable, but it proved a sad day for Hibernian, who were riding high in the League, confident that the title could be theirs. The ructions with Stein undid their self-belief and the Championship slowly slipped from their grasp as they ended the season fourth. The Scottish Cup was an even sadder tale, for they lost Stein just as they were about to enter the semi-finals. The football fates were obviously playing on Stein's side and had concocted a semi-final featuring three of his former teams: Dunfermline, Hibs and Celtic. Naturally, the Big Man was allowed to sit back as Hibernian and Dunfermline fought it out for the honour of playing Celtic in the final. Dunfermline won the day but their luck ran out at Hampden where Celtic emerged 3–2 victors. Within three months of arriving at Parkhead, Stein had won yet another trophy. The Big Man's name was now synonymous with sudden, unexpected achievement.

The task of stabilising forlorn Hibs was given to Bob Shankly, elder brother of the Liverpool manager, and one of a handful of people in whom Stein confided over the years. Like Shankly, Stein knew that his new club was in need of an urgent rethink. The statistics were revealing: since Stein left Celtic as a player, the club had suffered a decade of mediocrity without winning a single League title or Scottish Cup. Having ended that famine with the Cup final defeat of Dunfermline, Stein was determined that other trophies must follow quickly. Soon, the Glasgow Charity Cup was added to the silver collection at Parkhead when Celtic overran Queen's Park 5–0. It was another example of Stein using a middling trophy to instil confidence in the players and re-acquaint them with the forgotten habit of winning. Chairman Bob Kelly was overjoyed by the sudden resurgence of Celtic, but his countenance grew somewhat sterner when the Scottish FA requested Stein's services as caretaker manager of Scotland. The national team had reached a crucial stage in the qualifying rounds of the World Cup and desperately needed a figure of Stein's influence to inject hope and belief into tired legs. Bob Kelly was aware that the part-time post might well distract Stein from his commitments at Celtic, but he could not reasonably object to such an important and prestigious offer. With the express understanding that Stein would not abandon Celtic for Scotland, Kelly gave his consent. The Parkhead chairman had already concluded that Stein, and thereby Celtic, would benefit from the experience, both from observing foreign teams and spotting likely buys among the internationals chosen to represent Scotland. In retrospect, it was a peculiar arrangement: here was Stein preparing for his first full season as Celtic manager, with all the responsibilities and political changes that such a new post entails, and yet his ambitious club seemed content to allow him to travel across the world on international business. It says much for Stein's work-rate that the Glasgow club profited from their magnanimous decision.

Scotland had been drawn in a World Cup qualifying group with Poland, Finland and Italy and their chances of reaching the finals were slim. Fortunately, Stein arrived just in time to accompany his countrymen to two crucial away matches. A creditable 1–1 draw against Poland in Chorzow and a 2–1 defeat of Finland in Helsinki convinced many Scottish supporters that their team was world class, although Stein was less certain. His managerial influence over the side was severely circumscribed by the dictates of an anachronistic selection committee whose powers remained unchecked. For a time, this consideration seemed irrelevant, but the problem grew to crisis level on the evening of 13 October 1965. In a packed Glasgow stadium, the home crowd saw Celtic forward Billy McNeill score a potentially winning goal against Poland which remained unanswered until the closing minutes of the game. Then, suddenly, doleful Poland scored twice to transform imminent defeat into shock victory. The defence chosen for Stein had proven vulnerable both to sustained pressure and lapses in concentration. That bizarre assault left Scotland needing maximum points from their remaining two games against favourites Italy. Stein's knowledge of the Continental game served Scotland well in the first match which they won 1–0. Everything now depended upon a favourable result in Naples, which was akin to asking for a miracle. However, Stein was a specialist at producing shock reversals and his familiarity with the Helenio Herrera school of Italian football provided more than a grain of hope for an upset.

Unfortunately, Stein was defeated by events beyond his control. The eccentricities of the Scottish FA, injuries to key players and selfish bloody-mindedness on the part of the English clubs meant that half the Scottish squad was unavailable. After naming his team, Stein was forced to cross out the following stars: Law, Gilzean, Mackay, Crerand, Baxter and Stevenson. With the backbone of the Scottish squad removed there was no chance of beating a full strength Italy, so

Stein uncharacteristically aimed for a draw and the chance of a neutral play-off. The tactic backfired disastrously and Italy romped home 3–0, condemning Scotland in the process. Stein was disillusioned by the sorry affair and stoutly resisted official solicitations to continue as Scotland manager. He complained bitterly about the amateurish selection committee and the hopelessness of reaching a satisfactory arrangement with English clubs over the release of key players. The dilatory attitude of his employers was effectively summed up in their advertisement for Stein's successor: 'Scottish International Manager. . . might suit a man with outside interests'. The most prestigious position in Scottish football was still regarded as nothing more taxing than a part-time post.

Stein's disenchantment with the footballing authorities encouraged him to seek greater control at Celtic. From the outset, he demanded a free hand and insisted that the board have no veto on team selections. This was a major coup for Stein, ensuring that he had more autonomy than any manager in the history of Glasgow Celtic. Chairman Bob Kelly and his fellow directors were content to surrender chunks of power as long as Stein produced consistently good results. He did not let them down. By January 1966, Celtic had stepped up their Championship challenge by defeating deadly rivals Rangers 5–1. This result signalled a significant turning point in the history of Scottish football with Celtic threatening to emerge as the team of the decade. The Ibrox side managed to prevent Celtic from retaining the Scottish Cup but lost the race for the Championship. At that moment nobody could have foreseen that Celtic were on their way to establishing an incredible record-breaking run of nine consecutive League titles.

Prior to the 1966–67 season, Celtic embarked upon a tour of the United States and Canada and, while there, Stein let slip his latest grand plan. Rather improbably, he intended to mount a serious assault on the European Cup, genuinely believing that Celtic were capable of winning the trophy. All that was required, apparently, was a couple of new signings to boost the squad in preparation for the rigorous domestic and European programme. Few commentators interpreted Stein's boasts as anything other than false bravado. Celtic had recently competed in the European Cup Winners' Cup and fallen victim to Liverpool, who went on to lose the final to Borussia Dortmund. If Celtic could not win the Cup Winners' Cup, nor indeed the several Fairs Cups for which they had previously competed, what chance did they have in this superior competition? No British club had ever reached the final of the competition and yet Stein was blithely discussing Celtic's chances of victory. It seemed highly likely that Stein's only success would be in making a prize fool of himself.

Celtic's early exploits in the European Cup were impressive, though hardly taxing. Zurich went down 2–0 at Parkhead in a game that convinced Stein of their defensive vulnerability. He duly despatched an attacking formation to Switzerland for the second leg and Celtic won 3–0. Next up were French Champions Nantes, who lost 3–1 on both sides of the Channel. The celebratory rout was partially spoiled by the loss of ace striker Joe McBride, whose leg injury barred him from future competition. Stein responded to the crisis with his customary efficiency and immediately signed the talented Willie Wallace from Hearts. Nothing was allowed to weaken the strength and depth of Stein's squad, which would be called upon to perform footballing wonders early in the New Year.

While pursuing European glory, Stein had not neglected domestic competition. On the contrary, Celtic snatched the Scottish League Cup and found themselves well placed for a further League and Scottish Cup double. Locked in a battle for four trophies, however, Celtic seemed in immense danger of overreaching themselves. Rangers' shock defeat in the Cup at the hands of Berwick made them more desperate than ever to win back the Championship, and Celtic had to strain every sinew to maintain their title challenge. Fortunately, the players responded magnificently to Stein's instructions and pursued an aggressive, attacking policy which overwhelmed the opposition. The system was a throwback to Stein's days as a trainer, and many of the boys he had coached were now in the Celtic first team. The player/manager relationship was exemplary and possibly unique in Scottish football. Stein did not merely lecture his charges on tactical formations and set pieces but took players aside to discuss their particular problems and individual foibles. More importantly, he encouraged a form of group therapy, insisting that players openly discuss their game and consider the strengths and weaknesses of the side. In effect, he had inaugurated a football self-improvement course from which his team emerged stronger and more confident than ever.

The quarter-finals of the European Cup brought Celtic's first setback in the competition. The Yugoslav side Vojvodina played a tough, frills-free game which earned them a narrow 1–0 victory on their own ground. In the return leg at Parkhead they defended superbly, fending off Celtic's reckless, bombarding attacks down the wings and soaking up an ocean of torrential pressure. Eventually, it was a simple goalkeeping error which allowed Steve Chalmers to register a lucky equaliser. With Stein desperate to avoid a replay Celtic continued to surge forward and grabbed a late, fortuitous winner. The victory brought considerable relief to Stein for it allowed Celtic to continue their remarkable bid for four trophies in one season.

Celtic's progress in the Scottish Cup was aided by a series of home draws against small clubs. High-scoring victories against Arbroath, Elgin City and Queen's Park whisked them towards a tricky semi-final confrontation with Clyde, then lying third in the table. A replay was required before the Glasgow side won 2–0 and progressed to their third consecutive Cup final. With the season dragging on and the fixture list multiplying, Aberdeen had a strong chance of causing an upset but Celtic held firm and won 2–0. The grand slam beckoned.

The League Championship, so coveted by Rangers, began to slip from their weary grasp as the season closed. In spite of their Continental commitments, Celtic had played astonishingly consistently throughout the

League year scoring 111 goals and losing only two matches. They finally won the Championship with 58 points, the highest for nine years. Celtic had no easy run in the League; their hat trick of trophies was therefore all the more remarkable for being won in such an intensely competitive season.

Clinching the Scottish treble did not convince the football world that Celtic were capable of winning the European Cup. It was generally assumed that their blood and thunder style of play would be brutally exposed, both by the patient guile of the Continentals and the well-drilled regimentation of the Czechoslovakians. The semi-final paired Celtic with the army side Dukla Prague, whose iron-fisted defence provided a stern test. At Parkhead, Stein deployed an all-attacking formation whose crude assault on the Dukla goal wrought an impressive 3–1 victory. Dukla Prague were disappointed but not despondent, for British sides rarely fared well behind the Iron Curtain. Stein was equally concerned about the paucity of a two-goal cushion and elected to despatch a specially-prepared defensive squad for the return. Employing the negative tactics of the Continental teams he claimed to despise, Stein secured a thoroughly competent goalless draw which was enough to take Celtic to the final. The tactical change in Prague was sensibly expedient, indicating that Stein was not naive enough to pin his hopes on pursuing some ridiculous romantic notion of attacking football.

Even as they prepared for the European Cup final, Celtic were still regarded as the products of a primitive soccer nation. Their opponents were the majestic Inter-Milan, twice winners of the trophy in 1964 and 1965. A super methodical side, Inter boasted some of the finest players in the world and could justifiably describe themselves as a team of internationals. By contrast, Celtic were an all-Scottish side hopelessly ignorant of the tactical and temperamental quirks of other football nations. The overly optimistic Stein hoped that this contrast might somehow favour his gauche squad. For all their naivety, Celtic were at least a unified bunch whose cameraderie could be used to psychological effect. Stein played upon this imaginary advantage during the preparations for the final in Lisbon. While Inter were locked away in silent seclusion like Italian monks, the Celtic camp was an open house for well-wishers and Scottish sports journalists. Stein was in constant attendance throughout this period and gave the impression that he was unwilling to leave the squad for more than a few minutes. The relaxed atmosphere was never allowed to degenerate into slackness, and Stein's omnipresence ensured that the players were insulated from negative external influences without ever feeling caged.

Stein's success in maintaining team confidence and stoking national pride could not disguise Celtic's image as underdogs. There was a similar discrepancy between the reputations of the respective managers. Stein was not widely known outside Scotland whereas Helenio Herrera was a figure of international repute. Indeed, the Scot had even gone on a pilgrimage to Italy to sit at the feet of the great man and witness his legendary training methods. Now it was a case of the pupil returning to challenge the master, and their styles could not have been more contrasting. Stein had been unable to incorporate Herrera's method play into the Scottish game so he had adopted a more traditional attack using wingers to bombard the opposing goal. It was crude, unscientific and lacking in guile or subtlety but kept the Scottish crowds entertained with ludicrously high-scoring matches. Herrera intended to put an end to all the fun.

On the evening of the final Stein was determined not to be overawed by the brilliant Herrera. In a childish attempt to win a psychological advantage he commandeered the bench that the Italian had marked out as his own. When the indignant Herrera finally strode across the pitch there was an exchange of words, but the Big Man would not be budged. The Scottish players witnessed this farcical interlude and took great pleasure in the Italian's humiliation. The bullish behaviour of Big Jock reminded them that Inter-Milan were merely human and could be similarly upbraided.

The course of the game followed Helenio Herrera's expectations. Early in the first half Capellini was axed and Mazzola scored from the spot kick, after which Inter proceeded to close up shop. Herrera had perfected the system of containment and counter-attack and was confident that his side could clip Celtic's raiding wingers. At half-time Stein ordered his troops to continue in their attacking mode without resorting to desperate high crosses. The game increasingly resembled a siege and Stein knew that solid, striking blows from his front men offered the only possibility of success. If their commitment wavered or patience snapped then Celtic would be undone and in the confusion Inter might even score a second. The players responded sensibly to Stein's half-time talk and continued to penetrate Inter's defence with consistently accurate shots. The cumulative pressure eventually told when Tommy Gemmell blazed a powerfully hit ball past the Inter goalkeeper. The Italians failed to recover the initiative but seemed likely to take the game into extra time until Stephen Chalmers deflected a mishit ball into the net six minutes from the final whistle. Glasgow Celtic were Champions of Europe.

While the players bathed in champagne, the teetotal Stein surveyed the scene with quiet satisfaction. The superlatives were left to the loquacious visiting celebrity, Bill Shankly, who passionately informed his rival: 'You'll be an immortal'. Shankly was referring to Stein's accomplishment in becoming the first British manager to win the European Cup, but that was not the whole story. Other managers would follow in Stein's traces but none could approach the record of Celtic during that wondrous year. What they had secured was an incredible quadruple – a grand slam of every domestic trophy plus the premier European tournament honour. It remains an achievement unparalleled in British football history.

Intoxicated by the grandeur of Celtic's historic quadruple, Stein prepared his side for an ill-advised appearance in the World Club Championship Cup. This unofficial and troublesome trophy was inaugurated as a crude means of determining the globe's top soccer club by pairing the European and South American Cup holders in a two-legged play-off. The side that stood between Celtic and ultimate but meaningless glory was Argentina's Champions, Racing Club. The teams played the first leg at Hampden Park in October 1967 and the friction was tangible. Celtic adopted their customary style of fast attacking play, fully expecting to overwhelm the South Americans in the same way that they had broken down Inter-Milan. Racing, however, were far too clever to allow Stein's men the run of the park and employed a startling array of professional fouls, including body-checking, shirt pulling and the occasional punch. It was clinically executed intimidation no doubt designed to test the Celtic temperament. Racing were well aware that such tactics would not only distract their opponents but goad them into retaliating, thereby loosening their grip on the game. The South Americans were well tutored in the art of innocent pleading and could usually control their tempers at the right psychological moments and so escape the disapprobation of officialdom. The Scots had few answers to such skilled gamesmanship but shook off their aggressors long enough to score a single goal. It was a slender lead to take back to Argentina.

The sagacious chairman Bob Kelly had seen enough on the field to realise what might await Celtic in South America. With the protection of the players uppermost in his mind, he urged Stein to boycott the return match. His proud but reckless team manager would not hear of such a suggestion and persuaded the board to sanction the trip. It was to prove the most regrettable decision of his footballing career.

Great Britain was not the most popular country in Argentinian circles during 1967. The South American populace had not forgotten Argentina's unfortunate exit from the 1966 World Cup when the brilliant Antonio Rattin had been cruelly dismissed in a crucial quarter-final match against England. Equally galling was the unforgettably appalling attitude of Alf Ramsey who had denounced their talented side as 'animals'. The England team was subsequently ridiculed as 'pirates', while Scotland was regarded as an annexed colony tainted with the same contempt as its imperialist neighbour. That the Scots regarded England as their greatest and oldest footballing enemy was either not known or conveniently forgotten by their Argentinian opponents.

The tone of the return match was made clear by the actions of a hostile and partisan crowd. Long before the opening whistle Celtic goalkeeper Ronnie Simpson was felled by a flying missile and ruled out of the game. Stein merely shrugged his shoulders and produced a substitute from the dressing room. Foolishly, he still believed that Celtic could win the tie. Stein's faith was rewarded early in the first half when the tempestuous Jimmy Johnstone sauntered into the penalty area only to be rugby tackled by Racing's over-cautious goalkeeper. Against a deafening backdrop, Celtic converted the penalty and took a sizeable step towards the World Club Championship. Racing responded with an unhappy and irresistible assault on the Scottish goal. They scored twice in the second half and Celtic felt fortunate to end the game with an aggregate draw. It would have been politic to share the Championship trophy, but instead Stein agreed to play a deciding tie three days later in neutral Uruguay. Bob Kelly again advised Stein to surrender his grandiose plans, forget Scottish pride and go home. Convinced that Celtic's greater glory was only 90 minutes away, Stein somehow persuaded the board to ratify the fixture.

The third match was an unmitigated disaster. Racing were as expediently aggressive as ever, but on this occasion the Celtic players' tempers snapped. The fiery Jimmy Johnstone ruthlessly elbowed an opponent and was justifiably expelled from the field. His disgraceful lack of discipline angered the Uruguayan crowd and undermined the Scots' morale. Predictably, Racing took full advantage of their opponents' sense of injustice and frustration. They had long suspected that Celtic's fiery temperament could prove their undoing and this was confirmed when Bobby Lennox and John Hughes were also sent off in the second half. Towards the end of this ugly encounter Tommy Gemmell also received his marching orders but remained on the field, apparently unaware of the extent of the referee's displeasure. That this further transgression was not noted sums up the extent of the chaos. It was a lamentably self-destructive display from Celtic and a godsend to Racing who found themselves attacking eight angry, indisciplined and uncontrollable men. A single goal was more than sufficient to kill off this dishevelled green-hooped octet. Racing had emerged triumphant with an extremely cynical and brilliantly manipulative demonstration of controlled aggression and foxily executed professional fouls. They were truly the Champions of the World.

Celtic were rightly reprimanded for their atrocious behaviour on the field, where they had dragged the once-good name of British sportsmanship to an ultimate low. A shaken and deflated Stein was forced to apologise on behalf of his shamed team. He conceded that he had been mistaken in insisting that the game be played and acknowledged the foresight of Bob Kelly in attempting to cancel the fixture. Several of the players were fined, but it was Stein who was forced to drink the cup of humiliation to the dregs. He knew he had failed the most fundamental of all managerial tests: the ability to control the behaviour of his players. Four months before, his team had been hailed as European Champions and history makers and now they were regarded as a blight on the face of the game. It was one of football's cruellest reversals of fortune.

Following the year of the quadruple, Celtic surrendered the Scottish Cup in the first round, said an early farewell to Europe, but went on to win the Championship with a staggering 63 points, losing only one of their 34 games and completing the season with an incredible run of 16 consecutive wins. Their supremacy was such that Stein even had the audacity to nominate the Celtic B team for a place in the Scottish Second Division. Following the withdrawal of Third Lanark from the League, only 19 teams remained in the Second Division, thereby ensuring that one side would always have a vacant Saturday. Stein's proposal was designed to alleviate that problem as well as allowing his squad some decent competition. Predictably, his argument fell on deaf ears at the Scottish FA. The partisan Parkhead faithful interpreted the rebuke as genuine fear of the all-too-likely prospect of Celtic B effortlessly winning the Second Division title. It was not until 1975 that Meadowbank finally arrived to restore the Division to 20 strong.

Celtic's domination of Scottish football continued during the closing years of the 1960s. They won the domestic treble in 1969, a triumph made sweeter by a 4–0 thrashing of Rangers in the Scottish Cup final at Hampden. The cumulative success revived the dream of a second quadruple which came close to fruition in the 1969–70 season. The League Cup was effortlessly lifted and the Championship became a formality as traditional rivals Rangers faded alarmingly. In the end Celtic could afford to lose four games and still finish the season with an incredible 12-point lead thereby clinching their fifth consecutive title. Having beaten Rangers in the third round of the Scottish Cup, a third trophy seemed likely, but in the final a plucky Aberdeen upset the odds with a shock 3–1 victory. Stein was disappointed by this setback but took solace in the pursuit of a far more important trophy – the European Cup.

Celtic had good reason to believe that 1970 was to be their lucky year in Europe. In the second round of the Cup they faced the once-formidable Benfica of Portugal and established a powerful 3–0 first leg lead at Parkhead. Such was their dominance that the return was idly dismissed by many as a formality. Instead, Benfica came storming back and despite losing the injured Eusebio levelled the tie at 3–3. The Portuguese were desperately unlucky not to win the match in extra time and finally suffered the ultimate insult of seeing all their efforts lost on the spin of a coin. The value of such a reprieve to Stein's weary squad was inestimable and they vowed never to suffer such complacency again. After progressing to the semi-final they found their road blocked by a team more deadly than any that existed on the Continent.

Leeds United had emerged as the undisputed Champions of England and many maintained that they were the greatest club side of all time. Their ultimate ambition under the inspirational manager Don Revie was to win the European Cup, and few sides in the history of football had been better equipped to achieve that glory. Celtic's chances of defeating Leeds over two legs were dismissed outside Scotland as either unlikely or non-existent. Admittedly, Revie's squad was depleted by injury and fixture congestion but it was generally agreed that even a half-fit Leeds could overcome the Scottish Champions. The first leg at Elland Road proved an eye-opener which confounded the football world. Within two minutes Celtic opened the scoring against a team which boasted one of the finest defences and home records in European football. Leeds twisted every sinew in their attempts to win the game but failed to register even an equaliser. Celtic's shock victory was such an audacious coup that soccer cynics refused to accept its veracity.

The gods of Leeds were still tipped to reverse their bad fortune and win the return at Hampden. When Billy Bremner scored a scorching aggregate equaliser midway through the first half of the second leg, soccer sages nodded their heads and predicted an imminent onslaught. Instead, Celtic held their ground and John Hughes restored their lead early in the second half. Leeds' misfortune was completed when the rampaging Hughes accidentally bundled into goalkeeper Gary Sprake, who was soon taken off. Celtic scored again and found themselves proclaimed Champions of Britain. For the nationalistic Scots this victory was probably far more important than the European Cup itself. For years Scottish football had been derided as inferior and Celtic's string of titles were perceived by jaundiced English critics as fool's gold. Now they had beaten Super Leeds nobody would ever doubt their pedigree again. Their unexpected victory was not only a passport to the European Cup final but a major triumph for Scottish football.

The battle royal against Leeds made the final seem anti-climactic by comparison. Celtic were firmly established as favourites against the Dutch side Feyenoord, who had never played at this level before. In spite of their warning against Benfica, it was difficult to escape the conclusion that an air of complacency had once more infiltrated the Celtic camp. Prior to the game, several players were involved in intense discussion about merchandising rights and the amount of money that might be accrued from selling photographs of the Champions of Europe. The financial wranglings might have honed their footballing skills but instead they seemed distracted by the pound notes dangling before their eyes. When Tommy Gemmell scored an early goal Celtic looked set for a lucrative victory but Feyenoord fought back, equalised, and took the game into extra time. Celtic's customary flair and urgency seemed sadly absent and, as their concentration waned, Feyenoord struck with a killing winning goal. The lure of Mammon and the epic destruction of Leeds had conspired to rob the heart of the once rampaging 'Lisbon Lions'.

The European defeat hastened the demise of the great Celtic team of the 1960s but even during rebuilding Stein kept an iron grip on the Championship trophy. From 1970–75, Aberdeen and Hibernian joined Rangers as Celtic's main rivals but none proved successful in reclaiming the title. That Stein was capable of winning the League for nine consecutive seasons is a feat unprecedented in modern day football. It should be added that Celtic also appeared in six consecutive Scottish Cup finals (1970–5), winning four of them. In a country where the word 'double' is spoken with reverence, Stein achieved the honour on no less than six occasions – a remarkable feat. Heaping trophy upon trophy, Celtic seemed invincible in domestic competitions and it was difficult to conceive of a time when they would ever be superceded. The alarming regularity with which they won Championship and Cup honours made Stein's role seem less taxing than people assumed. As each year passed, however, the search for new players and fresh incentives became paramount. The nine-year Championship run was achieved primarily by hard work on the part of an indefatigable manager. It was only when Stein suffered a mild heart attack in 1973 that the public fully realised the strain that he faced with each passing season. Throughout this period he remained a footballing fanatic and continued to appear at junior and reserve matches always hopeful of unearthing new talent. Few doubted that his indestructible team would win their tenth consecutive title in 1975, but it was not to be.

Celtic slipped out of the Championship race, ending up third behind a revitalised Rangers and improving Hibernian. Although the end of an era beckoned, Stein softened the blow by winning both the domestic Cup competitions. The close season had been designated as a period of reassessment in which Stein intended to plot the restoration of the Championship. Such plans were shattered on 5 July 1975 when Stein was involved in a serious car crash. The passengers included Glasgow bookmaker Tony Queen, Stein's wife Jean, and Bob and Greta Shankly. Miraculously, only Stein and Queen suffered serious injuries and both recovered after a period of convalescence. The crash effectively precluded Stein's involvement in the 1975–76 season, so the task of wresting the title from Rangers, in the newly-formed Scottish Premier League, was left to assistant manager Sean Fallon. The disruption caused by Stein's sudden departure was reflected in the results and Celtic ended the season without a single trophy. It was their first dry run since 1964.

Stein returned to Parkhead one year after the crash to start building another new team, which included the brilliant Kenny Dalglish. Spurred on by a determination to prove that his injuries had not affected his judgement, Stein duly netted his favourite League and Cup double, leaving Rangers as forlorn runners-up and beaten finalists. It was the perfect comeback.

Expectations of a new epoch of Celtic dominance were to prove chimerical. The success that Stein had come to expect from the club evaporated as key players such as Kenny Dalglish, Lou Macari and Davie Hay drifted southwards. Having won the double, Stein suffered Sean Fallon's fate of failing to win a single trophy in the next season. Even more alarmingly, Celtic slumped to fifth in the League, a sure indication that their traditional supremacy had ended. Realising that further radical changes were required, the 56-year-old Stein agreed with the Celtic board that the manager's job might be better suited to a younger man. With a tinge of regret, he handed over the reins to his former captain Billy McNeill.

It was anticipated that the Celtic board would present Stein with a directorship, but this was never ratified. Instead, they suggested the post of commercial director. The offer was greeted with a mixture of incredulity and contempt by the Big Man who could never envisage himself as a 'glorified pools vendor'. Sadly, he left his beloved Parkhead a bitter, disillusioned figure, convinced that he had been treated cavalierly. He had fully expected to be kept on in an advisory capacity and would no doubt have proven an effective managing director or consultant scout. Like many managers, however, he learned that football clubs generally prefer expediency to sentiment. The retirement of Stein's great champion Bob Kelly had weakened the manager's influence at boardroom level and the new directors concluded that Celtic FC could survive and thrive without the guiding hand of the Big Man.

In retrospect, Stein may have stayed too long at Celtic for his own good. His Championship victories during the 1970s exuded an air of the inevitable which cruelly distracted from his Herculean efforts in sustaining the grand title run. In financial and prestigious terms, he might have been better advised to accept the managership of an English club during his later years. Certainly, his status would have been enhanced by association with a top English side. Both Manchester United and Coventry City had previously attempted to win his hand but Stein was always governed by a misplaced loyalty to Celtic and a fussy concern for family commitments. His departure from Parkhead hardened his heart, however, and before long he was ready to accept an offer from an eminent English First Division club.

Leeds United were sorely missing the silver trophies that had been collected during the glory days of Don Revie. Since his departure for the England job, they had suffered the disastrous 44-day reign of Brian Clough and watched impatiently as successive managers vainly attempted to restore lost greatness. The Leeds chairman Manny Cussins was an avuncular figure who saw in Stein an elder statesman capable of emulating the Championship feats of the enigmatic Revie. Cussins' faith in Stein was demonstrated by the size of the wage on offer, plus a mouth-watering £1,500,000 allocation for the purchase of new players. For Stein, the challenge, the money and the resources presented an irresistible package and he gratefully accepted Leeds' terms.

Stein's move to England coincided with a major setback in Scottish football. The national side had recently been humiliated in Argentina where the World Cup squad had suffered defeat against Peru and scraped a fortuitous draw with Iran. The Scots' freewheeling, blasé antics had provoked severe criticism and although the team ended their campaign with an impressive victory against Holland, the earlier débâcles continued to rankle. When team manager Alistair McLeod proferred his resignation, the Scottish FA urgently required an experienced replacement who could restore national pride. One man seemed ideally suited for the post but he was already entering his second month managing Yorkshire's finest. However, when it became known that Stein was working without a contract, the SFA formally offered him the job. It was an unwanted dilemma for the Big Man who was enjoying the financial security and challenge of working with Leeds. Nevertheless, the opportunity to end his career as a national manager could not be ignored. The distraught Manny Cussins implored Stein to remain at Leeds and offered new financial incentives but the Big Man would not be bought. Although embarrassed by the circumstances of his departure, he elected to return to Scotland. For the luckless Cussins, it was a double nightmare revisited. Like Don Revie, Stein had finally sacrificed club for country and in a remarkable re-enactment of the reign of Brian Clough at Leeds, he had lasted exactly 44 days.

Stein's stated intent upon taking over the Scotland team was to produce an effective World Cup squad. He rightly observed that too much attention had been focussed upon Home Internationals and friendly fixtures against England, while the recent World Cup games had been approached as a happy jaunt. What Stein promised was a new realism to replace the absurd expectations and inevitable disappointment of previous World Cup adventures. Unfortunately, the cautious approach was not accompanied by positive results on the field. Scotland lost 11 of their first 18 matches under Stein, who missed the day-to-day involvement that he had previously enjoyed at club level. The brave experimentation that characterised his time at Celtic proved impossible with the Scotland squad yet he looked with optimism towards the forthcoming World Cup finals. Scotland had been drawn in a group which included Sweden, Northern Ireland, Portugal and Israel. Their hopes of progressing to the next stage had been enhanced by FIFA's decision to increase the number of finalists from 16 to 24. This meant that Scotland could reach the finals in Spain by finishing in the top two of the group.

Myopic commentators assumed that Portugal and Sweden would test Scotland but the real threat turned out to be Northern Ireland. In effect, the home countries cancelled each other out with hard-fought draws at Hampden and Windsor Park. The Scots proved more cautious against Continental opposition, however, and their impressive defensive record guaranteed qualification before the final group match against Portugal. Stein had kept his word and not even a lamentable display in the succeeding Home Internationals could detract from his impressive record in crucial matches.

The 1982 World Cup finals in Spain saw Scotland placed in a tough group with Brazil, Russia and New Zealand. The latter alone seemed easy meat but the memory of poor performances against lesser sides prevented Stein from uttering empty platitudes. His caution proved well-advised for the match was a topsy-turvy affair, although Scotland eventually won 5–2. The second match against Brazil was realistically a matter of survival rather than victory, but the Scots shocked the world by taking a 1–0 lead. Their glory was short-lived, however, and the Brazilians romped home in the second half overpowering their presumptuous opponents 4–1. The statistics now favoured Russia whose superior goal difference meant that they merely needed a draw with Scotland to progress to the next round alongside Brazil. Once more, Scotland caused an early shock when Joe Jordan opened the scoring in the 15th minute. However, Russia's patient probing proved telling in the second half heat and two opportunistic goals ended Scotland's campaign. A late reply from Graeme Souness enabled Stein to point out that his team had been knocked out on goal difference. In truth, they were well beaten and, unlike the previous campaign under Alistair McLeod, there were no excuses.

Stein betrayed no inclination to retire after Spain and the Scottish footballing authorities knew better than to sack such a valued elder statesman. Nevertheless, there was evidence to suggest that Stein's managerial career had run its course. He found it increasingly difficult to understand the mercenary attitudes of some of the younger players and found himself falling victim to soccer's generation gap. Another poor performance in the European Championships pinpointed the need for new blood, but Stein stayed on. He was determined to complete one last World Cup expedition.

The qualifying round for the 1986 World Cup matched Scotland with Spain, Iceland and Wales. It was a relatively easy group and Scotland were fully expected to qualify alongside Spain. Stein elected to strike early and threatened to win the group outright following explosive victories over Iceland and Spain. However, in February 1985, Scotland were pegged back 1–0 in Seville, with Stein complaining bitterly about the negative tactics of the Continentals. The result was far from unexpected, however, and Scotland remained firm favourites to qualify. All that changed on 27 March 1985 when Wales registered their first victory at Hampden Park for 34 years. It was a disastrous setback which underlined the difficulty of facing a fellow British side at world level. Stein took the result particularly badly and suffered what may have been a minor heart attack later that evening. The strain of taking Scotland through the most torturous period of their recent footballing history was an immense burden, particularly for a 63-year-old with a heart condition. A vital return match against Iceland in Reykjavik was another nail-biter which Scotland scarcely deserved to win 1–0. A missed penalty by the home side meant that the Scots needed a single point from Wales to scrape through. It would not be easy.

On the evening of 10 September 1985 Stein arrived at Ninian Park, Wales, where Scotland's World Cup fate would be decided. The absence of Graeme Souness, Kenny Dalglish and Alan Hansen added an unwanted element of drama to the proceedings. Could the depleted Scotland team survive a Welsh onslaught for 90 minutes? The answer came early in the first half when Mark Hughes thundered the ball past Scotland goalkeeper Jim Leighton. An avalanche of goals seemed certain to follow as the Welsh pressed home their advantage, yet the score remained 1–0.

The Scottish dressing room was uncharacteristically gloomy at half-time. Stein seemed oddly subdued and bemused by the turn of events. Nobody commented upon his apparent confusion, for the entire squad was in a state of disarray. Goalkeeper Jim Leighton had lost a contact lens and rather sheepishly admitted that he had left his replacement set back at the hotel. Assistant manager Alex Ferguson was both stunned and embarrassed: he did not even know Leighton wore contact lenses! The appallingly ill-prepared Scots seemed set for one of their most memorable self-destructive displays. Reluctantly, but sensibly, Stein replaced Leighton, which left him only one substitution option in the second half. Scotland now needed a miracle to prevent the Welsh from travelling to South America in their place.

The initiative gradually shifted in the second half as Wales became increasingly aware of the need to preserve their slender lead. Sensing their uncertainty, Stein made an inspired substitution, replacing Gordon Strachan with David Cooper. From that point on, the game opened up and ten minutes from time Scotland won a ferociously disputed penalty. The much-praised Cooper casually beat Southall and suddenly Scotland were Mexico-bound.

Seconds before the final whistle, Stein rose from his bench, then staggered into the arms of trainer Hugh Allan before being taken to the Ninian Park treatment room. Word quickly spread that he had suffered a serious heart attack. Fans gathered in grim silence outside the ground as the sad news was confirmed. The most famous football manager in Scottish history had performed his last soccer miracle. Jock Stein lay dead.

BRIAN CLOUGH

BIG MOUTH STRIKES AGAIN

The irrepressible Brian Howard Clough was born on 21 March 1935 in Middlesbrough, a home town he shared with his adversary Don Revie. The Northeast was a great provider of footballing talent, so it is less than surprising that Clough's entire family were soccer enthusiasts. His devotion to the game took the form of a ruthless ambition which was to carry him far from the backstreets of Middlesbrough. Initially, he joined the city's junior team in 1951 and signed professional forms a year later. His progress was forestalled by two years' compulsory National Service and, upon his return, Middlesbrough were promptly relegated along with Liverpool. Even in the Second Division Clough found it difficult to establish himself as a first team centre forward, although his goalscoring abilities were undeniable. Probably the first person to spot his potential was a recently-signed goalkeeper who would soon become his mentor.

Peter Taylor was an unusual type – a fading player who fancied himself as a potential manager. Having spent nine years at Coventry under the auspices of Harry Storer, Taylor had observed first-hand the tactics of a ruthless rhetorician and astute observer of talent. Storer did not suffer fools gladly whether at boardroom level or on the pitch. He liked his football played hard and chose players accordingly. What most impressed Taylor about the man was his uncompromising nature and his willingness to take a chance on unfashionable or difficult players. He taught Taylor the invaluable lesson of what to seek in a footballer: ruggedness, courage and a hell-bent desire to win. For his part, Taylor had already taken to studying individual players, intent on discovering whether he possessed the rare ability to predict greatness. Within weeks of arriving at Middlesbrough, he convinced himself that he had unearthed a rare talent in the person of young Brian Clough. Sensing a bargain buy, he magnanimously phoned his old friend Harry Storer and suggested he sign the lad to his latest club Derby County. Storer was sympathetic but recent forays in the transfer market had made him over-cautious, so he politely passed. His reasoning was laudably sensible: Taylor was an untrained scout and the boy Clough had yet to command a first team place. No doubt the kid was promising, but he couldn't be *that* good.

Within a year of Storer's rejection Clough would emerge as the leading scorer in the Second Division. Throughout the late 1950s, he immersed himself in the role of the heroic striker, egged on by the constant companion who expounded his soccer skills to any willing listener. Taylor was not merely Clough's greatest supporter but a teacher and fellow scholar in the unending quest for footballing knowledge. With few friends inside or outside the club, the duo spent their spare time endlessly talking about soccer, coaching youngsters and discussing their respective futures. Clough was entranced by Taylor's evident enthusiasm for his scoring skills and soccer prowess. He was constantly fishing for compliments and Taylor rose to the bait like a schooled sycophant. His sentiments were undoubtedly genuine, but in massaging Clough's ego he was not only magnifying the boy's confidence but exposing a hideous streak of soccer selfishness. Clough was never the most altruistic of players but under Taylor's influence he became a law unto himself. He acted as though he was God's gift to football and his team-mates grew increasingly weary of his self-centredness and insufferable arrogance. Clough was not above insulting his fellow professionals if their actions displeased him in any way, and his tone seemed so supercilious and calculatingly humiliating that it was not surprising that he bred enemies. Chief among them was centre half Brian Phillips who refused to be bullied by Clough and repaid his goal-hungry gamesmanship during team training with some much needed hard tackling. On one occasion, big-mouth Clough ended up grovelling in the mud much to his opponent's satisfaction.

Whatever his failings as a diplomat, Clough kept on scoring goals, increasing his tally with each successive season. His leadership or bullying qualities won him the captaincy of Middlesbrough, although it is doubtful whether he was suited to the post. The function of a captain is to inspire loyalty, commitment and hard work, but Clough was incapable of this. He was a thoroughly bad influence on team morale, showing at best disdain for his fellows, who neither knew nor liked him. Frustrated by Middlesbrough's perpetual mid-table status, Clough even had the audacity to criticise his own defence. Here he was, the prolific goalscorer, but it was like filling a bath with the plug out. His detractors retorted that results might have improved if he had occasionally helped his overworked defence instead of goal-hanging in search of glory. Such criticisms fell on deaf ears, for Clough was a scoring glutton. There is the oft-told tale of how he actually pushed one of his own players aside just to get his name on the score sheet. Such selfishness made him a folk-hero among the Middlesbrough supporters but a pain in the backside to his long-suffering colleagues. Among his sternest critics was coach Jimmy Gordon who quickly realised that Clough was spiralling out of his control. Nevertheless, Gordon must have admired Clough's charisma for he was to remain with him for the rest of his career.

Clough's insularity and appalling insensitivity towards his team-mates inevitably precipitated a minor players' revolt. A substantial number of the playing squad petitioned the club to remove Clough's captaincy, but their bid failed. The incident deeply upset Clough who usually found it easy to brush aside even warranted criticisms. Now he was forced to face a depth of dislike that punctured even his crocodile skin. A similar humiliation would be visited upon him years later by the players of Leeds United.

The rift at Middlesbrough encouraged Clough to request a transfer. He had hoped that his scoring feats would attract the attention of major clubs but suitable offers were not forthcoming. One of football's great imponderables is how he would have fared in the First Division. His supporters believe that he would have been a leading goalscorer but there is another school of thought that suggests Clough was merely a big-mouthed, lower-division striker whose mobility might have been severely lessened and his scoring opportunities stifled if he had played in the top flight. Clough's chances of exploding that theory were presented on two occasions when he was chosen to represent England. Significantly, he failed to impress on either outing and was never capped again. In a team which featured such greats as Jimmy Greaves and Bobby Charlton, Clough had little chance to rule the roost. His place was taken by the workmanlike Derek Kavan, who obviously impressed Walter Winterbottom and the England selectors. The nagging suspicion remains that, at the crunch, Clough simply wasn't good enough.

Clough's hopes of attracting an offer from a First Division club proved vain. Instead it was Middlesbrough's Second Division rivals Sunderland who won the hand of the disgruntled striker. The Middlesbrough players were grateful to see the back of him, while Clough was content to leave. Taylor, his main ally, had just moved down to Port Vale, so his transfer was well-timed.

Sunderland had spent heavily in a determined bid to retrieve the First Division status that they had lost in 1958. It was anticipated that Clough's prolific scoring would win them promotion at the end of 1962 but they finished a tantalising point behind second placed Leyton Orient, who went up with the all-conquering Liverpool. It was a bitter disappointment to Sunderland, but Clough and manager Alan Brown looked to the new season with well-founded optimism.

Sunderland continued their promotion challenge in what was to become one of the strangest seasons in Football League history. Boxing Day 1962 was celebrated in a blanket of deep snow which stretched disconcertingly across the British Isles, driven inexorably by blinding blizzards and a numbing coldness which demobilised public transport, raised the unemployment rate to a staggering 3.9 per cent and escalated the tragic incidences of hypothermia among the poor and aged. It also encouraged the footballing authorities to create a pools panel whose sole function was to predict the results of postponed matches. The vagaries of British weather meant that parts of the traditionally frozen Northeast were paradoxically still capable of hosting a football match.

On 26 December 1962, Middlesbrough had wisely closed their ground, but Sunderland went ahead with a fixture against Bury, much to the satisfaction of Clough who was anxious to get two points closer to the First Division. What had seemed like a good idea was rapidly transformed into a disaster. Sunderland suffered their first home defeat of the season and Clough was left sprawled in the mud following a clash with Bury goalkeeper Chris Harker. When the trainer ran onto the pitch he was dismayed by the sight of the striker's right knee. A superficial inspection confirmed that Clough's scoring days were virtually over. Sunderland continued their promotion challenge but again foundered at the final hurdle – pipped by Chelsea on goal average and a point behind Second Division Champions Stoke.

Clough fought hard to regain fitness and discover a means to compensate for the damaged ligament which had robbed him of his speed. His incentive was great because Sunderland were winning in his absence and after another hard season made it third time lucky with a promotion place alongside Champions Leeds. Clough managed to win his way back into the first team for a total of three games in the top flight, but he was merely a shadow of his Second Division self. His single moment of glory came with a goal in the 3–3 draw against Leeds, a result which would later cost Don Revie his first League Championship. Clough never looked likely to retain his place and ended his playing days on the sidelines. Sunderland were struggling in the First Division, a situation which prompted Clough to round on directors and barrack players. He was so quick to find fault that he rapidly lost the sympathy of his team-mates and taxed the patience of everybody at the club. Bitter, disillusioned and evidently feeling sorry for himself, Clough had been reduced to the level of a football footnote. He had no historical distinction whatsoever: no European campaigns, League Championships or FA Cups. Two desultory international appearances and one First Division goal were the sum total of his football achievements at the highest level.

Clough was still vainly shouting the odds when a new manager arrived in the form of George Hardwick. Observing the morose state of Sunderland's once-formidable striker, Hardwick decided to cure such self-pity with hard work. Suddenly, Clough found himself in charge of the youth team, a job that enabled him to pass down his footballing wisdom to impressionable adolescents. Among the most attentive listeners was John O'Hare, who would later help Clough win his first League Championship. At this point, however, the horizon did not extend beyond the FA Youth Cup and under Clough's guidance Sunderland reached the semi-final. Hardwick was impressed, but the club's directors had already hardened their hearts against the injured firebrand. When Hardwick left Sunderland in the summer of 1965, Clough was summarily dismissed. Deflated and doleful, he spent the next few months pondering his future as one of football's great losers.

Clough's ex-colleague Peter Taylor was suffering no such crisis in his footballing life. Since retiring from Port Vale he had fulfilled a long-standing ambition to become a manager. Even as Clough was collecting his belongings from his locker at Sunderland, Taylor was celebrating Burton Albion's victory in the Southern Cup final. The Burton directors were so impressed with Taylor's success that they offered him a new three-year contract. Early the next season, the club had eased its way to the top of its division, prompting Taylor to dream of further glories. It seemed only a matter of time before some inspirational director would pluck him from amateur obscurity and propel him into the mainstream of the Football League. Such reveries were interrupted by an unexpected phone call from an old friend. . .

The downward spiral of Brian Clough had been halted by former England centre forward Len Shackleton, a sports journalist on the *Sunday People* who recommended the mournful one to lowly Hartlepools United. The Fourth Division club had recently risen to an all-time high of 15th in the table and were looking for a hard-working young manager to inspire the players to even greater feats. Shackleton had observed the lethal combination of Clough and Taylor at Middlesbrough and suggested that it was time to reunite the pair. It was an extraordinary proposition during a period when team management was unheard of. Clough pursued the idea, however, and during a terse conversation with Taylor suggested they move to Hartlepools immediately. When Taylor learned of the terms on offer he was flabbergasted. Impoverished Hartlepools could barely afford one manager, let alone two, so Taylor would have to sacrifice his £41-a-week pay packet and settle for a measly £24 wage. Even worse, he could not officially enjoy the status of 'manager' and would have to suffer the indignity of being sneaked in through the back door as a glorified trainer. By any logical reasoning the offer was ludicrous, but Taylor's gambling instincts told him to accept the presumptuous proposal. So it was that a great management team was born to the most humble of Football League clubs.

Although Clough and Taylor were ostensibly football managers, a visitor to Hartlepools United would have been forgiven for mistaking them for manual workers. Much of their valuable time was spent redecorating the club, scrubbing out baths and plugging leaks in a roof that resembled a colander. Training sessions were less notable for tactical talks than earnest discussions about whether the club could afford a weekly supply of footballs and a freshly laundered kit. In spite of regular changes in the team, no miracles were forthcoming on the pitch and, by the end of their first season, Clough and Taylor realised the enormity of the task before them. Their League position said it all: Hartlepools had finished 18th in the Fourth Division, three places lower than the previous season. Fortunately, the directors seemed reasonably content that the club had avoided the humiliation of applying for re-election to the League for the umpteenth time. Clough and Taylor were forgiven. Things could only get better.

Taylor, the power behind the managerial twin throne, had poached a couple of his former players from Burton and was forever scouring his little black book in search of bargain buys. Clough had inherited some of his partner's persuasiveness and rather naively attempted to woo his old adversary Jimmy Gordon from his latest club, Blackburn Rovers. The coach was amazed by his cheek and pointed out that it would be madness to leave a thriving First Division club for a bunch of Fourth Division no-hopers. Although he resisted the evangelical beckoning of Clough on this occasion, Gordon was closer to conversion than he realised.

Clough's arrival at Hartlepools had brought a smattering of media interest as he was the youngest manager in the Football League. Even such minor newsworthiness entranced Clough and he found, to his surprise, that he was rather adept as a public relations officer. While Taylor worked quietly in the background, Clough attempted to raise cash and halt the dwindling Saturday afternoon attendance figures. A beguiling rhetorician, Clough embarked on a tour of working men's clubs, drumming up support and squeezing contributions from already half-empty pockets. He even persuaded a local brewery to sponsor Hartlepools and his indefatigable enthusiasm restored pride in a club which had seemed on the brink of extinction. From their pit, hopelessly near the foot of the Fourth Division, Hartlepools moved confidently to eighth place and jaundiced supporters were amazed to witness such undreamed of luxuries as a new roof and modern floodlights. The sweeping changes on the pitch were reflected by similar upheavals behind the scenes. Since joining the club, the managerial duo had found themselves in conflict with their imperious chairman Ernest Ord, who held Hartlepools by his purse strings. Yet, within a year, he was swept from power when Clough and Taylor won the unexpected support of a mutinous fellow director. It was their first taste of power politics at boardroom level and it instilled a fearless and rebellious air which they maintained throughout their managerial careers.

The rebuilding of Hartlepools was gradual but effective. Clough was no scout but he did discover one important asset at a youth trial. John McGovern had all the hallmarks of a talented and dedicated footballer and soon found himself heading towards Hartlepools' first team. Docile and impressionable, he regarded Clough as a father figure and gave the impression that he would follow the man to any club in the world. The importation of fresh, malleable players suited Clough's managerial style and before long he became settled. Promotion seemed a distinct possibility in the next few years and saviour Clough was a public hero in a town that he had grown to love. Taylor was not so sentimental about Hartlepool or the club. Restless and ever ambitious he sought a greater challenge and bigger wages. His key to the higher divisions lay in the hands of the influential Len Shackleton, who knew the soccer grapevine as well as any journalist in the land. An inveterate supporter of the Taylor/Clough amalgam, he was only too willing to recommend their services to capricious directors in search of new football diviners.

Sam Longson, the chairman of Second Division Derby County, listened intently to Shackleton's testimonial and, after meeting Clough and

Taylor, made an official approach to Hartlepools. Clough was reluctant to leave the Northeast but Taylor reminded him of the footballing resources available at Derby, which included a £70,000 budget for new players. Taylor already had a list of potential buys and convinced his partner that they were firmly set on the road to the First Division. Longson immediately established a rapport with Clough and looked on open-mouthed as the managerial duo set about restructuring the team. Interestingly, it was Clough, rather than Taylor, who first spent Derby's money by returning to his old club Sunderland for the talented centre half John O'Hare. The archetypal Clough player, O'Hare brought forth some effusive and self-effacing comments from his new manager: 'He has more skill in his little finger than I ever had in my whole body. A team of John O'Hares would win everything including the European Cup because the other team would never get the ball'.

The search for 'a team of O'Hares' sent Taylor back to Hartlepools where he retrieved the promising teenager John McGovern. Shortly before that he and Clough had made an early morning raid on the house of Tranmere Rovers centre half Roy McFarland in a confident attempt to finalise a £24,000 transfer. Although naturally cautious, McFarland was no match for the loquacious pair:

> They woke me up at my Liverpool home at two o'clock in the morning and persuaded me to sign for them. The boss and Peter never stopped talking. They paralysed me. I never had a chance to do anything else but sign for Derby.

The technique was habitual. Again and again, the eccentric managerial duo would set out on some transfer mission, infiltrate households, beguile and sweeten worried parents, convert suspicious wives and insist on sleeping on the floor until they left with the signatures of their prey.

The intended transformation of the Derby team continued remorselessly throughout their first season, but the results reflected a painful transition. Contrary to Clough's expectations, progress was not immediate and, as at Hartlepools, the duo ended the season in a lower League position than when they had arrived. Several Derby directors voiced their concern about the disappointing results, even though the club had reached the semi-finals of the League Cup, losing to the eventual winners Leeds. Typically, Clough was convinced that his team was steadily improving, although events elsewhere reminded him of what he had left behind. Rather improbably, Hartlepool had won promotion to the Third Division and, having dropped the 's' from their name, were looking forward to a new era.

Taylor distracted Clough from nostalgic thoughts of the Northeast by stepping up the buying campaign. John Robson was spotted playing parks football and whisked away from the grasping arms of Newcastle, and Alan Hinton was snatched from Nottingham Forest's reserves. By this time only three Derby originals remained: Kevin Hector, Alan

Durban and Ron Webster. What Derby now needed was a player of class and experience to organise this motley crew of youngsters into a cohesive unit. Clough and Taylor found the perfect candidate in Spurs' former captain Dave Mackay.

Mackay had intended to return to his native Hearts as a 33-year-old player/manager but was wary of the dangers of spoiling his old reputation. Clough's abrupt arrival at the Spurs training ground with an offer from Second Division Derby County solved Mackay's dilemma. He desperately wanted to continue playing and was finding the pace at Tottenham increasingly taxing as age and weight took its toll. Instead of adopting an attacking role at Derby, Mackay was surprised to find himself slotted in at the back:

> I didn't think anybody played with a sweeper because that was supposed to be taboo. Their 'tactical innovation' suited Derby and it was good for me. I'd never played in the Second Division before. But it was easy, a piece of cake.

With Mackay's confidence in full bloom, Clough and Taylor completed the team sheet with the recruitment of Willie Carlin to the front line.

Derby began their promotion campaign with some inauspicious performances and Mackay confessed that he was unimpressed by the side. Before long, however, the team began to gel and Mackay noticed how heavily the management relied on solid defensive tactics:

> Their motto was: 'Don't give anything away, everything else is a bonus'. They weren't worried too much as long as you didn't let a goal in. That's Clough and Taylor in a nutshell.

Mackay's view is confirmed by the League statistics for that season which show that Derby conceded less goals than any team in the lower three divisions. They lost only five matches and romped free of their challengers, winning promotion by seven clear points. For Clough it was a moment to be treasured and, in spite of all the achievements that followed, he still maintains that the 1969 Second Division Championship was the most memorable moment of his footballing career.

For the old warhorse Dave Mackay, the 1969 season ended with the prestigious Footballer of the Year award. His carefree adjustment to Second Division football had been facilitated by a kid gloves approach from Clough:

> I was treated totally differently from everybody else. It couldn't have been better. I had a day off on Monday when the rest had to train. While other players would get crucified by Clough there was never any suggestion that I played badly or did anything wrong.

Clough's handling of Mackay was typical of a manager unafraid of being accused of inconsistency or favouritism by his younger players. Derby were on a roll and nobody was yet willing to question the methods of the man who had won them promotion.

During the close season Derby prepared for First Division crowds by building a new stand with seating for 4,800 spectators. It was a memorable year for the fans as the club effortlessly rose to challenge Leeds, Everton, Liverpool and Chelsea for a place in Europe by finishing in fourth position. However, the dreams of Fairs Cup glory were shattered before they had begun when Derby found themselves under investigation by the footballing authorities. A club audit revealed a series of irregularities including petty cash transactions without chits, unauthorised payments for programme articles and a failure to lodge the contracts of three players with the League. The footballing commission concluded that Derby were guilty of gross administrative negligence and fined the club £10,000. Peculiarly, they also banned the club from European competition for a year, a decision which angered Clough and Taylor. The expulsion from Europe encouraged the managerial duo to concentrate on lesser trophies and in August they added the Watney Cup to the trophy shelves. It was a pulsating way to start a new season as well as paying for the club's administrative blunders.

In order to strengthen Derby's Championship challenge Clough once more approached his old antagonist Jimmy Gordon. The Blackburn trainer was impressed by the money available at Derby but sceptical of Clough's motives. The two had seldom seen eye to eye at Middlesbrough and were known for their single-mindedness. However, Clough needed a strong-willed coach capable of challenging his authority and pumping the adrenalin that was necessary to produce a Championship side. Gordon also played a key role in introducing Clough to the next Derby secretary, Stuart Webb. Another man with a very independent mind, Webb would later test the limits of Clough's influence at boardroom level. For the moment, the secretary was left with the unenviable task of restoring the club's administrative credibility although he also alerted Peter Taylor to another important signing.

Archie Gemmill, a diminutive outside left at Webb's previous club Preston, proved to be Clough's toughest signing to date. Rivals Everton were hot on the trail and to complicate matters Gemmill's wife took an instant dislike to the big-mouthed Derby manager. In a brilliant display of personal charm, Clough ingratiated his way into the Gemmill household and ended up in the spare room before pulling off another remarkable nocturnal signing. Within three months of arriving at the Baseball Ground, Gemmill won his first cap for Scotland and replaced Willie Carlin as Derby's midfield lieutenant.

The first half of the 1970–71 season was not a happy period at Derby. In October, Peter Taylor suffered a mild heart attack and by Christmas was forced to take time off to convalesce. While he contented himself reading the sports pages and watching football and racing on television, Derby slumped to sixth from bottom in the First Division.

Taylor's return to the club was not all sweets and roses. A temporary rift occurred between the managerial twosome when Taylor learned that Clough had been given a £5,000 pay rise by the Derby chairman. Sam

Longson had a strangely sentimental affection for Clough whom he treated like a surrogate son. For a time, Longson was Father Christmas to the Clough household, bestowing extravagant presents and providing perks which boosted his manager's already dangerously high self-esteem. From a distance, Taylor looked on, resentful, envious, indignant and worried. Suddenly, the most effective managerial partnership in the League was displaying an irreparable fission.

Longson's familiarity with Clough was to have serious repercussions for Derby County FC. The ageing chairman had made the terrible mistake of befriending a man whose primary managerial strategy was to buck authority. Clough interpreted Longson's geniality as a sign of weakness and a firm indication that the manager could conceivably control every aspect of the club. Soon, Clough was in turmoil with the company secretary Stuart Webb, who objected to the team boss sticking his nose into affairs that were beyond his preserve. More than once, Longson found himself cast in the role of peacemaker, but it was a wearying task for a 75-year-old man.

Longson's feelings about Clough became more ambivalent as the charismatic manager grew in stature. The signing of Colin Todd was a case in point. In returning to Sunderland to sign his former player, Clough had shown no hesitation in breaking the British transfer record with a £175,000 payment. Remarkably, however, he had completed the transaction before informing his doting chairman who was in the Carribean when the news broke. It was an inexplicably insensitive stroke by Clough which deeply hurt Longson who thereafter began to question the sagacity of his prodigious favourite.

The private pain over the Colin Todd affair was soon replaced by a more public humiliation for Longson. Since arriving at Derby, Clough and Taylor had successfully signed several players from nearby Nottingham Forest, including Alan Hinton and Terry Hennessey. Although the managerial duo had not systematically set out to drain emerging talent from their neighbours, the Forest directors became concerned about this trend. An official approach for Henry Newton was declined and worse was to follow with the protracted negotiations for England forward Ian Storey-Moore. Manchester United had come close to signing the player when Derby intervened with a counter offer. Storey-Moore, undecided about his choice of club, was quickly won over by the persuasive rhetoric of Clough and Taylor and hastily signed forms for Derby. Clough was triumphant until Forest chairman Ken Swales pointed out that the contracts were invalid without his signature. Undeterred by such formalities, Clough brazenly attempted to force the issue by presumptuously parading Storey-Moore before the Baseball Ground faithful and introducing him to the Derby team. The Forest directors were aghast and continued negotiations with Manchester United who eventually signed the player. Clough's theatrical bid failed, much to the chagrin of the Derby directors. Incensed by the bureaucratic wrangling that robbed him of his prey, Clough despatched a four-page protest to League secretary Alan Hardaker. Sam Longson was not amused and suffered further embarrassment when Derby were fined £5,000 for a breach of transfer regulations over the affair. This would not be the last occasion on which Clough's impetuosity and candour would strain the patience of his senatorial chairman.

The power structure at Derby had become an intriguing exercise in group dynamics. The uneasy alliance between Clough and Taylor improved or declined in symmetrical relation to the familiarity between chairman and manager. Taylor's sensitivity towards the issue is best exemplified by his clash with Longson following the purchase of Roger Davies from Worcester City in September 1971. The Derby chairman had sighed: 'Well, I hope you're right', a comment which Taylor regarded as a personal slight on his ability to pick a player. In a huff he told Longson to 'Go to hell' and stormed out of the club. Even the volatile Brian Clough felt that his partner had overreacted to what was an innocuous remark. Taylor was especially indignant that Longson's remark had been made over a paltry signing fee of £14,000. Here again, however, the chairman's view was by no means eccentric or unusual. The entire football world had been astounded by Derby's brash move in paying £14,000 for an unproven Southern League striker and even Clough himself was moved to comment:

> What Derby have done has set a new pattern in transfer negotiations. If fees for non-League players spiral then there will be only a select few clubs able to regard the Southern League as a potential source of talent.

Derby's backroom battles did not impede their progress in the League. Having pulled themselves from the relegation zone to a healthy ninth the previous year, they began the 1971–72 season among the front runners, undefeated in their first 12 matches. For several months, Clough insisted that Derby could not possibly win the Championship but even his scepticism eroded by Easter. Before the final run-in, the Derby board was dismayed to learn that Coventry City were intent on signing Clough and Taylor. The daredevil duo promptly threatened to accept the invitation, a suggestion that sent Longson scurrying to the boardroom to confirm a counter cash offer. While this was occurring, impatient Coventry lost hope of completing the transfer and pulled out of the proposed deal. In effect, Longson had provided a pay rise which turned out to be totally unnecessary. Yet again, the beleaguered chairman felt cajoled and outmanoeuvred by his former favourite.

The Coventry controversy coincided with Derby's defeat by Arsenal in the fifth round of the FA Cup. With only the Championship left to play for, Clough marshalled his troops for a grand assault. The club suffered only two setbacks in their last 11 matches and, more crucially, beat their major rivals Leeds and Liverpool. It was a valiant run without the luxury of a squad of substitutes to cushion the effects of injury and fatigue. Derby duly completed their fixture list with a humble 58 points and flew off to Majorca leaving Leeds with the formality of picking up a point at Molineux to clinch the League Championship and FA Cup double. As if to prove nothing is ever certain in football, Leeds actually lost, and on the same evening Liverpool squandered their outside chance by drawing at Arsenal. Derby had won the title almost by default! While the drama unfolded, Clough was enjoying his dinner at the Island Hotel in Tresco in the Scilly Isles. The Derby players were relaxing at Cala Millor, downing bottles of champagne in celebration of their unexpected good fortune. The entire scenario had an air of unreality about it as if history had been changed by sleight of hand. While Don Revie and Bill Shankly were claiming floodlight robbery, Clough was already musing on the prospect of European Cup glory in 1973.

Derby's Championship triumph made Clough more autonomous than ever. During the close season he again broke the British transfer record with the purchase of Leicester defender David Nish for a cool £225,000. Once more, chairman Longson was caught on the hop, unaware of the speed at which Clough was now moving. Further internal furore was forthcoming in September when Clough made an unprecedented attack on his own home supporters: 'They start chanting only at the end when we're a goal in front. I want to hear them when we are losing. They are a disgraceful lot'. The next day, Longson gave a press conference dissociating himself and the club from Clough's remarks and earnestly apologising to the Derby fans. It was clear to everyone in the game that something was amiss at Derby and rumours about Clough's future intensified when it was learned that he had refused to sign a new contract. The Champions' results were also alarmingly erratic. Although they had opened their European campaign with a 2–0 victory against unknown Zeljeznicar, a League clash with Leeds ended in a 5–0 humiliation. Clough kept the Derby board on edge for another month before finally agreeing terms and signing a new five-year contract. It was difficult to gauge his relationship with the Derby board at this point, but there were signs of a general disillusionment with the game. Early in 1973 he shocked the Derby faithful by announcing that he intended to leave football and seek a different job which would allow him more time with his family. Nobody was sure whether his sentiments were genuine or simply the words of an impulsive newsmaking manager caught on a melancholic afternoon.

Derby's faltering League challenge and FA Cup defeat by old enemies Leeds left Clough grasping for European silver. Against the odds, Derby had reached the European Cup semi-final and found them-selves in Turin facing Juventus. It was an evening of disaster: Derby were thoroughly beaten and both Archie Gemmill and Roy McFarland received bookings which barred them from the return leg. Peter Taylor was also in trouble, having crossed swords with the German referee and Juventus's Helmut Haller. It was left to the irrepressible Clough to sum up the evening in an aggressive untranslatable aside to the Italian media: 'I will not speak to cheating bastards'. As expected, the return leg proved beyond Derby's reach and Juventus kept a clean sheet to win 3–1 on aggregate.

Clough was by now a well-known television sports personality whose pithy, provocative comments amused and outraged armchair viewers throughout the land. London Weekend Television were so taken with his impish wit that they offered him a full-time job as a presenter. Clough declined, but agreed to appear on a part-time basis. He was now a regular on both *On The Ball* and *The Big Match* with two major networks vying for his time. Longson was disturbed by this development, particularly in light of Clough's recent outbursts. During the close season he had made an absurd and inflammatory attack on Leeds United by suggesting, without a trace of irony, that they should be demoted to the Second Division. Shortly afterwards, the normally well behaved Derby fans became involved in a violent confrontation with visiting Chelsea supporters. Longson was worried about the club's declining reputation and genuinely concerned that Clough's idle tongue might bring official censure. The manager he once admired was now beyond his control, and the two were barely on speaking terms. The cold war did not curb Clough's extravagant spending. On the contrary, he grew more ambitious than ever, launching himself into clandestine negotiations for the signatures of Bobby Moore and Trevor Brooking. West Ham manager Ron Greenwood assured his pushy counterpart that they were unavailable but not before Clough had offered a king's ransom.

Longson was unaware of Clough's latest excursion having being busy preparing his own ultimatum. A letter was despatched to the contumelious Derby manager guaranteed to provoke his wrath. Longson insisted upon vetting Clough's newspaper articles and restricting his television appearances to an absolute minimum. Clough's characteristic reply was to tender his resignation, along with that of his partner Peter Taylor. It was a provocative power play forcing the Derby directors to choose between their charismatic manager and millionaire chairman. It was no contest. Clough's vain hopes of unseating the chairman were quashed by directorial fidelity. The swaggering Derby manager was finally put in his place by a geriatric chairman whose power he had totally underestimated. Shortly afterwards, there was talk of Clough relenting on his refusal to minimise his media work but such protestations were academic. Longson had already won a famous victory and reduced Clough to the level of an ostracised, unemployed manager.

The Derby board acted quickly in appointing a successor to Clough and their choice was eminently sensible. Dave Mackay, the former captain, still commanded enough respect to navigate the troubled waters that threatened to sweep Derby into internal chaos. His first problem was the attitude of the mutinous players who seemed determined to reinstate their svengali manager. Upon being informed that they would not attend training, Mackay became incensed and threatened to play the reserve team against League leaders Leeds. Clough's ludicrously loyal squad eventually came to their senses when their union representative warned that they could suffer suspension for breach of contract. For a time, Clough fanned the flames of the protest movement that sprang up in the wake of his departure but, after all the public meetings, planned rebellions and ego games, all that remained was the bitter anti-climax of an impotent, futile cause. It was left to the dogmatic Sam Longson to put the protesters in their place:

> We will go into the Second Division with our heads in the air rather than winning the First Division wondering whether the club will be expelled from the Football League.

Fortunately, Longson's relegation worries proved unfounded. Derby went on to finish third in the table and unexpectedly rose again to win another League title in 1975, albeit with the lowest Championship points total for 20 years. Clough and Taylor always insisted that they missed the opportunity to take Derby to far greater heights, but Mackay still derides such views:

> Brian talked about how Derby could have become another Liverpool, but to me that's absolute crap. Derby were a good little team, all grafters, hard workers. Nothing more.

In the aftermath of the Derby débâcle Clough decided to recharge his batteries with a six-month holiday cruise before seeking a new post. Taylor, however, was intent on re-establishing his name immediately and within weeks the pair were back in business managing Third Division Brighton and Hove Albion. It was a commendable act of faith by chairman Mike Barber who offered excellent wages, solid financial backing and complete managerial autonomy. Clough's arrival captured the imagination of the coastal town and trebled attendance figures overnight. On 3 November over 16,000 spectators turned up for the first home game against York and the atmosphere resembled a carnival with colourful banners testifying to the brilliance of the controversial management duo. Within a month, however, the champagne start had gone decidedly flat, as Brighton suffered the terrible indignity of losing an FA Cup tie 4–0 to amateurs Walton and Hersham. Two days later Bristol Rovers visited the Goldstone Ground and thrashed the Seagulls 8–2. Clough could only voice his deep sense of shame for the players. His much-vaunted talent for transforming promising sloggers into passionate professionals was sadly absent.

Taylor reacted to the crisis at Brighton by embarking on a wholesale policy of replacement. It was his characteristic ploy in the face of poor results. While he scoured the country seeking new talent at bargain basement prices, Clough's relationship with the players continued to worsen. The gauche young lads were in awe of the great man but he showed them little sympathy or encouragement when the results failed to improve. Not content to lambast the team in the dressing room, he openly criticised them in public. Forgetting that they were merely Third Division artisans, he accused the players of not knowing their trade and added, with remarkable disdain, that they had shirked all moral responsibilities.

Clough might have been better advised to question his own motives and actions. While crucifying the players for their lack of commitment, he was quite willing to fritter his time away campaigning for the Labour Party in Derby. He even took time off to travel to America during February solely to watch the world heavyweight championship between Muhammed Ali and Joe Frazier. The following month he visited Iran where the Shah of Persia offered him £400-a-week to manage the national team. It was all fun publicity for Clough but set an appalling example to the youngsters at Brighton who marvelled at their manager's inconsistency in demanding commitment while acting like an overpaid casual worker.

Peter Taylor was disgusted with Clough's carefree arrogance and realised that his partner was ill-suited to the unglamorous grind of Third Division football. The inevitable parting of the ways came sooner than anyone expected, for in April 1974 the football world was stunned by the sacking of Sir Alf Ramsey. The FA invited Don Revie to take over, leaving Leeds United with the unenviable task of replacing the most successful football manager of the past decade. On 20 July, Clough unexpectedly found himself back in the headlines managing a Championship team with insatiable ambition. On this occasion, however, he travelled alone. Resisting the obvious financial and career advantages offered by Leeds, Taylor chose to remain with humble Brighton. After nine years of hard-won success, the Clough/Taylor bandwagon had abruptly derailed.

Clough's appointment at Leeds strongly suggested that the Yorkshire directors had taken leave of their senses. In the event, this was only half true, for the board was split on the issue. The engagement was largely at the suggestion of chairman Manny Cussins who made the fundamental mistake of assuming that a great club necessarily needed a big-time manager. Clough clearly had Championship credentials but there were a plethora of reasons why he was thoroughly unsuited to the post. First and foremost, he was Leeds' sternest critic and had spent the last couple of years heaping abuse on the admirably ruthless professionalism that had created the finest football team of the era. While discerning managers such as Bill Shankly and Matt Busby admired the awesome Don Revie, Clough showed him scant respect, especially on television where their exchanges were engagingly antagonistic. During the year prior to his appointment at Leeds, he had shamefully insulted Peter Lorimer, for no apparent reason, at a dinner held in honour of the Scottish international. Most galling of all had been Clough's disgracefully provocative suggestion that Leeds should be forcibly relegated to the Second Division merely because of a less-than-perfect disciplinary record. How well such a move would have benefited his own club Derby County.

Manny Cussins' amnesiacal disregard for Clough's opinions was puzzling enough, but his willingness to recruit one half of a split management team seemed beyond logic. In nine years as a professional manager Clough had relied heavily on his partner Peter Taylor. They were a complementary duo and nobody at this stage could gauge their managerial worth as separate entities. Leeds was the last club at which to commence an experimental solo career, but this was precisely what Clough was undertaking. Leeds' staunchest supporters hated Clough with a vengeance because of his unsavoury remarks about the club, while the players were simply bemused by his inappropriate recruitment. Even with Taylor, Clough would have struggled to overcome the prejudice he had so studiously engineered against himself. Without Taylor he was doomed; a paper king merrily led into a raging bonfire.

Clough urgently needed to make a good impression at Leeds but instead began his reign with a calculated snub. When the players turned up for pre-season training they were astonished and horrified to learn that their new manager was still indulging himself on a summer holiday. Allan Clarke summed up the incredulous feelings of the Leeds team in a curt stab: 'He should be here with us, not sunning himself in Majorca'. When finally he did return, Clough turned up late for the pre-season team meeting, thereby adding insult to injury. It was difficult to escape the conclusion that Clough was still mentally attuned to the lackadaisical life at Third Division Brighton.

The Brighton habit extended to his cavalier treatment of the team. Leeds was a smooth-running machine with highly self-disciplined players who time and time again had risen from title misfortunes and Cup disappointments to challenge for the highest honours. Their competitive spirit and team unity was above praise and beyond criticism. Virtually all the players had grown up in a supportive environment in which the manager treated them like mature and responsible adults. Under Clough they found themselves thrust back into the kindergarten. Internationals who knew their worth were suddenly talked down to like disobedient children. The initial team meeting was a classic example of Clough at his most unwittingly self-destructive. According to legend, Clough opened his account by calling the entire team cheats and suggesting that they should throw their cups and medals down the dumper because they had won them unfairly. For a team that had sweated blood for ten seasons such comments must have sounded grossly unjust. Allan Clarke did not recall this blanket condemnation and also disputes Peter Lorimer's suggestion that Clough spat on the memory of Revie by calling him names: 'He never criticised Don Revie. Never'. Clarke does not deny that Clough was abrasive during his team talk but also recalls instances of unexpected humility:

He admitted that he was absolutely petrified about coming to Leeds. That surprises you, doesn't it? Possibly, what he said at that first meeting was his way of *not* showing us he was petrified. He told us that what he had said about Leeds while he was at Derby County was purely and simply sour grapes. He knew Leeds were the best team in the country. He showed his respect for us by saying that.

If Clough showed flashes of self-effacement then they were quickly obscured by his customary bluntness. Clarke recollects one of his more piercing gibes:

He did say to Eddie Gray that if he'd been a racehorse he'd have been shot five years ago. I laughed at that, but Eddie took it to heart. I suppose I would have done too.

Several others in the camp felt that Clough's words were needlessly insensitive. Among them was the formidable Irish international Johnny Giles, a player for whom Clough reserved his most stinging barbs. Clarke recalls: 'He then had a go at Johnny. He said that he was a vicious player going over the top of the ball'. Giles, a superbly talented midfielder and the mainstay of the Leeds team, was unfazed by such naive criticisms and treated Clough with the silent contempt that he undoubtedly deserved. Hunter and the rest were equally uninterested in belated lessons in football etiquette. They knew their power and their worth.

What Clough expected to achieve through his unnecessarily confrontational display can only be surmised. He could hardly have been foolish enough to believe that seasoned internationals would knuckle down to his insolent aggression like recalcitrant adolescents. The criticisms were an insult not only to their skill and integrity, but their intelligence. Clough seemed to think that the only way to win over the Leeds players was to crush them like ants. It was an absurd and monumentally stupid way for a new manager to act and suggested that Clough was dangerously out of his depth in controlling such a highly organised and professional squad. His own uncertainty about his standing was revealingly summed up in the childish suggestion to his secretary that Revie's desk ought to be burned.

Within three weeks even the crocodile-skinned Clough recognised that he was in dire trouble. His failure to establish a rapport with the players and staff had not escaped the scrutiny of the directors whose countenance grew increasingly stern. Clough responded to the impending crisis by telephoning Peter Taylor and begging his former partner to come to Leeds immediately. 'Name your price', implored the distraught Leeds manager, but Taylor refused to be drawn and elected to remain at Brighton. Instead, Clough found an unlikely ally in Jimmy Gordon who surrendered his job at Derby and loyally reunited with his old sparring partner. Meanwhile, Clough set about restructuring the Leeds team in his own inimitably eccentric style. On 6 August, he broke the Leeds transfer record by signing Duncan McKenzie from Nottingham Forest for £250,000. Most agreed that it was an ill-advised move, for McKenzie was a talented individualist whose style was completely unsuited to the methodical play favoured by Leeds. Two weeks after signing McKenzie, Clough's spending reached the £500,000 mark when he summoned John McGovern and John O'Hare from the reserves at Derby County. In the meantime, he had attempted to offload the brilliant Terry Cooper, a move which appalled the supporters and directors alike. Even the acquiescent

Manny Cussins baulked at the idea and the proposed transfer was soon scrapped. The Leeds fans were not alone in the belief that Clough was intent on destroying the very fabric of the team. The season had barely begun and already Clough was attempting to transform Leeds United into Derby County. Such ructions might have proved tolerable were it not for Clough's failings in the most crucial area of all: scoring League points.

The season began on an uncharacteristic note when Leeds lost their first two League matches to Stoke and QPR. Clough seemed outwardly unconcerned by the shock defeats and brushed aside his critics with a witty riposte: 'Well, we'll just have to win the next 40 matches, won't we?' Clough was fooling nobody who knew the recent history of Leeds. The previous season they had been unbeaten in their first 29 matches, prompting football pundits to proclaim them the greatest club side of all time. It was fully expected that they would start the 1974–75 season like greyhounds, leaving their competitors crawling in the dust and praying that Leeds might somehow overreach themselves in their thirstless quest for trophies. The present scenario was very different and inescapably appalling. Leeds did manage a narrow victory over Birmingham but a return draw with QPR and a shock defeat at the hands of Manchester City saw them plummet to the relegation zone. A home draw against recently promoted and soon-to-be-relegated Luton was the last straw and Clough suffered a barrage of catcalls from the home crowd. Had the supporters owned a crystal ball they would probably have lynched Clough, for the Championship was eventually won with a paltry 53 points. Leeds had never accumulated less than 53 points since returning to the First Division in 1964 and could have had 11 consecutive Championships if every season had been this easy. Thanks to their inept start, the cushiest title for years was frustratingly squandered.

The Leeds directors did not require a fortune teller to prompt their next move. Disturbed by the dreadful turn of events they held a meeting with the players who were given a chance to voice their grievances. Clough was in attendance but left at the request of his more reticent critics. The private trial continued in his absence. Several players felt that such an unprecedented meeting was not the most dignified way for a football club to conduct its internal affairs, but the discussion continued. It was accepted that Clough was an enigmatic manager and his carefree approach and distaste for dossiers jarred with the methodically-minded players schooled under Revie. The critical probing meandered until the unlikely figure of Paul Madeley suddenly lost patience and summarised his feelings about Clough in three startling words: 'He's no good'. The chaotic meeting petered out and the directors retired to reach their inevitable conclusion.

On 12 September 1974 Clough was sacked and his sidekick Jimmy Gordon left shortly afterwards. The entire sorry episode had cost Leeds an estimated £180,000 in compensation. Chairman Manny Cussins provided the expected PR rationale:

What has been done is for the good of the club. The club and the happiness of the players must come first. Nothing can be successful unless the staff is happy.

The following week, Billy Bremner, along with assistant manager Maurice Lindley and coach Syd Owen, picked the team which was conspicuous for the absence of McKenzie, McGovern and O'Hare. As if to show Clough what they could do, Leeds thrashed Sheffield United 5–0. The press was full of references to 'player power', yet none of the players genuinely believed that they were responsible for unseating Clough. Clarke summed up their viewpoint in a quaint aphorism: 'A manager's future is dictated by the board'.

The dismissal from Leeds hardened Clough but also made him less cocksure of his abilities to survive alone. Four months elapsed before he finally returned to football taking over the reins at Second Division Nottingham Forest. The men behind the move were Brian Appleby and Stuart Dryden, a barrister and a magistrate who convinced themselves that they could keep Clough in order.

Clough took office on 6 January 1975 and was joined by Jimmy Gordon several weeks later. McGovern and O'Hare were quickly recalled from Leeds, who were pleased to release the players even at £60,000, less than half the figure they had cost the previous August. Clough struggled for the remainder of the season with Forest finishing in 16th place. Although the team improved steadily, the 1975–76 season was largely a time of consolidation. With Forest in eighth place, Clough realised that his best hope of achieving First Division football lay in a reunion with Peter Taylor. During the summer of 1976 Clough flew to Cala Millor and outlined his proposals to his former partner. Taylor had narrowly failed to win Brighton promotion from the Third Division and, sensing a new challenge, agreed to rejoin Clough.

It is no exaggeration to say that Peter Taylor's arrival transformed Nottingham Forest, for his explosive optimism permeated the entire club. The partnership completely revitalised Clough as well as relieving the burden of mulling torturously over possible transfer deals. With Taylor in attendance, the old maestro was free to concentrate his attention on motivating players and squeezing money from well-meaning directors. During the autumn, Forest bought centre forward Peter Withe from Brighton and centre half Larry Lloyd from Coventry. These were the big men chosen to provide the solid backbone to a promotion-chasing team. For once, Taylor was fortunate in not having to replace more than a handful of players. However, this did not mean that the side was ready-made for the First Division. A considerable amount of restructuring was required before the correct blend of players were neatly slotted into place. Tony Woodcock was moved upfront from midfield and rapidly emerged as a lethal goalscorer. With others, it was not merely a matter of repositioning but remodelling: John Robertson's move to the left wing was preceded by a profound change in his lifestyle. When Taylor first spotted the lad in training he took him aside and accused him of living out of a chip pan before adding that the title 'professional footballer' should be erased from his passport. Robertson was stunned at being dismissed as an overweight loafer but was forced to admit that he had fallen into complacency during seven years at Nottingham Forest. Responding to Clough and Taylor's shock tactics he lost weight, worked harder at his game and emerged as a key figure in Forest's later glories.

Clough and Taylor had a knack of exploiting small, money-spinning competitions as a means of instilling belief in their aspiring youngsters. During the Derby days the Watney and Texaco Cups had served as aperitifs for richer prizes so the managerial duo were keen to compete in the equally irrelevant Anglo-Scottish Cup. In December 1976, Forest found themselves in the final where they overran Leyton Orient 4–0 to take the trophy. Team confidence was now soaring as Forest prepared themselves for a post-Christmas assault on the Second Division Championship. Their prospects took an alarming downswing in February when news filtered through that Taylor and Clough were poised to return to Derby.

The bizarre idea to recall Clough and Taylor was the brainchild of Derby's new chairman George Hardy. With Sam Longson in the descendant, a new board of directors fell victim to the ashen rhetoric of the old protest movement. The ingenuous Hardy began his campaign in earnest but found Clough more demanding than he had anticipated. Taylor, an inveterate Derby supporter, seemed anxious to heal the old wounds and before long there was talk of rejoining the First Division club. Hardy convinced himself that he had won them over but on the day of decision Clough pulled a *volte face* and announced that he would be staying at Nottingham Forest. Hardy was shattered. It was difficult to escape the conclusion that Clough and Taylor had strung along the Derby board in order to exact a belated revenge. However, both parties denied any subterfuge, although the public courting cannot have failed to appease their wounded egos. Amazingly, Derby would later make another attempt to seduce their former employees with surprising results.

Forest enjoyed an impressive late run in the Second Division title race but looked certain to miss promotion by a point. What they required was a minor miracle similar to the circumstances that had won Clough and Taylor their Championship at Derby. Coincidentally, it was Wolverhampton Wanderers that were again cast in the role of unlikely saviours. Five seasons before, Wolves had prevented Leeds from salvaging the draw that they needed to overhaul Derby for the double. Now it was Bolton who sought to steal a point from the Midlands club in order to leapfrog over Forest into third place. As before, Clough and company had already departed on holiday before learning that Bolton had been beaten. Against substantial odds Forest were back in the First Division.

Clough and Taylor's priority after winning promotion was a full scale strengthening of their first team squad. In July 1977 the duo signed troubled Birmingham City forward Kenny Burns. Burns was falsely labelled as a problem child and inveterate gambler and Taylor suspected that the rumours were exaggerated. A known gambler himself, Taylor investigated Burns' background even going to the extraordinary lengths of stalking him at a race meeting. Satisfied that the erring lad was no liability, Nottingham Forest duly won his signature, transferring him from striker to sweeper along the way. Within 12 months the hard man was voted Footballer of the Year.

Taylor was also instrumental in acquiring Peter Shilton from relegated Stoke. As an ex-goalkeeper, Taylor always wanted the best and had spotted Shilton's pedigree many years before. His induction saw the end of Forest's regular keeper John Middleton, who went to Tommy Docherty's Derby in a £100,000 exchange deal for Archie Gemmill. Forest now had the basis of a Championship-winning team, although nobody in the First Division would believe that until early the following year.

Forest emerged as front runners early in the 1977–78 season but the doubters kept insisting that they would fade. A 3–0 hammering by Arsenal in September appeared to confirm their vulnerability, though Taylor blamed the defeat on a sloppy first goal caused by poor marking. The culprit, at least in Taylor's eyes, was Forest's burly centre half Larry Lloyd, one of the most tempestuous players at the club. Incensed by the post-match haranguing he received from Taylor, Lloyd threatened physical retribution and had to be verbally restrained. His short fuse also brought him into occasional conflict with the fiery Clough, most notably after a European game when the twosome had a silly argument over Lloyd's refusal to wear a club blazer. In spite of such aberrations Lloyd proved a sound investment and, according to defender Frank Clark, was less troublesome to Forest than observers supposed:

> Larry Lloyd was a bit of an awkward customer but the management was never afraid to take on a so-called 'problem' player. We had a dressing room full of experienced characters who helped Clough and Taylor a great deal in curbing the wilder instincts of some of the players. That may have happened by accident, but we always felt nothing happened by accident. It rained by their ordination. The dressing room was the key. None of the players could dominate there. If big Lloydy started getting above himself there were eight of us to take him down a peg or two before it ever reached the management. Clough and Taylor knew that you never win anything with a team of nice guys. You need a few characters in order to give the team its character. It's a mistake to have *too* nice a dressing room. What's needed is people in there who'll stir it up.

Forest's blend of experience and youth wrought a confidence which became increasingly noticeable as the season progressed. Forest lost for a third and final time that season in November against Clough's old enemies Leeds. From that point onwards, even Liverpool found it difficult to clutch their coat-tails. By Christmas, Forest had taken a five-point lead, a situation which encouraged Clough to joke: 'The last time Nottingham were five ahead of anybody was in a cricket match'.

Forest's Championship prospects were less threatened by Liverpool and Everton than the potential loss of their inspirational management team. For on 4 December Clough was interviewed for the vacant post of England manager. The defection of Don Revie followed by World Cup elimination forced the FA to seek a permanent manager and Clough was on the shortlist alongside Ron Greenwood, Bobby Robson, Lawrie McMenemy and, surprisingly, director of coaching Allen Wade. Clough was confident, even cocky, about his star performance at Lancaster Gate, although, in reality, he was a rank outsider. Some even claimed that his invitation was nothing more than a public relations exercise on the part of the FA committee. The case against Clough as England manager was overwhelmingly convincing. The selectors were not only seeking an experienced club manager but a diplomat capable of conducting himself with dignity on the world stage. Clough's public outbursts and apparent inability to shut his mouth about controversial football issues was obviously anathema to the conservative committee. Less than a week before his interview Clough had launched an untimely attack on the West Bromwich Albion board for failing to offer their manager a contract. The indignant chairman Bert Millichip retorted that Clough ought to mind his own business, a view with which the selection committee would undoubtedly have concurred. Even more alarming than Clough's vitriolic outbursts was the memory of his disastrous tenure at Leeds United. Surrounded by a squad of internationals, he had not only failed to secure decent results but alienated the players and forced the club to rid themselves of his disruptive influence. The impression remained that although Clough was capable of revitalising downtrodden clubs he was hopelessly out of his depth dealing with experienced internationals on a necessarily part-time basis.

The selectors, backed by the appointee Ron Greenwood, cleverly fobbed off Clough and Taylor with the management of the England youth team. After a year in which they clashed with various officials, the duo resigned this part-time post to concentrate on their increased commitments at Nottingham Forest. Over the next decade Clough's name reappeared occasionally as an outside contender for the England job but even Fleet Street was finally forced to concede that his chance had been and gone. Nottingham Forest continued their surge into the New Year and by February had extended their lead to eight points. Their consistency remained unaffected by injuries or abrupt positional changes on the field. Indeed, Frank Clark argues that Clough's unpredictability undermined opponents as well as instilling arrogance in the elder members of the first team:

They would put round pegs in square holes rather than change a tactical set-up. If you've got adaptable players you can do that. They had John O'Hare playing wide on the right in midfield. Nobody else would have done that. But Clough got away with it. He would dare to do anything. He once put me and Archie Gemmill as a front two which was preposterous – but we won the game 2–0.

Forest's new-found invincibility carried them through to the final of the League Cup where they faced the arduous task of overcoming Liverpool. The first match was a backs-to-the-wall goalless draw, with 18-year-old goalkeeper Chris Woods emerging as Forest's hero. Four days later Nottingham won the replay with a controversial penalty. Clough was quick to offset accusations of good fortune by praising his depleted team and stressing that they had fulfilled his primary aim of quali-fying for Europe. A far greater achievement was recorded three weeks later when Forest clinched the League title in their first season back in the big time. For Clough, this Championship was especially significant for he became only the second man in football history (following the great Herbert Chapman) to win the League title with two different clubs.

The Championship brought hopes of European Cup glory, but Clough could not have hoped for a worse first round draw as Forest found them-selves pitted against holders Liverpool. Few commentators expected Nottingham to survive, even after they had unexpectedly defeated the Merseysiders 2–0 at the City Ground. Although under tremendous pressure in the return at Anfield, Forest somehow managed to keep a clean sheet and record a famous victory. The defeat of Liverpool was the first sign that their buccaneering style of football had been replaced by a new expediency. Frank Clark recalls the changes:

> The year we won the title we got people forward and ran teams off the pitch. Then we developed an almost European style very close to the way Liverpool play. The management developed that initially in order to play against Liverpool. We would tend to sit back with nine men behind the ball and invite teams to come at us. For many years Liverpool had been the masters of soaking up punishment. We developed that and 'out-Liverpooled' Liverpool!

Clough and Taylor were never short of innovation and stunned the football world by introducing the concept of the mid-season break. Much has been made of the management's nonchalant attitude towards training during these winter breaks in Majorca but Frank Clark remembers that it was not all beer, sun and fun:

> It depended on the situation. Often it was a case of having a few beers and relaxing but we trained very hard out there. Harder than we trained at home. It certainly wasn't a complete rest. At other times they'd take us away and keep tight control over things socially. It seemed *ad hoc* but it was all very deeply and carefully thought out.

The freewheeling style enabled Forest to continue their winning ways until December 1978 when Liverpool finally beat them 2–0. It was their first defeat since November 1977 ending an incredible record-breaking run of 42 League matches unbeaten. A second Championship seemed likely for Forest, but they were outpaced by Liverpool who went on to break the First Division points record. Football records continued to tumble that season when Nottingham again smashed the British transfer record by signing Trevor Francis from Birmingham for £975,000. With VAT and additional levies the total cost was £1,150,500 ensuring Francis' immortality as the UK's first million-pound player. With his squad replenished, Clough continued his assault on two Cup fronts. In March 1979, Forest again reached the League Cup final where they encountered Southampton. It was a strangely topsy-turvy match with Southampton outplaying Nottingham in the first half and taking a 1–0 lead courtesy of David Peach. However, Forest found their legs after half-time and two goals by Birtles and one by Woodcock put the tie beyond Southampton's reach. In retrospect, the most intriguing aspect of the match was not the events on the pitch, but Clough and Taylor's eccentric preparatory tactics. Instead of ensuring that their lads were tucked up in bed early the previous evening, the management duo had insisted on plying them with bottles of champagne. Frank Clark recalls this extraordinary evening:

> When we got to the hotel they looked at the players and decided that they had to do something to relax everybody. Top level sport is played in the mind and if you're tense and uptight you can't perform to your full potential. They knew we'd be up for the day anyway. What they didn't want was us staying awake all night worrying. It was a natural thing for them to do but it was all calculated. It was psychology, a wild stab. You could only do that if you were very sure of your position. One or two of the lads weren't used to drinking champagne and we certainly didn't start off very well against Southampton!

Even more champagne flowed in May when Forest reached the final of the European Cup at their first attempt. The Swedish side Malmo played a tight game but Nottingham refused to be ruffled and won the trophy through a single goal from Trevor Francis. Following the match, Clough summed up another remarkable triumph:

> As far as my career is concerned tonight is a marvellous milestone, but it doesn't mean as much as the First Division title. The first time we did that at Derby was the highlight of my life and nothing will surpass it.

Clough and Taylor ended their second First Division season by signing a new four-year contract with Nottingham Forest. After years of turmoil, Clough at least had found managerial stability.

For a brief period in the 1979–80 season Clough seemed set for a battle royal with his board of directors over some unflattering comments he had made on the trials and tribulations of football management. Several directors felt personally affronted by his words and Clough had experienced enough problems in the past to realise the consequences of his conduct. After several weeks' silence he decided to play the humble diplomat and issued an official apology describing his outburst as 'not befitting a manager'. Self-effacement has never been Clough's strong point but on this occasion he displayed an astute understanding of the need for political caution. In future his clashes with the board would be more measured and invariably incisive.

1980 was to prove the end of Clough's recent golden era. A third consecutive League Cup final saw Forest denied by a plucky Wolves revelling in their role as underdogs. The European quest proved more fruitful, however, and Clough emulated Bob Paisley's achievement in winning the trophy two seasons in succession. With an inspired display of sustained defensive football, Forest held Hamburg at bay for most of the match having taken an early lead. It was the last trophy that Clough and Taylor ever won together.

It is difficult to determine precisely when the rift began between Clough and Taylor. The intensity of their shared passion for football created the semblance of a deep friendship that was all too often illusory. Outside the club gates they were little more than acquaintances and, like many great partnerships, they had a sufficient store of ill-feeling to subvert the largely positive aspects of their friendship. Once relations between them began to deteriorate, it was all too easy to rewrite the past from a detached viewpoint and seize upon the fleeting bad times as evidence of perennial disaffection. What happened at Nottingham Forest, however, more closely resembled an insidious disillusionment as each partner outgrew the other. The complementary aspects of their personality, which had worked so effectively in fashioning Championship-winning teams from undiscovered kids and bargain veterans, was now completely disjointed. No doubt, age and sated ambition played their part, particularly for Taylor who was six years older than Clough and had fulfilled his need to prove to the footballing authorities that his methods worked. Having won two Championships and a couple of European Cups was there any point in a wealthy 53-year-old with a heart condition driving himself into the grave? Taylor's greatest strength had been his talent-spotting but this was no mere innate ability but the product of endless hours spent traipsing across the country following up questionable tips and half-hunches and laboriously cataloguing the progress of obscure players and potential transfer bargains. In his final period at Forest, Taylor's characteristic thoroughness had been weakened by complacency and the cut-price players of yore had been replaced by a tiny herd of white elephants. The promising Asa Hartford found it difficult to adjust to the system at Forest, causing Clough to comment: 'He is running about all over the place with no discipline in his play'. Two months after arriving in Nottingham, Hartford was abruptly despatched to Everton forcing Taylor to admit that he had blundered: 'Hartford is one hell of a player and will fit in well somewhere. But Forest are too big to change their pattern for one player'. In February

1982, expensive strikers Justin Fashanu and Ian Wallace were also listed as potential transfers. Once again, Taylor admitted that they were not the right players for Forest. Whether such errors of judgement affected his decision is debatable, but two months later Taylor announced his retirement: 'I have been in football for 36 years and it is having its effect on me now'. For the first time since those dark days at Leeds, Clough was forced to carry on alone.

The relationship between Clough and Taylor was not improved by the latter's decision to emerge from retirement seven months later to manage Derby County. Clough was infuriated by the decision which he subsequently seemed to regard as treacherous, even though Taylor had offered to rekindle the partnership. The football gods responded to this managerial rivalry by engineering an FA Cup draw which paired Derby and Forest. Clough desperately wanted to win this grudge match but it was Taylor's Second Division opponents who triumphed. Derby were finally despatched by eventual Cup winners Manchester United but returned the following year to reach the quarter-finals. In spite of such impressive Cup runs, their League form remained indifferent and at the end of the 1983–84 season they were ensnared in the relegation net. Taylor had previously won a vote of confidence from his directors, but a new board demanded his head. The Clough/Taylor/Derby saga had finally ended on an anti-climactic note.

Clough's record at Nottingham Forest in the post-Taylor years has not been unimpressive. Despite various financial cutbacks, the club has remained in the top flight throughout the 1980s playing attractive football which has been warmly praised by Clough's critics. In spite of all the changes, however, Frank Clark recognises a familiar pattern:

> They still play in the same style where they concede space to you in your own half and funnel back behind the ball. Why they look a more attractive side now is because they've got extra pace in the team. When they hit you on the break they look great. But it's still just a slight variation on an old tactic. It's actually a very unsophisticated way of playing. They pass the ball and say: 'We'll let you play your own game because we think we're better'. When it comes unstuck they get a good hammering. Liverpool beat them 5–0 and everybody said it was a great display but they were able to do that because Forest allowed them to play and on that night Liverpool were much better individually. We had a classic game with them here [at Leyton Orient] because they do allow you to play!

Clough's continued success at Forest appears to have given the lie to the theory that he needed a partner to thrive. It should be noted, however, that Clough has surrounded himself with a number of men who have grown up alongside him at Forest. Alan Hill and Ronnie Fenton are far from yes-men and have established themselves sufficiently to argue with Clough and question his decisions where necessary. In a sense, they have taken over the complementary role that was previously the preserve of Taylor.

Although Clough need hardly worry about his standing in modern football it is noticeable that he has won only one major trophy as a solo manager: the Littlewoods Challenge Cup in 1989. After a decade of generally appalling FA Cup results, Forest finally broke their hoodoo in 1988 and 1989 when they reached the semi-finals. Sentimentalists waxed eloquently on Clough's desire to win that elusive trophy but Kenny Dalglish's Liverpool put paid to such vain hopes on both occasions. Clough's other major frustration has been the lost opportunities to experience international football management. No doubt he has long despaired of the England job but approaches from Eire and Wales have each tantalisingly passed. How Clough must have envied Jack Charlton in inspiring the Republic of Ireland to an historic victory over Bobby Robson's England in the European Championship. Had Clough been at the helm for that one his supporters in Fleet Street would probably have stormed FA headquarters. The Wales saga was almost equally frustrating, for Clough had clearly set his heart on the job. At one point he threatened to quit Forest if they refused him permission to accept the part-time post, but the directors called his bluff. Surprisingly, Clough resisted any temptation to criticise their decision publicly, remaining mysteriously tight-lipped throughout the affair. Clearly, his security at Nottingham Forest was uppermost in his mind and in May 1988 he signed a new two-year contract to extend his 13-year reign at the City Ground.

The prospect of Clough taking another management job becomes less likely with each passing season. Although Nottingham Forest have now been a limited company since June 1982, Clough still wields enormous influence at boardroom level. He has helped make Forest a stable yet friendly club with a family atmosphere which has been enhanced by the presence of his son Nigel, who has emerged as an exciting talent in his own right. Even a million-pound offer from abroad proved insufficient to buy the loyalty of Clough jnr. However, whether father and son will ever share a League Championship or FA Cup trophy remains to be seen. Brian Clough is now the same age as Taylor when he retired, so why does he carry on? Frank Clark has one convincing answer:

> He keeps going because he needs it. It's like a drug to him, but I don't think he'll go anywhere else. The club ticks over so smoothly now it virtually runs itself. What helps him is his style of management. His forte now is coming in after they haven't seen him for a few days and lifting the whole tempo of the club by his presence. When he walks through the door the atmosphere is electric. Not being there every day has helped him retain that intensity in the dressing room on match days. He still gets a great buzz out of the game and he needs that.

In summing up Clough's career it must be said that his achievements at Derby and Nottingham Forest are without parallel in the modern game.

No other manager has established two Championship squads from lowly Second Division clubs with limited resources and, in the age of the Super League, Clough's record is unlikely to be equalled.

BOBBY ROBSON
THE ROAD TO LANCASTER GATE

Robert William Robson may well be the last of the great 'coal mining' managers of British football. The mining communities of Scotland and the Northeast provided the backbone of great managerial talent in the UK stretching back to the early years of Matt Busby. Robson's family background is uncannily similar to those of his elder counterparts and reads like a self-consciously scripted manual for footballing success.

He was born on 18 February 1933 in the village of Sacriston, County Durham. His parents were strict Methodists who valued the puritan work ethic and reared their five children (all boys) to respect traditional family values. Robert's father, Philip, spent most of his life underground yet did not seek the escapist leisure activities usually associated with such a high risk occupation. Like Bill Shankly's father, he neither smoked tobacco nor drank alcohol and prided himself on an exemplary attendance record at work, which was all the more remarkable considering the health hazards associated with mining. Within months of Robert's birth the family moved to nearby Langley Park where they settled. Young Robson was the typical soccer mad youth who spent most of his free time enjoying street football. Like most schoolchildren he failed the 11-plus and was installed at the local secondary modern. His footballing pretensions might well have ended at that point, for Langley Park was not affiliated to any of the local school soccer leagues. It says much for Robson's enthusiasm that he was not offput by lack of competitive play but continued to train alone, honing his skills with rudimentary routines which would rapidly transform him into a player of poise and strength. He attended a couple of unsuccessful trials at the age of 15 but soldiered on and by 1950 found himself under observation from half a dozen prominent clubs.

Initially, Robson intended to remain in the Northeast with either Newcastle United or Middlesbrough but, like Bobby Charlton, he was eventually wooed southwards. The club that won his signature was Fulham, freshly promoted from the Second Division and eager to pit their skills against local rivals Chelsea. In those days, before freedom of contract, untried youngsters could not rely on football to provide a decent living, so Robson wisely elected to continue his apprenticeship as an electrical engineer. The dual commitment proved extremely taxing for a young kid fresh from school and still unused to life in the big city. Robson's increasingly noticeable weariness finally attracted the attention of Fulham manager Bill Dodgin, who advised him to choose between engineering and professional football. Robson was mature enough to discuss the implications with his parents before making the brave decision to stay in soccer.

Robson signed for Fulham in 1951, having avoided National Service due to ear trouble. Interestingly, his team-mate Johnny Haynes also boasted less than perfect ears, so Fulham fortuitously retained two of their best young signings from the period. Like most of the youngsters at Fulham, Robson was taken in hand by Bill Dodgin whom he remembers as a kind man with an engagingly positive approach to the game. In common with many managers of the period, Dodgin had a ready-made list of catch-phrases at his command and could frequently be heard screaming: 'The ball is round, pass it around'. He taught the boys the importance of perseverance and morale and his geniality was crystallised in another sporting aphorism: 'Happy when you win, smile when you lose'. Such managerial stoicism no doubt contributed to Fulham's strangely erratic form. Without doubt, Fulham were one of the great enigmas of English football. Amid their playing ranks were some of the most colourful names of the period, yet the side was perpetually troubled by relegation worries. At their best they were capable of beating the finest First Division side, but poor organisation blighted their progress. Their comic, music hall image was reinforced by the presence of chairman Tommy Trinder, a top comedian much loved by the London public. Trinder's infectious affection for the club translated itself to the supporters who always turned out to watch Fulham, even as they plummeted to the foot of the First Division. There were some glorious moments during Robson's first season, however, particularly in the FA Cup where Fulham were paired with rivals Chelsea in a fiercely fought fifth round encounter. After drawing 1–1 at Stamford Bridge, Fulham won the replay at Craven Cottage 3–0. Suddenly, the fans were dreaming of Wembley but their ever unpredictable team went out in the next round to finalists Blackpool. Given their individual flair and cultured play, it was surprising that Fulham did not enjoy even longer Cup runs in the 1950s. Tommy Trinder would back them heavily and inspired the same kind of media interest that Watford enjoyed after the appointment of the flamboyant Elton John. Alas, Trinder's witty ripostes were not sufficient to forestall Fulham's relegation in 1952.

Robson was not unduly concerned about dropping down to the Second Division mainly because Fulham retained its optimistic air and there was no great turnover of disaffected players. On the contrary, the club could reasonably boast one of the best teams in their Division.

They had inherited the uproarious Charlie Mitten from Manchester United after Matt Busby refused to allow him to play for the club. Mitten had been one of several players who sought his fortune in Bogota, a decision guaranteed to alienate the over-scrupulous United manager. A born comedian, Mitten's wayward behaviour was better suited to Fulham, which did little to quell his eccentric antics on the field. Mitten found kindred spirits in Tosh Chamberlain and goalkeeper Tony Macedo. Chamberlain was not averse to clowning on the wing and on more than one occasion actually left the field for a couple of minutes, which greatly amused the supporters. Macedo was also known to stop the heart of his manager when he indulged in a spot of acrobatic ball practice in the penalty area. It was small wonder that the crowds flocked to see the Saturday show.

Robson was more studious than his more outrageous team-mates but formed a sturdy striking partnership with inside forward Bedford Jezzard. As Robson grew older, he fell under the influence of the more tactically-minded members of the Fulham squad. Amazingly, Fulham not only included entertainers but budding theoreticians, most notably the garrulous, hard-working and knowledge-thirsty Jimmy Hill. Having trained under England manager Walter Winterbottom, Hill was already a good bet for success as a coach and manager. However, it was his organisational and administrative skills, particularly in his negotiations over the maximum wage, which would later propel him to media prominence. Robson listened attentively to his views and became even more intrigued by the potential for coaching after witnessing England's famous 6–3 Wembley defeat at the hands of the Hungarians. That match, in 1953, was a watershed in the history of British football, causing many managers to abandon the old-fashioned 'WM' formation in favour of the short pass and an open 4–2–4 game. Among the Wembley throng on that eventful evening was an entranced Ron Greenwood, another Winterbottom disciple who realised he was witnessing a fundamental shift in tactical thinking. In 1956, Greenwood left Championship-winning Chelsea to join Second Division Fulham and for a time the team contained two future England managers. Robson meanwhile immersed himself in the FA coaching courses which had risen in popularity since the Hungarian humiliation. Fulham contained a minor academy of football brains yet inexplicably remained a middling Second Division side. Their teamwork still displayed a discernible laxity and yet there was Johnny Haynes, boy idol, goalscorer extraordinaire and one of the best passers ever seen in the game. Fulham's flair was virtually tangible but somehow they failed to mount a consistent promotion challenge during the remainder of the 1950s.

Financial considerations finally convinced the Fulham board that they ought to sell Robson, who was swiftly picked up by West Bromwich Albion for £25,000 in 1956. Robson initially found it difficult to settle in the Midlands and his return to First Division football began with a resounding 4–0 defeat. The culprits were Manchester City, spearheaded by that shrewd tactician Don Revie, who was playing as a deep-lying centre forward in blatant imitation of the all-conquering Hungarians. Now three future England managers were caught up in soccer's latest tactical revolution. Robson's education continued when he was selected to play for his country against France in November 1957 and scored twice as England won 4–0. The experience enabled him to witness first-hand the work of Walter Winterbottom whom he learned to respect as an intelligent, meticulous professional with a flair for oration:

> Walter had a great depth of knowledge about the game and could impart it. He was down-to-earth and could keep in touch with the common player. He said things about football I could understand. He was an educationalist, never swore, kept things temperate and was a good man.

The quiet, almost professorial dignity and tactical rigour that Winterbottom espoused greatly impressed Robson and would be remembered later when he assumed the post of England manager. The goal hero of 1957, however, was disappointed to discover that he had been relegated to the reserves for the next international the following year. It was a particularly odd decision by Winterbottom, for England had just lost three prized internationals in the Munich air disaster. Two-goal Robson retrieved his place in time for the World Cup group matches against the USSR and Austria and, but for a couple of disallowed goals, would have taken his country into the quarter-finals.

Back at West Bromwich Albion, Robson was gradually acclimatising himself to the lack of razzmatazz that he had come to love at Fulham. Albion were a better organised club and, significantly, had appointed one of the best managers of the era: Vic Buckingham. Another master tactician, Buckingham had learned his trade under Arthur Rowe, whose push and run Spurs side had won the League title in 1951. Like Rowe, Buckingham had experienced Continental football having previously coached Ajax Amsterdam. Renowned as one of the game's great thinkers, Buckingham was also an exceptionally strong personality who could be a tough disciplinarian when players challenged his authority. Moreover, like Winterbottom, he fancied himself as a rhetorician. In later years, when he assumed the managership of England, a couple of Robson's less attentive players unkindly dubbed him 'Mogadon', in memory of his long-winded team talks. However, Robson's ramblings were essays in abridgement compared to those of the loquacious Buckingham who had the verbal stamina of a university lecturer. Robson was duly impressed by this talkative tactician who was one of the first managers to play open, attractive European football, adopting the Hungarian 4–2–4 system along the way. Albion were a formidable League and Cup side during the late 1950s but lost their edge when Buckingham was sacked after being named in a divorce action. The moral scheme for football managers has changed little since then, as

Tommy Docherty was to discover when he was ousted from Manchester United for a similar transgression a couple of decades later.

Robson stayed at Albion for a further three years after Buckingham's dismissal, but the club was never quite the same. A dispute over wages saw Robson replaced as captain by Don Howe and in August 1962 he was placed on the transfer list. Fulham immediately intervened with an offer of £20,000 and within days Craven Cottage welcomed back one of its young heroes.

Fulham had gone full circle since Robson's departure, having recently returned from the Second Division to resume their customary role as First Division strugglers. Comedian Tommy Trinder was still chairman and the club retained its music hall atmosphere. A much-told joke of the period was the amusing, 'What's black and white and keeps going down? Fulham Football Club'. In the season prior to Robson's appointment, Fulham had experienced their customary thrills and spills and, in a rush of form, they had powered their way to the semi-finals of the FA Cup where they faced double-chasing Burnley. The match went to a replay before unlucky Fulham surrendered 2–1, thereby missing a glamorous all-London Wembley final against the great Spurs. The fleeting glories of the FA Cup predictably distracted Fulham from their League commitments and they slumped to 20th place, missing relegation by a single point. Clearly, they were in deep trouble and Robson could not have been given a more testing First Division appointment.

Bedford Jezzard, Robson's former inside forward partner, had been promoted from the ranks to manager but could do little to change the club's legendary unpredictability. On one memorable occasion, Fulham hammered Ipswich 10–1. A couple of days later, the teams met again and Fulham lost 4–2. Those results summed up the frustration of Fulham's many managers since the War. In spite of their erratic performances, the team continued to attract its fair quotient of stars. The latest prodigy was a cheeky Londoner named Alan Mullery, who looked set to emerge as one of the best wing halves in the game. Yet, within two years, he was despatched to Spurs for £72,500, the money being used to build the Eric Miller stand. Robson was appalled by the decision which he felt severely damaged team morale. More importantly, it led to a confrontation between the management and the board. Poor Bedford Jezzard had been kept in the dark about Mullery's fate and was so indignant about such treatment that he resigned. Coincidentally, he was replaced by Robson's former mentor Vic Buckingham who took it upon himself to knock Fulham into organisational shape.

Buckingham flexed his managerial muscles by attempting to discipline the over-individualistic Fulham stars. He took particular exception to flashy Rodney Marsh who was soon sold to QPR where he blossomed. Buckingham did not distrust flair, however, a point he proved beyond doubt by signing the talented wonder boy Allan Clarke from Walsall. Clarke made his debut against Leeds United, the team that he would later join for a record-breaking transfer fee. Young Clarke was a quiet, some said moody, individual who, by his own admission, 'held back while learning my trade'. Yet, even he could play the comedian in the grand Fulham tradition. When the Londoners won a penalty against Leeds, captain Robson stepped up confidently to take the spot kick. The veteran was flabbergasted when Clarke, a 19-year-old rookie, earnestly admonished: 'Take your time, son!' The Tommy Trinder influence was pervasive and nobody could take Fulham seriously, least of all themselves.

By 1967, Robson realised that it was time to wind down his playing career in favour of a coaching or management post. The prospect of continuing in football had been implanted in Robson's mind as early as 1960 when Walter Winterbottom took him to one side with Don Howe and insisted that both players attend FA coaching courses. Robson was quick to respond to this sound advice:

> It always worried me what I should be doing. Professional footballers think they're going to play for evermore but it can suddenly come to an end and you've got nothing. I knew I had to do something so I qualified as a coach. By the time I finished playing, I had seven to eight years' coaching experience.

Robson's qualifications encouraged him to take a chance. Seizing a rare opportunity to work abroad, he accepted the management of a newly formed Canadian club, Vancouver Royals. His brief was to build a multi-national team of bargain buys but, weeks before the season commenced, the Royals encountered serious financial problems. New backers were sought and, amid the turmoil, a second manager appeared in the form of the legendary Ferenc Puskas. The language barrier, combined with various disagreements over team selection, made Robson's job impossible but there was no question of Puskas being ousted. In the end, Robson threatened to sue the Royals for breach of contract and returned home in disillusionment. His solicitors advised him to stay idle and fight for substantial compensation but Robson could not resist a timely offer from Fulham, who urgently required a new manager. His decision was to prove an astute career move. Ironically, the Vancouver Royals eventually went bust, so Robson would never have won compensation but merely suffered the continued depression of unemployment and mounting solicitors' bills. Now he had the opportunity to transform festive Fulham into a serious footballing force. It was not a task to be envied.

Fulham were already in trouble when Robson returned in January 1968, and four months later they suffered relegation. The slump continued as they plummeted to the foot of the Second Division. Suddenly, the 'What's black and white and keeps going down?' joke no longer brought smiles to the faces of the once-stoical supporters. Not surprisingly, Robson's first managerial job was short-lived and within seven months he was sacked. He has always claimed that his dismissal came at the instigation of the dictatorial director Sir Eric Miller, but it was the results on the field that sealed Robson's fate. Even today, he bristles with indignation at the supposed injustice of the decision:

> I thought it was the worst thing that ever happened to me. I'd been given a three-year contract and I was out in seven months, three of which were out of season! The directors panicked because we weren't on top of the Second Division. It made me very angry, but not bitter. I've never been a bitter person. But I was worried about where I'd gone wrong. Was I too soft with the players? I don't know. I'd gone back to a club I had left and that always makes things difficult.

Before his departure, Robson arranged the lucrative transfer of Allan Clarke, who unexpectedly chose Matt Gillies' Leicester in favour of Matt Busby's Manchester United. Fulham were left with a £150,000 profit and a team that ended up in the Third Division. On paper, Robson's first posting was an unmitigated disaster, but Allan Clarke seemed impressed by aspects of his performance:

> Bobby Robson was a young, inexperienced manager. At the time I went there he was always interested in that side of the game, obviously planning his future. I thought he'd go on to great things because he was a deep thinker about the game and always played like that. He had some good points: he knew the game and had played at the highest level. He was very thorough in his work and seemed able to get the best out of players. He knew exactly what he wanted. Obviously, he didn't get what he wanted, but that's another part of management. It just didn't work out for him. What happened to Bobby didn't surprise me. Nothing surprises me in football. Experiencing the sack at Fulham was important. I think that anyone who hasn't experienced the sack doesn't really know what management's about. Once you've experienced that, you never lose your enthusiasm for the game. I believe it makes you a better manager.

Robson agrees that the sack motivated him to prove his worth to the footballing community and he took the first opportunity to return to the game by applying for a job at unfortunate Ipswich Town. The East Anglian club had rejoined the First Division elite in 1968, but their limited resources made them unlikely candidates for long-term success. However, after three months' unemployment Robson was content enough to be back near the top. Still recovering from the unhappy period at Craven Cottage, he seemed a rather nondescript figure when chairman John Cobbold introduced him to his new players. Mick Mills recalls his own initial impressions:

> He appeared to me a very nervous man who was unsure of himself. I think it stemmed from his earlier experiences of management in Vancouver and at Fulham where he was pushed out. That hurt him a lot. He also knew that he was fourth choice for the Ipswich job. Billy Bingham, Jimmy Scoular and Frank O'Farrell had all turned

it down. So he didn't come in with a lot of confidence. It was a very difficult first two to three years.

Between 1969 and 1972, Robson had a couple of uneasy seasons near the bottom of the table and some dramatic moments in the Ipswich dressing room. Several of the older players, who had been brought up under that stern disciplinarian Bill McGarry, resented their new young manager and sought to test his mettle. As Mills observed: 'There were some wise old boys in the dressing room who would exploit any weakness'. Robson was tested on numerous occasions and soon realised that he could not win over all the dissidents: 'In management terms, I had to get them out before they got me out'. In a bigger club, the obvious answer would have been a speedy transfer but Ipswich's financial state was so parlous that they could not merely offload troublesome players. Robson was expected to wait until fresh talent emerged from the juniors or a bargain replacement was spotted in the lower divisions. In the meantime, he suffered. The insurgents knew that their age and temperament spelled doom and fought the changes that Robson intended to make. The new manager could offer them little assurance: 'They felt their future at the club was short and in truth they were right, but you can have no sentiment in football. If things aren't right, the wheel has to turn'. Robson's chief antagonist was the sturdy defender Bill Baxter, who was not above laughing at the team if they lost. On one occasion he sent Robson a message requesting a bottle of champagne to celebrate a defeat. When quizzed by the press he sneered: 'Ipswich are going to the dogs'. The friction obviously translated itself to the younger players, and Mick Mills recalls hearing whispers that he would be in for a rough ride. The 21-year-old's sole transgression was cocky presumptuousness in accepting Robson's offer of the captaincy. In such an inflammatory atmosphere, it was predictable that tempers would finally explode. When Irish right back Tommy Carroll found himself demoted alongside Baxter, the touch paper was ignited. Robson remembers the day of confrontation:

Every Friday the routine was to put up the team sheet. These two players went to the board, saw they weren't in the side and ripped up the team sheet! That is sacrilege: nobody defaces the players' notice-board. That's an unwritten law of football. They just ripped it apart, came up to me and rammed it in my face as if to say: 'Screw your team'. Suddenly, the thing blew up and there was fisticuffs. In order to protect myself I had to swing, didn't I? They were raging lunatics. They'd seen their names weren't on the team sheet and couldn't accept it. I wasn't proud of it, obviously. I would have avoided it at all costs but it was such an emotive thing. It's the only time it happened in my life and I'd say it's very rare in football. Some managers will have a slanging and swearing match, but not blows!

The big fight special crept into the more gossipy sports columns whose scribes betrayed amused incredulity at the notion of anarchy in homely Ipswich. The effect on the impressionable younger players could have been disastrous but fortunately they rallied around Robson, as Mills remembers:

We thought, 'Good man, you stood up for your rights and dealt with the toughest'. We all respected him for it because the two guys involved were troublemakers.

Not surprisingly, Baxter and Carroll failed to regain their place in the first team and were despatched forthwith. The board, which had been monitoring Robson's problems, provided a much needed vote of confidence with the words: 'Get rid of them'. The pair brought Ipswich £31,000 in transfer fees but as Robson concluded: 'It was a shame because they were very good players'.

Robson admits that it took three years for him to understand the role of the manager and settle in at Ipswich. From the outset, he was keen on developing the youth policy at the club and was extremely fortunate in not having to start from scratch. Chief scout Ray Tyrrell deserves considerable credit for providing Robson with a group of promising local youngsters who would later form the backbone of Ipswich's first team. Trevor Whymark, Mick Lambert, Roger Osborne, Brian Talbot and Colin Harper were all local lads scooped up by the discerning eagle-eyed scout. Tyrrell next brought in his own man Ron Gray and they plundered the Northeast for further talent. Robson was impresed with their system and the quality of their discoveries and eagerly joined in the late-night excursions to obscure football grounds all over the country.

During these transitional years of the early 1970s, Robson kept a tight rein on the purse strings, restricting his buys to the £40–60,000 mid-range bracket. Frank Clark, Jimmy Robertson, Allan Hunter, Rod Belfitt and David Johnson all boasted these modest price tags and it was their arrival that helped keep Ipswich in the First Division while talent emerged gradually from the junior ranks. In the meantime, 17 older players had left, an export to import ratio of over three to one. It was the start of an astonishing transfer programme which established Robson as one of the most successful wheeler-dealers in the modern game. Evidently, it was a reputation not easily won:

Handling the transfer market is difficult. It takes a while to get the business acumen. You're a common footballer, not used to buying and selling shares. Yet, suddenly you've got to be able to talk money and persuade people to sell players. I had to rejuvenate the youth policy, get to know the local schools and personalities, directors and press, personal staff and administration. That took time. I never bought a player unless I saw him. That was my philosophy. Some managers buy blind, I would never do that. How can they do it? You're handling a lot of money and I always felt that you should spend the club's money as though it were your own. At Ipswich I had to be right; it had to work. At the bigger clubs three out of four good signings would be fine, but I could never take that chance. *Every* buy had to come off. Our scouting had to be spot on: no chances, guaranteed players. Character as well as ability.

By the time John Carruthers took over as chief scout, Ipswich were investing a sizeable sum in the youth scheme which would flourish throughout the 1970s, much to the envy of Robson's rivals. Along the way, club discipline improved markedly as the juniors adapted to a routine and standard of behaviour learned from the soccer cradle. Mick Mills maintains that the East Anglian environment and modest nature of the club helped Robson stamp his own personality on the impressionable youngsters:

He organised very well, worked hard and I think that rubbed off on people. He got the best out of players and was fortunate in inheriting a lot of good, young lads who loved the club and were hard workers. They lived in an area of the country where you couldn't be jack-the-lad because nobody wanted to know jack-the-lads. There were no side attractions to make you into the wrong type, so we always got genuine players coming through. There were no superstars and we worked hard at our jobs.

Robson managed to retain many of his emerging stars, most notably Mick Mills who stayed the course for 13 years. Surprisingly, however, Mills suggests that it was not loyalty but circumstance, which kept him at the club. During his early years he seemed a likely transfer candidate and betrayed dissatisfaction with his role in the team. Robson employed him as a man-to-man marker which invariably meant surrendering his favourite full back position to contest the midfield. Mills complained that this prevented him from making any impact at international level and decided to seek a transfer. He maintains that both Manchester United and Leeds expressed interest, and a move to Elland Road seemed irresistible. Leeds were the best club side in England and looked likely to dominate football for years to come. After consulting Robson, however, he learned that a speedy transfer would not be forthcoming:

I was told I would be allowed to leave once a replacement had been found. As a manager now, I look back and wonder whether there was any genuine attempt to replace me.

If Robson was deliberately stalling then his timing could not have been better. After finishing fourth in the League for two consecutive seasons, Mills forgot all about transfers and committed himself to the greater glory of Ipswich. He was also pleasantly surprised to discover that he suddenly preferred playing in midfield. Having stabilised the captaincy, Robson felt more confident about fielding a side of long-term regulars. The biggest threat to Ipswich's success now centred on the manager's own commitment to the club.

The unexpected rise of Ipswich and their non-contracted manager inevitably provoked interest elsewhere. When illness forced Harry Catterick to leave Everton, the Merseyside giants leaned heavily in the direction of Suffolk. Robson wavered momentarily before his employers responded with a breathtaking offer. The Cobbold brothers now knew Robson's worth and in a remarkable commitment of faith offered him a ten-year contract. Ever since his troubled time at Fulham, Robson had placed security before most other managerial considerations so elected to remain with Ipswich. Speculation about his future did not stop in April 1973 for there were several big clubs in urgent need of inspired management. Derby County found themselves thrown into complete chaos in October 1973 following the resignation of Brian Clough and Peter Taylor. A replacement was urgently needed and Robson was one of several managers approached. He took one look at the constitution of the board and backed off in trepidation.

Several months later a far bigger post became available following the sensational resignation of Don Revie from Leeds United. Before assuming the England managership, Revie sought to stabilise Leeds by nominating Johnny Giles as player/manager. Giles was reluctant, however, so Revie turned to Robson and even offered to negotiate his deal. Revie was arguably the most astute businessman in football management history and promised to secure Robson a contract worth over two-and-a-half times his present salary. The Leeds board was equally keen, perceiving in Robson a stable, energetic personality whose dedication rivalled that of their departing supremo. Robson was sorely tempted by the offer, which promised financial security and a team of established internationals. He had less than 48 hours to reach a decision and much to consider. Leeds had just won the Championship in impressive fashion with a record-breaking 29-match unbeaten run from the start of the season. Critics called them the greatest club side of all time and they boasted an organisational efficiency that was the envy of every club in the Football League. Even the top Continental sides made them favourites to win the European Cup in the following season. How could Robson pass over the chance of a lifetime? His doubts stemmed largely from the pressure of following the almighty Don Revie, whose influence on the club was pervasive. Most of the players in the side had come through the youth ranks and never played for another manager. Whether they could adapt to Robson's ways at such a late stage in their careers played on his mind. After much ruminating he declined the offer, rightly recognising that his true forte lay in building a small club rather than taking on a managerial hotseat. Instead of replacing Don Revie, he would attempt to emulate his achievements at humble Ipswich.

Robson must have felt relieved at the start of the following season when his confidence in Ipswich was vindicated. While Revie prepared for his first match as England manager, Ipswich joined the League's front runners. By Christmas, the East Anglians were heading the table and there was talk of their first Championship since the golden days of Alf Ramsey. January saw the Championship speculation replaced by ambitious talk of achieving the double, for Ipswich had knocked out FA Cup holders Liverpool 1–0. Aston Villa were defeated in the next round, which took the Suffolk side to a quarter-final clash against Champions Leeds. They could hardly have asked for a tougher task. It took four gruelling matches of pulsating football before Robson's men emerged from neutral Filbert Street with a narrow 3–2 victory. This exhausting epic inevitably took its toll on their Championship chances as injuries mounted. The FA Cup semi-final against West Ham brought another unwanted replay before the depleted Ipswich squad finally went out 2–1. Robson was furious with the referee whom he felt had disallowed a couple of clear-cut chances. Wisely, he said nothing, for he was already under a charge of bringing the game into disrepute following an argument with Derby's Francis Lee and referee Bob Parkin. In the end, it was Derby County that completed his misery by pipping Ipswich for the Championship by two points. Fourteen years later, Robson still laments that lost opportunity:

> My one regret was not winning a Championship with Ipswich. On three occasions I felt we were the best team in the League but we couldn't win it.

What Ipswich lacked was strength in depth, but they could not afford a second string of expensive stars. If Robson spent £500,000 the turn-stile takings would never justify the outlay. It was an insoluble problem but Robson mastered the impossible equation with expert scouting and meticulous balance sheets. In October 1976 he splashed out £120,000 on Plymouth's Paul Mariner in what he still considers his best buy from an English club. His careful budgeting was rewarded with another two seasons of sustained excellence in which Ipswich finished sixth and third, respectively. The closing months of the 1976–77 season had proven particularly taxing as Robson's future at Ipswich was again under threat. In January, Everton intervened with a renewed bid to transport him to Merseyside. After eight years in East Anglia, the temptation to take up a new challenge was not easily dismissed and when Everton upped the stakes by offering a lucrative ten-year contract, Robson succumbed. Terms were agreed verbally and all that Robson required was 24 hours in which to inform the Ipswich board of his momentous decision. By the early hours of the next morning, however, he was horrified to discover that the story had been leaked to the *Daily Express* whose back page boldly proclaimed: 'Bobby Robson Goes To Everton'. The scoop proved profoundly embarrassing to Robson for he greatly valued his excellent relationship with the Cobbold brothers. Infuriated by Everton's apparent lack of discretion, he terminated negotiations at the last minute and immediately made his peace with the Ipswich board. It was a brave decision, and, for a time, Robson felt that his integrity might be rewarded with the League Championship. Appropriately enough,

Ipswich defeated managerless Everton soon after to maintain their title challenge with a crucial game in hand over leaders Liverpool. The cut and thrust League race went the full distance with Ipswich retaining pole position over Easter. Days later they fielded a team with three reserves and lost to Leeds. With Paul Mariner injured and Kevin Beattie the victim of facial burning following a bizarre bonfire accident at his home, Robson realised his luck had finally run out. Liverpool grimly hung on to take the title by a single point and almost went on to complete the treble. Once again, the Ipswich manager was left to mull over what might have been.

Attempts to lure Robson away from East Anglia continued from far afield. In October 1977, Saudi Arabia offered him an astonishing £70,000 a year to manage their national team, but still he resisted. When Ipswich unexpectedly dropped below mid-table later in the season, that refusal had a haunting ring. Fortunately, Ipswich's desultory League form was not reflected in their FA Cup games. For once, they received some relatively easy draws and sped towards the quarter-finals where they produced one of their finest performances of the season to demolish Millwall 6–1. The game was marred by disgraceful behaviour from a section of the Millwall fans who attempted to avenge their impending defeat with a hail of bricks. Following the match, Robson suggested his own solution to the hooligan menace: 'Turn the flame throwers on them!' This unguarded comment, made in the privacy of the directors' lounge, was picked up both by the press and the BBC, much to Robson's later embarrassment. His inflammatory aside caused a minor stir but, in truth, was little worse than the comments of other leading soccer managers who were invariably demanding the re-introduction of the birch and salutary custodial sentences for first time offenders.

The FA Cup semi-final saw Ipswich paired with Robson's former club West Bromwich Albion. It was a hard, gutsy confrontation which exploded into life early in the first half when Brian Talbot scored Ipswich's opening goal. Soon after, he was involved in an accidental clash of heads with Albion's John Wile and had to be removed from the field with concussion. Wile himself was streaming with blood but determined to carry on. There was no doubting Albion's bravery and, even after Mick Mills added a second goal in the 20th minute, Robson knew the match was far from over. West Brom responded with a penalty and pushed hard for an equaliser before being killed off by a late John Wark goal. After the match Robson celebrated his first semi-final victory with a tribute to the 'the old stagers Hunter and Mills'.

Ipswich completed their League programme only three points clear of the relegation zone so it was hardly surprising that fifth-placed Arsenal were firm favourites to lift the FA Cup. The bookies lengthened their odds during Wembley week when the East Anglians looked in complete disarray. Their injury-hit squad was at last approaching full strength when Robson announced his intention to recall the talented Colin Viljoen in favour of the popular Roger Osborne. The players resented this decision and vented their feelings in a lacklustre League match against Aston Villa, which they lost 6–1. Robson was angered by a display which he now claims was the worst he saw in 13 years as manager of Ipswich:

> Our best player was the 17-year-old apprentice goalkeeper, Paul Overton, who was making his debut. That tells you how badly the rest of the team played. Whatever you say about Ipswich, we'd always had 11 honest players who tried, but on that day their play showed that they didn't agree with my decision. I could see it after 20 minutes; we were 3–0 down by then. I rammed into them and said they hadn't been fair to Viljoen. It was a dreadful performance, especially just before a Cup final. Arsenal must have been laughing their heads off.

Robson denies that he acceded to the players' resentful whims, but there can be little doubt that they sabotaged his intended team selection. Ipswich captain Mick Mills, now a manager himself, surprisingly still supports the players' rebellious action:

> I was involved and I think we were right. It was proven we were right. He made the decision in the end and he made the right one. Our protest was correct and so was his decision. He could easily have said: 'I'm the boss. Up yours!' Everybody thinks a manager has to take the hard line but it isn't always right. You've got to be logical and let players know you're fully aware of what's going on and have given things a lot of thought. If he'd put too much emphasis on his authority, we might not have won the Cup.

Robson uses remarkably similar sophistry to gloss over his helplessness in the face of what was undoubtedly a crude players' revolt:

> I made my own choice! It was either Viljoen or Osborne. Viljoen was clearly the better player technically, he was exceptional. Osborne was a players' player, a solid workhorse, likeable and good for the team. I had to make sure that the team that went to Wembley was our best side. I wanted to win there. Because of the way they played against Aston Villa, Viljoen was too big a gamble. Maybe it was player power to a degree. Certainly, it was unfair on Viljoen, but Osborne was in.

The Viljoen/Osborne affair emphasised that even a manager of Robson's stature was subject to expediency in the pursuit of a trophy. In the event, the established midfield proved their worth against Arsenal. Robson described the final as a fairy tale for Roger Osborne who not only retained his place, but scored the only goal of the match. With only 13 minutes of the game remaining, the lad was buried beneath an avalanche of congratulatory bodies and had to be removed from the pitch after suffering a unique combination of 'emotion and sunstroke'. For Robson, the FA Cup was the culmination of nine years' hard work, vigilant scouting and careful husbandry, all of which had transformed a low budget club into worthy and consistently excellent winners.

Victory at Wembley did not distract Robson from the disturbing League performances of recent months. Ipswich had finished a lowly 18th and the possibility of further decline was underlined when Nottingham Forest trounced them 5–0 in the Charity Shield. With the dependable Hunter and Beattie paralysed by knee injuries and the disaffected Viljoen sold to Manchester City, reinforcements were urgently needed. The youth policy continued to throw up promising talent in the form of Alan Brazil, Russell Osman and Terry Butcher but the team required an additional touch of flair and experience. A new buy was long overdue and Robson found the perfect candidate during a close season tour of Holland. Arnold Muhren of Twente Enschede was a superbly fit and exceptionally talented player whose passing ability was breathtakingly accurate. Equally important to Robson was his price tag: a bargain £150,000. The outlay was recouped when Brian Talbot was transferred to Arsenal for a staggering £450,000. With money in the bank, Robson returned to Twente Enschede in February 1979 to secure Frans Thijssen for £220,000. It was an inspired move to pair Muhren and Thijssen, for all foreign players are apt to fall victim to loneliness and isolation in unaccustomed surroundings. The culture shock of East Anglia was severely lessened by the mutual support that the Netherlands team-mates offered one another and this was duly reflected in their match performances. Spurs had employed the same psychology in pairing Ardiles and Villa and both clubs benefited from their respective twin imports.

The Dutch duo brought a new sophistication to Ipswich's play which ensured respectably high positions in the League for the remainder of the 1970s. During the same period, Ipswich twice reached the quarter-finals of the FA Cup before losing to Liverpool and Everton, respectively. The side was now at its peak and began the 1980–81 season with a winning flourish which augured well for the approaching winter. Robson was pleasantly surprised to find himself still in England and contesting a title race, for only months before he had seemed destined for Spain. Barcelona had wooed him with a two-year contract worth £80,000 per annum. With lucrative bonuses Robson could reasonably expect an annual income in the six-figure bracket. The stoic John Cobbold had accepted his manager's decision but rightly claimed £200,000 compensation from the Spaniards. What seemed a watertight deal suddenly sprang holes, as Robson resignedly recalls:

> They wouldn't pay the £200,000! Barcelona *never* buy a coach. That was their attitude. The club was so powerful and magnificent that they felt they were already doing me a favour. It was a golden opportunity and I felt that in view of the hard work I'd put in at Ipswich that they'd say: 'Thank you very much. Off you go!' Instead, they took a hard stance. I understood it. I could have resigned and taken the job one month later but then I would have lost my reputation in

the area and maybe in football generally. A contract is a contract and I decided to honour it.

Even nine years later, Robson still regrets missing out on a move that would have completed his footballing education: 'It can never be, but the one thing I would have liked was two or three years abroad, as Terry Venables has done'.

It was some consolation for Robson that his team performed so well in Europe that season. Victories over Aris Salonika, Bohemians Prague, Widzew Lodz, St Etienne of France and Cologne took Ipswich to the UEFA Cup final for the first time in the club's history. Progress in the domestic competition was equally impressive as Ipswich pursued their own version of the treble. Early in the New Year they topped the League and drew title rivals Aston Villa in the third round of the FA Cup. A narrow 1–0 victory proved a curse in disguise, for the Midlanders were now free to concentrate on collecting League points while Ipswich faced a fixture list of Everest proportions. The East Anglians peaked in February, winning a string of matches which brought the treble within striking distance. As so often happens in such campaigns, however, fatigue and injury took their toll and at the end of March Ipswich surrendered two successive League matches to Manchester United and Leeds. Four days later, they lost again to West Bromwich Albion and the following week their FA Cup run ended in the semi-finals where Manchester City scraped through 1–0. The domestic double was now history.

Ipswich's title chances seemed dead and buried but, amazingly, they journeyed to rivals Aston Villa and won. It was their third victory over Villa during the season and now they needed only to pick up a handful of points from their remaining fixtures to fend off the Midlanders' challenge. Regrettably, however, they conspired to lose their last four League games in a heartbreaking close to the title race. The general feeling that Villa had virtually won the trophy by default was reinforced by their own anti-climactic final game at Highbury which they lost 2–0. Robson still grimaces at the memory of Ipswich's suicidal run-in to title oblivion:

Aston Villa! We beat them! Home and away! The League was ours! We were the better team but they actually won the title. They had a greater depth of players than us and Ron Saunders could put in more experienced men. When we came to a rocky period of injuries I had to play inexperienced youngsters. They'll do it for you in one match but not nine or ten. We were always two or three players short of a class squad. I should have won the treble that year.

Robson was not the first manager to lose the treble but the circumstances of his failure deserve scrutiny. Like his great predecessor Don Revie, Robson suffered ill luck, abnormally high injury lists and, perhaps most crucially, a lack of the managerial killer instinct. Both managers betrayed considerable tension in the dug-out and their teams seldom received their just deserts in cabinet silver. Like Leeds, Ipswich often gave the impression that even if a trophy was presented to them they might still find some way of losing it. Their late season fatigue was mirrored in the visage of their harried, overworked manager who had all-too-often slogged the length and breadth of Britain in order to keep the youth induction scheme at peak momentum. Robson's scrupulous industry and unflagging leadership were unquestionably admirable qualities but in strictly managerial terms they may also have been counter-productive. Mick Mills argues that the over-vigilant Robson was sometimes his own worst enemy:

> The one thing he never learned was delegation. When he came in he wanted to do everything himself and when he left he was still trying to do everything. This happened later as England boss too. Whether it was a lack of confidence in people around him I don't know. A lot of the time we felt he didn't recognise the good points in people or instil confidence by giving them their head. I particularly remember when he was confronted with losing Bobby Ferguson to Millwall. Bobby would only stay if he was made first team coach and that's when the manager asked Cyril Lea to step aside. But, having made a difficult decision, he then didn't recognise Bobby Ferguson's strengths quickly enough. He wouldn't give him complete control of the training and coaching. We always felt things went better when the manager was the overlord and Bobby Ferguson was the coach. That typified how he never really learned to delegate work in the right area.

Mills' reading may not be enough to suggest a fatal flaw in Robson's managerial make-up but there does seem evidence of organisational autocracy. The extent to which this may have undermined Ipswich's over-ambitious three-pronged thrust for silverware remains an intriguing, although ultimately indeterminable, consideration.

Robson was becoming frustrated with his growing reputation as the 'nearly man' of soccer management and desperately wanted another trophy to rest alongside the solitary FA Cup. Having failed to emulate Alf Ramsey's celebrated Championship feat at Ipswich, he was doubly determined to secure the UEFA Cup. His weary squad was placed under severe psychological pressure when their manager deliberately refused to refute rumours of a move to Manchester United. Lawrie McMenemy had recently declined the lucrative post, leaving Robson as the bookmakers' favourite. In reality, the proposed departure proved nothing more than a red herring designed to shock the team into providing a superhuman performance. The distracting talk of managerial moves might easily have upset the players' concentration to disastrous effect, but Robson was prepared to gamble for victory:

> I was trying to get the last bit out of the players at the end of a long season. I took a chance. Sometimes, you have to do that.

The team responded magnificently to Robson's rallying cry and tore into the Dutch side AZ 67 Alkmaar, scoring three first leg goals without response. The UEFA Cup seemed won but the talented Dutch proved a different proposition on their home ground. The gaping deficit forced them into attack from the opening whistle but four minutes into the game Frans Thijssen found space and effectively ended his country-men's hopes with a typically opportunistic goal. Even at 4–0 down AZ were not finished and played some spectacular attacking football before finally surrendering 5–4 on aggregate. Robson had won his second trophy at last.

During the summer of 1981, the Cobbold brothers rewarded Robson with an updated three-year contract, but his days at Ipswich were drawing to a close. He made one final tilt at that elusive League Championship only to discover Liverpool back at their brilliant best. Even as Ipswich settled into runners-up position, the Football Association had reached a momentous decision that was to rob the club of its finest managerial servant. The FA Committee had long since decided to appoint a manager of England who could also deputise as head of coaching in the old tradition of Walter Winterbottom. Following the retirement of Ron Greenwood, they made the logical decision of approaching Robson whose track record at Ipswich and exemplary behaviour in football generally made him a worthy successor. Patrick Cobbold was disappointed to lose his long-serving team manager and at one point made the rather fanciful suggestion that Robson might be able to do both jobs! However, the Cobbolds proved surprisingly cooperative throughout the transition and, in complete contrast to their dealings with Barcelona, neglected to request compensation. As Robson explained: 'It was patriotism. Duty calls. Barcelona meant nothing to my chairman, but England did. They didn't ask for a penny!'

After leaving Ipswich, Robson often stressed the financial stability that had accompanied his reign there. In October 1982, however, accounts were released indicating that the club had made a seasonal loss of £173,395. Strangely, the cost-conscious Robson was unaware of this fact, and seemed flabbergasted by the implications:

> Are you sure? In my last year, we lost money? We finished second in the League and made a loss? I can't believe it! It upsets me. Through-out my career in management I was building a football club as well as a team. I made money. All I can say is that we must have paid a big cheque out for the completion of a stand or something. The money wouldn't be 'lost' on the playing staff or players. It would have been spent on the club.

Robson's vagueness emphasises the crucial point that, for all their finan-cial juggling, football managers are seldom avid readers of balance sheets or accountants' annual reports. The loss is also a worrying indictment of the difficulties facing a poorly supported club, even one which rests near the top of the First Division.

Financial considerations relating to the buying and selling of players were now a thing of the past for Robson. As England manager, it was his team selections and motivational skills which suddenly took priority. Nevertheless, there was a touch of the frugal detectable in his initial policy decisions. Cossetted internationals perceived a streak of puritanism in the revised training sessions which required them to turn out regularly on Sundays. Even worse was the loss of their sumptuous West Lodge Hotel accommodation in favour of a new training centre whose relative sparseness almost provoked a players' revolt. Bisham Abbey boasted excellent sporting facilities, but the cramped bedroom conditions, lack of room service, and unavailability of private telephones proved intolerable. Robson accepted the moans with good grace and compromised by booking the players into a local Crest hotel. It was his first act of diplomacy as England manager and won over the hardier characters in the squad.

One person whom Robson did not win over was the temperamental Kevin Keegan. The famed England captain was widely respected throughout the game, not least by Robson himself. Nevertheless, it was clear that his international career was in the descendant. Realising that he could play no part in the European Championships two years hence, Robson elected to seek a replacement at the earliest opportunity:

> It was one of the toughest management decisions I ever made, even though I had no allegiance to him. Remember, he never kicked a ball for me.

Naively, Robson assumed that Keegan would remain on call and so neglected to pacify him with a private reassuring explanation. Keegan's reaction was predictable enough: he criticised Robson in print and vowed never to play for England again. He had previously walked out on England after being dropped in the early days of Don Revie's management and now history was repeating itself. This time around, however, there was no way back for the fatally proud goalscorer. Robson claims he wrote a conciliatory letter and that no reply was forthcoming. Although Keegan was guilty of impulsiveness, vanity and indiscretion, it was Robson who publicly suffered most from the affair. Rival managers from Ron Atkinson to Lawrie McMenemy expressed perplexity at this abrupt dropping while pro-Robson players, including Steve Coppell and Bryan Robson, argued that the ex-Liverpool star deserved special treatment. Even one year later, the ever-opinionated Brian Clough was demanding that Keegan be reinstated. The self-imposed exile proved permanent, however, although Keegan may yet take a vicarious revenge. In a recent newspaper article, he rather optimistically nominated himself as the next England manager! Sober commentators have so far taken a jaundiced view of his self-promoting protestations.

Robson's first task as England manager was to contest the qualifying rounds of the European Championship in a group comprising Denmark, Greece, Hungary and Luxembourg. He spoke with confidence of the ability of his players to win the trophy, and it was generally accepted that England were the strongest team in their section. The opening match in Copenhagen, however, revealed a Danish side who were far from pushovers. England came away with a lucky 2–2 draw, the implications of which bothered Robson. Already he felt terrible pressure far beyond his experiences as a club manager. Worse was to follow in October 1982 when England played a friendly against West Germany at Wembley, losing 2–1. The Germans, inspired by the majestic presence of Karl-Heinz Rummenigge had overrun their opponents and England's only reply had come from a late consolation goal. As a friendly, the match had little significance beyond nationalistic pride, yet Robson's reaction to the defeat was peculiarly mournful. He not only felt deeply depressed by the result but made the ludicrous and alarming suggestion that it was worse than Ipswich's various semi-final losses and missed League Championships. Seven years later, he maintains that these sentiments were not PR flannel, but genuine:

It was my first match in charge at Wembley. I'd seen England beat Germany in the World Cup final and was proud to be English. Now here I was in charge of the national team and we lost. It was a big blow to me. At the time I did feel it was worse than losing the Championship. I was so loyal, so patriotic and wanted England to win so much. There were about 68,000 people there that night and it really hurt.

It still seems remarkable that a professional manager of Robson's stature should feel so concerned about a match that was of virtually no consequence. That a single international friendly should be compared to a once-in-a-lifetime lost Championship is akin to managerial heresy. History will record Robson's missing League Championship as a significant and unfortunate failure in an otherwise illustrious career, but who remembers a friendly against West Germany? Contrary to what he says, there seems little doubt that his disappointment was completely out of proportion. Ipswich supporters and League watchers still reflect on those lost titles, whereas the friendly against Germany is a forgotten, lifeless statistic. Its relevance, if any, did not extend far beyond the following morning's papers and Robson quickly scotched any initial doubts about his credibility with emphatic victories over Greece and Luxembourg.

It was not until the first anniversary of his appointment to the England job that Robson suffered a negative result of true consequence. Denmark, having proven so unlucky in their home match against England the previous year, came to Wembley in September 1983 and won 1–0. That shock result effectively ended England's hopes of qualifying for the European Championship and Robson was predictably devastated. Days of depression followed as the result took on a morbid significance far beyond its importance.

Inaugurated in 1966, the European Championship has never had the cachet of its equivalent club Cup competitions, let alone anything approaching the awesome import of the World Cup. The public still tends to perceive the European Championship as a makeshift competition specifically designed to break up the long four-year gap between successive World Cups. If nothing else, it allows the European nations the opportunity to test their squads in a rather more competitive environment than that provided by an inconsequential friendly fixture. England have seldom progressed far in the European Championships which is another reason why it still fails to engross the Blighty public. At best it has the status of a mock examination, encouraging the national football community to pull its socks up in preparation for the real thing: the World Cup. Robson, of course, lacks the arrogance to dismiss this event as a halfway house competition of marginal interest. That is to be expected, but the degree of credence he invests in such matches is a cause for concern. The embarrassing defeat against Denmark was seen as no mere aberrant statistic but a result carved in stone. Even three years later, while he was compiling a copious *World Cup Diary*, the humiliating memory of Scandinavian superiority returned to haunt his Pepysian prose:

> Whatever I may or may not achieve in my footballing career, the blackest day will remain 21 September 1983. It was the worst moment I had experienced at any level in football. . . The 1–0 defeat was only part of it. The way the team played; the walk back to the dressing room afterwards; the abuse of the crowd; the feeling of total confusion all contributed to the desolate feelings. . . I was full of self-pity, all I wanted to do was to turn the clock back 24 hours. I looked at myself in the shaving mirror in the hotel bedroom next morning, feeling half numb and only semi-conscious. Perhaps, I thought, I live it too much, maybe I am too passionate about it.

Try telling Robson that the Denmark match or earlier West Germany defeat were merely minor setbacks on the road to the World Cup and he reacts with incredulity:

> Denmark and West Germany were big pills to swallow. Big items. They're not trivia, believe me. The whole nation's on your shoulders. I represent *you*. I'm conscious of that.

England ended their forlorn European campaign on a positive note with convincing victories against Hungary and Luxembourg. Robson's record of two defeats in 15 international matches was good; his bad press came as a result of losing both at Wembley. In a determined and courageous attempt to discover new talent he threw several youngsters into an away friendly against talented France and lost 2–0. A fallow period followed in matches against the home countries before England once more entertained foreign competition at Wembley.

It had been 17 years since the USSR last appeared at Wembley when they earned a creditable 2–2 draw. Their previous visit back in 1958 had ended in a 5–0 drubbing and it was expected that Robson's men would inflict another, albeit more modest, defeat. Instead, Bobby's Wembley hoodoo struck again and the Russians seized an historical 2–0 victory. A crescendo of anti-Robson chants drowned the final whistle as the England manager learned the inevitable price of consistent failure at home. It was a depressing night for Robson made worse by an after-match television confrontation with Jimmy Hill. The following week England were scheduled to leave for a South American tour prompting the loquacious Hill to grill his guest about the sagacity of the visit. What was the point? Why submit England to further humiliation? Hill's defeatist gibes were not entirely rhetorical, for England had suffered a high incidence of injuries and seemed ill-equipped to survive the visit with any vestige of dignity. Robson, of course, was fully aware that the tour could not be postponed at such a late date and countered Hill with the weary plea: 'We might learn something'.

The vagaries of international football have seldom been better summed up than in England's performances during the summer of 1984. As Robson eagerly points out:

We were on a hiding to nothing. We were going to Brazil with an inexperienced team which had just lost 2–0 to Russia at Wembley. Eight days later we beat Brazil 2–0!

The defeat of Brazil was undoubtedly one of the sweetest moments of Robson's entire managerial career. He had prepared for the game with an uncharacteristic banter, smiling and joking with South American journalists who refused to believe that the mad Englishman would dare play 4–2–4 against their great Brazilian side. 'Nobody comes here and does that', was their derisive cry, but Robson continued to smile. 'Well, we are', was his confident retort. He had already decided to thrust caution aside and play two wingers, John Barnes and Mark Chamberlain, backed by the midfield duo of Bryan Robson and Ray Wilkins. It was a bold experiment that upset Brazil and turned certain defeat into historic victory. Robson did not need reminding that England had never previously beaten Brazil in South America. In fact, they had not been beaten at home by anybody in over 25 years. The result effectively salvaged Robson's tarnished reputation overnight. One week before he had been ridiculed as a failure, now he was a national hero. International football breeds stereotypes of winners and losers but as Robson's career has persistently emphasised, the gap between the two at world level can be frustratingly thin.

The South America tour instilled a much-needed confidence into the England squad and convinced Robson to continue following his own instincts and long-term plans. East Germany visited Wembley for a friendly in September 1984 allowing England to break their home jinx with a 1–0 victory. The World Cup qualifying matches followed and during this golden period of Robson's management England successively defeated Finland (5–0), Turkey (8–0) and Northern Ireland (1–0). Hard-fought away draws against Romania and Finland brought no glory but valuable World Cup points. Only a major disaster could now prevent Robson from qualifying for his first World Cup.

The spectre of the Heysel Stadium tragedy was the backdrop to England's erratic performances later that year when they lost three consecutive friendlies. Once again, their confidence seemed to erode but they survived the last three qualifying games to finish top of their group. In retrospect, the match statistics were surprisingly good, and England emerged as the only European country to reach Mexico without suffering at least one defeat in the qualifying tournament. It was a notable feature of Robson's reign that quirky patches of poor form distracted from what was generally an impressive series of results.

World Cup preparations were not all that concerned Robson during his first few years as national manager. He had been a leading light in a scheme designed to provide professional coaching for boys aged between 11 and 14. The Centres of Soccer Excellence were greeted with considerable enthusiasm by the footballing fraternity and 19 First Division clubs immediately applied for licences. Since 1984, the scheme has flourished and Robson remains optimistic about future developments:

> I've devoted a lot of hours putting up schemes which will get kids to play football and will create a more technically adept player at a younger age. We've got 125 Centres of Soccer Excellence in the country now with about 5,000 boys registered. That's a massive number which beats rugby, cricket, boxing and hockey. We're laying great foundations for grass-roots football and I hope that the concept is right and that people will work to make it successful and produce players.

In addition to the Centres of Soccer Excellence, Robson is also involved in a coaching scheme directed at boys and girls as young as eight years. His efforts in furthering the game deserve to be remembered.

The lead-up to the 1986 World Cup could not have been better scripted. Between January and May, England romped through six consecutive victories against Egypt, Israel, Russia, Scotland, Mexico and Canada. Robson appeared to have discovered a winning formula which prompted several commentators to suggest that England might surprise the world. The critics were to be proved right, but for all the wrong reasons.

The draw for the World Cup finals was merciful to England. Placed in a group alongside Poland, Portugal and Morocco they could have few complaints or excuses. While last minute preparations were underway, Robson discovered a new and unexpected opponent in the form of his World Cup-winning predecessor. The enigmatic Sir Alf Ramsey penned a tabloid piece in which he censured Robson's selection and named his own squad which featured Peter Reid and Glenn Hoddle. Peculiarly, Ramsey had previously criticised their inclusion in a friendly against Scotland, leaving Robson feeling that he could do nothing right. Whether the contrasting brickbats were mistranslated tabloid-speak or genuine sentiments is difficult to determine, but Robson rightly argues that they were unworthy of Ramsey. Even today, he still seems mystified by Sir Alf's motives:

> It was very odd. I never spoke to him about it. We both live in Ipswich, 500 yards from each other, but he's a bit of a recluse. He's never around and I see little of him. I tell you I couldn't believe he would act that way. I couldn't understand it. It hurt me very much and I was disappointed in him. A lot of people around me were too. They couldn't believe he'd go to that level with that paper. . . If I leave and act like he did to the next England manager then I pray somebody gets a .22 and doesn't miss me!

Ramsey's barbs had a mockingly resonant ring at the end of England's opening match against Portugal. Unbelievably, the unfancied Portuguese won 1–0, and Robson concedes that they were unlucky not to have scored a second. Embarrassment was followed by disaster in the next match when lowly Morocco almost ended Robson's campaign in a startling five-minute spell before half-time. Having watched his lethargic team outmanoeuvred in the opening stages, Robson realised his worst fears when captain Bryan Robson was stretchered off with a dislocated shoulder. Minutes later, Ray Wilkins received his marching orders for childishly throwing a ball at the referee. By the interval, Robson had virtually abandoned any hope of winning the game and was praying for survival. The Moroccans obliged by failing to press home their advantage and contented themselves with a goalless draw. Rather appropriately, Robson immediately sent his players to a nearby monastery to contemplate the consequences of their performance. What they needed now was a miracle.

Back in England, the critics were already sharpening their knives in anticipation of Robson's execution. Under such headlines as 'Robson In Despair', the maligned manager was pictured lying beside a swimming pool aimlessly listening to a Walkman. The image evoked the air of a man who had apparently given up. It was difficult to escape the superstitious feeling that some mischievous soccer deity had stage-managed events so that Robson might suffer the same fate as Ramsey – defeat at the hands of Poland and subsequently the sack. Fortunately, Robson was rather more positive than the tabloids assumed and had got to work refashioning the England midfield. Instead of recalling Ramsey's worst moment in 1973, the match conjured up memories of Geoff Hurst's World Cup-winning hat trick of 1966. The new hero was Gary Lineker whose three first-half goals neutralised Poland's threat and sent England cantering into the next phase of the competition. Robson was all smiles and confident bravura. The man had reinvented himself once again.

England effortlessly reverted to their pre-final winning ways with another sound performance against luckless Paraguay who were ruthlessly dismissed 3–0. Now followed the real test against Argentina.

South American sides are notoriously difficult to beat in their own continent, yet the British press was confident that England had a sporting chance. The mood of the squad was buoyant and Robson sustained their positivism by presumptuously discussing arrangements for the semi-final. The match itself turned out to be an extraordinary affair. England were comprehensively outplayed in the first half and it was becoming increasingly difficult to imagine them penetrating the formidable Argentine defence. Only the most intense concentration had kept them in the match and Argentina looked capable of exploiting tired legs later in the game. The breakthrough came early in the second half, but it was surrounded with controversy. Diego Maradona ran into space and, with only Shilton to beat, headed the ball into the net. A couple of English players disputed the goal, but the game soon re-commenced. Later, the goal came under tedious scrutiny and slow-motion replays taken from cameras at a certain angle appeared to suggest that Maradona might have served the ball into the net with his right hand. When questioned on the matter he retorted with engaging humour that the goal had come from 'the hand of God'. A school of thought maintains that Maradona may have been referring to himself in that quote for within minutes he scored a second goal which looked suspiciously like the work of a being invested with divine qualities. From the half-way line, the stocky striker literally bulldozed his way through no less than five players to score the most brilliant goal seen anywhere that decade. Argentina now seemed capable of running up a rugby score but, strangely, almost imperceptibly, the match turned. Maradona and his cohorts visibly relaxed assuming the game was over and England found a fresh sense of urgency. Robson, after some prevarication, threw on both his wingers, Chris Waddle and John Barnes, and the match instantly metamorphosed into a frantic, all-action kitchen-sink-throwing drama, uncannily reminiscent of a mid-1950s FA Cup tie. Argentina seemed baffled by the wild and whirling wingers and amazingly conceded a goal. They still looked capable of crushing England if they chose to flex their muscles and Maradona was unfortunate not to secure his hat trick with another telling run. In the end, Argentina had done enough, although Lineker came dangerously close to equalising in the closing stages. Argentina unquestionably deserved their victory, despite their controversial first goal, but England had shown a pugnacious spirit which was as admirable as it was surprising.

Robson's squad left Mexico with the flattering words of their manager ringing in their ears. He was equally gushing several months later, even going as far as declaring that he felt closer to them than any other team of players in his long career. It was an extraordinary statement when you consider the years he spent at Ipswich building up the club and grooming players to compete with the top teams in the country. Can you imagine that other great club man Don Revie actually admitting that he preferred England's amorphous squad to that of his beloved Leeds? Surprisingly, Robson still does not retract his eulogy or concede that it was nothing more than spontaneous, misguided flattery:

> It's true that there were players at Ipswich I got to know over the years. But I'm very passionate about my country. With England we were playing for the biggest stakes so the feeling between myself and the players was that much closer and deeper than it had been at Ipswich. It was more traumatic. I felt so close to those players in 1986. We'd been together for two years, then day in and day out for seven weeks in Mexico. Living there was very condensed: football for breakfast, dinner and tea. It was non-stop. And I felt so sorry for them. I knew the sacrifices they'd made in difficult circumstances in Mexico. To get knocked out the way we did was a bit galling. I felt sorry for them, a bit sick, because they didn't deserve it. In football you don't always get what you deserve.

At least Robson emerged from the finals with his dignity and reputation fully intact. The same journalists that had blasted him in the early stages of the campaign were now claiming that, all things considered, he had done rather well. A place in the quarter-finals was no disgrace and no more or less than England deserved. Beneath the media magnanimity, however, there lurked a distasteful and thoroughly reprehensible xenophobia. The rabid curs of the shameless street excelled themselves with savage, hysterical, jingoistic and self-righteous denunciations of the brilliant Maradona who was ludicrously labelled an ignoble cheat. The disputed 'hand of God' goal may have ended England's World Cup dream but it also provided the perfect excuse. Even Robson found himself fantasising about what might have been against Belgium in the semis and previous arch-enemies West Germany in the final. Injustice, imagined or otherwise, is a welcome panacea to the depressed and defeated.

Robson built on his experiences at World Cup level to prepare a side that he was confident would blossom in the European Championships in 1988. For two years all went well. England won consistently, sometimes seemingly effortlessly, and the newspapers generally expressed confidence in a team that they claimed was the most accomplished since 1966. The qualifying stages of the European Championships saw some stupendous results that even had Robson reeling:

> Hopes and expectations were high. Everybody was full of optimism. I thought we had a good team. We had! We went to Yugoslavia and won 4–1. You don't do that unless you've got a good side. We were so positive.

After completing their six qualifying games, England had dropped only one point and had a staggering goal difference of 19–1. On this form they looked a good bet to go all the way and perhaps win the European Championship.

What happened next was nothing less than the most traumatic night-mare of Robson's reign thus far. Placed in a preliminary group with Eire, the Netherlands and the USSR, England were favourites to proceed to the next round. Instead, they fell at the first fence to 25–1 outsiders Eire in Stuttgart. Ray Houghton's sixth minute goal proved sufficient to win the match, which was followed by mob misrule and 107 arrests. Days later, England lost again to the Netherlands and were out of the Championships. Adding shame to defeat, they were also thrashed by the USSR and finished bottom of their group. It was one of the worst series of England results in living memory and all the more shocking because of its unexpectedness. It is only on reflection that you realise Robson's entire tenure has been characterised by baffling and unpredictable form. Up until 1988, the bad results were always portentous of incredible reviv-als: the defeat at Wembley at the hands of the USSR in 1984 had been followed by victory over Brazil in South America; the poor start to the 1986 World Cup was followed by excellent performances against Poland and Paraguay; even the ultimate exit via Argentina was partly salvaged by a late revival. Given these shock reversals perhaps we should have been psychologically prepared for the obverse results. Having topped their preliminary group with 19 goals, it was perversely appropriate that England should come bottom in the next phase and score only twice. The fluctuating and frustrating form may be explained away for various rea-sons but its consistent recurrence is a mystery. Not surprisingly, Robson could see no pattern in these results that made any logical sense:

> That's football. That's the unpredictable game we play. There is no pattern and it will never change. It will always be like that. The game is a glorious uncertainty.

How sweet life would be if football managers could genuinely accept such fatalism. Unfortunately, bad luck is never an adequate excuse as Robson discovered at the post-match press conference:

> After the third defeat I faced the press and a little guy on my right said: 'Mr Robson, can you tell me why it is that you've got million-pound players like Lineker, Beardsley and Robson and you can't win a match. Can you explain *that*?' He had half an hour to think about that question. He threw it at me live. I had two seconds to think of an answer. You haven't half got to be clever and witty. You can't let them rattle you.

When pressed to provide an explanation, Robson had a ready-made list of excuses which sounded plausible:

> There's certain things I can't talk about. It's just the way it went. It was an amalgamation of many things, I suppose. How do you know that Beardsley and Barnes are going to play poorly when one's Footballer of the Year and the other runner-up? To be honest, I think they were burnt out in the summer. But we weren't to know that until they were

in the Championships. We missed Terry Butcher. Lineker, who was our best goalscorer, didn't perform well. He had hepatitis which we didn't know about. Two days later he's in hospital. Hepatitis! It had been in his body for six weeks. No wonder he kept complaining about being tired and feeling awful. We now know why, don't we? We went into those Championships with confidence. The mental approach was fine. It was just a bizarre result in the first match from which we never recovered. We played well enough against Holland to win it but lost in the last 15 minutes and were out. It was just the way the bloody deck fell.

Robson's apologia does beg the question of England's preparation for the Championships. Why weren't Beardsley or Barnes found out in training or practice matches if they were truly burnt out? Why weren't more stringent medical checks carried out on the lackadaisical Lineker before he reached the playing field? Perhaps, as Robson's words hint, England were a little too confident going into the Championships and underestimated the tenacity of the competition. Finally, if the mental approach really was 'fine', then how does one explain the third collapse against the USSR? Having being knocked out of the competition by the Netherlands, England had the opportunity to salvage their dignity with a reasonable display but instead played an atrocious, almost wilfully poor, game. That third defeat left Robson requiring all the sophistry of a barrister to talk his way out of trouble. Not surprisingly, the press was unmerciful and the old cries of 'Robson Out!' were resurrected on the back pages of a number of tabloids. The England manager tried to take a jaundiced view of this latest outbreak of vitriol, but he admits that it was a considerable strain:

> The most difficult part of my life at the moment is to withstand this pressure from the press. They're not really giving me ideal working conditions. I work in a hostile environment. I've got the experience now not to let them eat away at me. They've got papers to sell and that's all they're interested in. But it's still very hurtful and you know it's going to hurt your family. That's never easy. I'm concerned for them. To be honest, I try not to read the papers too much. If you do, it can affect your judgement. So if it's abusive, I don't read it.

One newspaper that Robson did read was the *Sunday Times*. There, at least, he might have expected to receive a less hysterical response than from the ravenous tabloids. Instead, he witnessed a stream of highly charged language from that doyen of football commentators Brian Glanville. The learned Glanville was so disgusted with England's attitude and performance throughout the Championships that he spent an entire paragraph castigating their 'spineless' play. Robson still seems astonished and hurt by the ferocity of the attack:

> Glanville! He seldom comes to press conferences and things like that and does it all away from the scene. He's been particularly

uncomplimentary and nasty. It was savagery! He's just asked to have an interview. Interesting that! He's actually asked to see me. I don't know how to handle it, whether to kick him in the balls or say yes!

Glanville was subsequently granted an interview and apparently escaped with his testicles intact.

One lingering memory of the 1988 European Championships was Robson's forlorn and strained appearance throughout the unhappy proceedings. What made the image particularly poignant and apposite was the contrasting picture of an exuberant and perpetually contented Jack Charlton. Seldom in the history of football management have there been two more strikingly different temperaments on opposite benches than this Northeastern pair. While Robson looked under sentence of death, Charlton consistently smiled at the so-called 'pressures' of international management. He assured the press that, although he might one day die in the excitement and struggle of attempting to catch a prize fish, he would never shuffle off this mortal coil while sweating over the result of a football match.

Few who knew Charlton's recent history could disagree with the Eire manager. While his fellow managers fretted about their future he exuded a carefree confidence that was both refreshing and appealing. He had the air of a man who had solved the secret of success in football management. During his short spell in the hot seat at Newcastle United he adamantly refused to be bullied either by the press or the luckless supporters. When a section of the crowd decided to pressurise him with the chant 'Charlton Out!', the wily Northeasterner happily called their bluff and abruptly resigned. The St James' Park faithful have been regretting their stupidity to this day. The message was loud and clear: 'Don't mess with Big Jack'. Rather than seeking another appointment, the insouciant one returned to his fishing and gave no indication of missing big-time management. Football needed him far more than he needed football. It was the perfect response. His appointment as Eire manager was as surprising as it was inspired. By all accounts, he goes about his job with the same almighty confidence that has characterised all his recent footballing activities. Nobody dares criticise him without good reason for fear that he might tell them to stick their job. Journalists report with amusement that Big Jack finds it difficult to remember his players' names and treats international assignments with a steadfast nonchalance more befitting a five-a-side tournament. Perhaps it is this extraordinary confidence and mature realisation that football really *isn't* a matter of life and death that has inspired his squad. Their record under his management is exemplary and only a late slip against Holland prevented the players reaching the European Championship semi-finals. In beating England, the World Cup-winning Charlton became a national hero in Eire and met the honour with customary unruffled acceptance.

Contrast all this with Robson, the England manager, who appears to care more, work harder and worry himself to near insomnia. For all this commitment, however, it was his team that foundered. Maybe that is the flaw in his managerial make-up – he cares *too* much. Can it be that his overt concern for good results actually has a detrimental psychological effect on the players and may even cause them to freeze on the big occasion?

The shift of emphasis from the players to Robson himself has been a noticeable feature of post-Championship reporting. Unfortunately, the tone has been neither analytical nor sympathetic but unconstructively derisive. The England manager attempted to stabilise his team against Denmark by playing carefully and ensuring a victory. In the circumstances risks were out – the result was all. A barely convincing 1–0 victory over Denmark was enough to satisfy Robson for the present, but the press saw it as little compensation for the European Championship fiasco. What followed was little better. England travelled to Saudi Arabia for a low-key friendly against the national side and drew 1–1. It was hardly a match worthy of extensive comment, but the tabloids went berserk. At least during the Championships journalists had concentrated on the football, now the focus was on Robson alone. Ridicule and character-assassination were par for the course as Robson was photographed with a fez superimposed on top of his head accompanied by a joke about dunces. The *Sun's* headlines 'England Mustafa New Boss' and 'Desert Prats' turned it all into a big joke, but Robson responded with deadly seriousness and a self-effacing nobility:

> I came here believing we would beat Saudi Arabia. It was never going to be easy. You lot think we can walk over teams and win four or five-nil. *You're dreaming*! I understand how the people at home must be feeling. How do you think I feel? I'm frustrated, I'm irritated. But I must not let those feelings overtake me. I must stick with the players and keep going. That's exactly what I intend to do.

Brave words they were, and much needed. Robson had played several youngsters in Saudi and was right to try out a new approach in light of the European disappointment. An international football manager should be judged on the important matches and Robson has been rightly criticised for some of England's early World Cup games and the full-scale collapse in the European group matches. Saudi, however, was inconsequential and irrelevant. It was an excellent and much-needed opportunity to experiment. If England had lost the game and Robson thereby learned something of value that would have been far more important than winning without learning anything, especially as certain questions about the team urgently needed answering. Robson needs to risk tactical changes and possible defeat in order to progress and resist any temptation to play safe in friendlies just to satisfy Fleet Street. His present task is the extremely difficult one of placing principles before populism and following through a necessarily radical programme in order to achieve his aims.

Robson maintains that he was perfectly correct to experiment in Saudi and his forthrightness deserves respect. What he now needs is a return to form during the crucial World Cup qualifying matches. The first of these, following the white heat of press criticism, was a tense affair against Sweden which ended in a goalless draw. Robson was stoical about the result:

We should have won 2–0. We played very well in the second half. Had we scored one goal, it would have been a different script. I was disappointed and I knew that the next morning's papers would turn on me. We'd lost in the European Championships and with this big game against Sweden we *had* to win at home. I knew that, the players knew that. But we didn't: we lost a point and they gained one. They were fortunate.

Predictably, the press responded to this latest dropped point by heaping yet more ridicule on Robson, who found himself caricatured as a 'Plonker', a nickname that will stick in tabloid prose for some time yet. Even the quality papers could not help noticing the manager's apparent confusion in the post-match conference when he referred to Sweden as Denmark and expressed concern about the 'defeat' when England had actually drawn. On radio, a concerned *Sport On 2* commentator warned that unless the press eased off they might drive Robson to a nervous breakdown. So is he cracking up? I could see no evidence of it during several hours spent at FA headquarters and Robson himself claims he was in good psychological shape on the evening of the Sweden match:

I was pretty normal, I think. Cracking up? They took that line and sent people along to see me make a slip and that was their story. Too much was made out of it. It was just a slip of the tongue; it's easily done. By giving them a press conference they can use that against me, which they did after Saudi Arabia too. I thought, 'Why do that?'. . . It's hard to take, particularly when you think it's unfair. They've been very personal against me. I don't know why because I've always accommodated the press very well. They'll find the next man won't accommodate them like I have. I've been good to them and tried to give them stories. Now it seems to have worked against me. Alf treated the press with contempt and wouldn't help them. I've been helpful. It would appear that they get you in the end anyway. . . It's all about results. You know what the job is? WIN!

If football management is a continual learning process then 1988 may well turn out to be the most important year of Robson's soccer life. He admits that it is only experience that has kept him afloat amid a sea of vitriol and agrees that had the anti-Robson campaign reached similar heights at an earlier stage he would have stepped down. Lately, he has grown more philosophical, although he is still far from the Buddha-like tranquility of Jack Charlton. At least he has no happy delusions about the future:

> It's getting worse. I've seen it every two years. The media pressure in '84, '86 and '88 has gone up in leaps and bounds. It's staggering. You've got to be clever and tough to handle it. The European Championships were bad and the World Cup will be worse, although I can't imagine how! You go into a press room and there's 250 journalists from all different countries. You've got 50 tape recorders on your desk and that's just the front row. There's five or six camera crews all filming live so if you brush your hair or stumble on a word it's all on tape. If Alf Ramsey moved into that now, he wouldn't believe it compared to what he had. It's out of all proportion.

There is a growing belief among international managers that it is now impossible to survive more than two World Cups. Typically, Robson is not quite ready to concede that point:

> You can stomach three World Cups if your percentage of winning is right and young players keep coming through. But there is a limit. You'll do two and think: 'I've done my stint'. The job will be given to an experienced man so you'll have to be about 45 when you start. After two World Cups you'll be in your mid-50s and I think ten years is a good stint. Alf had nine – that's the longest, I think. This is my seventh year and that's in the modern game. That's the equivalent of 15 years in Alf Ramsey's time.

With such experience, Robson can afford to take the long view and place the recent European Championships in a realistic perspective. But what has he learned from it all?

> What do you learn? We got off to a bad start in the World Cup and recovered. We got off to a bad start in the European Championships and didn't. So it's very important to win your first match. We've tried twice and haven't done it. What do you learn? It's a good question. You've got to keep a clear head, cope, keep your nerve, select well, keep working your players and make sure the amount of training and preparation is right. Then, hopefully, you can put those players in a confident scene in which they feel they can rely on one another and are a good team. Then you've got a chance of winning. They must have character because once they pass that white line there's little you can do. They've got to accept the responsibilities and take chances. It's about players having the right character and temperament. It's about players.

No doubt Robson will continue to elicit extreme reactions from the media, but his position looks secure. Unlike Sir Alf there is no wonder manager of the stature of Don Revie waiting in the wings with a cabinet full of trophies and promises of greatness.

As Robson concludes:

I was a manager for 14 years before I got this job. To have the same track record as me the next guy would have to have been in charge of a First Division club side for at least 14 years, finished second in the League in his last two seasons and qualified for Europe over ten. How many managers in this country have that track record?

It is a frightening thought.

Robson's future as England manager was placed under greater scrutiny following newspaper allegations in June 1989 suggesting that he had involved himself in an adulterous affair with a divorcee. Fully realising the implications of such a scandal, irrespective of his innocence or guilt, Robson hinted that he might resign before receiving a public vote of confidence from the FA. One year away from the World Cup finals, the pressures on Robson, both personal and professional, continue to mount.

BOB PAISLEY

THE ELDER STATESMAN
OF BRITISH FOOTBALL

Robert Paisley was born on 23 January 1919 in the Durham mining village of Hetton-le-Hole. His childhood and adolescent years were not dissimilar to those of Matt Busby, Bill Shankly or Jock Stein, all of whom hailed from mining communities with strong traditions of soccer excellence. Paisley was particularly fortunate in his choice of school, for Eppleton Senior Mixed did not attempt to emulate the independent sector by enforcing a 'rugby only' policy but prided itself on its standing in the county soccer league. Before the age of 14, Paisley had collected no less than 13 school medals, a figure he relishes with as much pride as the plethora of League Championships and European Cups that would later grace his managerial years. His school record was sufficiently impressive to attract the interest of Wolverhampton Wanderers, who duly signed him in 1933. It was, however, no big deal. At that time, football clubs had a reputation for signing any schoolboy that moved and their commitment often evaporated before the ink had dried on the forms. Paisley was spared any false illusions by the urgent need to find a job. Predictably, he followed his father down the mines, but a pit closure several months later left him unemployed. A family friend came to the rescue by securing him an apprenticeship as a bricklayer with a local building firm. Such skills were to prove unexpectedly useful when Paisley later joined a dilapidated club called Liverpool.

By 16, Paisley was playing for Hetton Juniors and, during his two years at the club, he won three trophies. His consistency drew the attention of the top amateur side Bishop Auckland, then at their peak. Paisley stayed for a two-year stint during which he enjoyed the drama of competing for a veritable host of amateur trophies. The lure of professionalism had so far been resisted, although Spurs had almost signed Paisley during his final year at Hetton Juniors. In May 1939, however, manager George Kay intervened with an offer from Liverpool. The Merseysiders could do nothing with Paisley until the close season, so they allowed him to fulfil his commitments with Bishop Auckland, who were desperately fighting for a momentous treble. At that time, league regulations insisted that a team had to complete its fixture list by the final day of the season. Unbelievably, Auckland's success in cup and league competition had left them with the Sisyphean struggle of completing 13 matches in a fortnight. So intransigent were the footballing authorities that they would not set a precedent by allowing Auckland even 24 hours' grace. Paisley and the first team were fit enough to punish themselves with 11 of the games while the reserve side turned out for the other two. In a remarkable sequence of results, Auckland clinched their league title, won the Amateur Cup and, against the odds, competed alongside such greats as Newcastle, Sunderland and Middlesbrough before lifting the Durham Professional Cup. It was a spectacular achievement and the most gratifying way of ending an eventful amateur career. As he celebrated this illustrious treble, Paisley could never have imagined that 38 years later he would be one match away from completing a similar landmark as a First Division manager.

Paisley's budding professional career at Liverpool was interrupted by the outbreak of the Second World War. He managed to play only two reserve games before receiving his call-up papers and remembers this period at Anfield as one of difficult adjustment. Fortunately, there was one person at the club whom Paisley found easy to approach for counselling: Matt Busby. The first team captain was a solicitous soul and, having come from a similar background to Paisley, well understood the problems that faced the youngster in adjusting to the big city. As Paisley remembers: 'He was a very stable man and over the years I've known him he was always available to give advice'. When Busby and several of his first team joined the Territorials, Paisley was hopeful that he might 'join their crowd', but instead he ended up in the anti-tank regiment of the Royal Artillery at Rhyl, Wales. In 1941, he was despatched to Egypt and also saw action in Italy. Back in England, he was stationed at Tarporley, Cheshire and played in many exhibition games alongside his old mentor Matt Busby. The War also introduced him to his wife-to-be Jessie Chandler and the couple were married in 1946. All in all, it had been an eventful six years, and although Paisley had lost a sizeable chunk of his playing career he was still young and fit enough to win a place in Liverpool's first XI.

Paisley could not have hoped for a more exciting First Division debut than that offered by the 1946–47 season. The 27-year-old wing half suddenly found himself in a team that had unexpectedly emerged as leading contenders for both the FA Cup and League Championship. Convincing Cup victories over Walsall, Grimsby, Derby and Birmingham had taken the Merseysiders to a semi-final clash against Burnley. Old lags recalled that the Lancashire side had prevented Liverpool from lifting the trophy in the final immediately preceding the First World War. Now, in the first semi-final after the Second World War, history repeated itself as Burnley again won 1–0. Liverpool were left to contest what was probably the most dramatic League Championship finale in football history.

Paisley's team had played exceptionally well during the early stages of the season but in December plucky Wolves dismantled them 5–1 at Anfield. That disastrous result was followed by the big freeze as numbingly cold weather devastated the League programme. Liverpool contested five matches before the icy onslaught strangled the fixture list and they lost the lot. The severest winter for decades could not have come at a worse moment for English football as the government had seen fit to ban midweek matches in its fight against workers' absenteeism. The cumulative postponements, the fuel crisis and wrecked train schedules conspired to prolong the season into the early summer with the worst-hit teams lagging far behind their opponents in uncompleted games. Liverpool were among the stragglers and in the final phase of the season found themselves fifth in the table with only three of their remaining eight fixtures at home. A remarkable winning sequence followed which took them to the brink of the Championship. Along the way Paisley had put paid to Matt Busby, who was hoping to celebrate his first year as manager of Manchester United with the League title. The top of the table was as follows: Manchester United 56 points; Wolves 56 points; Liverpool 55 points. However, United had completed their fixture list and it was mathematically impossible for them to remain in first place as Liverpool and Wolves were set to face each other in what appeared a Championship decider.

The match promised to be the most exciting League fixture for years. Wolves, the home side, were slight favourites and needed only a draw to clinch the title. Moreover, their 5–1 defeat of Liverpool earlier in the season provided a strong psychological advantage. Unconvinced by such statistics, the Kop pointed to Liverpool's excellent away form during the past few weeks. The neutrals, if there were any, would probably root for Wolves, whose captain Stan Cullis was hoping to secure a League winners' medal in his final game as a professional. In the event, the match turned out to be a debilitating duel in the sun, with June temperatures soaring to the 80s. Liverpool secured a comfortable 2–0 half-time lead but Wolves replied with an early second-half goal and the match reached a thrilling climax. Resisting tremendous pressure, Liverpool finally denied Wolves the point that would have given them the title.

However, although Liverpool now topped the table with 57 points, their inferior goal average allowed another team a chance of glory. Stoke City had crept into fourth place with 55 points and still had one more fixture to play two weeks later. The action now switched to Bramall Lane where Sheffield United would decide the destination of the Championship trophy. The vagaries of English weather again played their part as the pitch had been swamped by torrential rain. Nervous Stoke conceded a goal within two minutes but soon equalised, and looked likely winners. Instead, Sheffield killed them off with a late winner from winger Wally Rickett. Liverpool, meanwhile, were actually playing a local cup final against neighbours Everton. When the news broke over the loudspeakers, Bob Paisley celebrated by kicking the ball over the main stand. The Kop invaded the pitch as Billy Liddell, Albert Stubbins, Jack Balmer and the rest danced across the turf in jubilation. The referee was hard-pushed to complete this suddenly irrelevant Liverpool Senior Cup final, which the new Champions also won. It was the perfect end to an exhausting season.

Liverpool were a solid, efficient side but several of the players had seen better days. During the late 1940s they had slipped to mid-table mediocrity but threatened to end the decade with a flourish. The 1949–50 season began with a spectacular record-breaking run of 19 undefeated games as Liverpool looked firm favourites for the League Championship. Early in the New Year, however, their form declined and they eventually slumped to eighth position. What was more frustrating was that they were only five points behind Champions Portsmouth, who topped the table with one of the lowest totals of all time. The FA Cup provided the opportunity for a resurgence of excellence, and a fortunate draw against lowly opposition propelled them to a quarter-final clash against Blackpool. The absence of the great Stanley Matthews gave the Merseysiders a slight edge which they exploited fully to win 2–1. Media attention now focussed upon their semi-final opponents. Everton's impressive progress in the FA Cup had provided the possibility of the first all-Mersey final but, unfortunately, the teams were drawn together in the semis. A vast crowd gathered at neutral Maine Road to witness the grand clash and it was Bob Paisley who opened the scoring with a neat lob early in the first half. Billy Liddell added a second and suddenly Liverpool were back in the final for the first time in 36 years. Manager George Kay fully intended to keep an unchanged side but in the end there was one casualty: Bob Paisley. The unfortunate wing half remembers the circumstances leading up to his pre-Wembley mishap with resigned regret:

We went up to Newcastle the week after we'd won the semi-final and I did my knee in. I'd played 36 League games before that and then I got the knock. I probably wasn't 100 per cent but I'd gladly have got on with it. I didn't get the chance. I was dropped. That's the way it goes. I've never had much luck with the FA Cup.

Although Paisley could have played in the final he concedes that his injury was 'dicey' and, in an era before substitutes were permitted, it would have been foolish for Kay to risk a 10½-man team. There was no happy conclusion for Liverpool that season. Arsenal outplayed them at Wembley and won convincingly 2–0. It would be another 15 years before Paisley again accompanied Liverpool to Wembley and on that occasion the result would be very different.

Paisley retired as a footballer in 1954 and would probably have returned to bricklaying were it not for his interest in physiotherapy. During his final year as a player he had taken a correspondence course and received permission from Liverpool to attend a hospital for a couple of hours every afternoon in order to gain practical experience. It was an astute move from Paisley at a time when the prescribed panacea for on-field injuries had not progressed far beyond a hot towel, a sponge and a bucket of water:

> I thought if anything in the game needed a boost, it was the training. In those days, there were really some rough merchants. They weren't equipped with much knowledge. If you could run or kick somebody, that was it.

After falling from the first team into the reserves, Paisley was grateful to be appointed as Liverpool's trainer in August 1959. Four months later, the club underwent a major change when the charismatic Bill Shankly arrived. Wisely, he retained the backroom staff and placed great faith in Paisley, who would later emerge as his chief lieutenant. Paisley's job extended far beyond the usual confines of a team trainer. He was adept at baffling referees with convoluted physiological theorising uttered in his inimitably incoherent style. While bemused officials offered him access to a player, the canny trainer would pass on vital information from the bench. Like a spy penetrating enemy camp, Paisley could reorganise Shankly's troops at an often crucial stage in the match. More vigilant referees were quick to detect his surreptitious coaching, but even then Paisley would attempt to gain the upper hand by berating them for their treatment of certain players or failure to spot imaginary infringements by Liverpool's opponents. The psychological intimidation was an extension of Shankly's rhetoric and built up Liverpool's reputation of invincibility at Anfield. In many ways the urbane Paisley was an unlikely mouthpiece for such Machiavellian gamesmanship, but as he wryly observed:

> The funny thing was people used to say about me: 'He's too quiet!' But I was never quiet on the pitch.

Paisley's expertise as a trainer made him an invaluable asset to Bill Shankly. It was Paisley who elected to allow Gerry Byrne to continue with a broken collar bone in the 1965 Wembley final that brought Liverpool their first FA Cup triumph. Remarkably, the injury remained undetected by the opposition for the entire match and it was Byrne's cross which brought Liverpool their first goal. Paisley was an expert at gauging the seriousness of an injury and advising upon the necessary period of convalescence. It was no coincidence that Liverpool had one of the most settled sides in the Football League. During their Championship-winning season of 1965–66 they used only 14 different players for the entire campaign and competed with similarly injury-free squads in the 1970s. Shankly was acutely aware of Paisley's contribution in this respect and at times regarded him as an all-healing witch doctor. His reverence is best summed up in a poignant story that Paisley recalls with affectionate incredulity:

During ten years as a trainer, Bill always encouraged me to do the medical work. But at Melwood he'd always talk to kids about football tactics. Anyone who wanted to talk football was fine, it didn't matter what age they were. I'll always remember one day he came in pushing a lad in a wheelchair. I can still hear Bill coming up the passage saying: 'Bob'll fix this!' The lad had been in a wheelchair for three to four years. It was a long-standing thing that he was never going to be cured of. I could have cried, not laughed. I felt sorry. Bill had so much faith in me.

Shankly's faith in Paisley was demonstrated by the trainer's promotion to assistant manager in 1970. Four years later, the great Shankly retired leaving his colleague the unenviable task of assuming control at Anfield. Any manager would have felt daunted by the prospect of following Shankly, and Paisley was no exception. He admits: 'I was quite content to go along as I was. The trainer's job would have seen me out. They had to talk me into it'. Paisley's reluctance was evinced by his refusal to accept a contract during his first 12 months as a manager.

The tricky transition from Shankly to Paisley went more smoothly than expected, but there were some teething troubles. Kevin Keegan recalls that the new manager was not the most popular figure at Anfield, having always been regarded as Shankly's hatchet-man. Of course, this problem was immediately solved by the shift in the power structure. Joe Fagan was promoted to assistant manager and told by Paisley: 'If you see anything that shouldn't be done – nail it'. The role switch meant that Paisley was less the troubleshooter than the man responsible for motivating the team and commenting positively on their performance. Consistency was all at Anfield and the pre-match talks continued to highlight the greatness of Liverpool FC backed by the firm conviction that they would always score maximum points.

Paisley faced his first managerial headache before the season had even started. The battleground was Wembley Stadium where Liverpool faced League Champions Leeds United in the FA Charity Shield. The awesome rivalry between the two great clubs was now a decade old and, although each side had the utmost respect for their illustrious opponents, the element of pride inevitably produced a high level of competitiveness. Not surprisingly, the Charity friendly was played in the spirit of a fierce Cup battle and, with discipline still lax after the summer break, tempers erupted on the pitch culminating in an exchange of punches between Billy Bremner and Kevin Keegan. The felony was compounded by the pair's petulant decision to remove their shirts in a provocative manner after being sent off by the referee. Paisley accompanied his player to the subsequent disciplinary committee meeting but had no magic wand to convince the FA powers of the need for clemency. On the contrary, both Keegan and Bremner received an unprecedented punishment for being sent off and for bringing the game into disrepute, which included a complete ban from football for one month and a £500 fine. Paisley compared their treatment to that dished out by the Spanish Inquisition.

Although Shankly had left Paisley a Cup-winning side, key changes were necessary to strengthen the team. Paisley's first move was to transfer the ever-troubled Larry Lloyd, who was sent to Coventry in return for £240,000. In retrospect, this turned out to be an unfortunate error, for Lloyd was subsequently transferred to Nottingham Forest where he spearheaded the most sustained attack on Liverpool's footballing supremacy over the next few years. Having obliquely despatched a Liverpool player into the hands of his enemies, Paisley unwittingly robbed another rival of a key defender when he signed Phil Neal. Prior to Paisley's intervention, Neal was planning to leave League football and join amateurs Kettering Town, then under the managerial auspices of Ron Atkinson. The flamboyant Ron would later emerge as Manchester United's manager and no doubt would have taken Neal along a similar route. Paisley's surprise buy was therefore both well-timed and ultimately damaging to Manchester United's Championship aspirations. Liverpool also struck lucky with John Toshack, who was placed on the transfer list until a failed medical resulted in his dramatic reinstatement to the first team. Soon, he formed a new striking partnership with Kevin Keegan which revitalised the team. Another important figure in the reconstruction was Ray Kennedy, the attacker whom Shankly had bought only days before his shock resignation. Initially, the ex-Arsenal player had found it difficult to adjust to life at Anfield and was soon demoted to the reserves. However, Paisley struck up a good relationship with the off-form star and in an inspired positional switch transformed him into a midfielder. Thereafter, his career blossomed and, by the end of the season, Liverpool looked strong contenders for future Championships. Considering the abrupt transition, Paisley had performed more than adequately in his first 12 months as a manager, but, surprisingly, he is still self-critical:

> That was the only year we didn't win anything. It was an awful season. I always put it down as a failure. We finished second in the League. If we'd done that with the previous directors they'd have been quite content. It would have been seen as a bonus. At the end of the first season, the directors said they'd give me seven years. There was a lot of rebuilding to do. They could have got somebody else from the outside but it's debatable whether they would have done. I never wanted to leave the club.

The 1975–76 season saw the emergence of Paisley as a managerial power to rival Shankly. Liverpool's progress in the League was impressive, but they were matched by the unlikely consistency of QPR mounting the first title challenge in their history. The Londoners fought till the bitter end, leaving Liverpool to secure a result at Molineux in order to win the title. When Wolves took a first-half lead it seemed that Paisley was heading for a second barren year. The Reds kept their nerve, however, and the weight of pressure finally told in the second half with three sparkling goals. Bob Paisley had won his first League Championship as a manager.

Even while the silverware was making its way to Anfield, Liverpool were poised for an unprecedented League and European double. Their solid form had taken them to the final of the UEFA Cup where they faced Bruges in a two-leg decider. At Anfield the Belgians almost ended the contest before it had begun by taking a shock 2–0 lead. Paisley realised that there was a problem on the field and, in a characteristically shrewd reshuffling, brought on Jimmy Case for John Toshack. Liverpool responded with three goals, although they still needed a draw in Belgium to lift the Cup. Paisley prepared his squad for a tightly-marked defensive display and the tactic worked sufficiently well to secure a 1–1 draw. Not even Bill Shankly had won two trophies in a single season, but new boy Paisley was about to make it a Liverpool habit.

There was a degree of puzzlement among the Kop faithful when Paisley signed Ipswich striker David Johnson in August 1976. Liverpool were already top-heavy with forwards but, as ever, Paisley was investing in the future. The charismatic Kevin Keegan had privately agreed to stay at Anfield for one more season before seeking his fortune abroad. Clearly, his sights were set on winning the European Cup and the squad that Paisley was carefully assembling suggested that 1977 would prove Liverpool's best chance to date. What nobody could have expected, however, was the most sustained attack yet on that most coveted of managers' dreams: the treble.

Paisley was at last finding his niche as a calm, confidence-inspiring manager who greeted each match with a quiet conviction in Liverpool's superiority. He had even adopted several of Shankly's mannerisms, including the tendency to blast the opposition when circumstances demanded. A tricky tie against Trabzonspor of Turkey was nonchalantly dismissed in a cutting aside directed at his hosts' hospitality: 'It's like a doss house. We're just here to give them a good hiding'. The xenophobic air was reminiscent of vintage Shankly and, as so often in the past, Liverpool were made to eat their words when the Turks won 1–0. Although Liverpool overcame Trabzonspor in the return, the result threw up doubts about their ability to lift the European Cup. Progress in the League stalled alarmingly during December when Aston Villa thrashed the Merseysiders 5–1. It was Liverpool's biggest defeat since 1963 and when they lost badly to West Ham three days later their title prospects seemed extremely suspect. Once the Christmas blues passed, however, Paisley galvanised the side for one of the most incredible runs in the history of English football. As Easter approached, the treble grew tantalisingly closer and even the pessimists agreed that Liverpool had a fair chance of achieving the seemingly impossible. What they faced was a gruelling title race and several stupendous Cup games on their way to two Cup finals.

The quarter-final of the European Cup produced one of the most memorable matches ever seen at Anfield. French opponents St Etienne held a 1–0 lead from the first leg and, with their immensely talented team of internationals, looked strong contenders for the trophy. Keegan brought solace to the Kop by scoring a fine goal during the first half to equal the aggregate score, but the French were far from beaten. In a second half remarkable for its pace and flowing football Bathenay replied with a scorching equaliser which gave Etienne the upper hand. With away goals registering as double in the event of a draw, Liverpool were left with the Herculean task of scoring twice against one of the finest teams in Europe. Kennedy managed to broach the French defence and score, but, as the minutes ticked by, that all-important third goal would not come. Surveying the play from his bench, Paisley decided to take a final gamble by substituting David Fairclough for the tiring John Toshack. The boy dubbed 'Super Sub' ably lived up to his name by scoring a dramatic winner less than six minutes from the final whistle. It was enough to convince Paisley that Liverpool were on the way to their first European Cup final.

The road to Wembley Stadium had proven exceptionally smooth for Liverpool, who faced no serious opposition until as late as the semi-final of the FA Cup when they were drawn against neighbours Everton. For Paisley it was a nostalgic reminder of 27 years before when he had scored a precious goal to take Liverpool to their first Wembley final. The 1977 re-match ended in that most agonising of results for would-be treble-chasers: a draw. With the fixture list piling up, Paisley gritted his teeth and an aggressive display in the return saw Liverpool emerge 3–0 winners. However, post-match celebrations were forestalled when the FA made the remarkable announcement that, in the event of a draw at Wembley, the final would not be re-staged until 27 June. Paisley was aghast at the consequences of forcing his players through five weeks' extra training and castigated the authorities in an intense outburst:

> I am not intellectual enough to find words to express my disgust at this stupidity. It is cruelty. The FA are taking blood from the fans and the players. They do not think we are human.

Paisley's bitterness and disappointment were understandable, for Liverpool were already preparing for the toughest end-of-season run in their long history. The squad was due to report for pre-season training on 12 July, a mere two weeks after the proposed 27 June replay. The prospect of keeping the players in peak form throughout June was inconceivable after such a draining campaign, but the FA refused to bow to his pleas. The prevailing logic forced Paisley to adopt a win or bust attitude towards the Wembley final which would have a marked bearing on the eventual result.

The thrust for the treble was maintained throughout April when Liverpool took nine points out of ten to establish a two-point lead in the title race. They grimly hung on until the end of the season before finally taking the Championship with 57 points, pipping Manchester City and Ipswich. Meanwhile, the semi-final of the European Cup had passed in a surprising romp as ineffectual Zurich succumbed 6–1 on aggregate. The treble was now only two matches away.

Prior to the Wembley final, Liverpool retired to Sopwith House near St Albans to prepare themselves for the psychological pressures of competing for the ultimate prize. Few teams had ever come as close as this to achieving the double, but even that awesome feat would merely be regarded as a half-way house. Paisley was on the brink of soccer immortality but he could not rid his mind of the consequences of a replay on 27 June. He had intended to dominate Manchester United in midfield by employing the ageing Ian Callaghan but the absolute need to avoid a replay persuaded him to alter such tactics. Finally, he dropped Callaghan and settled for an all-out attacking formation. It was a decision that he would later regret.

Manchester United were appearing in their second successive FA Cup final and, driven by the fiery managerial presence of Tommy Docherty, seemed determined not to lose out again. The 1977 final was won and lost in the space of five eventful minutes during the second half. United's Stuart Pearson pushed a shot under Ray Clemence's body to open the scoring, but within a couple of minutes Jimmy Case replied with a powerfully struck equaliser. Three minutes later, Paisley could hardly believe his eyes as a mishit ball deflected off Jimmy Greenhoff's body and ricocheted into the Liverpool net. The Merseysiders stormed forward and pinned United back in defence. Ray Kennedy twice hit the crossbar but the crucial breakthrough was not forthcoming. On 21 May 1977 Liverpool missed the double and surrendered the treble dream on the same afternoon. Paisley maintains that his team did everything but beat United, yet there is also a tinge of regret about the tactical shift that may well have cost Liverpool the game. For that change, Paisley is less critical of himself than the heartless officials of the FA whose ruling changed his mind at a crucial moment, thereby destroying the dream of the treble.

Paisley had only four days to transform his squad from beaten FA Cup finalists into European Cup winners. The stage was the Olympic Stadium in Rome where the Merseysiders faced the formidable German side Borussia Moenchengladbach. It was undoubtedly the most important game in Liverpool's history up until this point and the occasion was made all the more poignant as both Kevin Keegan and Tommy Smith were each saying their farewells. Behind the razzmatazz, Paisley's footballing brain was concocting an amusing tactical bluff. In an attempt to confuse the Germans he had included John Toshack and Alan Waddle in the squad, a firm indication that Liverpool would be relying upon aerial superiority, just as they had done against Borussia back in 1973. On the day of the match, however, the pair were dropped and Paisley reverted to the midfield-based team that he had intended to employ against Manchester United. The ploy worked remarkably well in the first half when Liverpool's domination brought a 27th minute goal courtesy of Terry McDermott. Borussia were far from downhearted, however, and emerged for the second half more resolute than ever. They equalised within minutes and enjoyed a frightening period of domination before Liverpool steadied themselves. With the match in the balance, the unlikely figure of veteran Tommy Smith soared above the Borussia defence to score a quite brilliant headed goal. From that point on, Liverpool assumed command, with plucky Kevin Keegan eagerly searching for a celebratory final goal. Eventually, he was floored in the six-yard box and Phil Neal converted the penalty to put the result beyond doubt. Liverpool were the Champions of Europe. For Bob Paisley, it was a moment to be savoured. While the players doused themselves in champagne, the former Durham miner refused to allow a drink to pass his lips. He was far more concerned with tasting the atmosphere of the evening and revelling in his new-found fame as the third manager in Britain to win the European Cup.

Amid the euphoria of the European triumph, the ageing warhorse Tommy Smith decided to postpone his retirement and play on for another season. There was no retraction from Kevin Keegan, however, and in June 1977 he moved to SV Hamburg for £500,000. The money was welcomed by the Liverpool directors, but the loss of the most famous footballer of the era placed a great strain on Paisley. Fortunately, the departure of Keegan coincided with an intriguing phone call from north of the border. Celtic manager Jock Stein told him that Kenny Dalglish was about to be placed on the transfer market. A delicate series of negotiations commenced between these two managerial powers, with Paisley playing the cautious, but interested, buyer:

> It was early days for me as a manager, but I knew Jock. We'd had some contact over the years. He'd been down to the club a few times and we had a good relationship. Liverpool were the only club he approached. Nobody else came in. I did more or less everything he asked.

Indeed, Paisley immediately curtailed his summer holiday in order to discuss the move with his Scottish counterpart. The good news was that Dalglish was keen to play for Liverpool, having established an affection for the club from the days when he attended a youth trial on Merseyside at the age of 15. It was clear to Paisley, however, that Stein was stalling and betrayed an extreme reluctance to surrender his talented goalscorer. Their discussion ended with Stein demanding further time in the hope of dissuading Dalglish from leaving Celtic. Paisley returned to Liverpool and sat tight in anticipation of further developments. Celtic, meanwhile, embarked upon a tour of Australia and, significantly, Dalglish was not included in the party. Stein had evidently failed to assuage his troubled *wunderkind*. Paisley immediately advised his board to phone Stein in Australia and finalise the deal. When the directors finally reached the

Celtic manager, he was in poor spirits. His team had played a couple of dreadful games, as if confirming their paucity of talent without the magical Dalglish. Paisley placed a call himself only to be told: 'Bob, if I can, I'll try to keep him'. Time was now running out for Liverpool, who wanted to sign their new player before 9 August in order to beat the European transfer deadline. Stein well knew the pressure that Paisley was under and agreed to conclude matters quickly. With the Liverpool board demanding an immediate replacement for Keegan, Paisley and his chairman John Smith attended a make-or-break late-night meeting at Parkhead. The Celtic board was amenable enough but the canny Jock Stein was not a man who could be bought easily, as Paisley recalls:

> No fee had yet been mentioned so we bid £300,000, which was the top bracket then, and all of them jumped at it, except Jock. He said: 'It's no good'. He knew what we'd had for Kevin Keegan.

Sensing his advantage, Stein insisted that Paisley and Smith retire to another room while he consulted with his directors. When the Liverpool contingent returned, they were informed that the £300,000 offer was not enough. Smith added 10 per cent to the price and was soon pushed further until he reached the staggering sum of £400,000. At that point, Stein suggested a further 10 per cent levy and the Liverpool chairman momentarily hesitated before announcing: 'We'll give you £440,000'. Thanks largely to the negotiating skill of Stein, the British transfer record had been broken again. Football wiseacres were quick to criticise Liverpool for their apparent spendthrift attitude and Derek Dougan summed up for the prosecution with a wounding indictment: 'How can football ask for government help when a club spends this kind of money for just one player?' Dougan had a point, but his criticisms would soon be swamped in an ever-increasing wave of lucrative transfer deals. The market value of players was rapidly increasing and, having received £500,000 for Keegan, Liverpool were merely replacing one player for another with a net profit of £60,000. Interestingly, however, Paisley maintains that Liverpool would have still pursued the Dalglish deal even if Keegan had elected to remain at Anfield: 'I think they'd have been prepared to take Kenny Dalglish and have a twosome. But Kevin did leave so it became a priority'. Although Stein deserves great credit for the deal, it is debatable who struck the better bargain. Dalglish confirmed Paisley's ambitious expectations and emerged as one of the finest players ever to grace the Anfield turf. Indeed, Paisley himself provides the ultimate accolade in claiming that his most important signing was also the greatest Liverpool player of all time.

The 1977–78 season began with Paisley complaining about the late night revelries of several of his players:

> The supporters are killing us with kindness and there are invitations for functions three to four times a week. I am going to have to draw the line.

On the field, however, Liverpool continued to show a consistency worthy of European Champions. Not surprisingly, the bookmakers made them firm favourites to run away with the League title. In November, however, they lost their one-and-a-half-year unbeaten home record when Aston Villa struck again. The League still looked a likely proposition though, with newly-promoted Nottingham Forest heading the table. Nobody believed that Clough's team had the depth of talent to sustain this impressive opening run but, as winter set in, they showed few signs of flagging. Paisley regarded 1978 as the 'year of the changeover', but his sights were still set on competing for the treble until Chelsea shocked the football world by unceremoniously turfing Liverpool out of the FA Cup with an emphatic 4–2 victory. The upset gravitated Paisley towards a trophy that Liverpool had previously scorned: the League Cup.

Liverpool's past performances in the little-loved Cup created by League secretary Alan Hardaker, were uniformly abysmal. From 1978 onwards, however, the trophy would become an annual favourite of the Liverpool fans. Liverpool's FA Cup jinx persuaded Paisley to think in terms of a mini-treble with the League Cup providing the easiest route to glory. As the season wound towards its climax, Liverpool were on course for a European and League Cup double but, surprisingly, the Championship was slipping away. Clough's Nottingham Forest seemed invincible and by late March virtually everybody agreed that they were certainties to lift the title. Journalists dogged Paisley for an admission of defeat but all they received was a humorous aside, reminiscent of Bill Shankly: 'I'm not conceding anything, the Forest players' legs might drop off'. Forest kept their soccer legs, however, and deservedly won the title to establish themselves as the new scourge of Liverpool. The surprise Champions and dethroned runners-up each fought their way to the final of the League Cup for a revenge match which Paisley was determined to win. Liverpool totally dominated the day but failed to score against a resolute Forest defence inspired by the gutsy Larry Lloyd. Paisley did not need reminding that he had been indirectly responsible for furnishing his opponents with one of their most important players. Four days after the dour Wembley draw, Forest shaded a tightly-fought replay thanks to a hotly-disputed penalty. Clough's side had achieved an unexpected double triumph in their first year back in the big time. Paisley was probably thankful that Forest were not involved in the only competition left for Liverpool to win.

The will to retain the European Cup was strengthened by the enticing prospect of contesting the final at Wembley. Liverpool had played some tough sides including Dynamo Dresden and Benfica before resuming hostilities with Borussia Moenchengladbach in the semi-finals. The Germans won the first leg 2–1 but were no match for Liverpool at Anfield. In one of their best European performances the Merseysiders cruised to a 3–0 victory and were now firm favourites to lift the trophy for a second successive year.

The Wembley confrontation was a repeat of the 1976 UEFA Cup final with Liverpool facing Bruges. What seemed on paper a classic match turned out to be a disappointing spectacle as the Belgians massed their defence in a vain attempt to frustrate Liverpool. Dalglish eventually prised open Bruges' sardine-packed throng to score the only goal of the game. The disappointment of losing two trophies to Nottingham Forest was forgotten as Liverpool celebrated another unique achievement as the first British team to win two European Champions' Cups. Paisley enjoyed the same honour and was now well on his way to becoming the most successful manager in football history.

One of the many secrets of Liverpool's success was the refusal to take success for granted. Paisley's response to a strong, solid team was invariably to reinforce its strength. The induction of £350,000-signing Graeme Souness from Middlesbrough underlined the point most forcibly. Liverpool now boasted the record transfer fee between two English clubs (Souness), the largest between two British clubs (Dalglish) and the biggest between an English and foreign side (Keegan). In spite of the impressive price tags, Paisley's aim was never to create a team of highly-paid football geniuses. On the contrary, he greatly distrusted excessive flair unless it could be harnessed to the overall good of the team. His philosophy of buying players is particularly revealing:

> There's always a fault you can find. The perfect player never existed. That's what I think. Like Bill Shankly, I always felt teamwork was most important. If you get too many individuals some of them won't tie up with anybody else. They still play as individuals and try to cut each other out. We'd always pounce on somebody like that and soon unload them. When you're buying players you must look closely at your team. You might put somebody in to help an international who you're trying to boost. That way you can raise two players, a star player and a moderate one who's doing a particular chore for the full 90 minutes. You might need somebody in the air or two centre backs, but you must balance them off. It's that blend you're always after.

Again and again, Paisley would complement the skilful and the workmanlike to build a perfectly integrated side. The 1978–79 squad was arguably Liverpool's best ever and yet they began the new season with some desperately disappointing results. In the first round of the European Cup they were drawn against Nottingham Forest and, although Paisley expected a tough match, it was generally assumed that Liverpool's experience would prove decisive. At the City Ground, however, Forest established an impressive 2–0 first leg lead as Liverpool fell into the trap of playing the game as though it were an English Cup tie. Football pundits still reckoned that Paisley's side would reverse the defeat at Anfield, but they underestimated the defensive tenacity of Clough's well-drilled squad who bravely held out for a goalless draw. For the third time in a year, Forest had stolen Liverpool's glory and would go on to lift the European Cup the following May. The Merseysiders barely had time to console themselves before they were ushered out of the League Cup by lowly Sheffield United. The season had hardly begun and already Liverpool had surrendered two trophies.

The early season shocks steeled Liverpool for their most concerted League challenge in years. Clough's Nottingham Forest were determined to retain the trophy and found themselves in the middle of a 42-match unbeaten run. Paisley thrived on such a forthright challenge, however, and by the New Year Liverpool were on course for a possible double. Their exemplary defence took them through to the semi-finals of the FA Cup without conceding a goal. There they faced the familiar enemy, Manchester United, in a fierce struggle which ended 2–2. With the replay at Goodison, Liverpool were favourites to reach Wembley but recent Cup history repeated itself when Jimmy Greenhoff scored another late winner to sink Paisley's hopes. At least the League Championship had become a formality with Liverpool taking the title on an emotional evening at home to Aston Villa. It was a match scripted by the gods, for that very day Paisley was celebrating the 40th anniversary of his arrival at Anfield. The sense of history swept Liverpool towards the brink of a thrilling Championship statistical record. Coincidentally, their final fixture was at Leeds United who needed at least a draw to protect their all-time 67-point Championship record. Liverpool were unmerciful that night and romped home 3–0 to end the season with an incredible 68 points. Although they could not match Leeds' League record of only two defeats in a season, Liverpool's defensive record was greatly superior. They conceded a mere 16 goals in 42 matches, scoring 85, with a goal difference of 69, a feat only matched in the First Division by the great Arsenal side of the 1930s. It is little wonder that the team of 1978–79 lays claim to be the greatest of Liverpool's Championship sides.

Throughout this period of unprecedented success for Liverpool, several of the old guard, including John Toshack and Emlyn Hughes, had been transferred to lesser clubs. Unlike many managers, Paisley did not believe in hanging on to old heroes, although he stresses that his motives were charitable rather than expedient:

> I always thought that if there was any money they could get I would leave them go early rather than putting them into the reserves. I don't think it's ever any good when they end up in the reserves.

While Liverpool were still reorganising the team in the wake of Hughes' departure, they again fell victim to early season European ennui. The culprits this time were the Soviets Dynamo Tbilisi, who came to Anfield looking like European Champions and were desperately unlucky to lose 2–1. Their pedigree was confirmed two weeks later in Russia where they beat Liverpool 3–0 with a breathtaking display of free-flowing football. Predictably, the Reds responded to this setback with some class performances in the League. Once Liverpool hit top gear they looked unstoppable and although Manchester United and Ipswich fought all the way, the Merseysiders would not surrender their title.

The umpteenth attempt to emulate Spurs and Arsenal by winning the double seemed more likely than ever, especially after Liverpool journeyed to the City Ground and destroyed their erstwhile rivals Nottingham Forest 2–0. After defeating Bury, Liverpool won a memorable quarter-final tie away to Spurs and suddenly Wembley beckoned. Semifinals are seldom walkovers, but when Liverpool and Arsenal met, the result was an epic series of four matches which threatened to delay the date of the final. The deadlock was eventually broken by Arsenal who narrowly won the fourth match 1–0 to rob Paisley of his first FA Cup final as a manager. Amazingly, he would never come close again, for over the next three years Liverpool failed to progress beyond the fifth round. Missing out on the most glamorous of domestic trophies was a bitter disappointment to Paisley, but he remains stoical about his lost chances:

> I had more luck with all the other trophies, but I'd have liked to have won that FA Cup. I was there with Bill as both a trainer [1965] and assistant manager [1974]. I'd have liked to have won one myself. You win everything else and miss the FA Cup, so you settle for that. That's the way it goes.

FA Cup failures may have prevented Liverpool from achieving elaborate trebles but there were still enough trophies left to keep the Kop content. A rather patchy season in the League saw Liverpool slump to fifth place, but their progress in the European and League Cups was impressive. It took a replayed final against West Ham before Paisley finally got his hands on the League Cup and the trophy remained in his grasp for the rest of his managerial career. This latest triumph was a sweetener before the European finale, which had developed into a veritable battle of the giants. The semi-final line-up was nothing short of extraordinary: Real Madrid, Inter-Milan, Bayern Munich and Liverpool. The script read like a potted history of the European Cup as these four combatants had between them won the trophy 13 times. While Milan overcame Madrid, Liverpool faced an uphill struggle against Munich who recorded a goalless draw at Anfield. Paisley was faced with selection problems in the return encounter and finally elected to throw in such unfamiliar names as Howard Gayle, Richard Money and Colin Irwin. The decision to drop star striker Ian Rush was based on the belief that the Germans' over-regimentation and fear of the unknown would prove their undoing. It was a bold gamble that worked. The reserve trio performed exceptionally well in the circumstances and, just as the match was drifting towards extra time, Ray Kennedy scored the killer away goal. Bayern grabbed an immediate equaliser but it was not enough. Paisley's unorthodox tactic had won the day and he was on his way to Paris for his third European Cup final.

The billing Real Madrid v Liverpool conjured up visions of a soccer feast, but the reality turned out to be severely anti-climactic. Real, contesting their ninth final, had won the trophy on six occasions with wondrous displays of open attacking football but the Rome match was a battle of defences. It was a case of 'nothing neither way' until the closing minutes when Alan Kennedy ended the agony with a brilliantly-hit winner. Liverpool's track record was now beyond the reach of any of their rivals, and their manager was achieving legendary status. No longer spoken of in terms of England alone, Paisley had transcended parochial soccer and was proudly hailed as the first manager to win three European Cups. In the year of Bill Shankly's death, his successor had reached what seemed scarcely credible summits.

The 1981–82 season brought further changes at Liverpool when the ageing, but still effective, Ray Clemence was replaced by the eccentric South African goalkeeper Bruce Grobbelaar. Phil Thompson and Ray Kennedy also departed and new names such as Craig Johnston and Mark Lawrenson began appearing regularly on team sheets. Liverpool's unparalleled League record clearly attracted many wide-eyed youngsters, but for Mark Lawrenson it was the club's efficiency rather than image, which won his signature:

> I was talking to Arsenal and Manchester United at the time. But the way Liverpool went about their business I signed before I saw their place. They were great and very down to earth. Bob Paisley and the chairman were very businesslike and simply said: 'We want you to come'. I was still speaking to Manchester United but they weren't sure how much money they had to spend. Ron Atkinson wanted two players to go to Brighton and me to go to Manchester United, so it was a bit up in the air. Liverpool were in: 'We're paying cash'. No contest.

After the high-powered dealings, Lawrenson was pleasantly surprised to discover that Liverpool was a homely club with a friendly, easy-going atmosphere. In spite of the mountain of trophies, Paisley betrayed none of the egotistical trappings that usually come with uninterrupted success. Lawrenson paints a portrait of a humble, but confident, helmsman:

> He was like my granddad, I suppose. He was probably the shrewdest person I ever met in football. I never had any problems with him or with anyone at the club. Half the time, if you didn't know who he was, you'd think he was just a guy who worked at the ground. There were no airs and graces about him. He'd turn up wearing his slippers in the office. That's how he went about his business. He knew his place.

Paisley may have had most of the desired qualities of a schooled manager, but one distinctive failing was his communicative skills. Journalists in search of a juicy quote were no doubt bamboozled by his rambling, incoherent style of speech and, according to Lawrenson, new players found it similarly difficult to follow his thought processes during team talks:

> By his own admission he's not the best communicator. He was a master of the unfinished sentence. Some team meetings you'd wonder exactly what he meant but his message managed to get through.

He had his own kind of language if you will. Sometimes, you weren't quite clear what he meant so you'd say to Joe [Fagan]: 'What's he on about?' Joe, who'd been there a long time, would say: 'Well he means *this*'. After a while you became used to it, but as a new player it was a joke.

Another transitional period saw Liverpool briefly hit a sluggish spell in the League and they could not resist the financial temptation of competing for the World Club Championship in December 1981. This notorious competition involving the European and South American Champions had degenerated into a brawling fiasco in the 1960s, so instead of home and away legs, the organisers had settled on a neutral ground. The venue was distant Tokyo and the fate of Liverpool was the same as that of every other British club who had attempted to win the competition. The Brazilian side Flamengo won convincingly 3–0 and Liverpool returned home wondering why they had bothered. Their League standing was already in peril and in the New Year they suffered a shock defeat in the European Cup. Amazingly, their vanquishers were CSKA Sofia, a team they had thrashed 6–1 on aggregate the previous season. The Sofians narrowly won a controversial match in their own country, which was most memorable for the unfortunate dismissal of Mark Lawrenson, the first Liverpool player to be sent off in 18 years of European competition. Paisley was uncharacteristically furious about the result and roundly condemned the men in black in a tone which echoed Shankly: 'The officials were the worst I have seen in Europe since the trouble we had with Inter-Milan in 1965'. The disappointment was partly alleviated by the re-acquisition of the League Cup but, as ever, the Championship remained a priority.

In January 1982, Liverpool stood ninth in the League with a paltry 27 points from 18 matches. The new youngsters expected some harsh words from the manager but were amazed by his self-control in the face of unfavourable results. Mark Lawrenson recalls Paisley's controlled temperament:

> He'd be more vocal on a Monday than a Saturday. If he did any ranting and raving, which wasn't that often, he saved it for Monday. I think he felt that there was a danger of things being said in the heat of the moment after a bad game. He'd like to think things through first. He had two very able lieutenants in Joe Fagan and Ronnie Moran who did a lot of shouting anyway. They had the famous bootroom where they chewed things over. Look at the experience of those three alone. They had it!

Paisley's ability to absorb bad results and still push Liverpool towards a seemingly lost cause is exemplified by the climax to the 1982 season. With Rush and Dalglish hitting form, Liverpool strung together 11 consecutive victories and overhauled Ipswich to win their 13th League Championship. As Paisley pithily concluded; 'I'm proudest of this one because there was so much to do'.

In August 1982, Paisley announced that the forthcoming season would be his last as manager of Liverpool. By then he would be 64 and he was ready to retire. There was a discernible jauntiness in his mood throughout that final year as if he was determined to enjoy his last 12 months whatever the outcome. In October, when Liverpool were unexpectedly defeated by West Ham, he joked: 'Perhaps they should move us down to 12th place and we'll start again'. Remarkably, had such a bizarre ruling occurred, Liverpool would still have won the Championship. They soon eased their way to the top of the League and kept extending their lead until they established an incredible 16-point gap between themselves and second-placed Watford. So convincing was their embarrassing lead that they squandered their closing matches, losing five of their last seven fixtures and yet still ended the season 11 points clear. An annoying defeat in the quarter-finals of the European Cup at the hands of Widzew Lodz of Poland and an FA Cup loss to Brighton left one last trophy for the shelf. The once-elusive League Cup was becoming a permanent fixture in the Liverpool boardroom and the players were determined to provide Paisley with a hat trick of victories. A tough and highly entertaining final against Manchester United saw the Merseysiders win 2–1 and, fittingly, it was Paisley himself who scaled the steps of Wembley to receive the trophy. It was a marvellous end to an astonishingly successful football career. Under Paisley's managerial aegis, Liverpool collected a remarkable 13 trophies in nine seasons: six League Championships, three European Cups, three League Cups and one UEFA Cup.

Paisley admits that he would have come out of retirement if Liverpool had slumped badly in the wake of his leaving, but with reliable Joe Fagan at the helm this was never likely. Joe Fagan had been at Anfield since 1957, and at 62 was the oldest managerial debutant in League history. According to Paisley, he was extremely reluctant to accept the post and it was clear that his reign would necessarily be short. For the general public, it was inconceivable that anyone could follow Paisley, but the same had been said when Shankly retired. Liverpool's strength always lay in their remarkable continuity, and, as Fagan demonstrated, there were always new peaks to surmount. In his first year, Fagan added a fourth consecutive League Cup to the Anfield shelves and brought Liverpool a third successive Championship, equalling the achievement of Huddersfield in the 1920s and Arsenal in the 1930s. He also won the European Cup and in so doing became the first English manager to win three major trophies in one season. It might not have been the 'classic treble' (European Cup, Championship and FA Cup) but it was a treble, nonetheless. Paisley had stamped his personality on the club by winning trophies *en masse* and his successors seemed determined to achieve the few remaining goals that had eluded the old master.

When Kenny Dalglish took over the managerial reins in 1985, he inherited a team still suffering the horrific consequences of the Brussels disaster. The European Cup final at the Heysel Stadium ended with a tragic death toll of 39 and afterwards Liverpool were banned indefinitely from further Continental competition. Denied European football, Dalglish could not pursue the immemorial dream of the classic treble, so concentrated on domestic trophies. Amazingly, he too entered the record books in his first year as manager. The elusive double that Liverpool had come so near to winning over the years was finally achieved in 1986, much to the chagrin of closest rivals Everton. Even more remarkable, in many ways, was the team of 1987–88 which won the Championship in devastating form, losing only two matches and equalling Leeds United's record run of 29 unbeaten League games from the start of the season. Dalglish also narrowly missed a second double when unfancied Wimbledon surprisingly outwitted Liverpool in the FA Cup final. Not for the first time, football commentators were claiming that this was the greatest Liverpool side of all.

Bob Paisley, who had seen a plethora of 'Super Liverpools' over the years, was less willing to make such extravagant claims:

> Now they talk about Liverpool being the best team ever, but it's so difficult to judge. I could say that I would fancy my chances against them with the teams I had, but that wouldn't be fair because I know everybody that's there now. They're doing well and I put it down to the fact that the First Division isn't half as good as it was. I don't care what people say! I've seen nothing other than about five teams, and it was never like that when we played. It only seems to have happened in the last three to four years. Is this the weakest First Division ever? Yes. But I can only talk about the last 50 years.

Although it is inevitable that Dalglish will be compared to Paisley and Shankly, it would be wrong to assume that he is merely following a well-worn managerial blueprint. Mark Lawrenson, who served under the last three Liverpool managers, recalls that Dalglish was quite willing to challenge and alter Paisley's familiar routine:

> Dalglish, more than anyone, changed things. With Joe, it had been a case of 'as you were'. Joe picked his best 11 players whereas Kenny played horses for courses. If it meant playing a sweeper at some grounds, we did. Joe stuck to 4–4–2 wherever we went, except the odd occasion in Europe, but with Kenny it was different. Frankly, you weren't quite sure when you won 5–0 whether you'd be playing the next week. With Bob, 'Yes'; Joe, 'Yes'; but Kenny, 'No, not sure'. It kept everybody on their toes. Kenny also wouldn't announce the team until one-and-a-quarter hours before the kick-off, which had never previously been done on a regular basis. He used to say: 'If there's 16 in the squad, I like to think there's 16 who think they might be playing'. He was single-minded enough to make that decision. He had to ostracise himself somewhat from the players but he was tailor-made for the job. He just stepped into it.

And so another era begins. Sitting at his Woolton home, surrounded by a bulging cabinet of silverware amassed during a lifetime of professional football, Paisley recognises that Liverpool FC is bigger than any individual manager, including himself. He has played a crucial part in the history of the club as player, trainer, assistant manager, manager, scout and consultant. While acknowledging the strength of the present squad, he will allow himself to be drawn sufficiently to pinpoint a possible weakness:

We don't go scouting as often now, but we should do. When Kenny took over I used to go off when there was something big. But now we're not being called out and this might be a fault. It doesn't matter whether you say yes or no about a player, you can always give an opinion. They're settling in now and forgetting people. There are things that are being left. It's surprising, really. But they'll get back to it. They'll find out soon enough!

The above comments were made at Paisley's Woolton home in September 1988. Judged in the context of his lifelong support for Liverpool, they seemed candidly critical. Taken out of context, they might have served as tasty tabloid tittle-tattle. I smiled inwardly at the thought of such imaginary headlines as 'The Forgotten Man Of Liverpool' and '"Dalglish Has Got It Wrong" Says Uncle Bob'. An exaggerated Paisley v Dalglish feud could easily be manufactured from a few isolated, oblique words. Fortunately, I was not a hungry journalist, low brow or otherwise. It was clear that Paisley wasn't wildly impressed with things at Anfield, but neither was he overtly critical. They might hit a troubled patch because of their recent scouting policy, but he seemed confident that things would work out fine.

Six months after our interview, tabloid reality imitated my authorial imaginings as Paisley offered a similar but more damning summation of the set-up at Anfield. Liverpool were trailing Arsenal, Norwich and Millwall by the proverbial street and Paisley's displeasure at their League placing spilled over into some ill-advised criticism of the manager and several players. The quiet man of football was predictably cast in the role of the damning godfather and felt so embarrassed by the storm-in-a-teacup controversy that he proffered his resignation as a director. The offer was diplomatically declined and, days later, Paisley, accompanied by the Liverpool chairman, turned up before a match and apologised to both Dalglish and the players. It was a characteristically self-effacing act from the most successful and humblest soccer manager of the modern era. Following Paisley's public sideswipe and subsequent apology, Liverpool abruptly reverted to their winning ways and threatened to sweep all before them until the tragic events at Hillsborough blighted their season. With 95 spectators crushed to death, it was widely believed that Liverpool would end their season there and then. Instead, they continued against a background of mournful remembrance, winning the FA Cup in an emotional final against neighbours Everton and losing the title to Arsenal in the last moments of their closing fixture at Anfield. It was a remarkably exciting and moving conclusion to a season which had proven, once again, the indomitable spirit of a football club whose name is now synonymous with tragedy and triumph.

GRAHAM TAYLOR

THE BACKWARDS
STEP FORWARDS MANAGER

Graham Taylor was born on 15 September 1944 at a farm in Worksop, Nottinghamshire. Two years later, the family moved to Scunthorpe, where his father became a sports journalist for the local paper. Some of Graham's earliest recollections are of Saturday afternoons spent in the press box of the Old Show Ground:

> My father was known under the pseudonym 'The Lincolnshire Poacher'. He followed Scunthorpe United, then in the Midland League, and as a five- or six-year-old I was taken to games. I was placed in the press box and part of my job would be to press a stop-watch when a goal was scored.

Even before he properly understood the rules of the game, young Taylor was granted a unique introduction to football. The Taylors were a sporting family and both Graham and his elder sister Christine were impressive young athletes. During his early teens, Graham moved increasingly towards football and received considerable support from his parents. Often, his Methodist mother, Dorothy, would rise at the crack of dawn for her job with the Post Office and then rush home to take her children to athletic meetings or youth team matches. In the meantime, her son was enjoying some adolescent fame as a promising soccer player:

> When I entered my teens I got an easy entrée into Scunthorpe United. I even trained with them during the summer. Their centre half, Dick Taylor, had seen me kicking a ball about as a kid. I'd been eating an apple at the same time and I was told off for that. He used to give me 6d for every goal I scored. All the players knew my father as 'Tommy Taylor the Reporter'. It was marvellous for my ego to be walking around the town and hear one of the players shout: 'Hey! Tommy's lad!' It was great to be recognised by the professionals.

The influence of Tommy Taylor upon his son's career can never be underestimated. Quite apart from encouraging his football, Tommy introduced the boy to the newspaper business. Graham often visited the offices of the *Scunthorpe Evening Telegraph*, saw the papers running off the press and listened in to the conversations of erudite sports journalists, as well as reading their copy. Years later, he would use those insights to considerable effect in his relations with the media:

> People have said much about me, but one of the more complimentary things has been my ability in terms of PR. I'm sure that comes from my father's newspaper background. I saw so many different aspects of the game: the playing, presentation and writing of it. There was a real atmosphere there. Those early influences were obviously very important.

Taylor's amateur record was fairly impressive. He appeared for Scunthorpe Boys and won a place in an England Under 15 team as a wing half. Further success playing for Lincolnshire Grammar Schools and an Under 19 England side convinced him that a professional career was on the cards. Although no academic, Taylor was progressing reasonably well in the sixth form and his father hoped that he might enter Teacher Training College. Such hopes were dashed at the end of the first year sixth when Graham decided to leave school without completing his A-levels:

> I felt that if I didn't get into football then, that I never would. Since then, there have been latecomers who have gone through college and university, but they're still the exception. Being greedy, I wish I could have gone to college and played professional football, but I'm a fellow saying this in his mid-40s. At that time it really worried me that I might not be able to get into football the following year.

Taylor's connections at Scunthorpe were not sufficient to attract the interest of manager Dick Duckworth, who passed on the lad. Grimsby Town's Tim Ward was impressed, however, and in July 1962, Taylor joined the recently-promoted Second Division club. It was a rather messy signing, for Ward was poised to move to Derby County only days later. He had considered taking Taylor with him but felt that it would be bad etiquette to poach the lad. Taylor recalls his gentlemanly manager offering him some parting advice: 'You only get out of the game what you put into it'. Before long, Taylor found out that this aphorism was not always true.

Taylor now portrays himself as an innocent abroad at Grimsby and soon after joining the club he received a rude awakening on the pitch:

> Looking back, I realise how naive I was. I'd come out of grammar school where it was three cheers for the opposition at the end of the game. I was very ill-prepared for professional football. I quickly found out what a selfish game it was and how you had to look after yourself. I well remember taking the ball off Jimmy Scott in a practice match. He was a very gifted former Manchester United player. All I got for

my sins was a deliberate kick on the calf which put me out of the game for three weeks. I had fluid on my calf and it was very painful. It was only later on that I realised here was a 34-year-old Northern Ireland international who'd played out his footballing life. He was getting a free transfer and he didn't know what he was going to do.

The need to accommodate senior players would soon thwart any chance that Taylor had of developing his own career. He made his debut for Grimsby against Newcastle on his 18th birthday but his hopes of succeeding as a wing half had already vanished. Unfortunately, Taylor was caught between two eras of football and became a victim of the new realism of the early 1960s. All his life he had played soccer in the traditional 'WM' formation and was originally signed to Grimsby as a wing half. Before long, however, the club adopted the more defensive 4-3-3 system and Taylor was pressurised into accepting a new position. Grimsby boasted an unwieldy playing staff and, according to Taylor, he was merely one of ten wing halves at the club. Against his better judgement, he agreed to slot into the team as a full back, although he was always ill-suited to the position and, indeed, would never play anything other than lower division football:

> That left me with a chip on my shoulder. It still rankles when people call me 'just a lower division player'. I'd done very well as a schoolboy and gone to Grimsby as a wing half and, just to satisfy them, I was made to play left back – a right footed left back. I was lucky to get a career out of the game. I think that was a credit to my ability. I often think, if only. . . but I ended up playing about 380 games in a position that I had to teach myself.

Grimsby stayed only two seasons in the Second Division, clinging perilously to 19th position, four points from relegation. The following season (1963–64) they were relegated on goal average and would not return to Division Two until the 1980s. The drop was soon followed by a change of manager and for two years Taylor served under a man whom he revered as a footballing guru: Jimmy McGuigan. Under McGuigan's watchful eye, Taylor rose to become club captain and the youngest FA coach of his generation. McGuigan was an ardent advocate of pure, attacking football and his perception and honesty had a marked effect on Taylor's attitude towards the game:

> If it hadn't been for Jimmy McGuigan my knowledge of and feeling for the game would not be what it is. He taught me that there was more to football than I had ever realised. It was a simple game, but there were things that you could appreciate and do off the ball as well as on it. He taught us to work as a team and explained that we all had a part to play as individuals within that team. Later, when I became a manager at Watford and Aston Villa, I had him scout for me. I could talk to him. Players and managers need people to talk to who aren't sitting at a desk. He was a pair of eyes for me that I always

trusted. He was the one person in football on whose recommendation I'd have signed somebody without seeing them. Here was a man who had experience, knew the game inside out and was, undoubtedly, the biggest influence on my footballing career. It was a body-blow to me when he died recently. I miss him greatly.

Having begun his career in the Second Division, Taylor rapidly plummeted to the Fourth. McGuigan had been unable to take Grimsby back to the relative big time and soon the club went through a fresh series of managerial appointments. McGuigan's failure to revitalise the team provided Taylor with another salutary soccer lesson:

We were probably too much of a footballing side in the Third Division and couldn't get results away from home. There was something missing. That taught me that you need players with strength who will go up to Crewe Alexandra on a wintry day and be able to dig out a draw for you. It's not all pure stuff, as people might think. If wind and snow is blowing you've got to have people who want to play. That Grimsby side under Jim McGuigan was excellent but it included people who didn't want to perform away from home. When Jim left, I couldn't see any future for me.

Taylor's disillusionment with Grimsby was intensified by the realisation that his five-year loyalty to the club counted as nothing:

You couldn't get anything from Grimsby Town. I found players were coming into the club and receiving signing-on fees whereas I'd been there for years and got nothing. The club didn't look after its own players. It was a system that rewarded everybody who moved on. There was little or no loyalty from the players who weren't being rewarded. They were given a benefit, but these testimonials were paid for by the public. The club wasn't giving you anything. My career had settled into the lower divisions, so I was willing to move to a Fourth Division club that was prepared to pay me more than I was getting at Grimsby. All I'd been asking for at Grimsby was to be treated the same as the new players that they were signing. After five years I asked for a benefit of £750. I spoke to Mansfield but then decided to go to Lincoln. They wrote into my contract that I'd receive £150 as a bonus. I just felt I had to get away from Grimsby.

Lincoln were a solid, average, Fourth Division side during the twilight years of Taylor's playing career. The directors were impressed with their 28-year-old captain, however, and in November 1972 he was appointed player/manager. It was something of a managerial baptism of fire as Lincoln drew five and lost two of their next seven matches. Stunned supporters, desperate for a win and frustrated by the board's apparently cheapskate decision to appoint an inexperienced manager from within the club, vented their wrath verbally. Chants of 'Taylor out!' rang around the stadium and Graham admits that he felt under tremendous pressure. With a wife, two children and a semi-detached to support, he shuddered at the prospect of unemployment. Fortunately, his chairman proved patient, the results gradually improved and Lincoln finished a comfortable tenth in the Fourth Division. Two more seasons in mid-table followed while Taylor engaged in a flurry of transfer activity. Close to a score of players left Sincil Bank during the interim as Taylor carefully constructed a team of experienced journeymen.

Among the imports was a mature central defender named Sam Ellis who would remain with Taylor for many years. Ellis had first encountered Taylor during his coaching course at Sheffield Wednesday and was duly impressed with the man's work. With his career evidently fading, Ellis was plucked from Mansfield and given the opportunity to spearhead Lincoln's assault on the Fourth Division Championship. Taylor was always a great believer in the importance of a thriving youth policy but it is interesting to note that, in fighting his way out of the depths, he relied largely on older players.

Taylor wanted a fearless, ambitious side and his desire was fully reflected in Lincoln's training methods, as Ellis remembers:

> In those days, Graham Taylor never worked on his defence really. All the work we did was forward play, getting balls behind people and getting crosses into the box. We were never taught the negative side of football and the stress was on teamwork: shadow play, 11-a-sides, forwards against defence, things you could relate to on a Saturday. There were none of these two against twos, one against ones and ten-yard squares. They could be useful but on Saturday afternoons you don't have ten-yard squares! He always wanted teamwork in an attacking way.

Taylor's work did not end on the training ground. Outside the club gates he was emerging as an adept public relations officer and the players were taken around the local foundries to drum up support. Ellis remembers that the squad enjoyed a good social life and a sense of cameraderie while also learning the need to be responsible to the public. Towards the end of 1975, Lincoln were winning regularly, gates were improving and reporters were witnessing the first signs of Taylor's ability to establish a 'community' club. As Sam Ellis reminds us, however, supporters always place good will a poor second behind good results:

> It's easy for people to talk about a 'family atmosphere' and a 'community spirit' but, believe me, you can only get that with a winning team. At Lincoln, he had a winning team, so he could create that atmosphere. You can't do that if you're losing week in, week out. However, there's no doubt that he had great PR ideas and could have worked on the commercial side and not just football. When he bought Peter Grotier in the Fourth Division, he actually got the fans to pay for him! They did charity walks and contributed

£16,000 of the £20,000 that he paid for him. That summed up the man and his relations with people. How many clubs could have got their supporters to buy a player? They not only wanted to do it, they clamoured to do it. We all learned so much from the man in charge.

Lincoln's grand run continued until the end of the season and they topped the Fourth Division with a record-breaking 74 points and 111 goals. Suddenly, Taylor was a minor celebrity manager and his progress caught the attention of clubs higher up the League. With their impressive scoring record, Lincoln looked a good bet to climb to the top of the Third Division yet they stalled in eighth place. Sam Ellis admits that the team needed strengthening but club economics precluded development. The board apparently felt that Lincoln had reached the limits of its expansion in the upper echelons of the Third Division and actually feared the implications of further success. Interestingly, Ellis does not censure the Lincoln directors for their financial timidity:

If that's the only thing they think they can handle and they level with the manager there should be no problems. If you're told you've got to sell players, you've got to sell them.

Taylor knew he could go no further with Lincoln but argues that a change in the composition of the board might have produced a more positive approach:

Lincoln could have gone on to the Second Division. There was within that club a man named Reg Brearley who subsequently became chairman and he could have taken Lincoln further with me as manager. There's a saying: 'Managers know when players must go'. Directors also know when players must go but what they *never* know is when they should go. Having done a good job many directors can never come to terms with their situation and realise that it's time to move on. That was what was wrong at Lincoln.

In April 1977, Taylor received the kind of invitation that most Third Division managers vainly fantasise about: the managership of a top ten First Division club. West Bromwich Albion were emerging as one of the most consistent teams of the late 1970s with genuine Championship and Cup aspirations. Their offer looked a godsend but, remarkably, Taylor turned them down. The crunch came during a meeting with the Albion directors when the chairman informed Taylor: 'We know all about you'. The Lincoln manager smiled inwardly while ruefully concluding: 'Well, I could have read the *Rothmans Football Yearbook* too! He knew absolutely nothing about me'. Negotiations swiftly broke down as Taylor refused to place himself in a position where he could be 'chewed up and spat out' like so many other overreaching lower division managers. His logic seemed strangely overcautious and what happened next convinced his detractors that he was a manager of limited ambition. For, less than two months later, Taylor agreed to join Fourth Division Watford.

The conclusions were inescapable: Taylor had received a golden opportunity to break into the First Division top ten, yet here he was perversely dropping down a level. Obviously, he did not fancy his chances with a big club, lacked ambition and, more crudely, 'had no bottle'. What Watford offered was a small club with a pop star chairman, Elton John, who was seemingly willing to throw his money around. For the cynics, the entire set-up looked a joke and a fitting resting place for Taylor, 'the lower division player' who had confirmed his standing as a 'lower division manager'.

Taylor appeared to be taking a terrible risk with his career but it says much for his self-belief that he never doubted his chances of success. He had the opportunity to earn bigger wages and lucrative bonuses working at West Bromwich Albion, but what primarily appealed to Taylor was that most crucial of managerial requisites – power:

> As a manager you've got to establish relationships with so many people. That's why a manager, in the main, wants total control. Otherwise, he's spending too much time trying to stabilise his position. At Watford, provided I had enough confidence, the money would look after itself. In my early days at Watford I needed the power to give me the chance to be successful. So, actually, when it came to the contract, the money was secondary to my thinking. If you're out of a job it doesn't matter what you *were* earning. Authority was therefore important. I needed the position of power to enable everybody at the club to get the situation right. A lot of people said: 'You're lucky to have Elton John as chairman'. You're only lucky if you have ability yourself. Many managers like to hide behind directors. You talk to them and they'll say: 'We're not successful – but it's not my fault! The chairman won't give us any money'. With every decision I would make, I could never say that. Success or failure at Watford would be down to me. If you're not being restricted on your buying, how can you complain? Everything was ideal as long as you were willing to accept the responsibility that a chairman like Elton John gives you. His attitude was: 'You're the manager, get on with it. That's what I pay you for'.

Taylor speaks with great enthusiasm of his empathy with Elton John and what emerges most clearly is the excitement of two people pursuing a shared footballing dream:

> At Watford I met a man who was as daft as me. Elton John wanted to take a Fourth Division club to the top and into Europe. I remember asking him: 'Have you any idea what that will cost?' and he said, 'No'. I told him: 'Well, you ought to say a million to start with!' And it actually cost him more. But it wasn't just financial backing to buy players. That wasn't his job. In ten years, Elton John invested money to buy players on only three occasions. All the other money was spent on the development of the ground, the backing. There was no thought in my

mind that we might not succeed. We seemed to have a kind of telepathy. Our whole purpose was not just going to the First Division but the concept of what a football club could be. That idea of developing a team as part of the community stemmed from Elton and myself. Nobody else.

Once Elton John and Graham Taylor had made their pact, the Watford dream became a cause. Taylor's first priority was to seek an assistant and by September a surprise candidate was appointed. It was shortly after securing the Watford job that Taylor had received a letter of congratulations from former Arsenal manager Bertie Mee. Although no longer active in professional football, Mee was still regarded with tremendous respect for having taken Arsenal to the double only six years before. Taylor had seen the Gunners at Wembley that season and had a superstitious affinity for the club stemming from his childhood. He had once dreamed of playing for Arsenal and throughout his managerial years retained a forlorn belief that he would one day manage the North London side. His sense of destiny was thwarted on both counts but that same intuition caused him to ponder Mee's motives in writing to Watford. Reading between the lines he convinced himself that Mee was subtly fishing for an opportunity to return to League football. Taylor could not think of a more suitable recruit. With a 'lower division manager' and pop star chairman at the helm, Watford urgently needed an experienced and respected elder statesman to bring the club credibility. Mee was willing to accept an assistant managership and assume responsibilities for the scouting and youth schemes which Taylor had been formulating. It was to prove a happy marriage of experience and ambition, but not everyone was convinced initially. Taylor remembers walking behind one person at the club who was saying to a colleague: 'They'll be bloody signing Alf Ramsey as a turnstile man next'.

The Taylor/Mee amalgam was far from a short-term PR exercise. The youth policy was immediately implemented and during the first season several promising lads were signed including Steve Terry, Kenny Jackett and Les Taylor. They would not emerge into the first team for several years and, as at Lincoln, Taylor relied on older, tougher players to start the promotion wagon rolling. Sam Ellis again found himself in a winning side and maintains that his former manager was following a strict pattern:

Everybody says 'The Watford Way', but this was what had been started at Lincoln. Part of his proven formula, certainly at the lower divisional level, was to get experienced players together. You look at his teams in the Fourth Division and you won't find many kids there. They didn't come through until much later. I think that was deliberate because the Third and Fourth Divisions are probably much more physical.

Ellis may be right, but it is also true to say that Taylor had little choice but to wait for the 'Watford Babes' to come through. He had not inherited a team of aspiring youngsters and so the first phase inevitably required older heads. As it turned out, Watford easily won promotion at the end of the season, a runaway 11 points clear of their nearest rivals.

Taylor was relieved to get out of the Fourth Division at the first attempt for he realised that a successful youth policy depended upon the improving status of the club. If Watford were to compete successfully in the youth stakes against such clubs as Spurs and Manchester United they needed not only excellent facilities but a first team that was on a roll. Plans were already underway to open a family enclosure and Mee was fully utilising his many footballing contacts in an attempt to step up the youth recruitment drive. As Taylor explains, Watford were unnervingly ambitious in their long-term thinking:

> Bertie Mee proved that we knew what we wanted. I hadn't just joined Watford to win the Fourth Division Championship. I didn't need Bertie Mee for that, I'd already won it with Lincoln. Believe me, I knew enough about the Fourth Division. What I didn't know about was the First and Second. So, initially, it was me taking Bertie around. I well remember going to Rochdale and him saying: 'Where is it?' It was a laugh and a joke. I used to tell him: 'This is my background, I know all about this'.

Mee would repay the educational tour four years hence, but in the meantime, Watford wasted no time in winning promotion to the Second Division. Even Taylor was slightly taken aback by the speed with which Watford were racing up the League tables and he secretly feared that the present squad could not sustain the momentum. It takes several years for a youth policy to reach fruition and Watford were in the Second Division with an ageing side. For one of the few times in his managerial life, Taylor spent heavily to save the club, and seriously blundered:

> I had lower division players who didn't know how to cope with the Second Division. Then I made a mistake. I spent a lot of Elton's money because it looked like we might get relegated. I bought what I thought were class players but they were really five-a-side players. Their training had been based on five-a-side because that's how Liverpool are said to play. But these were not Liverpool players! As a result, one or two had to go by the wayside. I learned my lesson there, but having wasted some of Elton's money we made up for it in a variety of ways.

Although Watford finished a lowly 18th, there was a general feeling that the relegation crisis was permanently over. Behind the scenes, chief executive Eddie Plumley was establishing himself as an astute administrator while Caroline Gillies was making history as one of the first women to succeed at a top club as marketing manager. Watford's organisation was both strong and adventurous with money pouring in from advertising revenue, lotteries and lucrative friendly matches. Everybody was working for Taylor's cause and ,with Elton John promising further money in the event of First Division success, stability was assured.

On the pitch, Taylor was still encouraging his players to believe in themselves and, as Sam Ellis remembers, the tactics were effective:

> Like any other manager he'd go through teams: strengths and weaknesses. But there were no six-page dossiers. In the end he'd always say: 'We're better than them'. If they had a certain weakness we would expose it. He was very thoughtful in the preparation of his own team rather than in the dissection of other teams. He was a very clever tactician, always playing to our strengths. Sometimes he might say a particular opponent needed attending to, but nothing more than that. He came up with a way of playing that was effective in every division of the League. Look at the teams that Watford knocked out of various cup competitions over the years before they reached the top. It worked.

By 1979–80 the first batch of youngsters were mature enough to hit the Second Division and players such as Kenny Jackett, Steve Terry and Nigel Callaghan all made an important contribution in taking Watford to ninth position. As the club ascended the table, the influence of Bertie Mee in the background obviously increased. Young Steve Harrison saw him as a 'guiding light', adding: 'He did very well for Graham Taylor in those early years. I think he was the old head on young shoulders. . . a stabilising force'. Sam Ellis also feels that Mee's contribution to the Taylor cause should not be underestimated:

> If you respect somebody's judgement, you listen to them. Having listened, Graham Taylor would certainly make up his own mind and make the final decision. Bertie Mee was very experienced and a very influential man about the place. But how much he influenced the gaffer's decisions is difficult to say. I used to love sitting and talking to him for hours. You could ask him questions and he'd always help you. He taught me a lot.

Mee's Arsenal connections proved crucial in the signing of several indispensable players. Sunderland winger Wilf Rostron had signed schoolboy forms with the Gunners during Mee's reign and was happy to rejoin his old master at the Hertfordshire club. Mee also recommended Pat Rice, whose leadership would prove inspirational in the final charge towards the First Division. The third crucial signing during this period was a 17-year-old unknown who played for Sudbury Court in the Middlesex League. John Barnes had attended a non-soccer playing school, Marylebone Grammar, and somehow escaped the surveillance of the country's leading scouts. Mee checked out the lad and after only 15 minutes concluded that he was Watford material. It was a tremendously lucky signing, for Barnes' family were about to return to their native Jamaica. As it turned out, Mee had an unexpected advantage over any potential rival for he knew Barnes' father. Ken Barnes, a colonel in the Jamaican army, had once managed the national side in the Central American and Caribbean League. Arsenal had visited El Salvador under Mee and played Barnes' side, only to see the match called off after half-an-hour when the over-excited crowd rioted. It was not an incident easily forgotten and provided Mee with a distracting inroad while discussing the future of young John Barnes. Barnes' parents trusted Mee and the move to Watford progressed more smoothly than might otherwise have been the case.

In April 1982, Watford clinched promotion to the First Division, and the best was yet to come. Taylor was now entering a territory far more familiar to Bertie Mee but he denies feeling excessively wary of possible usurpation:

> The danger of bringing in Bertie was that he could have influenced me on everything. He could have taken over because he was perceptive and an excellent negotiator. But I never feared him. Never. I appointed Bertie because I was certain of the role that he could play in the development of Watford FC. He was seldom involved in the playing side, apart from passing comments. We talked about the game but he never came onto the pitch at all. He saw what we were doing and was quite certain that it was right for the club. I'm sure it wouldn't have been right for Arsenal. But we weren't as mean as an Arsenal side, nor as defensive. There was no way we could ever have become a second Arsenal. I didn't ever worry about him taking over.

Nevertheless, Taylor admits that he was sufficiently concerned about the extent of Mee's influence to emphasise his own authority within the club:

> When a man has won the double everybody backs down when he says anything. I felt it was very important to show that there was only one manager there: *me*. Bertie was very strict, especially regarding punctuality. We had staff meetings sometimes in the mornings and I knew that if they started at 9am Bertie would expect everybody to be there. I would arrive at 9.10. I knew that Bertie could not get up and leave in that ten minutes. He would be talking to Sam Ellis who would be learning from that. But it also made it clear that I was not going to jump for Bertie, who can be very intimidating. The only person who could be late for that meeting was me, the manager. Sam and the others couldn't be late and Bertie, of course, never would be anyway. I deliberately let that get up his nose, but other people had to see it. He had become so used to his own organisation and delegation.

The promotion to the First Division coincided with Watford winning the FA Youth Challenge Cup. It was a clear indication that Taylor's youth policy had paid off. Unlike the debut season in the Second Division, there was no temptation to splash out superfluous sums strengthening the squad. Taylor, at least, was glad to be spared such an unsavoury spree:

> I don't like getting involved in the transfer market. . . I think when you sit down and start talking millions of pounds it takes the thing completely out of proportion. I'll work with the transfer market whatever standard it gets, but I'm not keen speaking to young men about earning millions. The whole purpose of Watford was to develop a youth policy and produce players that could play in the First Division. We were fortunate that quite a few did.

Apart from the money saved in transfer fees, Watford finalised a £400,000 three-year sponsorship deal with the trucking company Iveco. Another £400,000 was secured through season ticket sales, again underlining the fine work of Caroline Gillies and Eddie Plumley.

On the field, the players were well-disciplined and had clearly learned much from the coaching skills of Tom Walley and Sam Ellis. The training staff themselves had paid considerable attention to the advice and instruction of Taylor and Mee, and the communication between different departments at the club was exemplary. Sam Ellis was already sufficiently knowledgeable to secure a managerial post in his own right at once-great Blackpool. He concludes that Taylor maintained a close relationship with the players even while preparing for the logistical problems of succeeding at the top:

> The players had the utmost respect for him. He is a very approachable man, although some of the press and public might not think so. He always listened to players. They did as they were told and there was a certain amount of respect, possibly fear, but they could still speak to him. My job at certain times was to shield the pressures from the manager and if there was something I could do myself, I'd do it. Yet, I never had a player ask me why he wasn't in the team. The gaffer always told them. There's no way any of his staff can take credit for the relationship Graham Taylor had with his players. He did that himself and he was bloody good at it.

Watford made their First Division debut at home against Everton and won convincingly 2–0. Days later there was a 4–1 away victory at Southampton. Winning three of their first five games was fairly impressive, but, following a demolition job by Brian Clough's Nottingham Forest, most critics assumed that Watford would quietly drift towards mid-table. On 25 September, however, the entire First Division was awoken by an amazing result at Vicarage Road which read: Watford 8 Sunderland 0. The hero of the day was Luther Blissett, who scored his first hat trick for the club since joining as a schoolboy back in 1974. The result was sufficient to take Watford to third in the table behind Manchester United and Liverpool. Even at this early stage, however, the Merseyside giants were playing at their brilliant best and on the same day defeated Southampton 5–0. However, nothing could distract from Watford's achievement in inflicting on Sunderland a defeat which equalled their worst ever and Taylor was happy enough to savour such glory:

> When Watford reached the First Division it was the first time I'd been there too. We went bombing away and I couldn't stop them winning. I knew we'd suffer for that later, but, in many respects, it was the pay-off for players like Luther Blissett and all of us. I had to learn all about the First Division. Of course, even if you've played there you still have to learn about management, so it doesn't make that much difference. Later on, people said that getting to the FA Cup final must have been the greatest emotional moment for me. It wasn't. The greatest thing was winning promotion to the First Division. It had taken me a full 20 years from 1962 to 1982 to reach my target and achieve what I wanted.

Within a week of the Sunderland massacre, Graham Taylor's career took another upswing when he was recruited as manager of the England youth squad. The part-time appointment caused a wave of controversy as earnest football scribes spoke of the dangers of England 'B' transforming into a carbon copy of Watford. Even the FA's head of coaching Allen Wade entered the fray by proclaiming:

> Playing football the Watford way worries me stiff. It could kill the game. The minds of players are drilled to fulfil certain requirements, irrespective of their own inclinations. I don't want to knock Graham Taylor or Watford – quite the reverse. I admire what he has achieved with limited resources. The problem is that the Watford way shouldn't be the England way.

Taylor rightly felt that the fuss was ridiculous and consistently explained that the obsession with Watford's 'long ball' tactics had little to do with his task of supervising England's youngsters. Like many before him, Taylor found the job as England youth manager a taxing part-time post and later suggested that it was too distracting for a First Division manager. Although some managers might have clung to the position as a means of staking a stronger claim for the ultimate honour of England supremo, Taylor realised that this would be unfair to Watford. He duly declined Bobby Robson's invitation to continue after the European Championships and was relieved to be able to once more monitor the progress of his youth and reserve teams. The England sojourn had provided welcome experience but there was little doubt that

had Taylor continued beyond that first year his extensive commitments at Watford, not to mention his home life, would have been adversely affected.

Within weeks of accepting the England job, Taylor received further criticism when Watford made their First Division debut in London. The victims were Tottenham Hotspur whose optimistic title hopes received a serious setback when Watford departed from White Hart

Lane with a 1–0 win. The *Daily Mail's* correspondent Jeff Powell was particularly scathing in his summing up of Watford's crude, all-action style and unflatteringly described them as 'a pack of wild dogs smashing themselves into a brick wall'. Taylor dismissed the gibes as predictable tabloid stereotyping, but it is clear that the criticisms intensely annoyed him:

> Watford came into the First Division playing aggressive, direct, excit-ing football, with a lot of goalmouth incident. At the same time I was becoming a name and a threat to certain people and had to suffer this labelling that goes on. The criticism of Watford was most fierce from people like Jeff Powell who never once took time out to come and talk to me. . . Here was a manager who'd got some ability and articulacy, and he was involved in the international scene. 'Oh, my goodness, he's going to put the game back!' It's quite funny if you look at it. Absolutely ridiculous. Long ball, short ball, you either pass a ball over 30 yards or five yards.

Taylor knew his soccer history well and contented himself with the knowledge that Watford's tactics were hardly revolutionary or worthy of censure. Herbert Chapman's Arsenal and Stan Cullis's Wolves had suffered similar contemporaneous criticism only to be retrospectively applauded for their impressive achievements. Far from regimenting his players to murder the First Division with stifling tactics, Taylor claims he encouraged individuality. During training he admonished his squad with a reassuring: 'When the opposition's got the ball, challenge them in any part of the field you want to'. The idea was to discover precisely how good the First Division defences were when confronted by players who would not allow them to dwell on the ball. While critics complained that Watford's game was 'too frantic', the crowds responded with excitement to high-scoring games and a refreshingly buccaneering spirit. To this day, Taylor maintains that Watford's pluck forced the top teams out of complacency and allowed the crowds to see star players fully turning on their skills.

When Watford returned to North London three weeks after beating Tottenham and proceeded to dismantle Arsenal 2–4, even the sceptics paused for thought. As 1983 loomed, Watford were still in the top three, having completed half of their fixtures. It was at this point that Steve Harrison realised Watford were on their way to a place in Europe:

> I don't think anybody envisaged Watford finishing runners-up – that's a safe bet. But it didn't take us by surprise as it gradually unfolded. After Christmas we could see ourselves doing well because we'd played everybody else by then. We said: 'We're doing all right. We can match these sides'. Up until then it had been an unknown quantity.

As the season reached its final stages, Liverpool had already run away with the title and were 16 points clear of their nearest rivals. That deficit was eventually reduced to 11 points as the Merseysiders casually lost five of their last seven games. Meanwhile, Watford were heading for Europe and eventually pipped Manchester United for second place in the League. The statistics told their own story: won 22 lost 15 drew 5. Watford had played every game for three points or bust. Rather fittingly, the final game of the season had been against Liverpool whom they defeated 2–1. It was the perfect ending to Taylor's first Division One adventure:

> What capped it for me was beating Liverpool in Bob Paisley's last game as a manager. I kept the team sheet and I still have it at home. It seems a little thing, but if there was a man I did admire from a distance it was Bob Paisley. I thought he was a very knowledgeable and shrewd man about his people and football.

Much was made of Watford's astonishing achievement in finishing runners-up to Liverpool and there was a genuine danger of over-expectation the following season. Taylor still insisted that his side was probably mid-table quality and there was statistical evidence to back up that gut feeling. Indeed, Watford's overall points total was comparatively the lowest of any runner-up for 27 years. Significantly, their total would not have won them the Championship of any division in League history. In most other First Division seasons they would have finished a respectable sixth. Although they had never realistically challenged for the title, the winning of a European place was fully merited.

'The team that took the First Division by storm did not play in Europe the following year'. That was Taylor's disappointed summation of Watford's first and only European campaign. During the summer Luther Blissett, who had scored 27 First Division goals the previous season, was transferred to AC Milan in a £980,000 deal. His loss was disconcerting enough, but further problems followed. The team was ravaged by injuries and with the autumnal Pat Rice fading into retirement, a fresh influx of untried youngsters nervously held sway. Watford went to Kaiserslautern for their opening European fixture and were soundly beaten 3–1. Most commentators wrote off the Hertfordshire side at that point but Kaiserslautern could not contain their opponents in the return leg at Vicarage Road, as Taylor recalls:

> There was some arrogance from the West Germans and we beat them 3–0. Our kids turned them over. Nobody talked about style then.

The next trial was against tricky Levski Spartak of Sofia and this time Watford foundered at home, missing a penalty and coming away with a 1–1 draw. Incredibly, they again survived the return leg and pulled through 3–1 winners in extra time. The following day, the injury-hit Hornets placed a self-mocking advertisement in the *Times*: 'Wanted: Professional Footballers, men (or women) aged 18–80. . . preference given to applicants with two arms and two legs in working order'.

Taylor knew that his inspired youngsters were living on borrowed time and feared the worst when Watford were paired with an East European side in wintry December. Sparta Prague came to Vicarage Road and immediately established control with a 2–0 lead. The Hornets clawed their way back to 2–2, but a last-minute goal by the Czechs scotched their chances. A 3–2 defeat was an ominous result for Watford to take to Czechoslovakia, especially in sub-zero temperatures. Taylor recalls 18-year-old Neil Price facing the might of Sparta in only his second game for the club:

It was so cold that he asked for a long-sleeved shirt. We had strong discipline at Watford and our kit manager said to him: 'You effing get out there. We're all in short sleeves!' I said: 'Ah, I think we can find this lad a shirt'. He was just a kid. It was men against boys.

Sparta adapted to the freezing conditions more easily and powered into a 4–0 lead, eventually winning the tie 7–2 on aggregate. It was a comprehensive defeat but Taylor remembers one amusing incident which summed up the Watford spirit. With three minutes remaining, and Watford needing five goals to equalise, Taylor left the bench and telephoned the club doctor to announce: 'It looks like our European venture is over'. Even after hearing the score, the chirpy medic earnestly replied: 'Well, I wouldn't give it up yet, Graham'.

The sportsmanship of Watford fans has often been commented upon and their easy-going attitude has allowed younger players to blossom without feeling under pressure. Taylor recognises that 'they are not really a football town', but that too has certain advantages, for there is no history of hooliganism:

We sometimes thought that the Watford supporters should be more passionate. But with passion comes violence. The Hertfordshire people, by their nature, are neither passionate nor violent.

Steve Harrison, who has been through the club as a player, trainer and manager, concurs with Taylor's viewpoint:

I always felt that the crowd was very appreciative. That's the big difference between Watford and many other clubs. The Watford fans will stand and applaud you off the field if you've played well, whatever the result. That's unique in the football world. The public here will leave the ground with a smile if they're entertained. Obviously, results are the be-all of League status but these people enjoy good football. I've seen the crowd applaud the other side after they've scored a goal, which is correct. Graham Taylor formulated that way of thinking. It's a state of mind. It's always a warm feeling when I walk out onto the pitch because I know they're fair-minded people.

The willingness to play adventurous, fluid football has proven particularly effective for Watford in various cup competitions. After leaving the European stage and settling into a mid-table position, the club found a new road to glory via the FA Cup. In the third round they faced local rivals Luton, whose record against them was particularly impressive. As usual, the confrontation was a tight affair which required a replay before Watford pulled through 4–3 in extra time. From thereon, they had a magical draw, missing all the big clubs as they sped towards Wembley. Charlton and Brighton, both in the Second Division, were beaten convincingly, as were soon-to-be-relegated Birmingham. In the semi-final Watford avoided a couple of First Division superiors and found themselves facing Third Division Plymouth. The last club from lower than the Second Division to reach an FA Cup final was Southampton back in 1901–02. Lowly Plymouth had the chance to put themselves in the history books, but odds-on favourites Watford scored the only goal of the match. Now they faced Everton in the final.

The safe ride that Watford had enjoyed to Wembley convinced many people that their name must be written on the Cup. Everton were easily the more accomplished side but Watford looked to have the spirit and pluck to reverse current form on the big day. As it turned out, the game was a huge anti-climax and a far-from-happy experience for Graham Taylor. Two weeks before the final, his captain Wilf Rostron was sent off in a match against Luton and therefore automatically disqualified from appearing at Wembley. It was a frustrating and agonising blow for both Rostron and the club, as Taylor bitterly recalls:

> The lad was in tears, but I could do nothing about it. The secretary of the FA was 'looking into' the subject, but I knew the disciplinary procedure would not be changed.

Television glamorises the day of the final and newspapers are full of romanticised stories about wide-eyed players fulfilling their footballing dreams. For managers, Wembley is traditionally the setting of their greatest moments when years of toil are justified in 90 minutes of soccer drama. Of course, not all managers are entranced by the media razzmatazz and it is interesting to learn that Taylor felt thoroughly disillusioned even before his team arrived at the Wembley gates:

> Going up Wembley Way was a matter of driving very quickly and having a can of lager thrown at us by an Everton supporter. I thought to myself: 'This is Wembley? The Cup final?' The event as a whole was a disappointment. While everybody out there was singing 'Abide With Me' I was inside the dressing room trying to get the team going. As a manager you lead the team out but you're not important enough to go up those steps. When it's all over, people only want to know the winners.

The loss of Rostron severely reduced Watford's already dwindling hopes. Taylor claims that he probably had the youngest back four ever to appear at Wembley and could only watch helplessly as his injury-hit squad began falling to pieces and losing their collective nerve:

> I saw players in the dressing room *freeze*. Neil Price, who took Wilf Rostron's place, was one. I remember the trainer Tom Walley saying:

'Don't worry. He's all right'. He did a most unnatural thing. He lay on the floor and put his feet up on the bench to show he was relaxed. He was shaking his legs. I'd never seen anyone do that! It frightened me. He was just a kid. One year later I gave him a free transfer and told him, 'Well, you'll always have that runners-up medal'.

Taylor's memory of the final is an exercise in prosaic summation:

> The game as a whole wasn't great. We needed to score first. We had two or three chances but when they went in 1–0 at half-time it looked over. It was a pity that their second goal was allowed to stand because it killed the game off. I disagree with referees having these finals as their last games. If a referee is good enough he'll have had a Cup final before his last game. Far too many don't want to go out with controversy, so some of their decisions can be a bit slack. For the last 30 minutes of the match I just hoped we weren't going to lose 3–0 or 4–0. The game was dead.

The Wembley disappointment was at least tempered by some good news. In April 1984, Taylor signed a new six-year contract with Watford, and during the summer retrieved the heroic Luther Blissett from AC Milan for about half the price for which he had been sold.

The fee spent on Blissett was no extravagance for Watford, as they had ended the 1983–84 season with record pre-tax profits of £863,000. For the next three years the club remained a solid mid-table side and, by 1988, had set a new FA Cup record by winning through to the fifth round for seven consecutive seasons. Taylor was twice foiled in the quarter-finals, first in 1986 against double-winning Liverpool, and the following year against losing finalists Tottenham Hotspur. Watford had become perennial Cup favourites of the public and an inspiration to smaller clubs in search of glory. In Taylor's mind, his original cause had been achieved, but he still felt that the true message had been distorted by the press:

> What many people missed was that Watford FC was not just about a style of play, or winning various divisions or cups. The Watford Way was about the heart and soul of a club. It said that you could go from the Fourth to the First Division if you got the concept right. What really was important was the players, how they behaved on and off the pitch, the directors, the community, the supporters, the safety aspect – the whole presentation. Here was a club in which players themselves became a family and the club and the town became very close-knit. This was how a football club could be a community. For a decade we saw the philosophy of a club and that was my achievement.

The sense of accomplishment drove Taylor to seek a new challenge and, although he seemed settled for life at Watford, he shocked the footballing world by moving to relegated Aston Villa at the end of the 1987 season. Taylor admits that this was the most torturous moment of his managerial career. The night of decision was one that he will never forget:

> The hardest part was leaving Watford and taking a step down into Division Two. That really was frightening. I've never sweated so much at nights as I did for the first six months at Aston Villa. The night I agreed to take over I stayed at the chairman's house. By 6am I still couldn't sleep. Even now, I don't know what stopped me from walking out of that room in the morning and saying: 'I have made a terrible mistake. I'm sorry, I'm going home to Watford'.

Taylor's imagined retraction was not forthcoming and, in August 1987, he found himself studying form in the Second Division. Some people felt that Taylor would struggle to assert his authority at Villa Park, but he was sensible enough to distinguish between the needs of a community club like Watford and a city club of Aston Villa's size and power:

> I don't feel that I have to be in total control here at Aston Villa and neither do I want to be. I think it's wrong that any one person, including the chairman, should have that control. You just can't do it. To have one person responsible for the day-to-day decisions of a club this size is absolutely ridiculous. When I came here no way did I want what I had at Watford.

Before accepting the post, Taylor spelled out his conditions to the strong-willed Villa supremo Doug Ellis. Taylor respected Ellis's commitment to the club but insisted on one strict proviso: 'If you want to get involved in day-to-day decisions, make sure they're not the footballing ones'. Having defined his responsibilities, Taylor recruited trusty Steve Harrison and began the awesome task of stabilising a relegated team.

After returning from a pre-season trip to Sweden, Taylor took a closer look at the club, which only confirmed his worst fears. Behind the powerful exterior there lurked a situation of near chaos. The problems manifested themselves in a myriad of minor ways. When the club physiotherapist left, Taylor was amazed to discover that he took his equipment with him. Incredibly, he owned some of the hardware presently in operation and a cheque had to be drawn hastily to purchase new medical equipment to the tune of £7,500. Meanwhile, injured players were sent to the local hospital for ultra-sonic treatment. Taylor could only shake his head at the absurdity of it all and soldier on in increasingly urgent attempts to reorganise the club.

Bookmakers suggested that Aston Villa had a strong chance of winning promotion but Taylor was unconvinced. On more than one occasion he publicly insisted that the Midlanders were not good enough to return to the First Division. He now claims that such protestations were not only accurate but euphemistic:

> This was a club heading for the Third Division. People said it couldn't happen to Aston Villa, but it had already happened to Wolverhampton Wanderers. The playing side was a complete shambles. We had

11 players who seemed to be permanently injured. Steve Harrison helped me enormously. I left the football pitch to him initially and turned over the players and the backroom staff.

Taylor strengthened his squad by spending a total of £900,000 on Derek Mountfield, Gordon Cowans and Chris Price. Among his earliest signings was Alan McInally from Celtic, who soon showed his worth by scoring 19 goals in 19 consecutive matches. Villa proved something of an enigma during the first half of the season, struggling at home, yet winning consistently away. Taylor blamed this on the size of their stadium which housed 48,000, but only attracted crowds of around 25,000. Half-full is also half-empty and with the visiting supporters placed *en masse* behind one goal, the home fans' cheers were all too often drowned out.

In spite of Villa's erratic home form, they reached the top of the table in the New Year before stuttering towards an automatic promotion place in May. It was an amazing last day of the season with Villa straining to secure a point against Swindon while their kamikaze rivals Middlesbrough and Bradford both lost at home. The hardest year of Taylor's managerial life had ended in unexpected triumph.

While Aston Villa regained their First Division status, Taylor's former club found themselves relegated. Watford had appointed Dave Bassett as Taylor's successor and at the time this seemed a sound move. Bassett was another ambitious young manager who had taken unfashionable Wimbledon from the Fourth Division to the top half of the First. His career record paralleled that of Taylor in certain ways and deserved respect. The ability to achieve so much with limited resources suggested that he might be the perfect manager for Watford. Unfortunately, Bassett proved over-eager to stamp his personality on the club and, in retrospect, wrought too many changes too quickly. Football cynics may argue that Taylor foresaw Watford's doom and was astute enough to leave the club with his reputation intact. However, it is difficult to pinpoint any glaring signs of impending relegation at the time of his departure and Taylor is quick to defend his name against accusations of managerial expediency:

I left a side that averaged ninth place in the First Division and, apart from Everton, no team had a better recent record in the FA Cup. There were no contractual problems there when I left. The argument that Watford needed to change upsets and disturbs me. I know that was not true. There was no necessity for those players to leave. What happened there, I don't know, but experienced First Division players left the club.

Although Taylor's oft-stated aim was to establish Watford as a club that would stay in the First Division for the next decade and ultimately challenge for the League Championship, he does not regard their relegation as disastrous. On the contrary, he maintains that Watford's present position accurately reflects all that was promised in the mid-1970s:

I achieved my ambition at Watford over those ten years. Certain principles were set up which I think will continue. Watford were relegated but, by the time your book is published, they may well be back in the First Division. We knew that we couldn't guarantee continued success but we hoped to establish a club which, if it dropped to the Second Division, had a chance of coming back into the First. Ultimately, Watford can be thought of as a First or Second Division club. Its days of being a Third or Fourth Division club are probably over.

While Watford continued the chase for promotion under Steve Harrison, Taylor was still remodelling Aston Villa for survival in the top flight. They had an erratic season in the First Division with an alarming tendency to squander two-goal leads and draw matches that they should have won. Overall, however, Taylor seemed reasonably satisfied with the team's performance in the circumstances:

We've now established the ground rules. They know what is expected of a good professional and there is discipline on the field. We have turned the thing around, but only somewhat. We've played in a manner where one week we look a top six side and the next we look like a bottom six side. It was a shock when we came up in one year. We've just started here. There's a lot of work left to do.

Precisely how much work is required to strengthen Aston Villa is a debatable point. What does seem likely is that Graham Taylor will not be the manager to take the club into its next phase. Football managers are notoriously vague about their future, but the most successful ones at least learn to appreciate the relative security of a long-term appointment at a big city club. One of the perks of a brilliant managerial career is that you probably won't be sacked at the first sign of a crisis. Past success buys time, even though it may not ultimately save your head. Taylor has arguably earned the prospect of a long stay at Aston Villa yet, even at this early stage of his reign, he is candidly speaking about leaving. Amazingly, he even seems willing to name the day:

I've no intention of staying here for ten years! I'm looking to get as much done in the next four years as possible. Whatever we do during the next three years, I don't expect to be the manager of Aston Villa FC after 1992. That's contrary to what I've said at an earlier stage, but it's not contrary to my philosophy. I worked at Watford for ten years, a quarter of my life. How much longer am I going to be a football manager? If I can leave Aston Villa in a position where somebody can take them on to attack the Championship, that's fine. If we could do that in the next two years, great, but, whatever happens, I'm looking to other things. It never worries me that people think: 'Why is he doing that?' I'm not bothered. People thought I should have gone to West Bromwich Albion when I went to Watford. The accusation was that I lacked ambition and couldn't control First Division players and internationals. A lot of rubbish, really. Nonsense. But you can fall into such traps if you're not steady. Accusations won't bother me. This is my life.

It is generally accepted in football that Taylor is the most promising candidate for the job of England manager whenever Bobby Robson finally retires. However, it would be wrong to assume that Taylor is impatiently or expectantly awaiting that opportunity. Now that his children have grown up he posits the possibility of a spell working for a Continental club, although he admits that such an appointment would be of necessity short term: 'I would find it very difficult to stay abroad permanently. I like my country and am happy here'.

Revealingly, Taylor stresses that it would be myopic to label him as 'just a football manager', for in the back of his mind something more ambitious is evidently brewing. Taylor has always taken an unorthodox route to achieve his aims and, analysing his asides, he may be preparing another oblique career move. Make of the following what you will:

There are other things outside football management and other aspects of my life that I'm not prepared to discuss with you. There are also things in football that don't involve team management. It may be that I could put myself forward into those positions. I'm not prepared to say anything further than that. What is important is that I'm not going to be a football manager for the rest of my life.

Reading between the lines, Taylor seems to be looking towards an administrative post, although how far away that may be is unclear. As with other figures in this book, I spent some time discussing the importance of coaching and management courses with Taylor and lamenting the merry-go-round of hirings and firings. The continued need for a genuinely powerful union to regulate the selfish scramble for managerial power brought an animated response. 'Maybe that's the job for me', he suggested. He was probably joking, but I wouldn't swear to that.

Looking back over Graham Taylor's career, there is one crucial item missing from his *curriculum vitae*: a major trophy. Critics will maintain that he needs to win an FA Cup or League Championship to bolster his claims for the England job. They may be correct, but I would wager that the post will be offered to him in any case. His credentials may look suspect on paper but there is no doubting the quality of his managership. For the past two decades he has been a fearless rejuvenator of troubled clubs, with a career development that resembles a series of circuitous roads. The strategy has been habitual. Again and again, Taylor has taken a backward step forwards by deliberately dropping to lower clubs and then moving steadily upwards. From Third Division Grimsby, he went to Fourth Division Lincoln, won promotion back to the Third, dropped down again to take on Watford, traversed confidently to the First and then slipped back to the Second to rescue Aston Villa. By any standards of modern football management, it was extraordinary conduct. Most managers instinctively strive to reach the First Division at the earliest opportunity, often with scarce regard to the consequences of their actions. Taylor has never been a casualty of the management game because he has insisted on playing by his own rules. Logic dictated that he should choose First Division West Bromwich Albion in favour of Fourth Division Watford, but Taylor had the confidence and foresight to take the longer route. It is seldom commented upon but Taylor presently has the longest consecutive managerial record in the Football League. John Lyall of West Ham was longer at one club and Brian Clough, despite his period of unemployment between Leeds and Brighton, has served the most years, but for totally uninterrupted day-to-day management at club level, Taylor can claim the prize. For 17 unbroken years he has displayed a courage, consistency and self-belief worthy of an international manager. Perhaps it is appropriate to leave the last word on Taylor to Sam Ellis, whose attempts to revitalise lowly Blackpool are a sharp reminder of the struggles that faced his gaffer in earlier times:

> Graham Taylor's strengths are his positive attitude and honesty. All through his career his players have given their bollocks for him. Along the way some people might have a low opinion of him but there won't be many. It'll only be a selfish reason if they have. There's bound to be some people who'll pick holes in him but, as far as I'm concerned, there's no way you can criticise his career or success.

WHAT MAKES
A FOOTBALL
MANAGER?

The preceding ten case studies have shown some great managers in action, with a cavalcade of lesser lights and important influences among the supporting cast. If there is a twin theme that runs through all these stories it is instability and paradox. The manager is at once all-powerful and utterly helpless: a god to his players, the public face of the club to the media and supporters, but, ultimately, just another employee whose fate may be in the hands of a capricious chairman or an amorphous board of directors. The paradoxes implicit in his role are reflected in his dualistic nature. The perfect football manager, if such a creature exists, is a veritable Janus: intuitive yet empirical; cautious with money, yet willing to spend millions; street-wise but never intellectually intimidating; sensitive to his players' problems, yet capable of giving them a terrible roasting; professionally remote, yet close enough to directors to get what he needs from them; animated and reflective in both defeat and victory; a skilful negotiator and a sympathetic, eager listener; ever loyal to individual players yet ever willing to sacrifice them for the ultimate good of the club.

This strange, hybrid creature has not always been easy to spot on the road to managerial godhead. Certainly, personality is no guide. Newspapers and the television like to present managers as cocky, confident and charismatic, and some of their favourites over the years have included Bill Shankly, Malcolm Allison, Tommy Docherty, Brian Clough, Ron Atkinson and Terry Venables. All of them were good for a star quote and their extrovert nature and unquenchable enthusiasm for the game appeared to suggest that these were essential attributes for successful management. However, this happy band of colourful characters have been more than matched by a contrasting array of quiet, thoughtful and dour personalities. Alf Ramsey, Bill Nicholson, Dave Sexton, Bob Paisley, Jim Smith and Kenny Dalglish all reached the top of their occupation with a mixture of guarded understatement and pained reticence. Others, such as Matt Busby, Don Revie, Joe Mercer and Graham Taylor have proven adept PR managers with an ability to train the spotlight on their clubs rather than themselves. All these categories of manager have produced extremely successful teams proving beyond doubt that you cannot discover a great manager simply by measuring the size of his mouth.

One common feature of virtually all soccer managers has been their extensive knowledge of the game, although this in itself is a relatively recent phenomenon, and by no means obligatory. In bygone years, when national soccer drew far bigger crowds, it was not the manager that chose the team but a board of directors who knew no more about the game, and often considerably less, than the average supporter on the terraces. Many managers were virtually desk-bound, but this did not prevent them from winning Cups and League Championships, even if their tactical awareness was very basic. Since the early 1950s, the track-suited manager has replaced his ivory tower predecessor and this revolution has been accompanied by a greater stress on the so-called 'science' of the game. Managers know their football now, even if they may know little else, for they have been playing and watching the game all their lives. Despite this equation, there is no direct correlation between soccer skills and managerial achievement. Most of the characters in this book were useful players, but few would describe themselves as the cream of their generation. Indeed, it is possible to argue that footballing genius may even be an impediment to successful management. Quite apart from the pressure that a former star faces from the terraces, he may well feel frustration in attempting to inject instinctive skills into the legs of workmanlike players, whose performances might otherwise be improved by more prosaic training methods. From Tommy Lawton, Stanley Matthews and Billy Wright through to Jimmy Greaves, George Best, Denis Law and beyond, the legends have either studiously avoided management or foundered under the weight of directorial or public expectation. The 1966 World Cup squad included a lively battalion of would-be managers, yet only Jack Charlton made the top grade. Bobby Moore, Bobby Charlton, Geoff Hurst, Martin Peters, Gordon Banks, Nobby Stiles and Alan Ball either strove vainly for success or languished in obscurity with small clubs. Conversely, a wealth of minor footballing talent, not to mention non-League players, have reached surprising heights, including Walter Winterbottom, Bertie Mee, Lawrie McMenemy, Lennie Lawrence and Graham Taylor.

Many of football's more accomplished managers have appreciated the need to re-evaluate what they learned as players and seek new strategies. Bill Nicholson, a strong workmanlike player, fashioned a team with flair and the ability to harness individual genius; Don Revie, a cultured sportsman, created an aggressive and ferociously competitive squad; Brian Clough, a supremely volatile and ruthlessly selfish individualist, demanded exceptionally high standards of discipline and organisation from his various sides; and Graham Taylor, who played for most of his career as a defender, specialised in teams noted for their attacking, entertaining football. Managers, who have not looked to the field to discover complementary aspects of their playing personalities, have all too often found their mirror opposites beside them on the bench. The urbane Matt Busby was flanked by the roaring Jimmy Murphy; loquacious Bill Shankly appreciated the undemonstrative industry of Bob Paisley; cheery old Joe Mercer enjoyed his greatest moments with the ostentatious and hard-training Malcolm Allison; and swashbuckling Terry Venables, for all his experimentation with new, improved players, long retained a loyal lieutenant, Allan Harris. The contrasting parallels are informative for they underline the methods by which untutored ex-players may confront the paradoxes implicit in the managerial process.

Role-reversal and the quest for a complementary partner are important strategies in football management but these usually reach fruition several years into a career. Most of the managers in the preceding studies have not achieved instant success but taken their clubs from the depths of the Second Division, or lower, to Championship or Cup glory. History tells us that steady success over a long period makes a great manager, whereas first appointments at big clubs are usually doomed to failure. In spite of the casualty rate, many clubs still believe the myth that a great player can make a great manager. Remarkably, the normally cautious and highly successful Merseyside clubs, Liverpool and Everton, have recently gambled on Kenny Dalglish and Colin Harvey, respectively, to prove that debutant appointments really can survive and thrive in the soccer firmament. It will be several years yet before Dalglish and Harvey may justifiably rank themselves alongside Shankly and Paisley or Catterick and Kendall, although thus far their records are impressive. With Dave Stringer presently performing wonders at Norwich perhaps the concept of the small-time apprenticeship is not as necessary as history tells us. Not surprisingly, this issue elicits sharply differing reactions from various managers.

It may be nine parts sophistry and one part human nature but most managers inevitably maintain that their career strategy is the correct one. Whatever position they happen to find themselves in, they will be quick to advertise its merits. Third and Fourth Division managers will stress the ruggedness of the lower leagues; Second Division managers of long standing will claim that theirs is the most exciting and competitive and they may even deride the First as a streamlined Super League; the First Division manager will naturally insist that the top flight is the only place to be. As for the ideal starting point, that is another matter of partisan conjecture. The following viewpoints provide some idea of the range of opinion.

Managers today have to live with people who are impatient for success. In football there is no way you can get success overnight. I always wanted to manage a Third or Fourth Division club as my first job in management, even though famous players can get a position on the strength of their names. They get a great club but it's suicide. All the great managers have learned management. Those were my feelings when I went into management.

Allan Clarke, whose cv *as a manager reads: Barnsley, Leeds, Scunthorpe, Barnsley.*

Your ego will always say you're good enough to manage a First Division club. You'll tell yourself you're good enough. It's easy to say otherwise but if an opportunity had come I'd have taken it. Allan Clarke must be a clever man who knows his strengths and weaknesses. Most jobs come up in the lower divisions anyway. One thing I would never have become is a player/manager. That's an impossible job. The failure rate is very high.

Sam Ellis, long-time manager of Third Division Blackpool.

I think you should aim for the top right away, the higher the better. It might turn out to be your only job anyway and you may prove good enough to say there. I'd rather serve my apprenticeship at Tottenham than Halifax. There's only one division to be in as a manager and that's the First. I'd rather make mistakes in the top ten of the First Division than at the bottom of the Third or Fourth. A top club has resources and if you're struggling you can spend money. You may not spend it wisely, but at least you're given the opportunity. No disrespect to Halifax, but if you go there and find you're struggling what can you do? Apart from playing the tealady and the groundsman, you're stuck.

Mark Lawrenson, whose first 12 months in football management took him from the First Division heights to non-League soccer and finally abroad to North America.

Is it better to start off as a manager in the First Division? It depends. There are clubs and clubs. If you go to Manchester United or Everton, or even Newcastle, there is such intense outside pressure from the public and media that if you are a bit naive you can really be caught out. Yet there are clubs in the First Division that don't have those kinds of pressure. I wouldn't say Manchester City or Leeds United or Chelsea in the Second Division are any easier than Southampton, Coventry or clubs like that. Some clubs just don't have as many outside pressures.

Mick Mills, manager of Second Division Stoke City since June 1985. As a newly-appointed manager, he had to stabilise a recently relegated club that had won only three of their last 42 League games and amassed a record low 17 First Division points.

Is it better to start off as a manager in the First Division? Graeme Souness and Kenny Dalglish would say 'yes'. The big scene can be made for certain people. Dalglish had the backing at Liverpool. Souness went into the big scene and handled it. The clubs must have said: 'This fellow's capable – he can do it'. It depends on who the guy is. Dalglish and Souness were big players always associated with big teams. If they'd gone to Halifax I don't think they'd have survived! They wouldn't have bothered with that. They wouldn't work on youth policies and wheel and deal in free transfers. They'd never been brought up like that. It would have been foreign to them. They were from the top flight. They always travelled first class. Of course, if you go in at their level and fail, I don't know where you go. Other managers are happy to stay up till two in the morning, trying to get a better player. It's a different style of management. Taking a club into the First Division is always very rewarding because you know it's down to you. You brought the club up and haven't inherited a great side. It's your return for all the hard graft you've put in and it gives you an infinitely better feeling.

Bobby Robson, manager of England, who, in common with Mark Lawrenson, suffered relegation from the First Division and the sack within months of his first appointment.

Who's to say who is right or wrong? It's difficult for a top player and it hits them hard to think, 'You're starting again, pal!' You may have to go down and take a drop in salary and some people won't do that. They'll go straight in at the top and try to stay there. But even if they do and they're continually successful, there's only one way for them: down. Realistically, very few can start at the top and stay there. You need to win something quickly. So how do you learn about management in the *real* sense? Real management isn't about going into a big club and having bags of money to spend, even though there are horses for courses. We all know about the one-year successes. There is no success over one year. No lasting success. There's just a medal on the table.

Graham Taylor, manager of Aston Villa, who once turned down a First Division club and willingly dropped down to the Fourth.

If managers find it difficult to agree on where to start a career then, once they do begin, the dilemmas multiply tenfold. Enough has been said here about the contradictions of football management to foster the defeatist notion that it is solely a matter of trial and error. If the right personality finds the right club at the right time, then surely all will be well. Of course, it cannot be all luck, for too many managers have performed consistently well with a number of clubs to be relying on the vagaries of fortune. All football managers, no matter how good or bad, are faced with a range of similar problems. Resolving those problems is a skilled process involving a finite number of considerations and requiring a methodology that is consistent and effective. Although it may never be possible to manufacture a model soccer manager, it is possible to pinpoint those characteristics that have proven most common in determining managerial success over the years. The essential elements of football management may be broken down into a variety of sub-categories as outlined below.

DEFINING OBJECTIVES

It took three years before I understood the role of the manager.

Mark Lawrenson

I've totally changed direction from where I started off. I thought I knew what it would take to be a manager and what was right and wrong about football and footballers but since becoming a manager I've just started learning. For the first six months I didn't know anything about management.

John Duncan

The biggest thing you learn from other managers is what *not* to do.

Mark Lawrenson

I know very few businesses where you can put a man in and he assumes automatic control almost straightaway. He's given it. That produces little continuity of policy in football. A new manager, just by the nature of events, can come into a club and what has been created there over ten years can go straight out of the window because of the power that he is given. But he's very vulnerable if his objectives are not successful. There's your power and vulnerability.

Graham Taylor

Before a manager signs with a club, it is important that he is clear about his objectives, particularly in relation to those of his employers. A former World Cup star dreaming of taking an unfashionable team into the European Cup final is of little use to a club struggling against insolvency at the foot of the Fourth Division. Many clubs prefer stability to success and require a level-headed manager who takes as much pride in the balance sheet as the score sheet. Other clubs, with big stadiums and sizeable gates, may be stuck in the Second Division, impatiently awaiting their return to the big time. What they may require is an inspirational manager, a big spender with a keen eye for talent. It is crucial, therefore, that the manager knows, not only the financial commitments offered by the club, but precisely what the directors require of him over a long period. Too many managers accept the first job offer that becomes available and glibly trust that things will work out. Unless the board and the manager are in fundamental agreement about their respective aims, the appointment will be embarrassingly short term.

After reconciling the philosophy of the club with his own principles, the manager must formulate a policy. Without clear directives about all his activities, his work will fail. He cannot replace a team overnight even if their style of play, character and general attitude are totally opposed to what he needs. Changes usually have to be exercised gradually, but the manager must always know what he is intending to achieve and budget his money and time accordingly.

COMMUNICATION

Press conferences are like President Reagan at the White House making a speech on disarmament. The media pressure is unbelievable. It's all part of the job.

Bobby Robson

When I was a player as a young lad, trying to make a name for myself, it was nice for the manager to have a word in my ear just before I went out for each game. As a manager you're paid to gee up players before a match. You might get one player who's withdrawn and another who is very lively, but you must be able to communicate with them. Any successful man in any walk of life has always learned things from somebody else. I'm a good listener. I'll always listen to good advice.

Allan Clarke

As a manager you've got to establish relationships with a lot of people – chairmen, boards of directors, secretaries and administrative staff. They've got their eyes on you. . . People have said much about me, but one of the more complimentary things has been my ability in terms of public relations.

Graham Taylor

A football manager is a public figure who must be capable of representing himself coherently and persuasively in front of the press, the board of directors and, most importantly, the players. In order to translate his plans into actions, the manager must convey his requirements at every opportunity, both on the training field and during team talks. Many inexperienced managers fall into the trap of assuming that once they have made a point, it does not need repeating. Players can have notoriously short memories, however, and each team talk should include a reiteration of the manager's basic principles. As well as articulating his own needs, a manager must be sympathetic towards the demands of his directors, players and staff. He should know as much as possible about the people he works with and the problems that they are facing. Good communication should not be confused with pontification and the manager must be willing to listen to the opinions of his directors, staff and players and never forget that he can learn from their experience.

CO-ORDINATION AND DELEGATION

The art of management is getting people into your system.

Sam Ellis

Nowadays you're supposed to be a coach, manager, psychologist, travel agent and even an accountant.

Mark Lawrenson

Most directors at other clubs don't do much except attend board meetings, but every director here at Blackpool has a specific responsibility. We've a director in charge of the medical side and the press; a financial director; a person who does ground mainte-nance and an ex-policeman who is police liaison officer. At every board meeting you can turn to one director who'll have a dossier. It's a good system. The directors work voluntarily, but they have an active part to play in the club. They like that; it involves them. Too many sleeping directors aren't good for a club. I believe that no one person (chairman, manager or player) should become the dominant figure all the time. Here, we've got a happy medium. We haven't got players who want everything, a manager who wants to grab every bit of glory, or a chairman who wants to take over and wield the axe. That does happen at some clubs and it's wrong and very dangerous.

Sam Ellis

This is a frightening job. Unless you can get some people to work on your behalf to win sufficient matches – you're out.

Graham Taylor

Perhaps the most crucial talent in a football manager is the ability to bring ideas and people together in order to accomplish an organisational goal. The process will have already begun if the directors have chosen a suitable manager for the job. He, in turn, will be expected to surround himself with a competent team, both on the field and in his office. This requires considerable knowledge of the football world. The choice of players is not simply a question of apportioning appropriate funds or getting the best bargain presently available on the market. Economic astuteness must be allied to an intuitive understanding of precisely what the team requires for success. Blending players is a fine art and requires the skills of a seasoned matchmaker. The best managers in football history have expertly aligned the rugged and the cultured, the workmanlike and the brilliant, and the wayward and the consistent in order to produce a perfectly balanced side. An unco-ordinated team of star buys will merely produce erratic, mediocre and disappointing performances.

In addition to co-ordinating a team, the manager is responsible for selecting and organising his backroom staff. In determining the degree of responsibility that he bestows upon his colleagues, the manager may encounter unforeseen problems. Many overscrupulous managers insist upon involving themselves totally in every decision relating to the team. This is commendable to a degree but may backfire. The more successful a club becomes, the more matches it plays in a season, and this can impose a tremendous workload on an already overburdened manager. If he tries to do everything, he will stretch himself to breaking point and the result will be snap decisions and, inevitably, mistakes. The efficient manager understands the function of delegation and does not become obsessed with surrendering chunks of power. As long as a manager defines precisely the authority that he is bestowing, then there should be no conflict with his backroom staff. This is a lesson that applies equally to club chairmen and directors, some of whom fail to compartmentalise the specific power and responsibility that they are offering a manager.

LEADERSHIP

If you get a situation where it's them and us, then the team will let you down.

Mark Lawrenson

The one thing about management is that you've got to be absolutely confident about yourself, even if you turn out to be wrong. You must feel certain that what you are doing is right.

Graham Taylor

From the first day Kenny Dalglish took over he said: 'On the pitch, I'm a player, you can say what you want to me. But, off the pitch, remember I'm the manager'. He had to ostracise himself.

Mark Lawrenson

It's very important to try to keep at a distance when you first come into management. I was a player too, which makes it more difficult. If you try to be completely adrift, then you'll take away all the humour from the dressing room on a Saturday afternoon. If you're a nasty bugger, the team may completely dry up and the spirit goes. So I had to be very careful not to divorce myself from them completely. One thing I never did though was socialise with the players. We never went out for drinks or meals together. If we travelled abroad I never went out with them, I always remained with the staff. That was important. Now I'm not playing, it's doubly important that they don't get too close to me. It's the same with the board and the directors. Don't get socially involved! That can be very difficult because they will invite you everywhere, even into their homes. You must accept some invitations, but I will never make a director or a chairman my best friend.

Mick Mills

I don't think you can model yourself on anybody else. You'll be found out if you try that. There's a lot of that in football, particularly from those who've played under very strong personalities. They end up having such a strong admiration for that person that they forget what they themselves are like as personalities. People who've played under Shankly or Clough may say: 'I want to be like him!' You can't. You can learn some things, but you can't start talking like him. If you're not naturally an aggressive man, you can't be aggressive; and if you're not naturally a comedian, you can't be the joker in the pack because nobody will laugh. You've got to believe in yourself and your own personality.

Mick Mills

I believe that one of the signs of a great manager is his ability to obtain the respect of his players, and to be able to hammer those players within the confidential walls of the club when they let him down, without letting them down or attacking them through the media.

Liam Brady

Leadership requires confidence and the ability to win the interest and respect of other people, most crucially the directors and players. Traditionally, football managers have been expected to wield a considerable amount of power over their players and a certain degree of aggression is expected. The younger manager is particularly prone to insubordination problems unless he exercises his authority in some emphatic fashion. Even Bobby Robson was reduced to physical violence in order to assert his control over a potentially rebellious team. Bill McGarry liked to place his fist underneath the chins of potential insurgents, while Harry Catterick had his team clocking on in the morning and fined them for every minute they were late, as though they were factory workers. It is not necessary to intimidate players to such a degree that they scurry around like frightened schoolchildren, but the responsibilities of the manager are such that he cannot afford to be undermined. The best form of leadership comes not from bullying but through active involvement with the players in an authoritative and consistent fashion that wins their respect and admiration. The case studies of Revie, Shankly and Busby show how effectively this can be achieved.

CONFLICT

The majority of managers get the sack. Realistically, it's a question of how long I manage without getting the sack.

Mark Lawrenson

Let them find another miracle man. I'm convinced now that football management is a rotten business. I've slogged away, saving the club money and teaching kids to play football. Then I'm slammed by shareholders who never watch us. I don't mind criticism but this situation makes me sick. Perhaps I should fight back. I am a fighter, but the blow this time has flattened me. Deep down I know I've done a good job. It grieves me that a man who wins five shares in the club at a raffle can cause so much upset.

Dick Graham, resigning manager of Colchester United

I get very frustrated here at Barnsley. I've had to sell players and solve financial problems. When a club sells a good player there's only one person that suffers – the manager. If I haven't got the players, my job becomes even harder. I'm always interested in quality players and strengthening the squad, but they've got to be in our price range. We won't borrow big money from the bank. There's no short cut or overnight success. We run things as a business. We're making progress. We're not a force at the minute, our youngsters aren't ready. Our board, like any board, wants success. I try to do a good day's work for a good day's pay.

Allan Clarke

If you lose every week you don't have charisma. It's success that builds that charisma and you can soon lose it. Look at Big Lawrie. The bottom line is success and results. The public don't give a toss unless you're winning. Supporters may, once in a while, appreciate that you've played well and been unlucky. But, if that happens four times in succession, things soon change. It may seem unjust but so are lots of things in life. Your past record counts for nothing in football if you lose seven games on the trot. Whoever you are, you are under pressure. Ultimately, you're dependent upon the strength of your board, the strength of their convictions and morals. They can stand you being criticised, but once the criticism turns on them for employing you, then you're on thin ice.

Sam Ellis

I work in a hostile environment. It gets easier over time which is why I say my job has to go to an experienced man. If he's inexperienced, he'll be dead within two years.

Bobby Robson

The worst part of my managerial career was leaving Leeds. A sad day that, it hurt. But I believe it made me a better manager. It was sad that I wasn't given the time to do the job that I went back to do, which was to rebuild that club. You can't do that in two years. I wanted eight or nine players. I only brought in four in two years and only paid money for three of those.

Allan Clarke

When I joined Lincoln in 1972 there were 22 or 23 players alongside myself. Suddenly, I'm the boss. I didn't set out to move those players on but, within 18 months, there were only about three left!

Graham Taylor

As a manager you can come across difficult people who are disruptive and you've got to get them out. But it's no use just getting rid of players. The problem is replacing them and getting money for them. I had to wait and see and take my time.

Bobby Robson

Resolving conflicts and juggling priorities are two of the more strenuous tasks that face a football manager. He is at once responsible to his directors, his staff and the players whom he oversees, and each of these parties will be making different demands upon his time and commitments. Keeping these conflicting priorities in order is one of the severest tests of a manager's skill. A football manager who claims that all priorities can be satisfied without prejudice to each other is either a fool or a liar. Some priorities must inevitably take precedence, but none can be ignored. For example, a manager may face an outbreak of player power in the dressing room, a coach who is about to be poached by a rival club, a press backlash, a run of losing games and a board of over-cautious and critical directors. What can he do? He knows that he ought to eliminate the sources of disequilibrium in the dressing room, sell the players, appoint a new coach, cajole the directors into injecting more money into the club and convince the press that the crisis can be turned around. In this scenario, the manager already seems doomed, for the problems are multiplying and will soon overwhelm him. Probably part of his nightmare has stemmed from ignoring the priorities that he initially found too difficult or time-consuming. If there are disputes with players, problems with finance, or personality clashes with staff or directors, they must be tackled at the earliest opportunity. At no time can the manager allow himself to be distracted. He must learn to order his priorities and act upon them accordingly, yet be equally willing to analyse and revise his decisions as circumstances change. Like a politician bombarded with conflicting demands, he must retain a consistent sense of purpose through all the chaos of adjustments and revisions until some form of resolution has been reached. Should he be seen to fail, the inevitable result will be his dismissal.

INNOVATION

When you become a football manager you must always plan. It's best to assume that you'll be at your club for the rest of your life. The facts will show that you won't, but you must try to assume that you will be. Then you'll work for it. You will become committed.

Graham Taylor

I've had to play kids here because of the economics of the club. We've had to sell kids too. I like to think I favour a youth policy. It gives you players and a feeling for the club. If you buy players in, it can take you a while to instil that fervour for the club itself.

Sam Ellis

Everybody says a youth policy is innovative and a good idea, but it costs money. You get what you pay for. You can't run a youth policy without resources. When a club has a financial problem the first thing that tends to go is the youth policy. The first team is what draws people through the gates and brings revenue into the club so that has to have priority. If it's a case of survival, the youth policy has to be neglected. We've kept it going on a piecemeal basis here at Orient. It takes three to four years to set up a youth policy and see any fruits from it. The average tenure of an English manager outside the First Division is about two years. Some of them will think: 'Why should I butt my head against a wall for somebody else?' There are managers like that and you can't blame them.

Frank Clark

Obviously, the priority must be the first team. But if you prune anything, you don't do so from the bottom. Because of the pressures that managers face, it's very difficult for them to have a concept of the whole.

Graham Taylor

To progress you've got to play youngsters and that's always a gamble. You risk losing the match if you play too many. I did it once and we were hammered.

Bobby Robson

A football team, and indeed, a football club, cannot remain static, even after winning a League Championship and European Cup. The manager can never rest on the greatness of the moment but must be continually seeking new ways to improve his side. The most successful managers in this book were not associated with one team, but three or four, sometimes over a decade or more. The cheapest and most effective way of ensuring continuity is through the introduction of a regenerating youth policy. This requires the manager to think long-term even while he is struggling in an occupation renowned for its rapid turnover of staff. The manager must also be aware of the developments taking place at other clubs both at home and abroad. He must always be ready to discard old procedures and avoid the temptation merely to follow the herd. Innovation inevitably requires a manager to take calculated risks. Perhaps the classic example in modern day football was Matt Busby's insistence on discarding his ageing side in favour of the untested Busby Babes. That one action inspired a generation of managers to accept and adopt the concept of the soccer crèche. The most innovative managers deserve the highest commendation because their actions will transcend the parochial limitations of one club and revolutionise the entire game.

THE CURSE OF
MANAGERIAL
INFIDELITY

The late League secretary Alan Hardaker was once asked to define the qualities of a successful football manager and his reply was characteristically blunt: they must be 'devious and ruthless and selfish'. Hardaker maintained that the pressure on managers was so intense that they could not afford to be too troubled by conscience. Having observed the greats over many years he wearily concluded: 'Most managers come into the game intending to be honest, but too many of them discover that life becomes a little easier if they bend the rules'. Although Hardaker was renowned for his cynicism, his words were still a searing indictment of the amorality of soccer management. Interestingly, his observations caused no bitter furore and passed virtually unnoticed back in 1977. Two years later, a rather less authoritative voice was heard addressing a Football Writers' Lunch with a similar catechism:

> The morals in football are very different from other jobs. It is the law of life and sometimes the only way to survive is to tell lies. There are lots of times when managers are honest, when they are fantastic company. But there are lots of times when they are cheats.

The speaker was the ever-provocative Tommy Docherty in his favourite role as after-dinner philosopher and footballing iconoclast. Although his words were no more invective than those of Hardaker, and considerably less influential, his fate is illustrative. He was severely censured for implicitly damning his colleagues as 'liars and cheats' and unceremoniously expelled from the Football League Executive Staffs' Association. The punishment of Docherty was by no means unexpected for it reiterated a fundamental soccer law which says that a manager must always appear a model of moral excellence.

Docherty's much-publicised fall from grace emphasises the peculiar position that a football manager occupies. A barrister in the High Court once argued that the only saints in British soccer were to be found in the sobriquet of Southampton Football Club. In practice, however, the

FA, and more surprisingly, club directors and chairmen, require an exceptionally high standard of conduct from their managers. Even as the carousel of sackings continues uninterrupted, the FA accuses aggrieved and outspoken managers of bringing the game into disrepute. The clubs demand absolute constancy even while they may be driving a dagger into a manager's back. The press can be equally censorious, particularly when confronted with what they perceive as disloyalty. The sad case of Don Revie is a chilling example. Here was a man pilloried by the soccer fraternity and general public for accepting an offer from abroad and brilliantly turning the tables on his employers by leaving them without a manager to axe. Revie's defection, deplored by so many, is placed in a less lurid light when viewed in the historical context of multitudinous managerial sackings. Indeed, it may even be defended as a Machiavellian retaliation, an apt and ultimate revenge for every manager dismissed and discredited over the years. Who but a fool would put nationalistic pride before self-interest in an occupation in which expediency and the seeming inevitability of the sack are the only constant truths?

The curse of managerial infidelity illustrates the hypocrisy and cant at the centre of football's moral scheme. Until such time as all football clubs treat their managers with faith and long-term commitment they can hardly expect the same in return.

The major gripe that managers voice is the peculiar way clubs choose to appoint them. Scant respect is given to those managers who have taken time to gain coaching or management qualifications and, as a result, promising courses suffer from accusations of irrelevancy. Club chairmen will appoint whomever they like, often selecting a well-known player or fashionable name and blatantly ignoring their absolute ignorance of management basics. The blunt Alan Hardaker once noted that many League managers find great difficulty completing a simple form correctly. It is hardly surprising that most appointments are so short-lived when the level of competence required remains unstated. Most sensible soccer commentators maintain that aspiring ex-players should undertake some form of formal qualification before being let loose in the offices and on the training fields of a League club. Several of the managers in this book have campaigned vociferously in favour of coaching and management courses, but club directors continue to appoint neophytes in perverse preference to better qualified candidates. Graham Taylor is not alone in believing that this is a political manoeuvre by club directors, perpetrated to weaken the strength of the managers' union FLESA (Football League Executive Staffs' Association). The union, in common with the Professional Footballers' Association, has made some commendable attempts to regulate the sorry tale of managerial sackings by encouraging its members to take specialised management courses. There is nothing revolutionary in this idea as similar, and considerably tougher, courses have long been in operation in Italy and West Germany. In the German system, no coach can obtain a job in the Bundesliga until he has passed five stages of certification which usually takes four years.

Allen Wade, the FA's director of coaching, launched a similar scheme in 1982 and it has been steadily improved during the intervening years.

Although coaching courses are a godsend to aspiring track-suited managers, many of the potential applicants are either too lazy or too tired after a hard season to avail themselves of such an excellent service. That great champion of FA badges, Bobby Robson, could not even persuade his captain Mick Mills to take time out and enrol, which may be some indication of the general apathy among players. Unfortunately, it is often the best players who miss out on the course due to international commitments during the close season and this is a problem that needs addressing. Mills, at least, was fortunate, for he found time to join a summer school management course run by the PFA. This much-needed scheme takes the player from the training field into the uncharted area of office administration. The student learns essential management theory with particular stress on how to conduct business with his chairman, directors, players, commercial staff, and various outside agencies such as the police, community representatives and the press. Apart from grappling with the complexities of inter-personal relations, the course deals with more basic skills such as how to conduct a telephone conversation and write a business letter. One suspects that the late Alan Hardaker would have heartily approved.

In order to invest their courses with greater credibility both FLESA and the PFA have brought in expert guest speakers, including Bill Nicholson, who provided a revealing insight into the pitfalls of club management. Bobby Robson was so impressed with the scope and depth of the management course that he actually attended as a student. His conclusion would not have been out of place in an advertising campaign: 'I was a very experienced manager and I learned a lot from that course'.

If only such courses could be made compulsory then the fiasco that masquerades as football management would be revolutionised overnight. Although perfect managers cannot be produced on a conveyor belt, you can save many from the embarrassment of incompetence and stupidity.

An influx of qualified managers would prevent the job marketplace from degenerating into a lottery. At present, the players' and managers' unions are virtually impotent because the clubs continue to dictate terms. Managers are often sacked midway through their contracts and frequently have to fight to win any compensation. Meanwhile, they are replaced by other managers who turn a blind eye to the implications of their own actions. Naturally, the clubs are reluctant to accept any union proposal that might curb their own power, especially the suggestion that only qualified personnel be appointed. Newly recruited managers are no better, for they will not unanimously agree to boycott clubs that refuse to honour long-term contracts. The irony of this situation is that the clubs would ultimately be far better off economically if they could resist the endless managerial purges and establish a system that guaranteed a regular flow of management talent. They would still have the option to sack incompetent managers as frequently as they wished, but paying out compensation for the remainder of their contracts would prove a costly business. Such an arrangement would encourage clubs to look more critically at their own recruitment policies and try to ensure that they made sensible appointments from the outset, as well as providing harried managers with the security of knowing that they would not be summarily sacked at the first hint of a crisis. The final grand irony of football management is that in resisting the power of the unions, the League clubs are ultimately slashing their own wrists and unwittingly creating and perpetuating a deplorable standard of managerial mediocrity.

INDEX